Bait and Switch

Human Rights and U.S. Foreign Policy

Other titles in the Global Horizons Series
Edited by Richard Falk, Lester Ruiz, and R.B.J. Walker

International Relations and the Problem of Difference
Naeem Inayatullah and David L. Blaney

Methods and Nations: Cultural Governance and the Indigenous Subject
Michael J. Shapiro

The Declining World Order: America's Imperial Geopolitics
Richard Falk

Bait and Switch

Human Rights and U.S. Foreign Policy

JULIE A. MERTUS

Routledge
Taylor & Francis Group

NEW YORK AND LONDON

A volume in the series *Global Horizons*, edited by Richard Falk, Lester Ruiz, and R.B.J. Walker

Published in 2004 by
Routledge
29 West 35th Street
New York, NY 10001
www.routledge-ny.com

Published in Great Britain by
Routledge
11 New Fetter Lane
London EC4P 4EE
www.routledge.co.uk

Library of Congress Cataloging-in-Publication Data

Mertus, Julie, 1963–
    Bait and switch : human rights and U.S. foreign policy / by Julie Mertus
        p. cm. -- (Global horizons)
Includes bibliographical references (p.) and index.
    ISBN 0-415-94850-9 (HC : alk. paper) -- ISBN 0-415-94851-7 (PB : alk. paper)
    1. Human rights. 2. Human rights--Government policy--United States.
3. United States--Foreign relations--1989- I. Title II. Series.

JC571.M444 2004
323'.973--dc22   2003022338

CONTENTS

ACKNOWLEDGMENTS

This book could not have been written without the support of the United States Institute of Peace (USIP), which awarded me a Jennings Randolph Senior Fellowship but, more important, provided me with the most stimulating and diverse collegial environment I have ever encountered. I am grateful to Joseph Klaits for his thoughtful counsel, to Virginia Bouvier for her thorough feedback, to Timothy Docking for his gentle prodding, and to Daniel Serwer and Kurt Bassuener for continually bringing me back to the Balkans. In addition, I am grateful for the insights of fellow fellows, including Sonja Biserko, Lieutenant Colonel Donna Boltz, Jean-Marc Coicaud, Graham Day, Neil Hicks, Michael J. Matheson, David H. P. Maybury-Lewis, Brenda Pearson, Robert Perito, Dana Priest, David Scheffer, Eric Schwartz, and Henryk Sokalski.

This book also would not exist without the support of my colleagues at American University's School of International Service. In particular, I thank Patrick Jackson, Renee Marlin-Bennett, Shoon Murray, Lucinda Peace, and Paul Wapner for reading and reviewing various parts of the work, and to Kathy Schneider, Steve Silvia, and the members of the Ph.D. research seminars of 2002 and 2003 for their feedback on presentations based on this work. I also thank Louis Goodman, Nannette Levinson, and the administration of American University for their support, in particular for the award of a summer writing grant. Finally, I gratefully acknowledge the leadership of Abdul Aziz Said, whose strong faith in humankind has inspired me.

A team of research assistants from American University also contributed substantially to this work: Maryanne Yerkes on the interviews and survey that form the heart of the book; Ruth Reitan on Chapters 1 and 2; Daniel Chong and Kevin Klock on Chapter 3; Maia Carter, Laurie Rosenberger, and Jane Gindin pitch hitting on spots throughout the manuscript; and last but not least, Eve Bratman who worked on the entire manuscipt at the final stages. Thank you, thank you, thank you.

I would also like to thank Michael Peters and the organizers of the 2002 Council on Foreign Relations NATO trip for facilitating my field research in the American sector in Kosovo; Lynda Boose for providing me a temporary home at Dartmouth College to work on this project; and the MacArthur Foundation for its support of my fieldwork in Kosovo in the mid-1990s, an experience that also informs this work. I am also grateful to the organizers of the panels at which this work was presented; that is, at the 2003 and 2001 conferences of the American Political Science Association, the 2002 and 2001 conferences of the International

Studies Association (papers presented with Maia Carter in 2002 and Daniel Chong in 2001), and the American Society of International Law conferences in 2003 and 2001.

This work also benefited from the insight of the participants at several additional conferences, most significantly at meetings sponsored by the McCormick Tribune Foundation; the Woodrow Wilson Center; the United States Institute of Peace; the Council on Foreign Relations; the Fulbright Association; the Rockefeller Institute; Catholic Relief Services; the Norwegian Institute of International Affairs and the International Peace Research Institute; the Institute for the Study of International Migration at Georgetown University and the American Red Cross; the Carnegie Council on International Ethics; the Latin American Studies Association; the University of Notre Dame Hesburgh Center for International Studies and the Joan B. Kroc Institute for International Peace Studies; the Minda de Gunzberg Center for European Studies, Harvard University; the Jackson School of International Affairs; the U.S. Air Force Academy; West Point Military Academy; the MacArthur Foundation; Women Waging Peace; Carnegie Commission on Preventing Deadly Conflict; Women in International Security; and the Halle Center for International Affairs, Emory University.

I appreciate the insight of all the 150-some people who agreed to be interviewed for this book. Those who agreed to be named are included in a list at the end of the book, and there is not enough space to thank them all again here. However, I would like to single out Lieutenant Colonel Jeffrey Walker, Lieutenant Colonel Richard Lacquement, Jr., David Stewart, and Martina Vandenberg, who not only agreed to be interviewed but who read and contributed suggestions for the redrafting of sections of this text.

Richard Falk, Jack Donnelly, Rhoda Howard, and Thomas Weiss should be singled out for providing crucial feedback on early versions of this work, and Joelle Balfe for lending a keen editorial eye to the entire text, but in particular to the conclusion. I would also like to thank Robert Tempio and Allison Taub for their attention during the editorial and production process.

In addition, the author acknowledges and appreciates the efforts of Tom Cushman and the *Journal of Human Rights*, which published a portion of Chapter 4 as "Raising Expectations? Civil Society's Influence on Human Rights and U.S. Foreign Policy," *Journal of Human Rights* 3 (2004): 21–40, and Mark Boyer and *International Studies Perspectives*, which published a portion of Chapter 1 as "The New U.S. Human Rights Policy: A Radical Departure," *International Studies Perspectives* 4 (2003): 371–384.

Although many people provided input on this text, far more than I can name here, the mistakes are mine alone. I have done my best to tell a story accurately and fairly, and I welcome comments emailed to me at mertus@american.edu.

Above all I thank Janet Lord for her input into the text as well as her undying encouragement; my children, Lynne and Daniel, for their new eyes on the world, which have improved my vision; and Peggy Lord for her unbelievable support with daily life.

A careful reader will note that many interviews were conducted for this book in 2001 and then again in 2003. For my family, 2002 was a very difficult year. My father, better known as Grampy Dan, died that year. It was his world travels and strong faith in the common dignity of mankind that inspired me to take on this work.

This book is dedicated to my mother, Marilyn Mertus, in honor of her own strength and with gratitude for her encouragement of mine.

Julie Mertus
Washington, D.C.

ONE

INTRODUCTION: ALL THAT GLITTERS . . .

This book is about the future of human rights in U.S. foreign policy. Many fear that the era of human rights ended the day terrorists turned jet planes into weapons of destruction and flew them into the World Trade Center and the Pentagon.[1] Or, many believe, human rights ended shortly after September 11, 2001, when the United States retaliated with unilateralist policies in violation of international standards, under the assumption that they could establish the rules for the rest of the world.[2] I disagree, but in a way that may be slightly confusing for the reader looking for a clear thumbs up or thumbs down on human rights. I contend that human rights are still important for U.S. foreign policy. The United States is in fact still leading the world on human rights, but in the wrong direction, promoting short-term instrumentalism over long-term ethical principles, double standards instead of fair dealing, and a fearful view of human nature over a more open one. An increasingly sophisticated array of nongovernmental organizations (NGOs) and other leaders in civil society continue to demand that human rights ideas be more fully incorporated into U.S. foreign policy. To some extent, these advocates have succeeded in framing public policy choices in human rights terms, but too often competing interests eclipse human rights considerations. Human rights talk has not been accompanied by human rights behaviors.

This is not the book I set out to write. When I began this project in the fall of 2000, I intended to test the thesis that human rights norms had a significant impact on both the White House and the Pentagon because they had become "deeply embedded," or, if you prefer, "institutionalized." I thought I would find that human rights norms had, in Martha Finnemore and Kathryn Sikkink's words, "become so widely accepted that they [had been] internalized by actors and achieved a 'taken-for-granted' quality that [made] compliance . . . almost automatic."[3] I was particularly interested in analyzing how human rights norms shape the identity, interests, expectations, and behaviors of Americans who make, implement, and influence decisions concerning military intervention and other forms of American involvement across state borders. I had high hopes of finding human rights deeply embedded in U.S. foreign policy. I discovered that human rights norms had shaped identities, but that human rights were not a taken-for-granted factor in shaping behavior. In particular, I discovered that the American public would tolerate and even participate in behavior running contrary to human rights tenets.

The events following September 11 assured me of my failed thesis, but the interviews I conducted in and around Washington, D.C., long before then had already tipped me off that something is seriously awry with the way the United States "does" human rights. Policy makers may talk about human rights now more than ever, but the talk does not lead to consistent human rights abiding behaviors and decisions. The manner in which human rights have been understood and applied threatens to strip human rights ideas of their central content. While many of the government policy makers and military officers I interviewed for this book genuinely identified with being "on the side of human rights," their vision of human rights accommodated double standards: one for the United States, and another for the rest of the world. In other words, human rights are something the United States encourages for other countries, whereas the same international standards do not apply in the same manner in the United States.

In the course of my research, I discovered that when I said "human rights" and when many of the governmental actors I was studying said "human rights," we were referring to two different things. I was referring to an understanding of human rights that, as explained below, incorporates three fundamental principles: the equality principle, the human dignity principle, and the moral worth principle. In contrast, the people and institutions that I was studying were most likely referring to a short list of American values, to be projected and applied to others in line with American national interests. By explicitly or implicitly understanding human rights as something done "out there" and to "other people," and in failing to apply human rights norms to the United States on equal terms, they were undercutting the core nature of human rights.

Although the rhetoric on human rights has changed from presidential administration to administration, manifestations of American exceptionalism appear in every presidency. Harold Hongju Koh, assistant secretary of state for democracy, human rights, and labor during part of the Clinton administration (1998–2001), stresses that some forms of American exceptionalism present little danger to the future of human rights.[4] For example, that the United States has a distinctive rights culture and often uses distinctive legal terminology is not troubling. Indeed, the distinctiveness of the United States may benefit human rights claimants.[5] However, the use of a double standard may be devastating both for U.S. human rights foreign policy and for the future of human rights. Koh points to at least four problems with a double-standard approach to human rights: (1) the undercutting of U.S. ability to pursue an affirmative human rights agenda; (2) the co-optation of the United States into condoning or defending other countries' human rights abuses; (3) the weakening of the United States' claim to lead globally through moral authority; and (4) the undermining of the legitimacy of human rights norms.[6] It is this double standard form of American exceptionalism that is the subject of the present book.[7]

To understand how human rights have become so tarnished, this book examines three groups of actors: (1) U.S. civilian policy makers; (2) the U.S. military; and (3) U.S.-based NGOs and other members of "civil society" concerned with human rights.

The framework of the book is organized around the three sets of actors under study. First, it begins with the executive branch and analyzes post–Cold War trends in human rights and U.S. foreign policy, noting continuities and discontinuities among administrations and underscoring the impact of Congress, the media, public opinion, and other contextual factors. Second, it examines the impact of human rights ideas on the U.S. military during the same time period, underscoring changes in behavior and identity. Third, it turns to trends within civil society and searches for specific examples of the ways in which civil society has influenced human rights and U.S. foreign policy.

Instead of relying solely on secondary sources, I draw from more than 150 interviews conducted over the course of the last three years,[8] a written survey with a similar number of respondents, primary documents, and my own field notes from work in the former Yugoslavia. My goal is to provide a readable account of human rights and U.S. foreign policy that will speak to a wide range of readers interested in world affairs as well as scholars and practitioners concerned with norm formation. With the exception of this introductory chapter, the theory driving this analysis remains in the background. The remainder of this chapter clarifies the definition of "human rights" and outlines the theoretical orientations informing this study. This theoretical discussion provides the underpinning foundations for the analysis on the whole, though it is possible to read any of the chapters that follow in isolation.

CLARIFYING TERMS

This section begins with a brief discussion of how the idea of human rights is employed in this study, introducing universalism and particularism concepts that are applied to the analysis of civilian and military actors that follows. It then turns to the two main theoretical influences for this work. First, the "English school" provides a good starting point for thinking about the nature of human rights in today's deeply troubled world. Second, the school of thought known as constructivism sheds light on how norms shape the identities, interests, and expectations of actors.[9]

Human Rights

The idea of human rights has resonance in many different ideological and cultural traditions.[10] As a base line, human rights require a certain conception of individual agency and autonomy, human nature, and rationality.[11] R. J. Vincent has explained this notion of "rights." As Vincent notes, "A right in this sense can be thought of as consisting of five main elements: a right holder (the subject of a right) has a claim to some substance (the object of a right), which he or she might assert, or demand, or enjoy, or enforce (exercising a right) against some individual or group (the bearer of the correlative duty), citing in support of his or her claim some particular ground (the justification of the right)."[12]

As Tim Dunne and Nicholas Wheeler have observed, disagreement on human rights centers on the last factor, the grounds on which rights are justified. Human rights advocates make the foundational case for human rights based on notions of common morality,[13] a singular "human nature,"[14] human dignity,[15] "universal social facts,"[16] equal creation, and equal brotherhood. Some human rights advocates point to a divine or "natural" origin for human rights,[17] while others search for more secular evidence,[18] examining historical practices and discovering similarities among diverse cultural traditions,[19] as well as in state practices.[20] Others take a more pluralistic and pragmatic approach: one does not need to reach a conclusion on the source of human rights in order to believe in human rights enforcement.[21]

Many advocates for social justice underscore the pragmatism behind framing claims of the oppressed in human rights language. Amy Gutmann points out that Article 1 of the Universal Declaration of Human Rights does not assert one foundation for human rights, but many, and each of these foundations is open to multiple interpretations. Recognition of the plurality of religious and secular foundational arguments for human rights is essential in a pluralistic world. "When foundations are treated as more important to honor than the rights themselves, and disagreement about foundations becomes a cause for violating rights," Gutmann warns, "then idolatry of abstract ideas, quite apart from the practical consequences of such idolatry, becomes a serious political problem."[22] The real-life consequences of recognizing or failing to recognize a human right should always be a prominent concern.[23]

The Core of Human Rights

To the extent that human rights adherents can find agreement on the content of human rights, it is in relation to three fundamental precepts. First, adherence to human rights requires acknowledgment of the dignity of individuals as individuals. That this principle focuses on the individual does not negate the importance of community. Individuals are not free-floating entities; they exist and derive meaning through social relationships and communal responsibilities and duties.[24] The identification and enforcement of human rights thus depends greatly on community. As Jean Bethke Elshtain notes, "[Rights] are woven into a concept of community" and "are intelligible only in terms of the obligations of individuals to other persons."[25] The idea of human rights, however, necessitates recognition of the agency and identity of the individual that may exist apart from the community. A human rights framework insists that "essential to [each individual's] dignity, and to a life worthy of a human being, is the simple fact that they are human beings."[26]

The notion that each human being should be treated with dignity solely because he or she is human requires acceptance of a second principle: the moral equality of human beings.[27] "Since all human beings have dignity and need common conditions of growth," Bhikhu Paarekh observes, "their claims to them deserve equal consideration and weight."[28] Equality is inherent to human rights because it informs day-to-day application of human rights norms. The equality principle requires states to apply human rights norms to the behaviors of all states, friend and foe alike, and to accept scrutiny of themselves under the same standards.

The third integrally related principle pertains to the notion of moral worth. This is the idea that all humans have value and, therefore, all can make a contribution to society. This notion of worth and the related concept of equality do not mean that all people are treated the same or that all benefits and burdens in society must be distributed in identical fashion. Differences in treatment may still exist, but any differential treatment must respect the moral worth and dignity of individuals.

The universal nature of the individual dignity, equality, and worth principles is endorsed in several international human rights documents. The preamble of the United Nations Charter states that one purpose of the organization is to "reaffirm faith in fundamental human rights, in the dignity and worth of the human person, in the equal rights of men and women and of nations large and small."

The first line of the Universal Declaration of Human Rights similarly states that "recognition of the inherent dignity and of the equal and inalienable rights of all members of the human family is the foundation of freedom, justice and peace in the world." Similar recognition of the "inherent dignity" and "the equal and inalienable rights of all members of the human family" is found in the International Covenant on Civil and Political Rights and the International Covenant on Economic, Social, and Cultural Rights.

More recently, at the Second World Conference on Human Rights in June 1993, representatives of 171 countries reaffirmed these principles when they adopted a Declaration and Program of Action, which states in the second paragraph of the preamble that "all human rights derive from the dignity and worth inherent in the human person, and . . . the human person is a central subject of human rights in fundamental freedoms, and consequently should be the principal beneficiary and participate actively in the realization of these rights and freedoms."[29]

These international documents are clear: dignity is one core element of human rights, equality another, and worth a related third.[30] U.S. human rights policy has long gone awry by engaging in "exceptionalism," that is, in assuming that the United States should and will receive special treatment when human rights are applied in practice. The modern idea of human rights requires—indeed is premised upon—the presence of all three concepts. One cannot embrace the idea of human rights and also hold that these rights apply to some individuals, or that only some states have a responsibility to respect human rights.[31] At the same time, one cannot accept the idea of human rights and also accept that they are earned, or that some individuals may be more worthy of human rights than others. A necessary corollary is that one must be willing to apply human rights standards to oneself and, thus, that states will reject exceptionalism.

Human rights provide victims with increasingly influential political and legal strategies for articulating their demands. Human rights mechanisms honor the agency of victims by calling into action a system of rights and correlative duties. Under human rights law, victims become claimants who are permitted to bring claims against perpetrators and some bystanders. By using human rights mechanisms for achieving justice and addressing human suffering, victims are able to act nonviolently to improve their positions. Without such recourse, violations are likely to perpetuate conflict through cycles of revenge and retaliation.

While reference to human rights norms does not automatically resolve disputes, it provides a language and, in some cases, specific agreed-upon adjudicative and legislative mechanisms for the hearing of the conflict.[32] A rights-based approach treats everyone equally before the law and values all people on the basis of their inherent worth rather than viewing certain members of society as more dignified, and therefore "more equal," than others. Accordingly, a human rights approach forces states to recognize the worth inherent in others and give them equal opportunity to state their claims.

The achievement of human rights is *political* in the sense that human rights translate, reflect, and challenge claims to power.[33] Human rights are demands for power from all who invoke them, including states, groups "below the state" (i.e., NGOs and social movements), and those "above and beside the state" (i.e., transnational bodies).[34] Within state borders, human rights norms serve as a check on the power of government to do what it wills with its own citizens.[35] In Jack Donnelly's words, "Human rights is the language of the victims and the dispossessed."[36] The disempowered turn to human rights discourse because it so "successfully manages to articulate (evolving) political claims."[37] Across state borders, respect for human rights serves as both a check on and an enabler for coercive and noncoercive intervention. States that fail to abide by minimum human rights guarantees open themselves up to criticism, censure, sanction, and, in some cases, military intervention.

Human rights norms not only restrict states, the doctrine also enables states to adopt certain courses of action. In the post–Cold War period, state leaders turn to human rights discourse to articulate "national interests" and assert moral superiority.[38] Virtually no state leader will acknowledge human rights violations perpetrated by the state, but instead will cling to the identity of the state as a human rights supporter and upholder.[39] In fact, state leaders seeking legitimacy will claim that human rights norms support their actions.[40]

The human rights "rationales and justifications for behavior which are prof-fered, together with any pleas for understanding or admission of guilt, as well as the responsiveness to such reasoning on the part of other states,"[41] are indicative of the efficacy of human rights norms.

Particularism versus Universalism

Human rights can be seen as reflecting a cosmopolitan sentiment that every human being should matter equally in relation to all others, and thus that each human being should be given equal consideration.[42] Two competing humanitarian ethics are embodied in this trade-off: ethical universalism and ethical particularism. This section explores these two orientations and explains how U.S. human rights policy appears universalist but actually is particularist in orientation.

Universalism and particularism differ according to their emphasis on: (1) individuals as agents capable of making choices; (2) the significance of prior relationships to other individuals; and (3) the nature and application of prin-ciples of ethical behavior.

Ethical universalism views all people "as agents capable of making choices surrounded by a universe of other such agents."[43] The relationship of individ-uals to one another may be significant in establishing ethical standards for behavior on a less "fundamental level." However, on a basic level, the duties that individuals have toward one another are determined by "general facts about other individuals," and not by any particular facts about their relation-ships. For example, my duty to feed a hungry person is determined primarily by the fact that the person is hungry and that I have food. That the hungry person is my relative, my neighbor, or my student does not matter on a basic level in determining this duty.

In contrast, ethical particularism "invokes the different picture of the ethical universe, in which agents are already encumbered with a variety of ties and commitments to particular other agents, or to groups or collectivities, and they begin their ethical reasoning from those commitments."[44] In this case, we begin our ethical reasoning by "taking account of the various relationships in which we stand to others."[45] Thus, that the hungry person is related to the person with food, while not determinative of the existence and nature of a duty, may be a highly significant relational fact in the duty calculus.

David Miller suggests that we can discern the core differences between these two approaches by understanding what the universalist will identify as the main weakness in particularism and, conversely, what the particularist will identify as the main weakness in universalism. Of central concern to the universalist is the apparent disregard of ethical particularism for reason in favor of sentiment, prejudice, and convention. More troubling is the failure of the particularist to search for a set of principles that could establish duties and guide conduct consistently and the unwillingness of the particularist to subject the purported existence and perceived nature of local relationships to rational scrutiny. This, notes Miller, leads to two dangers: "One is moral conservatism, the sanctification of merely traditional ethical relations, based on the interests of dominant social groups, on outmoded philosophies, or perhaps on sheer ignorance. The other is incoherence, where the ethical demands that stem from the relationships of different kinds are not brought into any rational relation with one another, so that a person who follows a particularist ethics would receive no guidance in cases where he was pulled in one direction by one set of obligations and the opposite direction by a second set."[46]

A particularist human rights policy deters the redress of social injustices and deters progressive social changes. Particularism supports the interests of dominant social groups by protecting their rights to the neglect of the rights of less powerful and unpopular minorities. By emphasizing the territoriality of values, particularism makes geography destiny. "If we adopt this perspective," Ken Booth warns, "the chessboard of international relations—and hence the politics of human rights—will be entirely synonymous with the geography of meaning."[47] Although spatial relationships are important, people move in many spaces and frequently alter their spatial relationships over time. Given this dynamic movement, "local" culture is never "pure"; rather, it is influenced by and, in turn, influences international culture.[48]

Particularly troubling for universalists is the manner in which a few elite spokespersons articulate the specific dimensions of a people, deeming themselves qualified to state the "real interests" of the group. And yet, those advancing the particularist claim often do not genuinely and legitimately represent those on whose behalf they are making the claim. The problem of cultural authenticity is complicated by the fact that cultures are not static but are constantly in flux.[49]

The main criticism that particularists have of universalists could be summed up as follows: the world simply does not work in a universalist way. For ethical particularism, it is implausible to assume that human beings exercise moral agency in the manner demanded by ethical universalism. Human beings are not equipped to determine moral duties by reflecting on the human condition in the abstract. In the real world, people are not detached and wholly autonomous creatures. Further, individuals are rarely motivated by purely rational considerations. Ethical duties are in fact determined by personal identity; considerations about who we are, where we come from, and to which communities we belong greatly influence our ethical reasoning.[50]

Where universalism insists that ethical motivations be grounded in rational convictions about morality and not influenced by sentiments, prejudices, and prior relationships with the objects of the duty, particularists insist that these often irrational motivations must be present. After all, one can only have rights as a member of a particular group and tradition and, it follows, one can only respond to rights violations as a member of a group. Far from being an abstract, individualistic-oriented rulebook, ethical life is a "social institution whose principles must accommodate natural sentiments towards relatives, colleagues, and so forth, and which must rely on a complex set of motives to get people to comply with its requirements—motives such as love, pride, and shame as well as purely rational convictions."[51]

Those who reject ethical universalism vis-à-vis U.S. human rights policy offer several lines of criticism, yet a common element is that the social relationships and particularist sentiments motivating behavior on human rights issues is highly significant. In today's post–Cold War era of globalization, they argue, recognition of the particular communal context is essential for avoiding human rights imperialism.[52] While globalization has entailed an increasing interdependence and a degree of norm convergence at the world level, it has also had the contradictory impact of increasing the fragmentation of states and peoples.[53] The ability of powerful states like the United States to make credible military threats, to persuade other countries to join in economic sanctions, and to offer enticing economic inducements puts pressure on local decision making. Local traditions and values, threatened by encroaching global moralism, must be protected. Thus, as a survival tactic in the increasingly interconnected world, economic, social, and cultural networks have formed to resist imperialism and to promote their own collective interests.[54] In this context, critics of universalism assert, the forced impositions of outside ideas about human rights on local matters may result in retrenchment and reactive nationalism that can lead to human rights disaster for minority groups.

Another argument for particularism takes a more pragmatic stance, and suggests that if one really cares about human rights, one must be at least a bit of a particularist. Some degree of particularism is necessary in order to determine the content of the duty at stake in any particular situation where rights are violated. Similarly, the general ethos of the United States determines the interests that it feels called upon to promote,[55] as well as the circumstances in which it takes risks in relation to those interests. Human beings in fact support human rights policies only when they see some self-interest at stake. This interest need not be related to money and power, but rather can be related to sentiment and identity.[56] The U.S. public, for example, tends to support humanitarian and human rights interventions when the photos of the suffering human rights victims "look like us" and/or "are us" in the sense that they are kin to at least some of us.

Human rights advocates in the U.S. government have long been criticized across the American political spectrum for their universalism. The problem, however, is that they are not universal enough. Many diplomats, U.S. State Department employees, and Pentagon spokespeople do indeed identify as being on the "side of human rights" and espouse the universal language of human rights, but they do so in defense of highly particularistic causes. Today the gap between what they profess to believe in (universal, aspirational rights) and what they actually represent on a political and operational level (particularist, relativist behavior) is enormous. In practice, they are not universalists, but exhibit demonstrably particularist behavior in carving out exceptions for their own actions based on a belief in the United States' special mission in the world. Through its self-perception as the morally and ideologically superior state, the United States advocates human rights for the world and state sovereignty for itself.[57] This being the case, why are human rights norms important at all? The theoretical schools of thought known as the "English school" and "constructivism" shed light on this question.

The English School

Hedley Bull, credited with the founding of the English school, has famously observed that theoretical inquiry into international relations is necessarily about moral or prescriptive questions.[58] While the trained social scientist may objectively and even dispassionately plan studies and gather data, moral and ethical questions inevitably enter into the analysis. None of us is a blank slate. We are individuals brought up in families and communities that have given us a sense of right and wrong and deeply rooted understandings of what it means to relate to one another in furthering the common good. Moreover, the desire to understand behaviors that violate our moral and ethical beliefs attracts many of us to the field of international relations. Although not explicitly prescriptive in nature, most of us hope that our work will do more than satisfy an intellectual curiosity, and will have some real-life application.

The question then is not *whether* but *how* norms should matter in the field of international relations. For the English school, norms are at the core of thinking about international relations. In contrast to scholars who envision an international *system* marked by ad hoc and functional cooperation, adherents of the English school speak in terms of an international *society* in which conduct is guided by norms expressing common sentiment.[59] Bull explains that a "society of states (or an international society) exists when a group of states, conscious of certain common interests and common values, form a society in the sense that they conceive of themselves to be bound by a common set of rules in their relations to one another, and share in the working of common institutions."[60] Other descriptions of international society emphasize that it is a socially constructed ideal, and that the governing norms may be interpreted differently by various actors and over time.[61] While the English school's understanding of international society is state-centric, some scholars writing in this tradition have suggested, as a modification to the tradition, thinking in terms of human relationships, thus moving beyond the state.[62]

While the centrality of norms in international society is fundamental to the English school, scholars differ according to their basic assumptions about the nature and function of norms. There are two main branches of the English school: the pluralist and the solidarist.[63] Proponents of the pluralist branch of the English school accept that the common principles for international social interaction are those related to security and coexistence—that is, sovereignty, nonintervention, and the nonuse of force.[64] For pluralists, these rather limited rules are rationally determined, fixed, and applicable only to state behavior; no space exists for human rights and humanitarian NGOs and other nonstate actors, regardless of their motivations. The solidarist branch of the English school challenges the ontological and epistemological bases of these rules. Solidarists suggest that the principles for interaction in international society are based on a broader principle of solidarity and are not fixed, but rather are susceptible to change along with their normative underpinnings. For solidarists, common moral principles can be identified that apply to both states and individuals. While some solidarists speak in terms of common moral values,[65] others refer to humanity and responsibility.[66] NGOs and humanitarian agencies are not only included in the cast of characters, but their actions can be grounded in altruism as well as cost-benefit analysis.

This book is influenced by the solidarist version of the English school and, in particular, in the commitment of solidarists to human rights as a key constitutive element of international society.[67] In addition to recognizing universal human rights directly as part of the ethical dimension of international society,[68] solidarist writings on legitimacy and justice offer indirect support for the centrality of human rights. They observe that the legitimacy of international society is linked to its commitment to justice. Wheeler explains that "[r]ather than see order and justice locked in a perennial tension, solidarism looks to the possibility of overcoming this conflict by recognizing the mutual interdependence between these two claims."[69] Human rights are one set of international standards that may promote justice and thus advance the legitimacy of international society. Conversely, as the present work seeks to illustrate, when human rights are poorly observed, this legitimacy is undermined. The manner in which human rights norms are observed is critical due to the created nature of social standards, procedures, and values. Because these principles do not exist apart from the community that recognizes them, one must analyze the circumstances and interactions surrounding their deployment. For this type of investigation, the English school alone proves theoretically inadequate.

Constructivism

Constructivism provides a lens through which to analyze the social structure of international society identified by the English school. For the purposes of the present study, constructivism is particularly helpful for understanding (1) the social environment in which norms operate; (2) the circumstances in which norms influence behaviors; and (3) the particular relationship between legal rules and norms. In brief, the English school tells us that norms matter and, at least according to the solidarists, human rights are of central concern. Constructivists stress that identities and interests matter and that actors are most likely to obey norms relevant to society. Perhaps more important, however, constructivists argue that what actors do, how they interact, and the manner in which they (and others) interpret their actions creates and changes the *meaning* of these norms. These dynamics are further elaborated upon in the following section.

An Environment Marked by Social Relationships

At the outset, constructivist theory helps us to think about the environment in which human rights norms are said to exist.[70] Rejecting the unidirectional roadmap analogy, constructivists propose conceiving of the international system as a dynamic network of social relationships.[71] One proponent, Alexander Wendt, explains that the international system contains three elements: "shared knowledge, material resources, and practices."[72] Further, he asserts that the identities and interests of states are not exogenously determined or perma-nently given, but are socially constructed products of learning, knowledge, cultural practices, and ideology.[73] In other words, states do not come to the international arena with identities, interests, and preferences predetermined; rather, their identities, interests, and preferences are continuously shaped through local and international interactions. The distribution of things, like corporate wealth and military arsenals, is similarly socially determined. Like everything else in the world, "material resources acquire meaning for human action through the structure of shared knowledge in which they are embed-ded."[74] The third element Wendt includes—practices—similarly underscores that social structures exist and acquire meaning only through lived realities: processes, interactions, and behavior.[75]

International structures and actors can be understood as mutually con-stitutive because the social construction process does indeed run in both directions.[76] States, through their interactions, help constitute the structure of the system, and the structure, in turn, shapes the identities and interests of states.[77] States' positions on human rights questions help shape the international system in which these norms are defined and enforced. At the same time, however, the international system influences the identities and interests of states that lead them to adopt certain human rights stances. This observation about mutually constitutive social construction runs con-trary to the assumption made by some liberal scholars that human rights policy is driven by a rational, interest-based calculation focused on interests and preferences related to autonomy and security.[78] While many states do engage in such calculations, what is missing from this analysis is that state interests and preferences are formed and continually reformed through the process of social interaction.

Robert Keohane explains the importance of this distinction to the study of the exercise and distribution of power. He notes, "Institutions do not merely reflect the preferences and power of the units constituting them; the institutions themselves shape those preferences and that power. . . . It is therefore not sufficient in this view to treat preferences of individuals as exogenously given: they are affected by institutional arrangements, by prevailing norms, and by historically contingent discourse among people seeking to pursue their pur-poses and solve self-defined problems."[79]

This orientation permits greater influence on norm compliance by nonstate actors.[80] As Margaret Keck and Katherine Sikkink have explained, nonstate actors may act strategically in trying to shape state interests and identities and, accordingly, to influence state behavior.[81] For example, the actions of human rights groups—such as documenting and publicizing human rights abuses and designing high-profile advocacy campaigns naming violators—may lead to a state's reassessment of its best interests. By including NGOs as one among several sets of actors, this book seeks to locate innovations and trends in NGO and civil society attempts to influence U.S. understandings of interest vis-à-vis human rights norms.[82]

Circumstances in Which Norms Influence Behaviors

Constructivist theory provides further insight into the relationships among human rights norms, identities, and behaviors and, in particular, why state actors comply with norms. Wendt, in a leading constructivist text, suggests three explanations given by neorealists, neoliberals, and idealists, respectively: (1) because they are coerced (they are threatened with use of force to produce and enforce a norm); (2) because they see complying as being in their interest (they calculate a cost-benefit analysis and determine there is an incentive to comply); or (3) because they regard the norm as legitimate (the norm becomes a part of who the state is). Only in the last instance are actors' identities constructed by norms; in the others, norms are merely affecting behavior or beliefs.[83] This framework provides a useful starting point for analyzing the circumstances most likely to promote norm compliance. While there is value in all three approaches, this book is most interested in searching for evidence regarding the last—that is, the extent to which human rights norms have become a part of the actor's identity.

The link between human rights identities and behaviors is complicated. An actor's behavior and identity are mutually constitutive in that behavior constructs an identity over time, yet the parameters of behavior are based upon that same identity.[84] Actors usually want to be seen as being on the same side of these norms and, consequently, may lay claim to the identity of norm enforcers or norm promoters.[85] Consequently, in order to make this claim, they may change their behaviors.

Actors may, however, have other reasons for complying with norms, such as fear of sanctions or other coercive measures. Even in such circumstances, their reluctant norm compliance has the (unintended) effect of promoting a human rights identity and, in turn, supporting larger human rights structures and processes.[86] Similarly, even attempts to use human rights in a hypocritical and self-serving manner may nonetheless serve to bolster human rights structures. To take one illustration, Daniel Thomas's study of the Helsinki human rights process demonstrates that although repressive states agreed to be bound by human rights norms in the belief that they could acquire international legitimacy without substantial compliance, "this 'empty' commitment nonetheless promote[d] local, transnational, and interstate processes that undermine continued repression."[87] Once they become part of structures and processes, human rights norms may assume a life of their own, and continue to exert influence even as conditions change. Because they become part of the social space, other actors can relate, not only with these norms, but also with other actors through these norms.

The norms that have the most powerful influence over an actor's identity and behavior are those that have become so deeply rooted that they can be said to be embedded in identities and structures and thereby internalized. Jeffrey Checkel has described this process as "social learning," that is, "a process whereby actors, through interaction with broader institutional context (norms or discursive structures), acquire new interests and preferences—in the absence of obvious material incentives."[88] Through social learning, not only are actors' identities transformed, but their interests are changed as well. Jeffrey Lego has pointed out that while states do have multiple identities (e.g., sometimes acting as doves, sometimes as hawks), states will choose which norms to follow according to an assessment of the norms' impacts on the most salient of state identities.[89]

Finnemore and Sikkink describe a three-step life cycle for norm influence.[90] They observe that "[c]hange in each stage . . . is characterized by different actors, motivations, and mechanisms of influence."[91] In brief, in the first stage, norm emergence, particularly influential people—"norm entrepreneurs"—"frame policy choices in human rights terms. In so doing, they call attention to issues or even 'create' new issues,"[92] and "attempt to convince a critical mass of states (norm leaders) to embrace new norms."[93] In the second stage, largely due to such factors as pressure for conformity, norms begin to "cascade" down to domestic society. Where in the first stage persuasion is used to encourage states to embrace new norms, in the second stage norms spread through a process of socialization. Finally, at the "extreme end of the norm cascade," norms are internalized.[94]

For foreign policy decision makers, this process holds great importance. "Once a norm becomes internalized in this way, it is not simply one among a number of considerations that must be added into the calculus of foreign-policy decision-making," Ward Thomas has explained, "it becomes one of the foundational assumptions on which that calculus is based."[95] Where norms become foundational assumptions, actors are pulled into compliance with them. This is so, not because of some specific incentives for compliance in a particular case, but because the actors have already determined that compliance will serve their interests and identities over the long run.[96] In such situations, the norm acquires a taken-for-granted quality in that compliance is expected and there is little contentious debate over the appropriateness of the norm.[97]

So how can one find evidence of norm embeddedness? This study is based on the assumption that what actors both do *and* say matters. As Thomas Risse and Kathryn Sikkink have demonstrated, dialogue, communication, and argumentation are essential mechanisms for the socialization of norms.[98] Rhetoric connected to reputation is particularly helpful for tracing norm socialization. Actors continually strive to communicate in a manner that enhances their reputation by, for example, portraying themselves as being in compliance with applicable norms. Wendt explains that "identities and their corresponding interests are learned and then reinforced in response to how actors are treated by Others."[99] This process is referred to as "reflected appraisals" or "mirroring" because "actors come to see themselves as a reflection of how they think. Others see or 'appraise' them, in the 'mirror' of the Others' representation of the Self."[100] Audie Klotz's impressive study of the influence of international norms on state stances on apartheid illustrates that concern for reputation can play a role in influencing human rights foreign policy.[101] Drawing on such works, this book considers how the United States presents itself to the world on human rights issues.

Cynics point out that the U.S. military's reference to human rights and humanitarian norms can at times be hypocritical and self-serving. This may be true. Nonetheless, the mere reference to the norms, as distinct from behavior indicating compliance, demonstrates a desire to be seen as promoting the norm and, thus, the importance of the norm for the actor's identity and interests. In the same vein, how a state's behavior within a regime is interpreted by others, what pleas for understanding or admissions of guilt are made, and how others respond to these claims are all component parts of explaining the socialization of a norm.[102] Thus, this study searches for references to human rights norms not only in behaviors, but also in speech, including interviews, public addresses, and memoirs.

The Role of Legal Norms

This book also develops the strand of constructivism that analyzes the role of legal rules and norms. In particular, it considers the legal rules pertaining to human rights. As explained above, constructivist theorists have found some norms to be "constitutive" in that they define the identity of an actor. Applying this insight to legal norms, Peter Katzenstein has explained that legal rules have constitutive effects when they "specify what actions will cause relevant others to recognize a particular identity."[103] Where norms are thought of not as constitutive but as merely "regulative," they operate as "standards that specify the proper enactment of an already specified identity."[104] To use Friedrich Kratochwil's oft-cited example, the rules of chess make the game itself.[105] One could play by other rules on the same board, but one would be playing a different game. In the same vein, constitutive international rules are said to be constitutive of the international system, defining the identities and interests of actors in the system. Good illustrations of rules that help form the identities of actors are the shared understandings that bestow recognition on states and their respective rights and duties.[106] Thus, for example, the sovereign equality of states is said to be a constitutive legal rule of the Westphalian system.[107] This rule could disappear, but then so would the Westphalian system.[108]

Constitutive legal rules define the interests and identities of international actors.[109] Constitutive rules determine "what constitutes relevant political behavior, what power is, and which dimensions of collective life are most significant."[110] In this sense they are part of the architecture of state identity. One need not define with precision the constitutive rules of the international system.[111] Instead, what matters here is the perception of "constitutive rules" and the identification of rule violators. To extend the example introduced above, this study is interested in how international actors that violate accepted norms of sovereignty define themselves, how others define them, and the expectations, behavioral patterns, and structures that emanate from such definitions. Those regarded as breaching sovereignty norms may be viewed positively as sovereignty-free actors, transboundary entities, and norm entrepreneurs, or they may simply be called international law breakers. This book examines not the mere existence of rules or compliance with rules, but also the perception of rules and the resulting expectations and behaviors reflected through processes.[112]

For this study, nonconstitutive legal rules hold equal importance to the extent that they also shape identities. Both legal rules and norms are important parts of the shared knowledge of a wide range of actors, and these actors define themselves within the community in relation to these rules. At the same time, the material resources and structure of society are created and manipulated by the actors' involvement with legal rules and norms. This book is particularly interested in how the process of human rights norm definition and enforcement demonstrates who we are as a society, what we value, how power is distributed, and how relationships are regulated.[113]

Process theory within the field of international law is somewhat analogous to constructivist approaches to the socialization and internalization of norms. Process theorists traditionally examine the horizontal legal process that occurs among nation-states interacting within treaty regimes.[114] But Koh, a leading scholar writing in this tradition, suggests instead a focus on the vertical process "whereby international norms become domesticated and internalized into domestic law."[115] Among law-abiding states, he notes a three-step process of "interaction, interpretation and internalization of international norms."[116] He has made the important observation that "[a]s transnational actors interact, they create patterns of behavior and generate norms of external conduct which they in turn internalize."[117] It is through a repeated process of "interaction and internalization that international law acquires its 'stickiness,' that nation-states acquire their identity, and that nations define promoting the rule of international law as part of their self-interest."[118]

Koh's project thus examines why states obey, and how law-abiding states internalize international law in their domestic and legal political structures. In contrast, this book examines how law-abiding non-state actors internalize international laws and norms into their identities and communities. Notwithstanding the different goals, Koh's detailed analysis of transboundary relations provides a useful framework for this study, which complements the constructivist orientation.

THREE ARGUMENTS

Using the tools described above, this book uses a close study of post–Cold War civilian policy making, military actions, and activist strategies to test three arguments.

First, human rights norms matter as they shape the identities, interests, and expectations of all three groups of actors (U.S. presidential administrations, the military, and the activist community). Of these three groups, the identity of the U.S. military has changed the most in casting off the traditional warrior image and adopting an identity of professionalism and humanitarianism. Moreover, just as human rights norms have impacted military identity and behavior, so too have changes in the military impacted human rights. By using human rights terms—at least sometimes—to define purposes or guide actions, the military does indeed play an important role in framing the debate about international problems and in making human rights arguments more socially available.

Second, American exceptionalism prevents human rights norms from progressing into consistent human rights behaviors. Although U.S. policy-making and military actors have long tended to pronounce themselves as universalists on human rights, they act as particularists, failing to apply human rights norms to their own behaviors. A view of human rights in which the doctrine applies only to others and not to oneself with the same consistency undermines the main tenet that human rights are to be applied to all equally. Thus, to the extent that the United States is leading the world on human rights by example, it is leading the world in the wrong direction.

Third, for the presidential administrations and the military, the trend toward the institutionalization of human rights norms has been influenced by numerous external actors who have become increasingly sophisticated in their activities. Civil society has a subtle yet significant impact on human rights and U.S. foreign policy. Largely due to the influence of civil society, human rights policy in the United States is today a rhetorically available idea, filled with hope and radiating culturally and morally loaded values.

Despite the creative and unrelenting efforts of human rights advocates, human rights have yet to become deeply embedded in institutions so as to have a "taken for granted" feel. This book explains this quandary: Human rights behavior is much harder to come by than human rights talk. Politicians deploy human rights rhetoric easily, but on closer inspection it turns out to be fools' gold.

ENDNOTES

1. Michael Ignatieff, "Human Rights as Politics," in *Human Rights as Politics and Idolatry*, ed. Amy Gutmann (Princeton, N.J.: Princeton University Press, 2001), 16.
2. Andrew Lui, "Do Human Rights Have a Future? A Study of Transformation in International Relations," paper presented at the Forty-fourth Annual Convention of the International Studies Association, Portland, Oregon, 2003.
3. Martha Finnemore and Kathryn Sikkink, "International Norm Dynamics and Political Change," *International Organization* 52, no. 4 (1998): 904.
4. Harold Hongju Koh, "On American Exceptionalism," *Stanford Law Review* 55 (2003): 1485–87.
5. Koh identifies another form of exceptionalism that is rarely of concern, the "flying buttress mentality"—that is, when the United States harms its own reputation by failing to agree with international mechanisms even as it complies with the substantive mandate of those mechanisms.
6. Koh, "On American Exceptionalism," 1487.
7. References to "American exceptionalism" in this text refer to this double-standard form.

8. See the list in the appendix. Note that many people interviewed who are in the military and government wished to remain unnamed.

9. Alexander Wendt and Raymond Duvall, "Institutions and International Order," in *Global Changes and Theoretical Challenges: Approaches to World Politics for the 1990s*, ed. Ernst-Otto Czempiel and James S. Rosenau (Toronto: Lexington, 1989), 51.

10. See Tim Dunne and Nicholas J. Wheeler, "Introduction," in *Human Rights in Global Politics* (Cambridge: Cambridge University Press, 1999), 1–28.

11. Jack Donnelly, "The Social Construction of International Human Rights," in *Human Rights in Global Politics,* ed. Tim Dunne and Nicholas J. Wheeler (Cambridge: Cambridge University Press, 1999), 71–102. See also Carlos Santiago Nino, *The Ethics of Human Rights* (Oxford: Clarendon Press, 1991), 141, 216.

12. R. J. Vincent, *Human Rights and International Relations* (New York: Cambridge University Press, 1986), 152.

13. See, e.g., Alan Donagan, *The Theory of Morality* (Chicago: University of Chicago Press, 1977); and Joseph Boyle, "Natural Law and International Ethics," in *Traditions of International Ethics*, ed. Terry Nardin and David R. Mapel (New York: Cambridge University Press, 1992).

14. See, e.g., Henry Shue, *Basic Rights: Subsistence, Affluence and U.S. Foreign Policy* (Princeton, N.J.: Princeton University Press, 1980).

15. See, e.g., Jack Donnelly, *Universal Human Rights in Theory and Practice* (Ithaca, N.Y.: Cornell University Press, 1989); and Rhoda Howard and Jack Donnelly, "Human Dignity, Human Rights and Political Regimes," *American Political Science Review* 80 (1986): 801–17.

16. See, e.g., Ken Booth, "Three Tyrannies," in *Human Rights in Global Politics*, ed. Tim Dunne and Nicholas J. Wheeler (Cambridge: Cambridge University Press, 1999), 31–70.

17. See, e.g., Michael Perry, *The Idea of Human Rights* (New York: Oxford University Press, 1998).

18. See, e.g., William F. Schultz, *In Our Own Best Interest: How Defending Human Rights Benefits Us All* (Boston: Beacon Press, 2001).

19. See, e.g., Bhikhu Paarekh, "Non-ethnocentric Universalism," in *Human Rights in Global Politics*, ed. Tim Dunne and Nicholas J. Wheeler (Cambridge: Cambridge University Press, 1999), 128–59.

20. See, e.g., Andrew Hurrell, "Power, Principles and Prudence: Protecting Human Rights in a Deeply Divided World," in *Human Rights in Global Politics*, ed. Tim Dunne and Nicholas J. Wheeler (Cambridge: Cambridge University Press, 1999), 277–302.

21. Amy Gutmann, "Introduction," in Michael Ignatieff, *Human Rights as Politics and Idolatry*, ed. Amy Gutmann with commentary by K. Anthony Appiah, David A. Hollinger, Thomas W. Laqueur, and Diane F. Orentlicher (Princeton, N.J.: Princeton University Press, 2001), xi.

22. Ibid., xxiii.

23. This argument about the relative unimportance of foundations should not be over-stated. The foundational basis for human rights does shape the content of the rights recognized and most avidly enforced.

24. Chris Brown, "Universal Human Rights: A Critique," in *Human Rights in Global Politics*, ed. Tim Dunne and Nicholas J. Wheeler (Cambridge: Cambridge University Press, 1999), 103–27.

25. Jean Bethke Elshtain, "The Dignity of the Human Person and the Idea of Human Rights" (book review), *Journal of Law and Religion* 14 (1999–2000): 53–57; see also Lisa Sowle Cahill, "Toward a Christian Theory of Human Rights," *Journal of Religious Ethics* 9 (1980): 278.
26. Donnelly, *Universal Human Rights*, 81.
27. David P. Forsythe, *Human Rights in International Relations* (New York: Cambridge University Press, 2000), 3.
28. Paarekh, "Non-ethnocentric Universalism," 149.
29. "Vienna Declaration and Programme for Action," presented at the World Conference on Human Rights, Vienna, June 14–25, 1993. United Nations General Assembly A/CONF/157/23. Available online at www.unhchr.ch/huridoca.nsf/(Symbol)/A.CONF.157.23.En?OpenDocument.
30. Donnelly, *Universal Human Rights*, 81.
31. Paarekh, "Non-ethnocentric Universalism," 149.
32. Ignatieff, *Human Rights as Politics and Idolatry*, 16.
33. Uprenda Baxi, "Voices of the Suffering, Fragmented Universality and the Future of Human Rights," in *The Future of International Human Rights*, ed. B. H. Weston and S. P. Marks (Ardsley, N.Y.: Transnational Publishers, 1999), 102.
34. See, e.g., Kurt Mills, *Human Rights in the Emerging Global Order: A New Sovereignty?* (New York: Palgrave, 1998); William Korey, *NGOs and the Universal Declaration of Human Rights* (New York: St. Martin's Press, 1998); and Richard Falk, *Human Rights and State Sovereignty* (London: Holms and Meier, 1981).
35. Ignatieff, *Human Rights as Politics and Idolatry*, 16.
36. Jack Donnelly, *International Human Rights*, 2nd ed. (Boulder, Colo.: Westview Press, 1998), 20.
37. Marie-Benedicte Dembour, "Human Rights Talk and Anthropological Ambivalence: The Particular Contexts of Universal Claims," in *Inside and Outside the Law: Anthropological Studies of Authority and Ambiguity*, ed. Olivia Harris (New York: Routledge, 1996), 35.
38. For an analysis of the impact of this shift toward human rights on U.S. foreign policy, see Steve Wagonseil, "Human Rights in U.S. Foreign Policy," *Journal of Intergroup Relations* 26 (1999): 30–31.
39. See, generally, David P. Forsythe, *Human Rights and Comparative Foreign Policy* (New York: United Nations University Press, 2000).
40. Nicholas J. Wheeler, *Saving Strangers: Humanitarian Intervention in International Society* (New York: Oxford University Press, 2000), 285.
41. Friedrich Kratochwil and John Ruggie, "International Organization: A State of the Art or the State of the Art," *International Organization* 40, no. 4 (1986): 753–75.
42. David Miller, *On Nationality* (New York: Oxford University Press, 1995), 49.
43. Ibid., 50.
44. Ibid.
45. Ibid.
46. Ibid., 56.
47. Booth, "Three Tyrannies," 53.
48. See, e.g., Michael Peter Smith and Luis Eduardo Guarnizo, *Transnationalism from Below* (New Brunswick, N.J.: Transaction, 1998).
49. See, generally, Richard A. Wilson, "Human Rights, Culture and Context," in *Human Rights, Culture and Context: Anthropological Perspectives,* ed. Richard A. Wilson (New York: Pluto Press, 1999).

50. Gertrude Himmelfarb, "The Illusions of Cosmopolitanisms," in *For Love of Country: Debating the Limits of Patriotism,* ed. Martha C. Nussbaum (Boston: Beacon Press, 1996), 72–77.

51. Miller, *On Nationality,* 58.

52. See, e.g., Norman Lewis, "Human Rights, Law and Democracy in an Unfree World," in *Human Rights Fifty Years On: A Reappraisal,* ed. Tony Evans (Manchester: Manchester University Press, 1998), 77–104, esp. 96–97.

53. See, e.g., Sol Picciotto, "Networks in International Economic Integration: Fragmented States and the Dilemmas of Neo-Liberalism," *Northwestern Journal of International Law and Business* 17 (1996–97): 1014–45.

54. I develop this argument in Julie Mertus, "From Legal Transplants to Transformative Justice: Human Rights and the Promise of Transnational Civil Society," *American University Journal of International Law* 15, no. 5 (1999): 1335.

55. Miller, *On Nationality,* 6, 8.

56. Richard Rorty has argued persuasively that adherence to the idea of human rights necessitates a certain amount of identification with the oppressed group; see Rorty, *Contingency, Irony and Solidarity* (New York: Cambridge University Press, 1989).

57. Harlan Grant Cohen, "The American Challenge to International Law: A Tentative Framework for Debate," *Yale Journal of International Law* 28 (2003): 562.

58. Hedley Bull, "Introduction," in *International Theory: The Three Traditions,* ed. Martin Wight (Leicester: Leicester University Press, 1991), 4.

59. Barry Buzan, "From International System to International Society: Structural Regime Theory Meets the English School," *International Organization* 47, no. 3 (1993): 233–36.

60. Hedley Bull, *The Anarchical Society: A Study of Order in World Politics,* 2nd ed. (London: Macmillan, 1995), 13.

61. Mark Hoffman, "Normative International Theory: Approaches and Issues," in *Contemporary International Relations: A Guide to Theory,* ed. Margot Light and A. J. R. Groom (London: Pinter, 1994), 27–44.

62. Martin Shaw, "Global Society and Global Responsibility: The Theoretical, Historical and Political Limits of 'International Society,'" *Millennium: Journal of International Studies* 21, no. 3 (1992): 421–34.

63. Timothy Dunne, *Inventing International Society: A History of the English School*; St. Anthony's Series (Basingstoke, England: Macmillan, 1998); Nicholas J. Wheeler, "Pluralist or Solidarist Conceptions of International Society: Bull and Vincent on Humanitarian Intervention," *Millennium: Journal of International Studies* 21, no. 3 (1992): 463–87.

64. Wheeler, *Saving Strangers,* 11.

65. See, e.g., Nicholas J. Wheeler and Timothy Dunne, "Good International Citizenship: A Third Way for British Foreign Policy," *International Affairs* 74, no. 4 (1988): 847–70.

66. See, e.g., Andrew Linklater, "Citizenship and Sovereignty in the Post-Westphalian State," *European Journal of International Relations* 2, no. 1 (1996): 77–103.

67. R. J. Vincent, *Human Rights in International Relations* (New York: Cambridge University Press, 1986).

68. Wheeler and Dunne, "Good International Citizenship," 847–70.

69. Wheeler, *Saving Strangers,* 11.

70. See John G. Ruggie, *Constructing the World Polity: Essays on International Institutionalism* (New York: Routledge, 1998); Nicholas G. Onuf, W*orld of Our Making: Rules and Rule in Social Theory and International Relations* (Columbia: University of South Carolina Press, 1989); Friedrich V. Kratochwil, *Rules, Norms, and Decisions* (New York: Cambridge University Press, 1989); Alexander Wendt, "Constructing International Politics," *International Security* 20 (1995): 77–78.

71. Alexander Wendt, "Anarchy Is What States Make of It: The Social Construction of Power Politics," *International Organization* 46 (1992): 405–7.

72. Wendt, "Constructing International Politics," 73.

73. Harold Hongju Koh, "Review Essay: Why Do Nations Obey International Law?" *Yale Law Journal* 106 (1997): 2650 (discussing Wendt and the constructivist and "international society" school of international law).

74. Wendt, "Constructing International Politics," 73.

75. Ibid.

76. Anthony Clark Arend, "Do Legal Rules Matter? International Law and International Politics," *Virginia Journal of International Law* 38 (1998): 107–29.

77. Ibid.

78. Andrew Moravcik, "The Origins of Human Rights Regimes: Democratic Delegation in Postwar Europe," *International Organization* 54 (2000): 217–52.

79. Robert O. Keohane, "International Institutions: Two Approaches," *International Studies Quarterly* 32 (1988): 379–82.

80. See, generally, Margaret Keck and Kathryn Sikkink, *Activists beyond Borders: Advocacy Networks in International Relations* (Ithaca, N.Y.: Cornell University Press, 1998).

81. Ibid. see esp. 887–917.

82. See, e.g., Christian Reus-Smith, "The Constitutional Structure of International Society and the Nature of Fundamental Institutions," *International Organization* 51 (1997): 555–69; Audie Klotz, "Norms Reconstituting Interests: Global Racial Equality and U.S. Sanctions Against South Africa," *International Organization* 49 (1995): 451; and Martha Finnemore, "International Organizations as Teachers of Norms: The United Nations Education, Scientific, and Cultural Organization and Science Policy," *International Organization* 47 (1993): 565.

83. Wendt, "Constructing International Politics," 73.

84. See Arend, "Do Legal Rules Matter?" 129.

85. See, generally, the work Keck and Sikkink, *Activists beyond Borders.*

86. Thomas Risse calls this process "argumentative self-entrapment," in which state actors fall into the spiral of becoming increasingly accountable to their own assertions of being norm promoters; see Risse, "Let's Argue! Communicative Action and International Relations," *International Organization* 54 (2000): 32.

87. Daniel Thomas, *The Helsinki Effect* (Princeton, N.J.: Princeton University Press, 2001), 3.

88. Jeffrey Checkel, "The Constructivist Turn in International Relations Theory," *World Politics* 50, no. 2 (1998): 324–48.

89. Jeffrey W. Lego, "When Norms Matter: Revisiting the 'Failure' of Internationalism," *International Organization* 51 (1997): 31–63.

90. Finnemore and Sikkink, "International Norm Dynamics," 895.

91. Ibid.

92. Ibid., 897.

93. Ibid., 895.

94. Ibid., 904.

95. Ward Thomas, *The Ethics of Destruction: Norms and Force in International Relations* (Ithaca, N.Y.: Cornell University Press, 2001), 38.

96. In this sense, the ethical tradition behind behaviors could be viewed as "rule utilitarianism," not act utilitarianism. Rule utilitarianism holds that the "correct rules are those the general observance of which maximize utility." See Anthony Ellis, "Utilitarianism and International Ethics," in *Traditions of International Ethics*, ed. Terry Nardin and David R. Mapel (New York: Cambridge University Press, 1992), 158–79.

97. Finnemore and Sikkink, "International Norm Dynamics," 895.

98. See Risse, "Let's Argue!" 1–39; see also Thomas Risse and Kathryn Sikkink, *The Power of Principles: The Socialization of Human Rights Norms in Domestic Practice* (New York: Cambridge University Press, 1999).

99. Alexander Wendt, *Social Theory of International Politics* (Cambridge: Cambridge University Press, 1999), 327.

100. Ibid.

101. Audie Klotz, *Norms in International Relations: The Struggle against Apartheid.* (Ithaca, N.Y.: Cornell University Press, 1995).

102. John G. Ruggie, *Constructing the World Polity: Essays on International Institutionalization* (London: Routledge, 1998).

103. Peter Katzenstein, "Introduction: Alternative Perspectives on National Security," in *The Culture of National Security: Norms and Identity in World Politics*, ed. Peter Katzenstein (New York: Columbia University Press, 1996), 5.

104. Ibid.

105. Friedrich V. Kratochwil, *Rules, Norms, and Decisions: On the Conditions of Practical and Legal Reasoning in International Relations and International Affairs* (Cambridge: Cambridge University Press), 26.

106. See Restatement (Third) of the Foreign Relations Law of the United States, Sec. 201 (1987).

107. Stephen A. Kocs, "Explaining the Strategic Behavior of States: International Law as System Structure," *International Studies Quarterly* 38 (1994): 535.

108. Some commentators would say the Westphalian system has already disappeared. See, e.g., the essays in Gene M. Lyons and Michael Mastanduno, eds., *Beyond Westphalia? State Sovereignty and International Intervention* (Baltimore: Johns Hopkins University Press, 1995).

109. Wendt, "Anarchy Is What States Make of It," 391.

110. Paul Wapner, "Politics Beyond the State: Environmental Activism and World Civic Politics," *World Politics* 47 (1995): 319.

111. I would argue only that the very search for such matters as "central principles," "nonderogable," *erga omnes*, or *jus cogens* proves my point: international actors are drawn to perceiving some legal rules as constitutive and others as less important; the identity of many actors and structures are based on such categorizations (or rejection of such categorizations). See, e.g., the now classic debate over "relative normativity" in international law, which was initiated in Prosper Weil, "Towards Relative Normativity in International Law," *American Journal of International Law* 77 (1983): 413, and the responses in Theodor Meron, "On a Hierarchy of International Human Rights," *American Journal of International Law* 80 (1986): 1, and in John Tasioulas, "In Defense of Relative Normativity: Communitarian Values and the Nicaragua Case," *Oxford Journal of Legal Studies* 16 (1996): 85.

112. This study thus departs significantly from the traditional international law require-
     ments for norm formation. While international relations scholars commonly examine
     how rules are socially constructed, international lawyers adhere to the traditional twin
     requirements—state practice and *opinio juris*—for the formation of customary inter-
     national law. Where state practice is lacking, international lawyers may stress *opinio
     juris*. They may also look for evidence of intent in treaty law, treaty negotiations,
     international standards, and other "soft law," or attempt other tactics to dodge the
     practice requirement. See, generally, Michael Beyers, *Custom, Power and the Power
     of Rules: International Relations and Customary International Law* (New York:
     Cambridge University Press, 1998); Jordan J. Paust, "Customary International Law:
     Its Nature, Sources and Status as Law of the United States," *Michigan Journal of
     International Law* 12 (1990): 59; see also Theodor Meron, "The Continuing Role
     of Custom in the Formation of International Humanitarian Law," *American Journal
     of International Law* 90 (1996): 238–39.

113. Philip Allott explains the constitutive nature of power as "a power over consciousness
     itself, through its control of society's reality-forming, as well as the power to embody
     the values derived from such reality-forming in legal relations and to interpret and
     apply those legal relationships authoritatively." See Allott, *Eunomia: New Order for
     a New World* (Cambridge: Cambridge University Press, 1990), 210.

114. See, e.g., Abram Chayes and Antonia Handler Chayes, *The New Sovereignty* (Cam-
     bridge, Mass.: Harvard University Press, 1995).

115. Harold Hongju Koh, "The 1998 Frankel Lecture: Bringing International Law Home,"
     Houston Law Review 35 (1998): 623–35.

116. Harold Hongju Koh, "Why Do Nations Obey Law?" 2599–2603.

117. Harold Hongju Koh, "Transnational Legal Process," *Nebraska Law Review* 75 (1996):
     181–202.

118. Ibid.

TWO

THE *LINGUA FRANCA* OF DIPLOMACY: HUMAN RIGHTS AND THE POST–COLD WAR PRESIDENCIES

Human rights have long been central to U.S. self-image.[1] The Declaration of Independence's proclamation of "inalienable rights" is, in fact, an assertion that certain rights are neither granted by government nor subject to removal by government. And from the beginning, U.S. foreign policy has been concerned with projecting a positive image of U.S. national identity and values. As Arthur Schlesinger observed, "Americans have agreed since 1776 that the United States must be a beacon of human rights to an unregenerate world. The question has always been how the U.S. would execute this mission."[2] It would be wrong to assert that U.S. foreign policy has only recently assumed an interest in human rights—that interest has been there all along. What is new is the frequency with which the United States has invoked human rights as rhetorical justifications for its actions.

The relationship of human rights to U.S. foreign policy has traditionally been framed in terms of national interests. One could say that today U.S. national interests solidly include the promotion of human rights and the disassociation of the United States from regimes that are abusive on human rights issues.[3] Or one could assert that in U.S. foreign policy national interests may be trumped by "moral sensitivities," including caring for fundamental human rights.[4] Regardless of whether one sees a redefinition of national interest or a greater accommodation of moral considerations, the United States does in fact rhetorically invoke human rights concerns in its foreign dealings with increasing frequency. In the words of Chester Crocker, "human rights have become part of the furniture when it comes to U.S. diplomacy."[5] U.S. diplomats invoke human rights rhetoric so frequently that, to some extent, they have built up expectations that the United States will demand compliance with human rights norms. Advocates thus frame U.S. policy options in human rights terms with the hope that this framing will generate attention and influence outcomes.[6]

The framing of policy choices in human rights terms, however, must compete with alternative ways of interpreting the problem and, worse yet, the general public accepts these alternatives as viable choices. To put it bluntly, human rights are not the only game in town, and quite frequently other games garner more attention. Kathryn Sikkink has pointed to the post–World War II pressures of anticommunism and the segregationist sentiment among conservative states in the nation as "more powerful clusters of ideas/interests" blocking adoption of a strong U.S. human rights policy.[7] Even after these ideas subsided, Sikkink observes, "human rights ideas did not totally displace earlier interpretations of national security, but rather continued to exist with them among some members of Congress, the executive, and the general public."[8]

After the September 11 attacks on the World Trade Center and Pentagon, human rights ideas must also contend with the pressures of antiterrorism and the willingness of the general public to accept double standards when justified by antiterrorism claims.[9] Yet doomsayers who bemoan the end of human rights are clearly wrong. Even with competition from alternative ideas, the promotion and protection of human rights norms has remained a legitimate concern of U.S. foreign policy, albeit one with stiff competition for attention.

The continued presence of human rights as an influential policy theme during skeptical administrations can be explained by both the institutionalization of such rights and their centrality for American identity. This does not mean that each presidential administration has embraced human rights and responded in a consistent manner to human rights concerns. On the contrary, the story of human rights in U.S. foreign policy is one of perpetual tension and resistance, of interpretation and reinterpretation. This chapter explores the nature of this dynamic process, exposing the way in which it involves both acceptance of and resistance to human rights.

While also outlining earlier historical developments, this chapter focuses on the development of U.S. human rights foreign policy in the post–Cold War presidential administrations of George H.W. Bush, Bill Clinton, and George W. Bush. For each administration, the chapter considers four questions:

1. *What was inherited?* How do institutional legacies from previous administrations constrain the new administration in its development and deployment of human rights policy? (A somewhat more detailed background is provided with the first post–Cold War president, George H. W. Bush, simply because he is the beginning of our narrative and the history each president inherits is cumulative.)

2. *What was retained, and what was changed?* In what ways did the new administration either continue to use the human rights institutions of its predecessor, or conversely, deride the human rights stance of its predecessor in order to distinguish its own goals, objectives, and the country's interests? What specific changes were made to existing institutions or programs, and which new ones were created in the process of using this norms-based language?

3. *What were the constraints?* What constraints or influences can we identify based on the expectations and demands of other actors, including U.S. allies, citizens of the country being targeted, American citizens, government employees, the military, nongovernmental organizations (NGOs), the media, and so on, that moved the administration toward employing or ignoring human rights norms?

4. *What was the degree of norm embeddedness?* Does the evidence suggest that human rights norms are "embedded" in the sense that they have a taken-for-granted quality in influencing policy choices? To what extent will the public sacrifice human rights norms for competing approaches?

PRESIDENT GEORGE H. W. BUSH: HUMAN RIGHTS AND THE NEW WORLD ORDER (1988–1992)

The foreign policy of the United States and the machinery for its formulation and execution must change in order to meet the challenge presented by a dramatically altered international environment.

—Undersecretary of State James Rogers, quoted in David P. Forsythe, "Human Rights Policy: Change and Continuity"

What Was Inherited?

In his assessment of human rights in U.S. foreign policy from 1945 to the inception of the first Bush administration, David Forsythe points out a number of problems that would influence the human rights policies of President George H. W. Bush. Although human rights ideas had been resonant among Americans since the country's founding, American fondness for human rights presented two fundamental problems in foreign policy.[10] At first a reluctant great power and then a more willing superpower, the United States faced the traditional conflict between the commitment to human rights on normative grounds (because they are "right")and the demand that power be exercised or conserved for other interests.

The United States had painfully discovered that although American and international versions of human rights are equally important in an interdependent world, these versions are not necessarily the same. This discovery left the nation with three awkward choices: (1) ignore the differences and pretend that international human rights norms converge perfectly with American values; (2) confront the difference and assert the superiority of the American way of thinking and being (for example, in asserting that civil and political rights warrant more attention than economic, social, and cultural rights); or (3) acknowledge the differences and reform American laws and practices to meet international standards. While the last tactic has never been politically popular in the United States and thus used with extreme rarity, President Bush and his administration had the first two approaches at their disposal, along with a growing number of human rights specialists who could help Bush make his case.[11]

Within the diplomatic core, Bush worked with a number of seasoned political veterans whose careers had been formed by the anticommunism fight. Among them was Secretary of State James Baker, who had been chief of staff in Ronald Reagan's first administration. Lawrence Eagleburger and Brent Scrowcroft were also key players on Bush's staff. They followed in close association with Henry Kissinger and were likewise ideological devotees of détente politics.[12] Bush did, however, choose an advisor to the United Nations Commission for Human Rights, Marc Northern, who was a strong supporter of human rights principles. Northern addressed the commission stating, "The U.S. makes no apology for insisting that where human rights are concerned, every nation, including my own, must be held to the highest standard. . . . We stand ready to help those governments committed to human rights move ahead."[13]

Development of State Department and Congressional Roles

In designing his own policies on human rights, Bush also had to contend with a Congress and State Department that had become increasingly interested in human rights. The willingness of the State Department to engage in human rights issues was a radical departure from earlier times. Under the administrations of Richard Nixon and Gerald Ford, the State Department had opposed the creation of a human rights bureau,[14] and only a single desk officer worked on U.S. positions for UN issues concerning human rights.[15] At the same time, Secretary of State Henry Kissinger was openly hostile to including human rights in American foreign policy concerns.[16] Appearing on the television show *Face the Nation* in 1976, he defended U.S. support for abusive regimes, commenting, "You cannot implement your values unless you survive. . . . Wherever we can, we are trying to nudge [these regimes] in a direction that is compatible with our values. But to pretend that we can simply declare our values and transform the world has a high risk of a policy of constant interventionism in every part of the world and then sticking us with the consequences."[17]

American diplomats rarely criticized oppressive regimes before the administration of Jimmy Carter, and Kissinger made an example of one who did—Ambassador David Popper. When Popper raised human rights concerns to Chilean officials in 1974, Kissinger made sure that his response, "Tell Popper to cut the political science lectures," was widely circulated.[18] Not surprisingly, during this period the United States played a decidedly destructive role in promoting human rights abroad, increasing aid to a range of dictators involved in "dirty wars."

Congress grew increasingly concerned with the glaring absence of human rights on the U.S. foreign policy agenda and by American support for brutish regimes, which included the U.S. backing of the military junta in Greece, support for martial law regimes in South Korea and the Philippines, and U.S. ties to dictatorships in Latin America, including support of the overthrow of a democratic government in Chile and the installation there of a repressive regime.[19] Under the leadership of Congressman Donald Fraiser of Minnesota from 1973 to 1978, the House Foreign Affairs Committee spurred the enactment of a series of legislation linking human rights to U.S. military and economic assistance to other nations. Specific requirements were created for certain countries with histories of abusing human rights, such as Argentina, Chile, and Uruguay. "Because of the mistrust of the executive," John Salzberg's study of U.S. human rights legislation concludes, "even after Carter's election, the legislation became increasingly specific."[20]

Another mechanism used by Congressman Fraiser was the power to hold public hearings in order to influence presidential administrations recalcitrant on human rights issues. The Subcommittee on International Organizations held more than 150 hearings with more than 500 witnesses, examining the human rights records of such countries as Argentina, Chile, Cuba, El Salvador, Indonesia, Israel, Nicaragua, South Korea, and the Soviet Union.[21]

The new flurry of hearings on Capitol Hill was accompanied by changes at the State Department. In 1976, Congress mandated the creation of a new bureau in the State Department[22] and required the secretary of state to promote human rights through U.S. foreign policy.[23] Modest steps were taken to strengthen the weak human rights bureaucracy, but the first coordinator of the new State Department Bureau of Human Rights and Humanitarian Affairs was "really 'no factor' in administration policy-making."[24] Unavailing in its desire to elevate the status of human rights concerns within government, Congress responded by passing legislation elevating the rank of the position to an assistant secretary position.[25] It was in this manner, through the persistence of Congress, and not through any presidential initiatives, that the institutionalization of human rights in U.S. foreign policy began.

The Carter Years: Human Rights Take a Stand

The human rights climate that George H. W. Bush inherited predated the Reagan and Carter years. While President Carter did not initiate the U.S. human rights foreign policy agenda, he did bring an unprecedented presidential commitment to the issue. As Kathryn Sikkink has noted, "Virtually all of the essential human rights legislation was already in place when he took office."[26] All that was needed was for the president to make use of it. In his inaugural address, Carter declared, "We have already found a high degree of personal liberty, and we are now struggling to enhance equality of opportunity. Our commitment to human rights must be absolute, our laws fair, our natural beauty preserved; the powerful must not persecute the weak, and human dignity must be enhanced."[27] The rights the administration sought to address, Secretary of State Cyrus Vance announced in 1997, included

> The right to be free from governmental violations of the integrity of the person. Such violations include torture; cruel, inhuman, or degrading treatment or punishment; and arbitrary arrest or imprisonment; . . . denial of fair public trial and invasion of the home;
> The right to the fulfillment of such vital needs as food, shelter, health care, and education;
> The right to enjoy civil and political liberties; freedom of thought, of religion, of assembly; freedom of speech; freedom of the press; freedom of movement within and outside one's country; freedom to take part in government.[28]

Never before had an American presidency endorsed such a broad list of rights. President Carter's rhetorical allegiance to human rights raised the human rights agenda to public prominence.[29]

The main human rights tactic employed by the Carter administration was one of "public diplomacy," a vast improvement over his predecessor's "quiet diplomacy," which often entailed doing nothing.[30] Combining traditional diplomacy with symbolic actions, Carter's "public diplomacy" on human rights was often at the highest levels of government. In his memoirs, he explains that "whenever I met with the leader of a government which had been accused of wrongdoing its own people, human rights was on the top of my agenda."[31] Nonetheless, during the Carter administration, security and economic interests could be invoked both to support as well as to trump human rights concerns.[32] "This contradiction," Forsythe writes, "helps explain his reluctance to use economic sanctions on Idi Amin's brutal rule in Uganda . . . , and his early reluctance to a congressional effort to link human rights to World Bank and other multilateral loans."[33]

The new human rights bureau at the State Department faced considerable obstacles in the Carter years. The first Assistant Secretary for Human Rights and Humanitarian Affairs, Patricia Derian, was "not warmly welcomed" at the State Department.[34] While Carter had tried to support human rights by elevating Derian's position to the assistant secretary level, clashes between the staff of the human rights and geographic bureaus were frequent, particularly over Latin America. The most significant change in human rights practice at the State Department at this time was the implementation of congressionally mandated human rights reports. Human rights staff members were charged with writing annual country reports on the human rights records of specific states and with monitoring related foreign policy decisions, such as whether improvements in a country's human rights record merited continued foreign aid. While many of the State Department publications were criticized as selectively serving other American foreign policy interests,[35] the reports were seen as conditioning the Foreign Service and State Department cultures to be more sensitive to these issues. This sensitivity continued throughout the Carter administration, even as the Iran hostage crisis and U.S.–Soviet relations eclipsed human rights concerns at the end of the term.[36]

Throughout the administration, the United States played an increasingly active role in United Nations and inter-American human rights bodies,[37] creating worldwide public expectations that the United States would continue to be an active member in these fora. Carter also undertook the important, although largely symbolic, step of signing two controversial covenants on human rights, the UN Convention on the Elimination of All Forms of Discrimination Against Women and the UN Covenant on Economic, Social, and Cultural Rights. (It was not until 1984 that the Senate ratified its first international human rights treaty, the Convention on the Prevention and Punishment of the Crime of Genocide, which was adopted by the UN General Assembly in 1948 but languished in Congress for many decades.) Although human rights had entered U.S. foreign policy before Carter took office, he was the first president to make the institutionalization of human rights a central concern.

The Reagan Years

The Reagan administration proclaimed at the outset that it would undo the Carter human rights legacy and, in particular, rein in the human rights work of the State Department. Forsythe writes, "Reagan went out of his way to invite to the White House, and display prominently in the Washington press corps and society, friendly authoritarians from South Korea, Zaire, Liberia, etc.—all who had been given the cold shoulder from Carter."[38] Reagan also signaled his degree of respect for human rights with his initial nomination for head of the Bureau of Human Rights. Perhaps one could find no better person to undermine human rights than Ernest Lefever, an avowed critic of human rights legislation who openly advocated doing away with the annual country reports on human rights practices (even though they were mandated by Congress).[39] The Lefever nomination, however, proved to be a wake-up call on human rights for the Reagan administration. Having underestimated the support for human rights both within and outside government, the administration was surprised when the Senate Foreign Relations Committee rejected Lefever's nomination with a vote of thirteen to four.

The Reagan administration revisited its objection to human rights. Secretary of State Alexander Haig, who had previously flaunted his disdain for human rights by excluding human rights staffers at his State Department meetings, delivered a major address "declaring that human rights were 'the major focus' of the administration's foreign policy."[40] The administration also intentionally leaked a high-level internal State Department memo calling for renewed commitment to human rights in U.S. foreign policy.[41] While the Reagan administration cast about trying to reinvigorate human rights policy after the Lefever episode, the human rights bureau "languished as the 'laughing stock' of the State Department."[42] Nonetheless, human rights would not go away.

The appointment of Elliot Abrams as assistant secretary of the Bureau of Human Rights and later as assistant secretary of state for inter-American affairs simultaneously salvaged the institutionalization of human rights in the State Department while also undermining the credibility of human rights discourse. Abrams, a Washington establishment insider who knew how to influence the foreign policy agenda, would uphold the institutional mechanisms of the State Department's role in shaping policy. However, recognition of human rights as a legitimate agenda item within the administration and State Department did not lead to a consistent human rights foreign policy in line with international standards. Abrams seized upon human rights as a useful tool for promoting his own anticommunist ideological agenda in Latin America and the Caribbean. He supported U.S. assistance to the contras, a force on record for using tactics in clear violation of international human rights standards, to overthrow the Sandinista government of Nicaragua. He also advocated for funding the military government of El Salvador and supervising its war against a popular leftist rebellion. In the congressional investigations that followed disclosure of the Iran–contra conspiracies, Abrams was accused of withholding information from Congress.

The self-serving manner in which Abrams used human rights to advance policy goals is characteristic of the entire Reagan administration, which abruptly changed course on human rights after the first year in office. In 1981, UN Ambassador Jeanne Kirkpatrick, who had previously defended U.S. assistance for authoritarian regimes, wrote that "not only should human rights play a central role in U.S. foreign policy, no U.S. foreign policy can possibly succeed that does not accord them a major role."[43] The Reagan administration, however, defined human rights far more narrowly than the Carter administration, omitting any mention of economic rights.[44] Foreign policy was set by pragmatists within Reagan's administration and thus human rights were advanced inconsistently and only in places where it was ideologically correct to do so, and where major economic or security interests were not a factor.[45]

Accordingly, Ambassador Kirkpatrick and other members of the Reagan administration could criticize communist regimes for human rights violations while continuing to support rightist dictators with economic and military assistance. This explains a somewhat surprising finding made by statisticians analyzing the relationship between the amount of U.S. aid and the human rights conditions within the potential recipient countries. One would expect to find fewer human rights abuses in countries receiving large aid packages, both because the United States supports friendly countries (its friends are not supposed to engage in human rights abuses) and because aid is conditioned on observance of international human rights standards. Yet during the Reagan administration, large amounts of U.S. aid (that, is, aid given to rightist dictators) was associated with a deterioration in human rights observance.[46]

Although the public diplomacy that had characterized the Carter administration disappeared, human rights continued to be invoked in bilateral relations in subsequent administrations.[47] Under the Cold War paradigm, the Reagan years were dominated by interventionist policies that were often quite destructive to human rights in practice, but were legitimized by claims that the United States was supporting middle-ground politicians rather than radicals. This dichotomy is witnessed in, on the one hand, the United States supporting the contra revolution in Nicaragua and sending aid and arms to Afghanistan and Angola, and, on the other hand, Reagan sending aid and arms to President José Napoléon Duarte in El Salvador, a centrist Christian Democrat who sought democratic reforms. Late in the administration, Reagan acknowledged the abuses of authoritarian leaders such as Augusto Pinochet in Chile and Ferdinand Marcos in the Philippines, and went so far as to encourage Marcos to step down from power.[48] When the Reagan administration backed the Haitian coup in 1986 that removed Jean-Claude "Baby Doc" Duvalier, the United States declared its new policy: "The American people believe in human rights and oppose tyranny in whatever form, whether of the left or the right."[49]

The Reagan administration reoriented the human rights agenda by interlacing American exceptionalism throughout. The very definition of human rights was altered to focus narrowly on the civil and political rights most familiar to the American system. Decisions to engage another country in human rights discussions were based even more squarely on larger American interests. The United States refused to apply international human rights standards to its own behavior, placing its own national sovereignty above the value of human rights as an international norm. Domestic practices in violation of human rights in the United States included measures of discrimination against racial minorities, such as cutting back equal opportunities in education and fair housing, and the enormous discrepancies in the incarcerations of the nation's blacks (versus whites), which were magnified after the onset of Reagan's drug war.[50] In this altered form, however, the ideas promoted by the Human Rights Bureau spread to the rest of the State Department bureaucracy. "By the end of Reagan's second term," one close observer concludes, "human rights were accepted as an important component of the American national interest."[51]

President George H. W. Bush thus inherited an ambiguously complex legacy in which his immediate predecessor had created and projected an image of disdain for international organizations, laws, and norms. Reagan's foreign policy revealed hypocrisy with respect to condemning communist regimes for human rights abuses while remaining silent on those of authoritarian allies. During this time, a distrustful Congress mobilized to ameliorate the damage caused by the executive branch's stance on human rights, and the Department of State and the Foreign Service grew ever more sensitive to human rights themes. This legacy undoubtedly shaped and constrained Bush's own policies with respect to human rights.

What Was Retained, and What Was Changed?

Initially, it seemed like great changes were ahead in the new administration. President George H. W. Bush promised that the United States would benefit from the "new world order" made possible by the end of the Cold War. While members of the administration had absorbed the Cold War suspicions of international institutions, they saw an unparalleled opportunity to advance U.S. interests by controlling the agenda. Bush explained, "The new world facing us [is one] devoted to unlocking the promise of freedom. It's no more structured than a dream, no more regimented than an innovator's burst of inspiration. If we trust ourselves and our values; if we retain the pioneer's enthusiasm for exploring the world beyond our shores; if we strive to engage in the world that beckons us, then and only then, will America be true to all that is best in us."[52]

To a large extent, the focus of the Bush administration was an *economic* new world order. Walter Russell Mead explains that this could be characterized as the Hamililtonian globalist school. Indeed, Bush set about developing "a worldwide trading and finance system based on the unchallenged might of America's military forces and on the dynamism of its economy."[53]

The foreign policy of the Bush administration was also influenced by the more multilaterally minded Wilsonian school. Mead explains that for Wilsonians, a "vast and systematic intensification of American political and economic interests around the world" entails such measures as "promoting the rule of law, the spread of democracy, and the construction of a genuine international consensus against aggression and the protection of human rights. . . ."[54] Many members of the administration believed that a link existed between the trade interests of the United States and the existence of democracy and rule of law in other states. So it was within the context of a globalist agenda focusing on economic interests, but also heeding the need for democracy promotion, that human rights concerns emerged.

President Bush's overall foreign policy record vis-à-vis human rights is difficult to characterize.[55] One the one hand, he criticized Bulgaria for its treatment of minority Turks, and pressured El Salvador to control death squads and other paramilitaries.[56] Yet on the other, he downplayed rights violations in China and renewed its most-favored-nation trade status following the Tiananmen Square massacre,[57] and virtually ignored human rights violations in Iraq prior to the Persian Gulf War.[58] Bush also opposed proposals for reductions in foreign aid in 1989 to African countries with old-guard dictators, such as Kenya (Daniel arap Moi), Somalia (Siad Barre), and Zaire (Mobutu Sese Seko).[59] Human rights issues also came back to haunt Bush when he was reproached by Bill Clinton during the 1992 presidential campaign for returning Haitians who were fleeing their country and for failing to take decisive actions in Bosnia.[60]

In the Western Hemisphere, Bush did use international mechanisms to advance certain human rights concerns, such as the Santiago Declaration on collective security for all democratic governments in the Organization of

American States (OAS), of which the United States was a signatory. Bush also used the OAS and the UN to expand peacekeeping and electoral assistance operations in South and Central America, specifically in Nicaragua, El Salvador, and Guatemala.[61] Nevertheless, Bush's involvement with the OAS was always instrumental. As comparative human rights scholar Forsythe has noted, "the United States has supported [OAS programs] as it sees fit, but without fully integrating itself into OAS human rights activities."[62] The United States has neither ratified the OAS American Convention on Human Rights nor accepted the jurisdiction of the Inter-American Court of Human Rights.

This erratic policy position can best be explained by highlighting a continuity between Bush and his predecessor: like Reagan's policy team in his second term, Bush's advisors—National Security Advisor Brent Scrowcroft, Secretary of Defense Dick Cheney, and Secretary of State James Baker—were pragmatists with regard to human rights.[63] In places like El Salvador and the Occupied Territories in Israel, Bush showed more attention to human rights than Reagan. Yet in Iraq, Bush strongly opposed the trade sanctions being considered by Congress in 1990, as Saddam Hussein was still seen as a strategic ally in maintaining a stable Iran. Furthermore, Bush publicly protested the Tiananmen Square crackdown while privately sending assurances that relations would continue with Beijing.

When there was no conflict of interest, Bush did act on human rights grounds. Bowing to intense international and domestic pressure, in the spring of 1991 Bush did support military involvement inside Iraq and the eventual creation of a zone of Kurdish autonomy where, with the help of the UN, Kurdish rights achieved a degree of protection.[64] In a flip-flop of policy, Bush made a direct appeal to human rights norms in his depiction of Saddam's atrocities against Kuwaiti civilians—acts that, according to Bush, demanded U.S. military action. He charged that while the international community sat back and waited for sanctions to have effect, Hussein "systematically raped, pillaged, and plundered a tiny nation no threat to his own. He subjected the people of Kuwait to unspeakable atrocities."[65] Hussein's actions were a "throwback to another era, a dark relic from a dark time."[66]

Once the war was over, realist power equations seemed to dampen Bush's enthusiasm for putting a stop to continued "throwback behavior." Bush was slow to react to Hussein's continued attacks of the Shiite populates in southern Iraq and the Kurds in the north, concerned that a disintegrating Iraq would strengthen Iran.[67] Assistance for these groups came only after media coverage spotlighted the civilian slaughters.[68] Furthermore, U.S. military actions helped reinstate the autocratic ruler of Kuwait, forgoing the opportunity to make any serious demands toward democratic reform in that country.[69]

In the realm of treaty law, Bush's record was mixed. He signed and sent to the Senate the UN Convention against Torture and obtained consent to ratify that treaty as well as the International Covenant on Civil and Political Rights (ICCPR), which had been signed by Carter. However, following the pattern it set for itself with earlier treaties, the United States accompanied each signing with a series of "RUDs"—"reservations," "understandings," and "declarations."[70] The government used this device to declare, among other things, that the United States shall abide by only those provisions compatible with the American constitution and that are in conformity with existing American law.[71] U.S. treaty making has been likened to Russian matrioshkas—wooden dolls that can be twisted apart at the middle to reveal any number of smaller, nested dolls—because it requires interpreters "to penetrate layer upon layer of reservations, understandings, and declarations that pose progressively greater obstacles to achieving the goals of the treaty."[72] The U.S. reservations to the ICCPR specifically permit the United States to deviate from international standards by allowing hate speech in line with American free speech jurisprudence, the use of the death penalty for persons under the age of eighteen, and sentencing of a convicted criminal to the sentence proscribed at the time the crime was committed even when a lighter sentence has since been enacted.[73] The UN Human Rights Commission found that the United States' reservations to the ICCPR go too far, making them incompatible with the object and purpose of the covenant and therefore in violation of international law.

Throughout his term, then, Bush seemed reluctant to abandon the triumphant American exceptionalism so central to the Reagan presidency. While he was more focused on the creation of a new world economic order than his predecessor, Bush continued to apply human rights norms in a selective and self-serving manner, continuing the trend set in the second Reagan administration.

What Were the Constraints?

As the Soviet Union collapsed, the United States emerged as the sole world superpower. President Bush set about casting the United States in terms that he thought our allies and would-be foes demanded—that is, of a "principled" hegemon, actively engaged and leading the world toward greater democracy, prosperity, security, and multilateral cooperation. The world, according to Bush, was calling for strong U.S. leadership because it is trusted to be fair, restrained, and moral in its use of power.[74]

Public opinion proved to be a significant impetus for Bush's human rights foreign policy. Like presidents before him and since, he had to contend with "the American self-image of an exceptional people who stand for freedom around the world."[75] The notion that Americans opposed human rights and international institutions has been proven wrong.[76] On the contrary, human rights discourse was particularly attractive to the public in the wake of the Cold War, when Americans were searching for their bearings and a new self-definition. According to the Program on International Policy Attitudes (PIPA), an independent research center affiliated with the Center on Policy Attitudes and the Center for International and Security Studies at the University of Maryland, the percentage of Americans considering human rights a very important priority for U.S. foreign policy rose at the end of the Cold War.[77] With a very strong majority of Americans feeling that promoting human rights served U.S. interests, human rights advocates within the Bush administration had a strong platform from which to frame their arguments.

The media also served to shape the nature of U.S. policy on human rights issues, although the exact extent of media influence during this time period is debatable. Research on the actual impact of media coverage on policy choices demonstrates that the so-called CNN effect is often overstated.[78] It is widely asserted, for example, that the "unrelenting" media coverage, rather than moral outrage, caused the Bush administration to reverse its policy and authorize U.S. peacekeeping troops to intervene to stop the famine and social disintegration in Somalia in 1992.[79] Yet in the case of Somalia, there was not much media coverage before the decision to act, and thus media coverage cannot be credited with prompting the intervention. To the extent that "television inspired American intervention in Somalia," political scientist Jonathan Mermin explains, "it did so under the influence of government actors . . . who made considerable efforts to publicize events in Somalia, interpret them as constituting a crisis, and encourage a U.S. response."[80] The media does prove influential, but only in limited cases. Where policy certainty exists, media coverage cannot force policy change.[81] However, where the administration remains uncertain about its policies and the media coverage empathizes with the victim, media coverage may in fact drive policy.[82]

Human rights advocates also influenced how American human rights foreign policy developed during the Bush administration.[83] The reforms introduced in the State Department in the 1970s drew more attention to human rights in American foreign policy, and the expertise and influence of foreign policy officers on human rights was growing.[84] The work of Assistant Secretary of State for Human Rights and Humanitarian Affairs Richard Schifter, to take one illustration, led to improvements within the UN Human Rights Commission, which ultimately transformed the commission's investigatory rigor.[85] Or, to take another example, Jim Bishop, Schifter's replacement as acting assistant secretary of state for human rights and humanitarian affairs, is generally credited with improving the administration's human rights policy on Africa and, specifically, for drawing attention to Somalia.[86] While the human rights supporters within government did not exercise appreciable policy setting, they did find some success in obtaining specific goals in the Bush administration, in contrast to the Reagan era.

What Was the Degree of Norm Embeddedness?

Ultimately, however, the inconsistent and ideological response of the Bush administration to items on the human rights agenda signals a lack of norm embeddedness. As will be explained further in Chapter 3, the military under George H. W. Bush was slow to protect civilians in other parts of the world. When confronted with evidence of ethnic cleansing and other gross human rights abuses in Yugoslavia and Somalia, Bush urged "prudence."[87] By the time the United States acted, however, the ethnic cleansing, detention camps, and massacres of Bosnian civilians, and the famine and social upheavals in Somalia, had been widely publicized by the media, and the Bush administration was perceived as doing "too little, too late."[88]

Bush's actions often failed to live up to his ideal-laden rhetoric. On one hand, the United States was seen as—or, rather, wished to be seen as—the great leader of the civilized world and a beacon of freedom. On the other hand, Bush depicted the United States as a warrior on constant guard "to defend civilized values" in the face of the "jungle's" assault.[89] He tried to create and maintain fear, warning, for example, that "the Soviet bear may be extinct . . . [but] there are still plenty of wolves in the woods."[90] The threat to the American way of life was seen as ongoing: "There will be other regional conflicts. There will be other Saddam Husseins."[91]

Bush's mindset has been described as one of "neo–Cold War orthodoxy." He believed that human rights factored into this worldview insofar as the United States was the only superpower with the power and moral responsibility to solve international problems.[92] As Bush declared in his 1991 State of the Union Address, "Yes, the United States bears a major share of leadership in this effort. Among the nations of the world, only the United States of America has had both the moral standing, and the means to back it up. We are the only nation on this earth that could assemble the forces of peace. This is the burden of leadership—and the strength that has made America the beacon of freedom in a searching world."[93]

Bush viewed human rights as one set of concerns that the United States must tackle. In doing so, he looked not to international human rights, but to norms already found in U.S. law and culture. While he spoke often of "shared interests" and "shared ideals," they were always those of "our great country."[94] Human rights advocates had made progress during the Bush administration, but American exceptionalism was still the informing principle behind U.S. human rights foreign policy.

BILL CLINTON: HUMAN RIGHTS AND DEMOCRACY (1992–2000)

With the passing of the cold war, all of its [negative impact] has changed. The basic principles of human rights and democracy must no longer be debated with impunity. Nor shall they be blinked at for the sake of some geostrategic goal. Rather, they must be restored to their rightful place in the relationship among nations.

—John Shattuck, assistant secretary of state for human rights and humanitarian affairs in the Clinton administration, quoted in David Forsythe, "Human Rights Policy: Change and Continuity"

Forget the "new world order." Forget "enlargement." Forget "assertive multilateralism." The votes have been counted, and the most prominent theme of America's emerging foreign policy is neomercantilism. Foreign policy for the next two years will be an exercise in the art of the possible, and what's possible is anything that has tangible benefits for the American public.

—Anthony Lake, national security adviser in the Clinton administration, quoted in Tim Zimmerman and Linda Robinson, "The Art of the Deal: Forget Idealistic Foreign Policy. The Name of the Game Is Trade"

What Was Inherited?

Bill Clinton inherited from George H. W. Bush a legacy of value-laden foreign policy, U.S. leadership, and international infrastructures presupposed by collective engagement.[95] Cold War institutions were firmly intact and, to some extent, strengthened. Bush had concluded that the North Atlantic Treaty Organization (NATO), the "G-7," the International Monetary Fund (IMF), and the World Bank (i.e., the Bretton Woods institutions) came into their own in the post–Cold War era, fulfilling his new vision and serving their original mandates.[96] Clinton inherited this policy of "collective engagement and shared responsibility" through these institutions;[97] and, perhaps most important, he inherited the expectation that the United States would act in concert with them.

Bush, being the committed globalist that he was,[98] also left office with U.S. troops deployed in more countries abroad than at any time since the administration of Harry Truman. Clinton, the foreign policy novice, became the commander in chief of U.S. Marines stationed in Somalia, Navy and Coast Guard personnel ringing Haiti, and Air Force servicepeople monitoring the no-fly zone in Iraq and preparing for the Bosnian airlift.[99]

Clinton also inherited a more complicated and contested foreign policy establishment. As one scholar of the post–Cold War presidencies summed up, "During the cold war era, the president and his advisors directed foreign policy, but in the post–cold war era members of Congress and other powerful groups have become highly visible actors in the process. There are now numerous actors clamoring to act in the name of the United States."[100] This infusion of new actors, ideas, and agendas serve—in James Scott's words—to "make foreign policy making more like domestic policy making: subject to conflict, bargaining and persuasion among competing groups inside and outside government."[101] This pluralist trend was well in place by the time Clinton took office.

What Was Retained, and What Was Changed?

Like his predecessor, Clinton was "staunchly globalist."[102] He was elected to office, however, with a mandate to be a different kind of globalist—one who would bring greater awareness of social issues to the Hamilitonian economic agenda and greater appreciation of Wilsonian-style engagement in international consensus and cooperation. Candidate Clinton declared that human rights would be a cornerstone of foreign policy under his leadership.[103] He criticized the Bush administration's policies in Iraq, Serbia, China, and Haiti and distinguished himself by offering a foreign policy oriented toward democracy and human rights promotion and working with international organizations.[104] Specifically, Clinton vowed to press China on its human rights record by linking the renewal of most-favored-nation trade status to improvements in human rights.[105] He urged Bush to seek the UN's approval for air strikes to protect relief aid delivery in Bosnia.[106] On every international issue, from democracy to human rights to intervention in humanitarian disasters and nuclear nonproliferation, Clinton claimed Bush had done too little too late, and pledged himself to be resolute on human rights values when confronted with competing interests.[107]

Upon taking office, Clinton immediately set to work cleaning shop, filling many key positions with people with strong human rights backgrounds. The position of secretary of state was first filled by Warren Christopher, a political veteran of human rights policy in the Carter administration, and then by Madeleine Albright, who brought to the position experience on democratization and a strong devotion to human rights.[108] The human rights portfolio in the Clinton administration was also advanced by Assistant Secretary of State for Human Rights John Shattuck, who came from the American Civil Liberties Union, and his successor, Harold Hongju Koh, an international law professor from the Yale University Law School with very strong credentials on human rights. Defense Secretary Les Aspin's record supported more attention to democracy and humanitarianism at the Pentagon.

Other impressive appointees with a commitment to human rights included Timothy Wirth, the former Colorado senator who led the new Office of Global Issues at the State Department; Morton Halperin, appointed to head the Office of Human Rights at the National Security Council; and Halperin's successor, Eric Schwartz, formerly of Human Rights Watch. Equally important, in addition to appointing strong human rights advocates at the top of key institutions, many new hires at the mid-range level had experience in human rights NGOs.[109] "All of a sudden it was like—BANG!," one advocacy director in a human rights organization remembered, "And after so many years of being ignored, State was calling us. They had to talk to us."[110]

Policy Shift: Democratic Enlargement

The change in personnel and increased openness to human rights was accompanied by a significant policy focus on democratic enlargement. While Presidents Reagan and Bush had favored promoting democracy, President Clinton embraced democracy promotion, including human rights, as a cornerstone of his entire foreign policy portfolio. Clinton explained that the key to peace and prosperity was "enlargement"—that is, expansion of the community of democratic states.

President Clinton explained the policy in his 1994 State of the Union address. "Democracies don't attack each other," he noted, and therefore "the best strategy to insure our security and to build a durable peace is to support the advance of democracy elsewhere."[111] The vision of democracy promoted by the Clinton administration was democracy American style, linking free markets to the political freedoms characteristic of the American form of government. In practice, this blended privatization and open-trade projects with minimal guarantees of civil and political rights and free and fair elections. The emphasis on "market democracy" assumed that political freedom would be enhanced by economic liberalization and that the rule of law and protection of basic freedoms would be the foundation of a successful economy.[112] Overt promotion of these tenets increased after the bailout of the Mexican peso in 1995, and especially after the Asian economic crisis of 1997. In these cases, an explicit connection was made between corrupt and despotic governments and faltering economies. Through this approach, human rights issues were brought into discussions of trade and economic relations as never before.

In a speech at Johns Hopkins University in September 1993, National Security Advisor Anthony Lake delineated the four components of "enlargement of the world's free community of market democracies," noting, "First, we should strengthen the community of major market democracies—including our own—which constitutes the core from which enlargement is proceeding. Second, we should help foster and consolidate new democracies and market economies, where possible, especially in states of special significance and opportunity. Third, we must counter the aggression—and support the liberalization—of states hostile to democracy and markets. Fourth, we need to pursue our humanitarian agenda not only by providing aid, but also by working to help democracy and market economics take root in regions of greatest humanitarian concern."[113] The idea of democratic enlargement would be implemented largely by tagging "democracy" onto other issues; for example, in the NATO enlargement debate, the United States insisted that applicant countries meet certain democracy benchmarks.[114]

The bureaucratic rearrangements that followed the announcement of the doctrine of democratic enlargement served to elevate the importance of democracy promotion, and in so doing detracted attention from human rights. The Center for Democracy and Governance, for example, was created at the U.S. Agency for International Development (USAID), and when Clinton's attempt to create a position of assistant secretary of defense for democracy and peacekeeping at the Department of Defense was thwarted by Congress, a special assistant for democracy was named at the National Security Council.[115] Similarly, the bureau in the State Department focusing on human rights, formerly known as Human Rights and Humanitarian Affairs, changed its name to the Bureau of Democracy, Human Rights, and Labor.

As the expansion of democracy became official policy, changes in orientation and behavior were noted among some of the more idealistic members of Clinton's policy team. For example, Madeleine Albright abruptly toned down her moralizing internationalist rhetoric against genocide and instead adopted what one analyst has described as a "realpolitik maverick," denouncing the slow reform of the UN and downplaying the role of UN peacekeeping.[116] Secretary of State Christopher, however, was concerned that the "enlargement" policy made no provisions for either human rights or peacekeeping. While he largely reiterated National Security Adviser Anthony Lake's four-point doctrine, Christopher nonetheless emphasized not only the continued support of democracy but also the defense of human rights. "Our commitment is consistent with American ideals," he stated. "It also rests on a sober assessment of our long-term interest."[117]

Both Christopher and Albright have been described as "basically pragmatic individuals, like Clinton, who adhered publicly to the principles of democracy and human rights but steered toward a policy of realism much of the time."[118] Measured in terms of rhetoric, the investment in democracy was enormous, but in terms of actual dollars spent, it was small. Compared with military spending, democratization and human rights received only a small fraction of government spending. Figures from the State Department indicate spending on democracy assistance at $580 million in 1998, with increases to $623 million and $709 million in 1999 and 2000, respectively. Nevertheless, these levels of support for democracy assistance did not reflect the Clinton administration's grand rhetorical commitment to a policy of democracy enlargement. When compared with the 1999 appropriations of $21.6 billion for International Affairs and $276.7 billion for the Department of Defense, the dollar amounts are minimal.[119]

Under the Clinton administration, the development of market economies was a top priority. As Clinton explained, "In this new era our first foreign priority and our domestic priority are one and the same: reviving our economy. . . . I will elevate economics in foreign policy, create an Economic Security Council . . . and change the State Department's culture so that economics is no longer a poor cousin to old school diplomacy."[120] This economic-centric foreign policy left Clinton open to accusations that he had picked up where Bush had left off. Richard Falk saw the policy as evidence of a "rightward lunge on matters of national security and foreign policy." Falk warned that "[t]he Clinton Administration, with only minimal efforts at disguise, is the architect of this market-oriented design for the New World Order."[121]

The democratic enlargement doctrine was never designed to promote human rights and democracy everywhere: as a politically viable concept, enlargement had to be aimed at primary U.S. strategic and economic interests.[122] Yet Clinton's campaign promises of holding fast to human rights principles raised expectations that would lead to a hard letdown. As Falk put it in his scathing critique of Clinton's mislabeled "democratic enlargement" doctrine, "Clinton has reoriented the Democratic Party as a party dedicated to serving the economic elite of the country and accepting the U.S. role as guardian of global capitalism interests. [They] have abandoned welfare capitalism in favor of a late Twentieth Century version of comprador capitalism at the expense of the most vulnerable members of our society and of genuine democracy abroad."[123]

In their assessment of the impact that these enlargement programs have had, David Forsythe and Barbara Ann Rieffer have tentatively concluded that U.S. democracy assistance has had little discernible impact on democratization but was nevertheless highly intrusive into foreign societies' economies.[124] The democratization initiatives predominantly consisted of small grants to isolated projects for short time periods, while funding for market restructuring substantially outweighed the support for democratization initiatives. "This raised the questions," they note, "of whether democracy assistance was the moral fig leaf covering other motivations like American pursuit of profit (not to mention the workings of laissez-faire ideology)."[125]

Thomas Carothers reached a similar conclusion in his studies of U.S. policy toward the former Soviet bloc. He found that the emphasis was by and large on economic reform and security concerns and the advancement of democracy was only a secondary goal.[126] The democratic enlargement policy was also seen by some as having a stifling effect on advancing a culture of human rights, particularly in those countries already deemed "democracies."[127] Rather, critics asserted, the Clinton policy settled for a proliferation of "illiberal democracies."

Human Rights and Trade

Following the pattern set by the democratic enlargement policy, the Clinton administration's record on human rights and trade is mixed. Although Clinton campaigned strongly in favor of linking trade agreements to human rights improvement, his record was poor, particularly in comparison to his two immediate predecessors. A 1999 study of foreign assistance found that "[h]uman rights considerations did play a role in determining whether or not a state received military aid during the Reagan and Bush administrations, but not for the Carter or Clinton administration. With the exception of the Clinton administration, human rights was a determinant factor in the decision to grant economic aid, albeit of secondary importance. . . . Human rights considerations are neither the only nor the primary consideration in aid allocation."[128] While exceptions to the general rule existed—for example, in 1997 the United States suspended foreign assistance in Cambodia and conditioned aid to Zaire due to human rights concerns[129]—the Clinton administration generally refused to permit human rights abuses to stand in the way of advantageous trade.

Perhaps the greatest human rights policy reversal took place over China.[130] In 1996, the Clinton administration announced it would apply economic sanctions against China for failing to protect intellectual property rights as obligated under a 1995 agreement. In response, China backed down and undertook immediate steps to enforce the agreement. It was clear then that economic sanctions could have impact on China. Nonetheless, while the United States has used its economic and political might to isolate Burma and Cuba on human rights grounds, these same considerations were not permitted to sour relations with leading trading partners such as China.

Instead, Clinton succumbed to business lobbying efforts and adopted an approach of "engagement" with China, delinking the most-favored-nation status from the human rights record.[131] This reversal was essentially a return to the approach of the Bush administration.[132] Clinton had an opportunity to redeem himself on China when, during U.S.–China summits in 1997 and 1998, he spoke out forcefully on Chinese policies including such issues as forced prison labor, the denial of freedom of religion, and the occupation of Tibet.[133]

But the administration failed to use summit negotiations to secure significant Chinese reforms.

Perhaps, not surprisingly given its record on trade, the Clinton administration did not push international financial institutions on human rights. With regard to World Bank and IMF policy, Forsythe notes, "The United States has always been the most important state in these two IFIs [international financial institutions] and bears considerable responsibility for their record on human rights."[134] As an illustration of this power, in 1997 the U.S. government blocked an IMF loan to Croatia due to the state's failure to indict war criminals and protect the rights of minorities. In the Clinton era, that sort of intervention was rare, and there were only limited changes in these organizations' positions vis-à-vis human rights. While the World Bank began to embrace the rhetoric of good governance, this was largely measured in fiscal responsibility rather than in the promotion or defense of human rights. The IMF was even more reluctant to address notions of human rights, much in keeping with the past. The Clinton administration did little to challenge these anti–human rights positions, and pressed for giant increases in IMF funding as a response to the Asian economic crisis, without any sort of human rights, labor rights, or environmental protections emphasized in U.S. funding of the institution.[135]

Human Rights and the United Nations

Since the end of the Cold War, the United States has consistently—and often successfully—asserted its views on human rights in the UN Security Council, General Assembly, and Human Rights Commission.[136] One cornerstone of the Clinton administration was the belief in the benefit of U.S. participation in UN institutions. Human rights concerns were best aired through international bodies. Harold Hongju Koh, Clinton's assistant secretary of state for democracy, human rights, and labor, credited the president with playing an essential role through supporting international institutions and catalyzing human rights networks in particular.[137] Increased U.S. involvement in UN bodies in the Clinton years led to four major changes involving human rights.

First, the United States led the Security Council to greatly expand the scope of Chapter VII of the UN Charter: "In effect, many human rights violations essentially inside states came to be viewed as constituting a threat to or breach of international peace and security, permitting authoritative Council decisions including the deployment of force and sometimes limited combat action."[138] With the Iraqi Kurds (during Bush, Sr.'s term), Somalia, the former Yugoslavia, Haiti, and Rwanda, the consistent application of Chapter VII brought human rights to a more prominent standing in the international community. By narrowing the ability of states to use "state sovereignty" to shield them while committing human rights abuses, this development elevated human rights above national boundaries to a point where the international community could intervene on the grounds of human rights. As a result, human rights gained status as standards that could and would be enforced by the international community.

Second, under Clinton the United States led the way in expanding the concept of UN peacekeeping under Chapter VI of the UN Charter, leading to second-generation, or complex, missions in Namibia, El Salvador, and Cambodia, though in the case of the last credit may fall at least equally to President George H. W. Bush. Notes Forsythe, "[I]n many situations the United States led the United Nations in seeking not just peace based on the constellation of military power, but a liberal democratic peace based on many human rights."[139] With the endorsement and often the participation of the United States during the Bush and Clinton administrations, postconflict activities have "*broadened* laterally in terms of the policy goals and sectors that are implicated, *deepened* in terms of their involvement in the internal workings of societies, and *lengthened* in terms of the stages of conflict when it operates."[140] Through a series of presidential directives (see Chapter 3 of this volume), "Clinton made peace operations a centerpiece of U.S. foreign policy."[141]

Third, the United States was the prime impetus behind the creation of the international criminal courts for the former Yugoslavia and Rwanda. In creating these courts, "the United States rejuvenated the idea of individual criminal responsibility for violations of the laws of war, crimes against humanity, and genocide."[142] The United States was the primary funder and supporter of these courts. Although the support of the United States for a permanent international criminal court later wavered,[143] the Foreign Relations Authorization Act, Fiscal Year 1994 and 1995, recorded the following "Sense of the Senate on the Establishment of an International Criminal Court":

1. The establishment of an international criminal court with jurisdiction over crimes of an international character would greatly strengthen the international rule of law
2. Such a court would thereby serve the interests of the United States and the world community
3. The United States delegation should make every effort to advance this proposal at the United Nations.[144]

Finally, under the Clinton administration the United States used the UN General Assembly as the forum for advocating for the new office of high commissioner for human rights in late 1993.[145] The first high commissioner, José Ayala Lasso, however, was roundly criticized by human rights groups for failing to speak out against abuses.[146] Mary Robinson, the high commissioner after Lasso, however, successfully used her position to disseminate information about human rights and offer technical support to countries requesting assistance. This position of high commissioner is quite dependent on the role taken by the high commissioner himself or herself. Likewise, U.S. financial support for this office has also been irregular, in large part due to congressional pressures and uneven domestic support.[147]

International Instruments

Clinton's record on human rights treaties and other international instruments is mixed. Despite its promises, the administration failed to push for Senate ratification of the UN Convention on the Elimination of All Forms of Discrimination against Women (CEDAW) or the UN Convention on the Rights of the Child. Nor did the United States join any of the major International Labor Organization conventions guaranteeing core labor rights to organize and engage in collective bargaining. Clinton refused to sign the Ottawa Land Mine Treaty, bowing to pressure from the U.S. Army, who contended that it would undermine military effectiveness. Finally, Clinton refused to support a treaty banning the recruitment of child soldiers because the Pentagon disagreed with the eighteen-year-old age minimum for recruitment.[148]

When the Clinton administration did take a stand on human rights, it did so on issues that were largely settled or where the investment of political capital was low. For example, Clinton indicated that he would support the UN Covenant on Economic, Social, and Cultural Rights, a treaty that had been pending before the Senate since the days of the Carter administration.[149] This treaty will likely never make it out of the Senate Foreign Relations Committee due to the expansiveness of the rights it entails—such as food, clothing, shelter, and medical care. Accordingly, although the administration's rhetorical support was a significant change from the prior administration, it was of little political consequence. To take another example, the Clinton administration did take credit for depositing the instrument of ratification for the UN Convention against Torture (CAT), and thus, triggered its implementation. However, it would be wrong to attribute the CAT wholly to Clinton since the vote on ratification had taken place under Reagan.[150]

The Clinton administration did invest political capital into advancing human rights when it ratified and implemented the UN Convention on the Elimination of All Forms of Racial Discrimination (CERD).[151] Undermining the importance of U.S. ratification of the CERD, however, were the many significant reservations the United States made to its terms, including one rejecting the notion that discriminatory acts could be determined by effect as well as intent.[152] In the words of one scholar, the CERD ratification was "largely empty gestures in terms of providing any additional enforceable rights for U.S. citizens and residents."[153] The importance of the United States ratifying CERD rested in the way it galvanized antiracism activists within the United States and brought their issues to the world stage.[154]

A related area of significant progress was in the creation of formal interagency coordination mechanisms on human rights issues. In 1998, Clinton signed Executive Order 13107, which calls for the implementation of all human rights treaties to which the United States is a party and establishing an interagency working group to make implementation more effective.[155] While Executive Order 13107 had been prompted by the International Covenant on Civil and Political Rights (ICCPR),[156] it proved extremely useful for the CERD as well. "The inter-agency working group was made necessary by the CERD treaty's reporting process," explains Margaret Huang, director of the International Advocacy and U.S. Racial Discrimination programs at the International Human Rights Law Group. "The State Department had to make this report on the status of race discrimination and the U.S. laws related to discrimination, but the State Department didn't have that information, so they needed to find a way to get it to them."[157] The interagency working group thus became a main source of information and a portal for input by civil society during the Clinton administration.[158] Human rights advocates point to these working groups and the general receptiveness of the Clinton administration to their work as one of the administration's major achievements on human rights.[159]

What Were the Constraints?

The degree to which the Clinton administration desired to participate in international institutions and to influence international lawmaking demonstrates that international norms and institutions were in fact influencing the administration. "Where there was an important international meeting, we were there—or we wanted to be there," a former staffer explained: "Of course we [saw ourselves as] on the right side of international law."[160] Significant exceptions existed during the Clinton years. For example, the United States' decision to use force against the Serbs without first gaining Security Council authorization undermined international law.[161] Yet for the most part, the Clinton administration was more concerned with international law and international institutions than its predecessors.

Congress proved to be the most important constraint on human rights policy during the Clinton administration. Not only could a Republican Congress often effectively undo many of Clinton's human rights policies, but it could also use well-placed threats to prevent him from fully implementing existing policies or creating new ones.[162] Members of Congress used both direct and indirect tactics to advance their agendas.[163] Direct tactics included entering into diplomatic negotiations and introducing legislation intended to have an impact on human rights (i.e., legislation on economic embargos of countries with poor human rights records). Indirect tactics included those designed to frame an issue to influence the outcome of major foreign policy debates—for example, portraying the International Criminal Court (ICC) not as a matter of accountability for perpetrators but as an attack on state sovereignty.

The increasing participation of Congress in foreign affairs questions put a check on what the administration could do. Congress assumed a more active decision-making role in U.S. foreign policy. For example, Congress played a pivotal role in the decisions to establish a new Cuba policy, reject the Comprehensive Test Ban Treaty, and refuse consideration of the Kyoto Protocol on global warming.[164]

The new Republican-led Congress of 1995 provides a good illustration of the constraining power of Congress. In an effort to cut the budget and also to thwart Clinton's initiatives, several projects that were a part of Clinton's democratic enlargement efforts, such as the United States Institute of Peace, the National Endowment for Democracy, and the Agency for International Development, were threatened with cutbacks from Congress.[165] This Congress indeed took its toll on Clinton's plans. As Arthur Schlesinger notes, "These freshmen legislatures showed a scorn for international affairs that was nativist, if not just short of isolationist. The new legislature jammed the brakes on Clinton's ambassadorial nominations, cut funds for the State Department and its overseas missions, drastically slashed American foreign aid, and insisted that two thriving departments—the United States Information Agency and the Arms Control and Disarmament Agency—be folded into the State Department to save money. Clinton capitulated on most of these issues."[166]

In addition to Congress, domestic politics and public opinion also played an important role in influencing Clinton's human rights foreign policy.[167] "Many of Clinton's major foreign policy decisions can be traced to domestic politics," according to Richard Haass.[168] If this assertion is correct, understanding the public mood toward internationalism throughout the Clinton years arguably carries great explanatory weight in considering human rights policies. As one journalist aptly noted, "Sometimes the Clinton administration's foreign policy appears to be driven almost entirely by domestic concerns."[169] In the post–Cold War era, Americans were growing less interested in engaging with the outside world.[170] Throughout the 1990s, the public was concerned with the domestic economy, and reducing spending on foreign involvement.[171] A 1995 national opinion poll showed that roughly one-third of the U.S. populace thought that promoting and defending human rights and democratization abroad was "very important,"[172] while most ranked domestic concerns such as illegal drugs and employment and security concerns such as the spread of nuclear weapons as more pressing.[173] Clinton's deference to public opinion,[174] even to the extreme point of "media panic,"[176] made his human rights foreign policy even more selective.

The business community proved to be one important constituency that the Clinton administration could not ignore. Clinton's initial resoluteness about his human rights and humanitarian-centered foreign policy quickly succumbed to a forceful lobby of business interests that encouraged the emphasis on trade liberalization and fostering "market economies." Big business lobbied hard, and ultimately successfully, for the delinking of most-favored-nation trading status and China's human rights progress.[176] As increased commerce became linked to political reform, the United States sought to open trade with countries with major human rights offenses.[177]

The Christian Right also played a potent part in the new American pluralism. Their foreign policy revival confronted Clinton with a sophisticated and well-organized agenda employing the instrumental use of human rights norms.[178] The Christian Right strong-armed the passage of specific legislation aimed at promoting religious freedom. Although neutral on its face, the International Religious Freedom Act of 1998 was concerned largely with members of the Christian faith.[179] Within the human rights establishment, the act elevated religious discrimination to a favored institutional position in the State Department, creating a separate Office on Religious Freedom and an ambassador at large for religious freedom. Among other measures, the new law also enabled the president to employ sanctions and other penalties against violators.[180]

The pressure that the U.S. Congress put on the Department of State to focus on religious freedom is indicative of the power struggles that occurred between the Republican-dominated Congress and the Democratic presidential administration. It also exemplifies an internal civilian power struggle of the United States: how, as a diverse nation that pursues equality for all people, to grapple with placing its own special interests above global human rights concerns. As explained further in Chapter 3, Clinton-era human rights policy practiced selective human rights assistance and intervention, which was determined not only by the president's executive decisions, but also derived from congressional pressures, domestic concerns, economic concerns, and public opinion.

In addition to public opinion, Clinton listened very closely to the wishes of his joint chiefs of staff. His decisions on the Ottawa Mine Ban Treaty, the ICC, and on the timing and nature of intervention in Haiti, Bosnia, and Rwanda were "as much due to the concerns of the Joint Chiefs as to opposition in Congress."[181] Clinton's troubles with the military had begun in the first months of his taking office, when he lost face in the controversy of admitting gays into the armed services. The explosive backlash within the military put Clinton on the defense in his future dealings with the military.[182] "From then on," says one of his former advisors, "he gave more deference to what the military leadership thought."[183]

All of these factors—congressional pressure, the pull of domestic politics and public opinion, the demands of big business and the Christian Right, and the concerns of the military—shaped, and to some extent, limited, Clinton's ability to promote human rights as a central and consistent concern in his foreign policy.

What Was the Degree of Norm Embeddedness?

The hallmark of the Clinton administration's human rights foreign policy was the linking of human rights concepts to national interests. Harold Hongju Koh warns against confusing "the real Clinton-Albright doctrine" with the "notion of humanitarian intervention"—that is, "commitment of U.S. military force to promote human rights in situations where there are otherwise no discernible U.S. interests." Koh writes, "In my judgment, this confuses the tip with the iceberg. The broader goal of the Clinton-Albright doctrine was to assert that promotion of democracy and human rights is always in our national interest. The goal of American foreign policy is thus to fuse power and principle, by promoting the globalization of freedom as the antidote to other global problems, resorting to force only in those rare circumstances where all else fails."[184] Under the Clinton-Albright doctrine, vital national interests became closely linked with human rights concepts such as the independence of the judiciary, the rule of law, and respect for basic freedoms of expression and association. Through this policy Clinton tried to have it both ways, portraying his "democratic enlargement" policy as a synergistic wedding of American values and interests: "I believe that . . . enlargement . . . marries our interests and our ideals."[185] The appearance of mutual support of these ideals and interests sometimes subsumed the framework of human rights, in lieu of the priorities of democratization and economic interests.

Many in the administration seemed to be involved in spinning this notion of synergy. Secretary of State Albright noted that the concept of human rights reflects the essence of civilization itself. Vice President Al Gore claimed that the United States stands for something in this world.[186] The integration of human rights into U.S. foreign policy, he contended, is "therefore a natural reflection of our own interests and values."[187] Shortly before Clinton's term ended, Samuel Berger, Clinton's national security adviser, condensed the enlargement doctrine and gave it a globalization spin: "The way for America to exercise its influence today is to build with our democratic partners an international system of strong alliances and institutions attuned to the challenges of a globalized world."[188]

As late as 1999, Steven Wagenseil, director of multilateral affairs for the Bureau of Democracy, Human Rights, and Labor of the State Department, recalled Martin Luther King, Jr.'s "Injustice anywhere is a threat to justice everywhere," and then stated, "This Administration shares Dr. King's vision."[189] Yet, after a half a decade of the "enlargement" doctrine, this depiction of Clinton as the global human rights activist rings hollow. As some observers have noted, "Whereas the Clinton administration has firmly rejected cultural and religious relativism, it has embraced the relativism of political and economic expediency."[190] While the Clinton administration made clear that it supported human rights, the rights it envisioned as top priorities coincided with American values and interests.[191]

While the Clinton administration talked about human rights more than previous Republican administrations, its human rights rhetoric often was not matched by its policy decisions.[192] In 1993, for instance, Secretary of State Warren Christopher stated that the administration would consider acknowledging the validity of economic rights, yet there was no subsequent policy action in this regard. Moreover, the executive branch's interagency human rights committee (established under Clinton) never actually functioned as intended.[193] And the "expedited removal" procedures of the 1996 immigration reform act, for example, conflicted with U.S. obligations under the 1951 UN Convention Relating to the Status of Refugees and undermined the stated U.S. position on the human rights of refugees.[194]

Nowhere is the disparity between rhetoric and action so pronounced as in the Middle East. To take just one example, in his first year in office, Clinton showed no interest in openly challenging the poor human rights record of the Israeli government, and was quick to assure the Israeli prime minister that he favored maintaining U.S. aid to Israel, which at the time boasted a three-billion-dollar price tag.[195] The administration did privately lobby the Israeli government on the closure of the occupied territories and certain other human rights issues, and it did comment publicly when U.S. citizens became the victims of abuse. However, the Clinton administration never commented publicly on the routine abuse to which Palestinian residents of the Occupied Territories were subjected during interrogations and in other day-to-day violations of human rights.

One human rights issue that did prompt public diplomacy was the administration's first foreign policy crisis. The Bush administration had voted in favor of UN Security Council Resolution 799 on December 18, 1992, to condemn the deportations of 415 Islamists and urged Israel to rescind them. Upon taking office, the Clinton team lobbied against Security Council sanctions on Israel. Notwithstanding the fact that Resolution 799 demanded the "immediate return" of all the deportees, Secretary of State Christopher brokered a deal where only 100 deportees would be permitted to return immediately. The Clinton administration's primary interest was on renewing the peace talks. "While this was logical," Human Rights Watch notes, "the U.S. at the same time weakened the cause of human rights by lending legitimacy to an inadequate Israeli appeals process. . . . Washington's generous annual aid to Israel bestows on it the authority, and the obligation, to be a public advocate for human rights."[196]

The Clinton administration was also particularly selective in its approach toward international justice and accountability issues, which are essential to the maintenance of human rights. U.S. particularism manifested itself in the government's support of the international tribunals dealing with atrocities where no American citizens are at risk, such as in Rwanda and the former Yugoslavia. When it came to the creation of the ICC, however, Congress was staunchly opposed and consistently attempted to cripple the institution, so that no U.S. citizens could be indicted for their crimes.[197] David Scheffer, ambassador at large for war crime issues of the United States and leader of the American delegation in Rome, put it simply: "The U.S. delegation has been and will continue to be guided by our paramount duty: to protect and advance U.S. interests."[198]

Human rights scholars and activists pronounced the Clinton record as "mixed."[199] On one hand, the willingness to assume great financial and political costs in humanitarian efforts such as those in Haiti and Rwanda was seen as a positive departure from previous administrations and reflected an unprecedented commitment to a human rights–based foreign policy. Human rights advocates noted a greater access to high-level policy makers and State Department officials, which translated into a growing capacity to influence the agenda. Moreover, they pointed to the increased willingness of U.S. diplomats to include human rights language and even specific human rights treaties in peace agreements. As George Ward observes, "After [the] Dayton [Peace Accords] there is the expectation that when there is a peace agreement negotiated [at best in part by] the U.S., human rights will be there."[200] On a more negative note, Clinton's actions failed to live up to his lofty rhetoric in three crucial areas: in bilateral strategies against countries that are human rights abusers, in the indiscriminate proliferation of U.S. arms sales abroad, and in the erratic positions taken toward multilateralism and the ICC.[201]

The Clinton presidency record reveals a "rhetorical policy, one consisting only of words."[202] Mark Danner observes that the president exposed the emptiness of his own policy: "As the President remarked one day in April [1995], 'The U.S. should always seek an opportunity to stand up against—at least speak out against inhumanity.' These verbs—to stand up against and to speak out against—Clinton blends together in a single sentence as if they were one and the same, in fact they are very different."[203] Clinton's interest in public images, in economic concerns, and in the expansion of democracy took priority over the international obligations of upholding and supporting human rights.

GEORGE W. BUSH: HUMAN RIGHTS AND THE WAR ON TERRORISM

Bush believes, whether it's domestic politics or international affairs, that if you have strength you exert it. You use it. You show it. . . . Signs of conciliation are going to be used by your adversaries as signs of weakness. Some intellectuals might write nice things about you, but your adversaries will use it to take advantage of you—that's his view. And that can work if you have that strength, but what you do along the way is you build lots of animosities, and you have all kinds of people who nurse their wounds and egos until you stumble and then are eager to jump on you with cleats.

—Norman Ornstein, resident scholar at the American Enterprise Institute, quoted in Anne E. Kornblut, "Defining George W. Bush"

To be a good president when it comes to foreign policy, it requires someone with vision, judgment, and leadership. . . . My goal, should I become the President, is to keep the peace. I intend to do so by promoting free trade; by strengthening alliances; and by strengthening the military to make sure the world is peaceful.

—George W. Bush, speaking at the New Hampshire Republican Party debates, December 3, 1999

What Was Inherited?

George W. Bush inherited a world distrustful of American military and economic dominance. Tension between the United States and its traditional European allies was mounting. This strain was due, in part, to the Clinton administration's reluctance to support several significant international agreements. Because Clinton had signed on to the ICC agreement at the eleventh hour over the objections of the Pentagon and the Republican-dominated Congress, U.S. participation in the ICC became a highly controversial issue and set the stage for a subsequent weakening of relations with the international community, and Europe in particular.[204]

The Bush administration also inherited a State Department with a greater capacity for and an enhanced interest in human rights issues. While the political appointees may have been adverse to international human rights standards, career officers were not. Thus, even critics of the State Department were praising improvements in its main work product on human rights abuses, the Annual Country Reports on Human Rights Practices, which offered reports on friendly and adversarial governments alike. Neil Hicks, a longtime critic of the reports, proclaimed, "The Annual Country Reports on Human Rights Practices are now, happily, largely free of the political distortions, favorable to key U.S. allies, that marred the reports in earlier years."[205] At the same time, the Bush administration inherited a Human Rights Bureau within the State Department that had little influence over foreign policy.

The Bush administration also found itself in a world filled with complex peace-building operations in war-torn areas. While earlier peace operations focused on such tasks as separating the warring factions, monitoring peace agreements and the provisions of emergency humanitarian assistance,[206] more recent "nation building" efforts were "multidimensional" and "increasingly interventionary in nature."[207] The public had grown weary of these interventions by the conclusion of Clinton's term. Yet at the same time, demands for U.S. involvement in new peace operations were on the rise.

What Was Retained, and What Was Changed?

In campaign speeches and debates where George W. Bush's lack of experience in foreign affairs was evident, he promised to rein in the excesses of Clinton globalism and be more humble on the world scene.[208] "Our nation stands alone right now in the world in terms of power," he said at a presidential debate in 2000. "And that's why we've got to be humble and yet project strength in a way that promotes freedom. We're a freedom-loving nation. If we're an arrogant nation, they'll view us that way, but if we're a humble nation, they'll respect us."[209] Expectations were that while the United States would still pursue its economic and political interests abroad, foreign policy concerns would no longer dominate the agenda. To the extent that the United States was engaged in the world, it would be to advance a narrower view of national interests.

There was a question as to how human rights would fit into the new administration's agenda. As governor of Texas, Bush had overseen the executions of more than one hundred people and had spoken out against U.S. involvement in international human rights treaties.[210] His early appointments would prove telling.[211]

People with Plans

At least three of Bush's appointees—Otto Reich, Elliott Abrams, and John Negroponte—had emerged from the Iran–contra affair of his Republican predecessors with spotty records on human rights. Otto Reich, Bush's special envoy for Western Hemisphere initiatives, was perhaps best known for his role as the former director of the State Department's Office of Public Diplomacy (OPD). Fairness and Accuracy in Reporting (FAIR), a media watch group, was one of many interest groups to oppose his appointment on the basis of his record of "media manipulation through planted stories and leaks . . . cajoling and bullying of journalists."[212] The OPD was permanently shut down in 1987 after Reich became ambassador to Venezuela. Now-declassified U.S. comptroller general's reports show that Reich's office had engaged in prohibited, covert propaganda activities.[213] Reich has also been linked to lobbying for groups that earned money for promoting laws on the U.S. embargo against Cuba. Political analyst Peter Kornbluh observed at the time of Reich's nomination that Reich "would become the key policy-maker interpreting and implementing legislation on Cuba, which he was handsomely paid to promote—a clear conflict of interest."[214]

A second specter from the Iran–contra affair is Elliott Abrams, now special assistant to the president and senior director for Near East and North African affairs and a key player in determining policy in Israeli–Arab relations.[215] He may be best remembered for his role in playing down, if not lying about, the human rights abuses of U.S.-supported dictators in Latin America.[216] Also, in the Iran–contra affair, Abrams perjured himself by denying that he was soliciting third-country support for the contras.[217] Abrams pled guilty to two misdemeanor counts of withholding information from Congress but was later pardoned by President George H. W. Bush.[218] In a response to the news of Abrams's 2001 appointment to the National Security Council's Office for Democracy, Human Rights, and International Operations, Canadian Member of Parliament Dick Proctor commented, "Talk about putting the fox in charge of the hen house." Proctor objects most strongly to what he believes is Abrams's complicity in the deaths of hundreds of El Salvadorians by the U.S.-backed military.[219]

While Abrams's questionable past was the focus of a number of news stories, the real story, notes *The Weekly Standard's* Fred Barnes, was the appointment of Abrams to shepherd a Middle East peace plan that he apparently opposes. Barnes quotes from Abrams's book *Present Dangers* (2000), in which Abrams writes, "American interests do not lie in strengthening Palestinians at the expense of Israelis, abandoning our overall policy of supporting the expansion of democracy and human rights, or subordinating all other political and security goals to the 'success' of the Arab-Israel 'peace process.'"[220]

Jim Lobe of the Inter-Press Service predicted that Abrams's hawkish politics would be likely to provide a more conservative balance to Secretary of State Colin Powell's dovish quest for peace. Abrams openly challenged the "land-for-peace" formula, opposed the Oslo peace process, and was described as an "American Likudnik" for his public support of the right wing Israeli party.[221]

Bush's choice for U.S. ambassador to the United Nations, John Negroponte, was a longtime colleague of Abrams and Reich. The *San Francisco Chronicle* editorialized that this appointment was most troubling because "the U.S. ambassador to the United Nations is the face America shows to the world."[222] *The Nation* wrote about Negroponte that "Bush has named him to represent the United States at an institution built on principles that include nonintervention, international law and human rights. Negroponte was a central player in a bloody paramilitary war that flagrantly violated those principles and was repeatedly denounced by the institution in which he would now serve."[223]

A 1995 article in the *Baltimore Sun* presented evidence that Negroponte, as the U.S. ambassador to Honduras, knew about horrendous human rights violations and crimes committed by government forces trained and supported by the United States. Former Honduran congressman Efrain Diaz Arrivillaga said he spoke several times about the military abuses to U.S. officials in Honduras, including Negroponte. "Their attitude was one of tolerance and silence," he noted. "They needed Honduras to loan its territory [for neighboring wars] more than they were concerned about innocent people being killed."

An intelligence unit within the Honduran government, called Battalion 316, trained and supported by the U.S. Central intelligence Agency (CIA), was responsible for much of the kidnapping, torture, and murder committed against the people of Honduras. Journalist Duncan Campbell wrote in 2001, as the hearings on Negroponte's nomination got underway, that "some members of the battalion had been living in the United States, but were deported just as Mr. Bush's selection of Mr. Negroponte was announced."[224] This eliminated any chance that they could be called upon to testify about their actions and their connections to Negroponte. In the end, the Senate Foreign Relations Committee endorsed Negroponte for the UN post, despite expressing some dissatisfaction with his responses to their questions. As one reporter wrote, "Negroponte, pressed on various human rights cases in Honduras and on what he discussed with the Contras, told the Senate committee he could not remember."[225]

Bush's appointment of John Bolton to the position of undersecretary of state for arms control, nonproliferation, and international security also sent a clear message that the administration had little interest in participating in international institutions on an equal basis with other states. Bolton had published several articles blasting international law and international treaties and institutions, including the ICC.[226] In 1998, he wrote in the *Wall Street Journal* that the "proposed International Criminal Court, a product of fuzzy-minded romanticism, is not just naive, but dangerous."[227] Bolton was also fiercely critical of U.S. involvement with the UN. He responded to the possibility that Washington could lose its vote in the UN General Assembly for failure to pay dues by asserting that many Republicans "not only do not care about losing the General Assembly vote but actually see it as a 'make my day' outcome."[228] Bolton, who stated himself that he "feels like a conservative in a conservative administration,"[229] is a strong part of the Bush team that delights in undermining international institutions if it means greater power for the United States.

The appointment of General John Ashcroft, Bush's pick for attorney general, would prove to be another abysmal moment for human rights. His far right politics and embrace of religious fundamentalism appealed to Bush's agenda. Ashcroft has been described as "the perfect hatchet man on civil rights enforcement."[230] Voters in his home state of Missouri elected their deceased governor to succeed Ashcroft in the Senate seat rather than endure another term of what critics referred to as his "Stone Age stance on civil rights."[231] In confirmation hearings, Ashcroft answered questions about statements he had made in an interview with the white supremacist publication *Southern Partisan*. According to FAIR, Ashcroft said that "David Duke represented the 'American ideal'; that slave-owners were concerned about the 'peace and happiness' of slave families; that ethnic groups from outside of Northern Europe 'have no temperament for democracy'; and that only 'Italians, Jews and Puerto Ricans' live in New York, not 'Americans.'"[232] In office, Ashcroft lived up to this reputation. Despite a February 2003 speech to a conference on the trafficking of women promising to "protect the victims of trafficking and to bring to justice all those who violate their human dignity,"[233] Ashcroft took steps to restrict opportunities for victims of gender-based human rights abuses to seek asylum in the United States.[234] After the war in Afghanistan began in 2002, he announced intentions to establish camps to indefinitely detain U.S. citizens who appear to be "enemy combatants."[235] Also under his leadership, the U.S. government interceded repeatedly in lawsuits on behalf of corporations accused of human rights abuses in developing nations. Ashcroft even spearheaded a campaign to limit or even end the ability of victims of grave human rights violations occurring outside the United States to bring civil claims in U.S. courts, severely restricting the reach of the federal legislation known as the Alien Tort Claims Act (see Chapter 4 of this volume).[236]

In addition to these widely publicized appointees from the Iran–contra era was a close-knit cadre of conservatives who had been working on a conservative foreign policy platform for years.[237] Candidate George W. Bush had promised to run the presidency like a chief executive officer: that is, he would set the broad strategies for others to implement. In seeking out experts to help him, the main criteria appeared to be experience and loyalty.[238] At the highest level, the experts brought two distinct visions of the United States' role in the world. Closest in ideological platform to Bush was Secretary of State Colin Powell's policy of restraint. He cautioned that the United States should conserve its power, avoid conflict, and engage only when doing so was necessary to advance national interests. The "Powell doctrine" for intervention also more specifically considered cost, level of public support, likelihood of success, and the existence of a coherent exit strategy.[239]

The new civilian leadership at the Pentagon, however, had far greater ambitions for an assertive, unilateral American foreign policy.[240] As Walter Russell Mead observes, under this view "[t]he ultimate goal of American foreign policy should be . . . to convert the present American hegemony into a more durable system."[241] Even according to this hegemonic power model, human rights did not disappear from the American foreign policy agenda.

However, the United States would enjoy greater latitude in picking and choosing its subjects of interest, focusing on human trafficking in Eastern Europe and the rights of Christians in Africa, and avoiding as it could such touchy subjects as reparations for slavery and the use of the death penalty.[242]

These two competing platforms would provide lasting tension in the Bush administration as it encountered new foreign policy challenges. He would seek to balance these tensions in announcing a new vision for human rights in American foreign policy that captured and expanded upon the exceptionalism of earlier administrations.

The Policy: "Dignity" and Providence

At the very beginning of his presidency, George W. Bush avoided human rights terminology, especially when it would place any legal obligations on the United States or bind U.S. action in any way. Instead, he invoked a more amorphous concept of "dignity." His inaugural address was a plea for Americans to remember particular tenets of U.S. history (real and imagined) and culture. The United States, he noted, was born from a "simple dream of dignity," and has long strived to be "a place where personal responsibility is valued and expected."[243] "Where there is suffering, there is duty," he declared. Drawing from scripture, he "pledged to the nation . . . a goal: When we see that wounded traveler on the road to Jericho, we will not pass to the other side."[244]

Bush proclaimed in his inaugural address that it is consistent with the American spirit to be "generous and strong and decent, not because we believe in ourselves, but because we hold beliefs beyond ourselves."[245] The source of these beliefs is not international human rights law or American commitment to multilateral institutions, but rather, the president suggested, providence—in his words, "an angel" who "rides in the whirlwind and directs this storm."[246] Emory University religion professor Steven Tipton observes that in Bush's inaugural address providence was one of the central motifs. "From beginning to end, as the inaugural address concludes," he writes, "there has been this providential angel riding the whirlwind of history—surprises, reverses, tragedies, catastrophes, calls to war, national emergencies, this providential angel in whom we trust. And beyond, we trust the authorship of the creator and the orderer of the universe and the orderer of history, too. That carries through from the Inaugural to the State of the Union to the National Cathedral and the other addresses that follow more or less immediately on 9-11."[247]

While the foreign policies of other administrations have been informed by the religious convictions of the president and his close advisors,[248] Bush's is unusual in the extent to which he justifies his policies based on scripture. Elaine Pagels, a professor at Princeton University, finds that "in recent memory, I cannot think of anyone who has used the language in the way that this man has."[249] At a national prayer breakfast, the president declared, "The Almighty God is a God to everybody."[250] In announcing the Columbia space shuttle disaster, he paraphrased Isaiah 40:26, "The same Creator who names the stars also knows the names of the seven souls we mourn today."[251] And in his 2002

State of the Union address he drew from a popular evangelical hymn in declaring, "There is power—wonder-working power—in the goodness and idealism and faith of the American people."[252]

Perhaps surprisingly, it was only after the events of September 11, 2001, that the Bush administration began to talk more directly about its specific vision of human rights. In so doing it embraced the mantle of the "city on the hill" delivering American values to a waiting world. In a speech before the Heritage Foundation on October 31, 2001, Lorne W. Craner, assistant secretary for the Bureau of Democracy, Human Rights, and Labor, told his audience that "maintaining the focus on human rights and democracy world-wide is an integral part of our response to the attack and is even more essential today than before September 11th."[253] Craner went so far as to assert, "We are proud to bear the mantle of leadership in international human rights in this century. . . ." The kind of human rights policies promoted by the admin-istration, however, are only those consonant with a narrow set of American values and interests. Craner clarified, "Our policy in this administration, and it is certainly true after September 11th, is to focus on U.S. national interests," which includes "concentration on advancing human rights and democracy in countries important to the United States."[254] The goal for U.S. supporters of democracy and human rights, noted Craner, is to "protect the values that underpin civil society at home."[255] Thus, though the Bush administration does not claim to be discarding human rights in the post–September 11 climate, it is also continuing the practice of U.S. exceptionalism.

In both the 2002 and 2003 State of the Union addresses, Bush drew on a notion of "human dignity" in the place of language about human rights obligations as a new policy term. These "dignity" obligations, he contended in the 2003 address, are at the core of the American character: "The American flag stands for more than our power and our interests. Our founders dedicated this country to the cause of human dignity, the rights of every person, and the possibilities of every life. This conviction leads us to help the afflicted, and defend the peace, and confound the designs of evil men."[256]

Following the pattern of many earlier addresses, Bush appealed to a reli-gious foundation for the "cause of human dignity." He declared, "As our nation moves troops and builds alliances to make our world safer, we must also remember our calling as a blessed country is to make this world better."[257] The "liberty" that the America strives to bring to others, he noted, is "not America's gift to the world, it is is God's gift to humanity." Deploying military troops based on a sense of a "calling" and of being "blessed" with "God's gift to humanity" represents a departure from appeals to action based on a sense of obligation grounded in international standards and enforced by mul-tilateral institutions.

The 2002 National Security Strategy, the thirty-one-page report submitted to Congress by the president at the end of September 2002, provided the most comprehensive explanation of the Bush administration's attempt to replace human rights with a peculiar U.S. notion of "human dignity."[258] While dif-ferent cultures have their own notions of what constitutes "dignity," Bush acted on the assumption that it is the American version of dignity that is universal. Yet the invocation of "dignity" instead of "human rights" is deeply regressive and, if accepted and repeated elsewhere, may overturn fifty years of progress in the development of human rights norms.

To be sure, the National Security Strategy is peppered with references to human rights, for example, promising to "press governments that deny human rights to move toward a better future,"[259] and predicting that "only nations that share a commitment to protecting basic human rights" will be assured future prosperity.[260] Yet "human rights" appeared as a vague matter of concern for other states; the administration's commitment to the applicability of the norm to the United States itself remains uncertain. In contrast to "human rights," "dignity" was outlined in detail. The National Security Strategy defined the "nonnegotiable demands of human dignity" as consisting of the following elements: "the rule of law; limits on the absolute power of the state; free speech; freedom of worship; equal justice; respect for women; religious and ethnic tolerance; and respect for private property."[261] The eclectic list is remarkable in that it is wholly divorced from any that has ever appeared in international human rights instruments. Through this unilateral reordering, the administration redefines who is on the side of human rights (those on the side of freedom, dignity, and capitalism) and who is against human rights (those on the side of tyranny and indignities).[262]

While the list declares that limits should be placed on the power of the state, little responsibility is conferred on the state to do anything to promote and protect rights, such as reducing the level of structural violence within society.[263] At the same time, under this formulation individuals have very little power to assert any rights claims against the state. The list itself is contradictory; it calls for "equal justice," but women are merely due "respect" and religious and ethnic groups are due "tolerance." Further, despite Bush's call for the "rule of law" and "justice," in the absence of a clearly articulated and recognizable set of norms, these rights are difficult to enforce, and create passive actors without the agency to make legal and political claims.

Far from reflecting a universal consensus, the Bush catalog of rights is a random rendition of the administration's current priorities. The listing omits nearly all of the human rights deemed "nonderogable" in international human rights treaties (and, thus, not subject to any exceptions such as national emergency or necessity),[264] including the right to life, freedom from torture, and freedom from slavery. Also missing is any mention of the many human rights associated with civic participation and democracy—a popular (and nonpartisan) tenet of American assistance abroad based on the belief that democracy brings with it peace and freedom. The single item that is elevated to a higher status than that recognized in international human rights law is the right to property. The inclusion of "property rights" in the new template and the exclusion of all other social and economic rights is consistent with the administration's overall policy agenda that makes U.S. trade and investment a key concern.[265]

In contrast to the National Security Strategy, multilateral instruments discuss human dignities within the context of broader human rights. The preamble of the UN Charter states that one purpose of the organization is to "reaffirm faith in fundamental human rights, in the dignity and worth of the human person, in the equal rights of men and women and of nations large and small."[266] The first line of the Universal Declaration of Human Rights states that "recognition of the inherent dignity and of the equal and inalienable rights of all members of the human family is the foundation of freedom, justice and peace in the world."[267] Similar recognition of the "inherent dignity" and "the equal and inalienable rights of all members of the human family" is reaffirmed in the International Covenant on Economic, Social, and Cultural Rights,[268] and in the International Covenant on Civil and Political Rights.[269]

More recently, at the Second World Conference on Human Rights in June 1993, representatives of 171 countries (including the United States) reaffirmed these principles when they adopted a Declaration and Programme of Action, which states in the second paragraph of the preamble that "all human rights derive from the dignity and worth inherent in the human person, and . . . the human person is a central subject of human rights in fundamental freedoms, and consequently should be the principal beneficiary and participate actively in the realization of these rights and freedoms."[270]

Human rights constitute one way of upholding human dignity, yet dignity alone is not sufficient for human rights.[271] As these international human rights instruments make clear, "dignity" is one core element of human rights, "equality" another, and "worth" a related third.[272] Yet this is where current U.S. human rights policy has gone awry. The modern idea of human rights requires—indeed is premised upon—the presence of all three concepts. One cannot embrace the idea of human rights and also hold that these rights apply to *some* individuals, or that only *some* states have a responsibility to respect human rights.[273] At the same time, one cannot believe in the idea of human rights and also believe that they are earned, or that some individuals may be more worthy of human rights than others. The new foreign policy announced by the Bush administration features championing "aspirations for human dignity" as a primary tenet of American foreign policy,[274] but absent from the policy is the full recognition of the principles of equality, worth, and equal value.

The Practice: Exceptional Exceptionalism

Indications that the Bush administration was on "rough ground" on human rights came early in the administration.[275] In 2001, for the first time since the founding of the UN Human Rights Commission in 1947, the United States lost its seat on the influential body. Three European countries were elected to the three slots reserved for Western industrialized nations. Because each country is elected by its own region, America's European allies were largely responsible for its defeat.[276] This result was viewed largely as a payback for years of U.S. manipulation of the commission's decision-making process to advance a U.S. foreign policy agenda. The U.S. representatives to the commission, critics claimed, would go so far as to attack the human rights records of countries they did not like while shielding regimes with poor human rights records when doing so advanced other American foreign policy concerns. Perhaps more surprising than the result of the vote was the arrogant reaction of the United States. Acting as if it were denied something to which it was automatically entitled, the U.S. Congress decided to withhold $244 million in dues owed to the United Nations. As Stephen Zunes has observed, this set a dangerous precedent: "Countries in the world are voted on and off various UN agencies and commissions with regularity, yet this is the first time a country has withheld funds because it lost a vote. Countries are obliged to pay their UN dues regardless of whether a particular vote goes their way. If every country withheld its dues because of the irritation of losing a vote on a particular agency or commission, virtually all funding for the world body would cease."[277]

The Human Rights Commission vote signaled that even European "friends" were not willing to give the United States greater international status than it already had.

Bush was elected on a campaign pledge to undo unnecessary treaties, and his view on international treaties swung between disdain and opportunism. He exhibited opportunism in calling for criminalizing the possession of biological arms and the creation of a UN procedure to investigate suspected violations, calling these "improvements" to the 1972 Biological and Toxic Weapons Convention, which banned germ weapons.[278] On the other hand, he demonstrated his disdain for international instruments on many other occasions. While initially supporting ratification of CEDAW, the administration has recently backpedaled on its support due to opposition from right wing antichoice activists.[279] Bush has also continued the opposition of the United States to the Mine Ban Treaty and has continued to oppose a ban on children under the age of eighteen serving in the military.[280] Furthermore, the United States has refused to ratify the comprehensive nuclear test ban treaty and has backed away from its commitments to Kyoto emission control standards that mitigate the effects of global warming.[281]

Another illustrative story of American exceptionalism under the Bush administration concerns the new International Criminal Court. In April 2002, the minimum number of ratifications necessary to bring the ICC treaty into force was met. The establishment of the court was celebrated in many parts of the world—particularly in the European Union—as "one of the most important human rights initiatives since the adoption of the Universal Declaration of Human Rights."[282] The United States had conditioned its support for the creation of a permanent ICC on the UN Security Council's control of cases submitted to the court. The U.S. proposal ensured that the court would not have jurisdiction over American nationals for crimes against humanity and war crimes. In Tina Rosenberg's words, that was an "everybody but us" position that would "invite the other nations of the world to look at the court as something that the United States has designed for its own purposes."[283]

This was understandably unacceptable to the members of the UN Security Council.

Having failed to create a fail-proof mechanism for exempting the United States from the court's jurisdiction, President Bush took the unprecedented step of announcing to the UN that he was "unsigning" the ICC.[284] Knowing well that this step still did not eliminate any possibility for the court to gain jurisdiction over a U.S. national, the Bush administration instructed its diplomats to pressure allies into signing bilateral agreements exempting U.S. soldiers from prosecution or extradition to the court.[285] These strong-arm tactics led to the cutoff of military aid to thirty-five countries who refused to exempt their personnel from extradition.

A sharp fight broke out between the United States and its European allies in the middle of 2002 when, as leverage in its attempt to gain immunity for U.S. peacekeepers, the United States vetoed a resolution extending the UN peacekeeping mission in Bosnia. This move successfully pressured the UN Security Council into agreeing to exempt U.S. peacekeepers from being arrested or going to trial under the ICC rules for a year, with the option of annual renewal.[286] When in June 2003 the exemption was renewed, Kofi Annan, secretary general of the UN, expressed his doubts about the renewal of the exemption, stating that he hoped that the renewal would not become a yearly routine, and that should that happen, "it would undermine not only the authority of the ICC, but also the authority of this council, and the legitimacy of United Nations peacekeeping."[287] American exceptionalism on peacekeeping has continued to draw intense criticism as the United States has been roundly criticized for unilateralism, undermining its relationships with allies and weakening international human rights norms.[288]

Human Rights and the War on Terror

The "war on terror" presented the Bush administration with an opportunity to rethink its engagement with the world. Candidate Bush had originally promised a more stay-at-home foreign policy wherein military troops would be deployed sparingly. "I don't think our troops ought to be used for nation building," he told the nation during the second presidential debate in October 2000. "I think our troops ought to be used to fight and win war."[289] On the campaign trail in February 2000, he stated, "I'm going to say to our friends if there's a conflict in your area, you can put troops on the ground to be peacekeepers and America will be the peacemakers."[290] Following through on this promise, in May 2001, the Bush administration withdrew 750 troops from Bosnia, and in May 2001, Defense Secretary Donald Rumsfeld announced that the military job was done in Bosnia and the remaining troops should be brought home.

The aftermath of the "war on terror" in Afghanistan and Iraq, however, brought the Bush administration squarely into the nation-building business. The administration tried hard to distinguish its approach from that of the Clinton administration, suggesting more of a "tough love" and "hands off" approach instead of the Clinton bear hug. "In some 'nation building exercises,' well-intentioned foreigners arrive on the scene, look at the problems, and say, 'Lets go fix it for them.' . . . This is the opposite of what the coalition is trying to accomplish in Afghanistan," Rumsfeld said in a February 2003 speech. "Our goal is not to create another culture of dependence, but rather to promote Afghan independence-because long-term stability comes not from the presence of foreign forces, but from the development of functioning local institutions."[291] But the Clinton administration had also promised to support local institution building and avoid creating a culture of dependence.[292] President Bush's approach to nation building in many ways suggested an even more intrusive approach to nation building than ever endorsed by the Clinton administration. In a speech before the American Enterprise Institute in February 2003, he suggested that the World War II allied occupations and reconstructions of Germany and Japan provided good models for the Middle East. "After defeating enemies, we did not leave behind the occupying armies, we left constitutions and parliaments," he reflected on the postwar occupation, adding "we established an atmosphere of safety, in which responsible, reform-minded local leaders could build lasting institutions of freedom. In societies that once bred fascism and militarism, liberty found a home."[293] American-style liberty could find a home, he implied, through similar wholesale occupations in the Middle East.

The Clinton administration's pattern for postconflict reconstruction was, in the words of one foreign service officer who served on postconflict reconstruction and development projects in both the Clinton and George W. Bush administration, "We go in and create a safe enough environment, build institutions, write laws, and hold elections."[294] The Bush administration altered the formula in three ways. First, there was no formula. Instead of exposing itself to accusations of following a poor plan for nation building, the Bush administration followed *no plan* for nation building. By the summer of 2003, with American soldiers still being killed and injured in a war that had long been declared "over" and the deployment of reservists in Iraq stretching longer and longer, military families grew increasingly frustrated,[295] and the American public wondered, "Where's the plan?"[296] While the Department of Defense had in fact drawn elaborate plans for postconflict scenarios in Iraq and Afghanistan, much to the bewilderment of the drafters of those plans the Bush administration failed to follow them. "There is no way the Bush administration should not have known that massive looting and chaos would follow the end of Saddam Hussein's regime," said one retired DOD employee who had worked on postconflict planning for Iraq, frustrated that the failure to follow his advice was resulting in the deaths of U.S. soldiers.[297] "I had told them that a post-Saddam Iraq would take ten years to stabilize, and 250,000 to 300,000 troops, but this administration said 75,000 troops [and promised they would be] in and out."[298] Other military and civilian foreign service officers interviewed for this project similarly spoke of being involved in creating plans for postconflict scenarios for Iraq that were never followed. "It was like [the Bush administration] was in denial," said one retired military officer.

Second, while light on planning, nation building Bush style was extra heavy on ideology. The administration made explicit that its support of democratization endeavors and post-conflict reconstruction would be tied to the promotion of American values, promising that those conflict areas moving most closely in line with American values would be rewarded. For example, in announcing a 50 percent increase in development aid in March 2002—the "Millennium Account," the president made clear that the aid was conditioned on support of American values.[299] Humanitarian organizations unwilling to declare their allegiance to American values need not apply for U.S. resources to work in Iraq—this was the message projected from the U.S. Agency for International Development during the Bush era.[300]

Third, the Bush administration also indicated its willingness to impose its desired version of postconflict democratization, employing military force as needed. Harold Hongju Koh, the former assistant secretary of state for human rights in the Clinton administration, testified before Congress in July 2003 about this troubling shift in policy.[301] "Since the U.S. invasion of Afghanistan, our democracy-promotion efforts seem to have shifted toward military-imposed democracy, characterized by United States–led military attack, prolonged occupation, restored opposition leaders and the creation of resource-needy post conflict protectorates," said Koh. He warned that at present, "a new and discouraging, four-pronged strategy seems to be emerging: 'hard,' military-imposed democracy-promotion in Iraq and Afghanistan; 'soft,' diplomatic democracy-promotion in Palestine; optimistic predictions of 'domino democratization' elsewhere in the Middle East; and reduced democracy-promotion efforts elsewhere."[302] Most troubling, Koh found, was the way in which the administration permitted its war on terrorism to soften its democracy-promotion efforts in such pivotal countries as Pakistan, Saudi Arabia, and Kuwait.

Compounding the negative impact of Bush's style of nation building was its go-it-alone attitude. Unlike its sudden embrace of (selective) nation building, there would be no Bush administration policy reversal on unilateralism. Its decision to seek UN Security Council resolutions condemning Iraq's defiance of earlier Security Council resolutions and authorizing the U.S.-led intervention may appear to demonstrate the administration's support of multilateralism. However, President Bush repeatedly made clear the U.S. intention to act alone, without UN Security Council approval. "Nations are either with us or against us in the war on terror," he said,[303] painting the world in black-and-white terms. As Laura Neack observes in her post–September 11 analysis of the foreign policy of the Bush administration, "Unilateralism remained the key operating mode, although the United States would fully expect others to fall behind it."[304]

In his 2003 State of the Union address, President Bush explained that the American approach to terrorism is utilitarian in nature. "America's purpose is more than to follow a process," he said, "it is to achieve a result: the end of terrible threats to the civilized world."[305] As the leader of the "free" world, he contended, the United States has unbridled discretion to make a utilitarian calculus in the name of the American people—and indeed all free people. "All free nations have a stake in preventing sudden and catastrophic attacks," he claimed. "And we're asking them to join us, and many are doing so. Yet the course of this nation does not depend on the decisions of others. Whatever action is required, whenever action is necessary, I will defend the freedom and security of the American people."[306]

In the same address, the president told his American audience that "we've arrested or otherwise dealt with many key commanders of al Qaeda." Even more ominous for the human rights of those arrested, the president declared, "All told, more than 3,000 suspected terrorists have been arrested in many countries. Many others have met a different fate. Let's put it this way—they are no longer a problem to the United States and our friends and allies."[307]

This "ends justifies the means" approach to terrorism has led to a crackdown on civil liberties in the United States, prominently in the Domestic Security Enhancement Act of 2003, which authorizes secret arrests, strips Americans of their citizenship for peacefully supporting groups deemed "terrorist," expands the basis for deportation without a hearing, and exempts habeas corpus provisions from the judicial review of certain immigration proceedings.[308] In the weeks following September 11, 2001, a massive domestic sweep of 1,100 mostly young Arab men by the Federal Bureau of Investigation (FBI) mirrored an aggressive international roundup of hundreds of al Qaeda suspects in fifty countries coordinated by the CIA and foreign intelligence services.[309] These and related actions have resulted in a general attack on civil rights both domestically and internationally on the part of the Bush administration and the military, including approving CIA assassinations, establishing secretive military tribunals, massive arrests of young Arab men, discussing (and perhaps implementing) torture as a "necessary" interrogation measure, and breaching the Geneva Conventions in the treatment of the detainees at the U.S. naval base at Guantanamo Bay, Cuba.

Concluding that executive orders do not preclude the president from "lawfully" fingering a terrorist for assassination by covert action, the Bush administration empowered the CIA to carry out such missions in its global campaign against terror, and expanded the range of potential targets.[310]

Bush signed an executive order on November 13, 2001, establishing secret military tribunals to try al Qaeda members and others accused of terrorism, citing "extraordinary times" and "national security interests" and protecting "the safety of potential jurors as reasons for circumventing the U.S. court system and international law.[311] Bush was passionately denounced by a small but loud chorus from both the domestic political Left and Right as well as by European commentators for this sublimation of human rights and overextension of executive power. As Anne-Marie Slaughter, dean of the Woodrow Wilson School of International Afairs at Princeton, has cautioned, "At a deeper level, such trials challenge Americans' identity as a people. Military commissions have been used rarely in the past, principally to try to hang spies caught behind enemy lines. Now such commissions are proposed as a long-term mechanism to achieve a principal war aim — finding and trying terrorists. But

America is also, according to Mr. Bush, fighting for the values embodied in its constitution, against an enemy that would destroy its way of life. How then can it violate those values in the process?"[312] The Washington, D.C., advocacy director for Human Rights Watch, Tom Malinowski, has warned that the order will open the door for the world's military dictators to follow suit. "In effect," he notes, "the administration has one critical choice: It can let Mr. Bush's order stand as it is, and let it become a virtual code of misconduct for authoritarian governments around the world. Or it can show what the U.S. system of military justice was meant to show: that America does not abandon its commitments to human rights in times of conflict, but affirms it as an enduring source of national strength."[313]

Along with the creation of the military tribunals, an aggressive FBI roundup was championed by Attorney General John Ashcroft. The Justice Department issued a list of five thousand young men who entered the United States since 2000 from, predominantly, the Middle East. At that, opponents cried racism and racial profiling. "This type of sweeping investigation carries with it the potential to create the impression that interviewees are being singled out because of their race, ethnicity or religion," stated Nihad Awad, executive director of the Council on American-Islamic Relations, an Islamic advocacy group based in Washington, D.C.[314] As allegations of unjust and unlawful treatment poured in to civil rights attorneys' offices across the country, a class action lawsuit was filed against the government for ethnic and religious pro-filing.[315] Immigration lawyers and human rights advocates have repeatedly submitted complaints of civil rights violations on behalf of detainees held in the Metropolitan Detention Center in Brooklyn, New York, where many men are being held without being charged for terror-related crimes while allegedly there is secret evidence against them.[316] Amnesty International issued a report on these detentions reiterating concerns over violations of international civil liberties.[317]

The press began floating articles about the frustration that both investiga-tors and many in the general public were feeling over the inability to get desired information out of the detainees. Some investigators began to complain that traditional civil liberties would have to be put aside if they were to extract information about the September 11 attacks and future terrorist plans.[318] One seasoned FBI interrogator lamented, "We are known for humanitarian treat-ment, so basically we are stuck. Usually there is some incentive, some angle to play, what you can do for them. But it could get to that spot where we could go to pressure [sic] where we won't have a choice, and we are probably getting there."[319]

Alternative tactics discussed concerned extraditing suspects to third coun-tries where "security service sometimes employ threats to family members or resort to torture." U.S. domestic law was cited for its disallowance of court-room evidence obtained through "physical pressure, inhumane treatment or torture." Furthermore, domestic law allows for victims to sue or for the government to charge battery. A former FBI agent complained, "You can't torture, you can't give drugs now, and there is a logic, reason, and humanity to back that. But you could reach a point where they allow us to apply drugs to a guy. But I don't think this country would ever permit torture or beatings."[320]

In January 2002, photos were released of Taliban and al Qaeda prisoners being held in what appeared to be "sensory depravation" conditions—in masks, earmuffs, heavy wool caps and gloves, with their hands and feet bound. The treatment of prisoners by the U.S. military at its naval base in Guantanamo Bay caused a worldwide outcry.[321] European diplomats, lawmakers, and analysts openly criticized Washington, and other European Union officials and the International Red Cross raised questions as to the physical and legal status of the prisoners. One ambassador charged the United States with "international law a la carte, like multilateralism a la carte. It annoys your allies in the war against terrorism, and it creates problems for our Muslim allies, too. It puts at stake the moral credibility of the war against terrorism."[322]

Human rights advocates have concluded that a number of countries, including China, Columbia, India, Indonesia, Singapore, Malaysia, Russia, Uzbekistan, and Israel, are using the U.S.-led campaign against terror as a cover to justify repression of all kinds, including that of nonviolent activism for democratic change.[323] Human rights abuses may even have been furthered in these nations, since the United States offered arms in exchange for support of the war on terror to many countries with dismal human rights records immediately following the announcement of the new war.[324] Restrictions on military aid were also lifted to countries, particularly those with large Muslim populations, who voiced support for the war on terrorism. [325]

What Were the Constraints?

The greatest influence on the Bush administration's decision making regarding human rights were the terrorist attacks on September 11, 2001. On one hand, the public expected the United States to be a leader on human rights, but on the other hand, the public demanded that the nation defend itself.[326] The war that ensued in Afghanistan, at least initially, won over many human rights advocates and scholars usually critical of U.S. interventionism. In a clear departure from his usual stance, Richard Falk stated, "This war in Afghanistan against apocalyptic terrorism qualifies in my understanding as the first truly just war since World War II."[327] Similarly, Harold Meyerson of the *American Prospect* credited Bush's strategy with being "a case where a liberal value became one of the strategic guides to the conduct of war."[328] Such "liberal values" were ones that "[kept] civilian casualties and other collateral damage to a minimum, that gave a high priority to humanitarian assistance for the people of Afghanistan and that played to feminists by focusing criticism on the Taliban's policy of oppressing women."[329]

To maintain public support, the administration explained the wars in both Afghanistan and Iraq in human rights terms. President Bush, cabinet members, and military leadership submitted to multiple interviews and gave numerous broadcast speeches emphasizing the delivery of U.S. relief supplies.[330]

To take one example, the turning point of public opinion on the war in Iraq was the media coverage over the rescue of American soldier Jessica Lynch. The media was ecstatic about Lynch's rescue, and the story gave the public an uplifting image of a courageous, young, and pretty American woman being saved from the hands of the enemy rather than the slow, agonizing war it had seen in the first few weeks of fighting.[331] The story of the battle to save Private Lynch, however, was an overstated affair. Media at the time portrayed her rescue as a daring mission of U.S. forces raiding a compound of Saddam Hussein's henchmen. As the dust from the fighting settled, however, the conditions from which Lynch had been gloriously rescued turned out, in fact, to have been not nearly so bad as depicted in media accounts. The "multiple gunshot wounds" that she had reportedly suffered were in actuality broken bones. The U.S. troops had rescued Lynch from an "undefended compound" (which was a hospital). Lynch, who was in the care of Iraqi doctors and nurses, had been well fed and cared for during her captivity.[332] One journalist observed that "Americans were primed to expect a story of rescue—not just because our president told us that we would save Iraq and ourselves, but because for more than two centuries our culture has made the liberation of captives into a trope for American righteousness."[333] The media's role in shaping public opinion was prominent. In Iraq, as with the bombing of Afghanistan, reporters were side by side with American forces; television coverage, with live images of the wars, was constant on many U.S. news stations.

Another factor influencing the administration's behavior was the vociferous debate over whether the United States should, or even, could, go it alone in Afghanistan and Iraq. Secretary of State Powell, his deputy Richard Armitage, and Anthony Zinni, envoy to the Middle East, advocated a "go slow" policy with regard to expanding the war on terror and working with international allies in our diplomatic efforts. A more aggressive stance was taken by Rumsfeld, Deputy Defense Secretary Paul Wolfowitz, Bush's counterterrorism chief Wayne Downing, and Cheney's chief of staff Lewis Libby, who advocated a quick, unilateral attack on Iraq.[334] The Rumsfeld camp's go-it-alone stance showed a victory of their influence on the president over Powell's camp. Furthermore, it indicated the dominance of the new foreign policy ideology of the United States, which is that while multilateralism may be one alternative, hegemonic action could be embraced and accepted regardless of the approval of international organizations such as the UN.

The Bush administration paid little attention to the numerous human rights NGOs that petitioned the UN's Committee on Human Rights to reprimand the United States in its 2003 report for treatment of detainees at Guantanamo Bay and in U.S. prisons in the war against terror, as well as the creation of U.S. military tribunals to try suspects. It also did not heed UN High Commissioner for Human Rights Mary Robinson's demand that the United States recognize the Guantanamo Bay captives as prisoners of war. On the contrary, the United States retaliated against Robinson by failing to support her reappointment.[335] Amnesty International is taking up the cause of those swept up in the FBI searches and detained indefinitely on supposed secret evidence in U.S. jails.[336] Some of these captives were children as young as thirteen years of age.[337] The Bush administration nonetheless managed to continue to justify its actions as being in line with national interests and the extraordinary efforts needed to fight the "war on terror."

Tugging at the Bush administration's desire to utilize American strength solely to promote U.S. values and interests abroad is broad support for humanitarian action within USAID as well as within other government entities involved in such issues, such as the U.S. State Department's Bureau of Population, Refugees, and Migration; its Bureau of Democracy, Conflict, and Humanitarian Assistance; and the Department of Defense's humanitarian officer. USAID, under the leadership of its new administrator, Andrew Natsios, insisted that humanitarian and democratization policies receive greater attention in areas of conflict and potential conflict. Natsios created a new bureau at USAID, the Bureau for Policy and Program Coordination, which housed program, policy, and administrative decision making under one roof.[338] He also made conflict a pillar of USAID's work, creating a transition assistance office and conflict management fund with the stated purpose of giving "greater latitude to experiment with 'non-traditional' approaches."[339] The United States would thus "take a stronger leadership role in shaping the practices of development relief, breaking from its traditional reluctance to embrace the more political aspects of relief operations."[340] Natsios's powerful leadership at USAID pushed the Bush administration to realize the link between development assistance and conflict, and to understand the U.S. national interest in responding to humanitarian crises. Although these crises were defined in terms of humanitarian and democratization needs, addressing them required paying attention to human rights concerns as well.

Under Natsios, USAID continued the creative work of the Office of Transition Initiatives (OTI). This outfit, which has been called USAID's "swat team" and "the entrepreneurial wing of USAID"[341] can work more closely with U.S. military and civilian authorities and do the kind of political work that many humanitarian and human rights organizations shun. OTI was credited for quietly supporting the broad range of Serbian NGOs, student groups, think tanks, labor organizations, and media that united to oust Slobodan Milosevic.[342] Although OTI took care to show that it appeared as if indigenous organizations were always driving events, many were, if not designed, at least heavily inspired by outside coaching and resources. OTI continued its innovative work in the aftermath of the American bombing stage of the Iraqi war. OTI sent in the first-ever U.S. human rights "response team" charged with "getting information and mitigating human rights abuses in a hot post-conflict environment."[343] Albert Cevallos, one of the leaders of the OTI team, notes that by identifying mass graves and property issues as "key points of potential conflict," OTI was able to "connect the dots" by linking "local and international NGOs" together and by providing resources to enable their projects to proceed. Cevallos expresses the attitude of many government employees working in post-conflict areas when he comments, "To some extent it does not matter which [presidential] administration I'm dealing with. I'm out there trying to do the thing I do best."[344]

Individuals and institutional efforts to integrate human rights into U.S. involvement overseas continued to develop rapidly during the Bush administration. Yet still there was much the administration could have done to support these developments. Increasing the resources and capacity of units with special expertise and a proven tract record on human rights promotion in transitional areas—such as OTI—would have been a good start. Addressing issues related to security, coordination, and sustained commitment over time would also have led to greater success. Yet while the human rights capacity of government agencies like USAID continued to improve, it was ultimately the Bush administration that called the shots, and the administration that continued to employ human rights in an instrumental and exceptionalist manner.

What Was the Degree of Norm Embeddedness?

The range of possibilities for human rights foreign policy is informed by three sets of choices: domestic or international definition of norms; unilateral or multilateral action; and a focus on application of human rights norms at home or abroad.[345] In applying domestic norms unilaterally to the behavior of certain (enemy) states, the administration of George W. Bush appears to be patterning itself after the second Reagan administration, which made similar choices on human rights policy. Indeed, the language of the new National Security Strategy is strikingly similar to statements on human rights made by members of the Reagan administration. For example, in a speech in February 1984, Secretary of State George Shultz explained that Americans, in contrast to other people, define themselves "not by where we come from, but where we are headed: our goals, our values, our principles." Freedom, Shultz said, is a central goal for Americans. In response to domestic expectations then, "moral values and a commitment to human dignity have not been an appendage to our foreign policy [in the Reagan administration], but an essential part of it, and a powerful impulse driving it."[346] This idea is echoed in President Bush's belief in what he terms "a distinctly American internationalism."[347]

Like the current administration, the second Reagan administration articulated the difference between the United States and its enemies in moral terms, as "the difference between tyranny and freedom."[348] Also, like the current administration, the second Reagan administration used international human rights norms strategically, as a tool for furthering its interests rather than as a means for evaluating its own behavior. The Reagan administration was not isolationist; rather, it supported "a commitment to active engagement, confidently working for our values as well as our interests in the real world, acting proudly as the champion of freedom."[349]

Comparing these words to those of the 2002 National Security Strategy, it may at first glance appear as if President Bush's staff took a page right out of the Reagan administration's foreign policy scrapbook. Notably missing, however, is a significant element of the Reagan human rights strategy—namely, the willingness to utilize, albeit selectively, international human rights treaties and mechanisms. While not fully embracing multilateralism, the second Reagan administration demonstrated at least a pragmatic understanding of the modern human rights regime. In the speech quoted above, Shultz made clear that the Reagan administration sought to use multilateral institutions as an "instrument of [U.S.] human rights policy."[350]

The second Reagan administration's commitment to multilateral approaches to human rights problems should not be overstated. It invoked treaties selectively, reading in the kinds of civil and political rights most familiar to U.S. constitutional law, and reading out economic, social, and cultural rights that are largely foreign to U.S. legal traditions. Nonetheless, the second Reagan administration still recognized the existence and potential importance of international human rights instruments and organizations. The decision of the administration of George W. Bush to depart from this practice is radically regressive.

At the same time, the administration carries forth the worst tendency of the first Reagan administration: the practice of overlooking gross human rights abuses whenever a government sides with the United States in a fight with an enemy. The Bush administration abruptly dropped its push for religious freedom in China when, after September 11, it needed intelligence information about Muslim militants.[351] Relations with the Chinese thawed almost overnight; as the *Washington Post* noted, "The U.S. relationship with China has changed almost as dramatically as that with Russia since September 11, and for some of the same reasons. Public prickliness has disappeared as the government of Jiang Zemin has supported the U.S. campaign against terrorism and even the bombing in Afghanistan—the first time China has supported a U.S. military action since the end of the cold war. In return, China, like Russia, expects new understanding for its brutal repression of a Muslim minority, the Uighurs, on the grounds that this too constitutes counterterrorism. And, as with Russia, the Bush administration appears ready to make important concessions."[352] In his October 2001 visit to Shanghai, Bush did gently remind his hosts that "the war against terrorism must never be an excuse to persecute minorities,"[353] yet these words were not backed with action. Freedom of religion would remain on the back burner.

Another example of the sacrifice of human rights in the name of security is present in the U.S. relationship with Russia. In recent years, U.S. officials have publicly criticized Russian human rights abuses in its war with the secessionist rebels in Chechnya. But in the wake of Moscow's offer to let the United States use its bases and airspace in the war against terrorism, Bush abruptly changed the policy, instead calling on rebels to cut their ties with "international terrorist groups" and to enter into peace talks with Moscow.[354] Bush went further to seek normal trade status with Russia, despite calls to link it with improvements in Moscow's human rights record.[355]

A similar regression of human rights practices occurred toward Uzbekistan. The U.S. government largely abandoned its concerns over the Uzbeki government's jailing of Muslim activists and religious freedom in that country. As

U.S. Air Force planes made this country its temporary home in the Afghan war, the Bush administration embraced its new ally.[356] In thanks, the country received $160 million in U.S. aid money for 2002, and in 2003 Bush lobbied Congress to lift trade restrictions on Uzbekistan.[357] However, as with China and Russia, the United States has not entirely sidelined human rights and democratic institution building, at least not on paper. In the "declaration of strategic partnership" signed between Secretary of State Powell and the Uzbeki foreign ministry, the government commits itself to broad political and economic reforms, including establishing a multiparty system, ensuring free and fair elections, promoting an independent media, judicial reform, and free market reforms. This agreement, then, is no different from what in a not-so-distant era was termed "democratic enlargement."

The twist with the Bush administration, however, was the manner in which American exceptionalism influenced policymaking. President Bush's belief that the world would be a better place if everyone would be more like the United States left a deep imprint on the way the United States approached the world. One illustration can be found in the document that was released as a companion to the 2002 National Security Policy clarifying the administrations new foreign aid strategy. *Foreign Aid in the National Interest: Freedom, Security, and Opportunity*, a USAID publication, suggests that the United States must foster development around the world because "life, liberty, and the pursuit of happiness are universal."[358] The gloss given to these "universals," however, is a particular American influence on property ownership and material wealth. The only right mentioned by name is "property."[359] The document makes its goals clear, declaring that "a world where all countries are becoming more prosperous would also be a profound affirmation of U.S. values and interests."[360]

CONCLUSION

The United States views itself as the moral leader of the world, and yet, under both Republican and Democratic administrations, it has employed human rights selectively, condemning the human rights abuses of its enemies while overlooking those of its allies. Each administration has objected to scrutiny of its own domestic violations of international human rights standards, including capital punishment for juveniles,[361] the use of shock restraints and other practices in U.S. prisons,[362] and, more recently, the treatment of terrorist suspects.[363] America continues to send more weapons and economic aid to oppressive governments around the globe than any other nation.[364] And, by ratifying fewer than half of existing international human rights agreements, the United States remains an outsider to many key human rights processes.[365]

Each administration has used different rhetoric to frame its human rights policy—rhetoric that has influenced public perceptions of that administration's approach to human rights policy. Because each president has invented new buzz words in an effort to brand as unique his approach to human rights and

U.S. foreign policy, the public perception has tended to focus on the differences of one administration from another, while failing to notice their similarities. Yet, upon careful examination, the differences between the presidencies are eclipsed by one overriding similarity: American exceptionalism, with the United States applying one standard of human rights to itself and another to the rest of the world.

Table 1 is a snapshot comparison of the post–Cold War presidencies. The rhetoric does differ considerably from administration to administration, as does the style and approach. For example, the pragmatic, nondoctrinal President George H. W. Bush tolerated NGOs and worked with international institutions, while his more doctrinal son George W. Bush took a more adversarial and unilateral approach. The Clinton administration had the strongest rhetorical policy on human rights, literally opening its doors to human rights advocates and openly identifying human rights as a central foreign policy concern. President Clinton also had the greatest respect for international law and institutions, signing treaties, for example, that President George W. Bush proceeded to unsign or ignore. Another critical factor affecting the approaches of different presidents has been each one's chosen source of guidance on human rights norms. Both President Clinton and President George H. W. Bush were globalists in their approach; they both recognized the legitimacy of international law, though Clinton more enthusiastically tried to shape it. In contrast, George W. Bush looks not to international law for guidance on human rights but to the U.S. Constitution and to providence.

Despite these differences in philosophy and approach to human rights, each president's human rights policy has ultimately been driven by the common theme of American exceptionalism. In all administrations, national interests trump the consistent application of a single standard for human rights. Furthermore, despite rhetoric to the contrary, each president has acted as if the United States is first among states that are less than equal. Human rights are envisioned as something applied to *others* in line with U.S. national interests. Even the Clinton presidency, which had a strong self-identification as a human rights presidency, suffered from a disconnect between globalist rhetoric and nationalist action—a disconnect that did not go unrecognized by rest of the world. Moreover, when under pressure, Clinton abandoned his idealist rhetoric altogether, as did the other post–Cold War presidents.

In no presidency to date can we say that human rights norms have been pervasively or consistently embedded in thought and action. Human rights have to some extent become institutionalized, but they do not have an automatic influence over identities, interests, and expectations. Ultimately, although their record on specific human rights issues has varied, every American president since Carter has used human rights in an exceptionalist and unilateralist manner that serves to undermine the idea of human rights. In particular, by exempting the United States from scrutiny under human rights norms, the administrations have undercut the notion that human rights apply to all on an equal basis. To the extent that the United States perceives itself as a human rights role model, it is setting a bad example for others.

TABLE 1

Snapshot Comparison of U.S. Presidencies and Human Rights, 1988–2003

	George H. W. Bush	Bill Clinton	George W. Bush
Human Rights Buzz Words[a]	New World Order; Freedom; Human Rights	Democratic Enlargement; Human Rights; Peacebuilding	War on Terror; Human Dignity; American Values; Freedom
Characteristics of Policy	Pragmatic; Managerial; Nondoctrinal[b]	Shifting Idealism; Rhetorical; Media/Public–Opinion Driven	Pragmatic; Doctrinal; Unilateral; Militarily Driven
Attitude toward NGOs[c]	Increasingly Tolerant; Partner or Combatant	Partnership; Source of Expertise; Cheap Service Provider	Adjunct to U.S. Policies or Adversarial
Emphasis of Human Rights Policy	Electoral Democracy; Market Reforms	Linking Economic and Political Reform	Electoral Democracy; Market Reforms
Strategies	Diplomacy; Institution Building; Sanctions; Assistance Conditionality	Institution Building; Participation in International Institutions; Delinking Aid; Adding Human Rights in Peace Agreement	Institution Building; Unilateral Intervention
Guidance for Human Rights Strategies	Shared Interests; Shared Ideals; U.S. as Leader of "Civilized World"	International Law; International Institutions; Regional Considerations	American Values; Providence
Trump Card for Human Rights	National Interests; Risk to U.S. Military	National Interests; Risk to U.S. Military	National Interests
Treaties	Signed Torture Convention; Ratified ICCPR	Signed Children's Convention; International Criminal Court; ICESCR[d]; Ratified Race Convention	Unsigned International Criminal Court

[a] Other buzz words used for human rights policies include *rule of law* and *democracy*.

[b] See United States Institute of Peace, "U.S Human Rights Policy: A 20-Year Assessment," June 16, 1999 (commens of Susan Bergman).

[c] Refer to Chapter 4 of this volume for more on NGOs.

[d] ICESCR = International Covenant on Economic, Social and Cultural Rights.

ENDNOTES

1. See, generally, Felix Gilbert, *To the Farewell Address: Ideas of Early American Foreign Policy* (Princeton, N.J.: Princeton University Press, 1961); Richard Rosecrance, *America as an Ordinary Country: U.S. Foreign Policy and the Future* (Ithaca, N.Y.: Cornell University Press, 1976).

2. Arthur Schlesinger, "Human Rights and the American Tradition," *Foreign Affairs* 57 (1978): 505.

3. Jack C. Donnelly, *Universal Human Rights: In Theory and Practice*, 2nd ed. (Ithaca, N.Y: Cornell University Press, 2003), 161.

4. Belinda Cooper and Isabel Traugott, "Women's Rights and Security in Central Asia," *World Policy Journal* 20, no. 1 (2003): 59–67.

5. Chester Crocker, interview with the author, August 16, 2001.

6. L. Kathleen Roberts, "The United States and the World: Changing Approaches to Human Rights Diplomacy under the Bush Administration," *Berkeley Journal of International Law* 21 (2003): 631.

7. Kathryn Sikkink, "The Power of Principled Ideas: Human Rights Policies in the United States and Western Europe," in *Ideas and Foreign Policy: Beliefs, Institutions and Political Change*, ed. Judith Goldstein and Robert O. Keohane (Ithaca, N.Y.: Cornell University Press, 1993), 162.

8. Ibid.

9. See Roberts, "Changing Approaches," 631.

10. David P. Forsythe, "Human Rights in U.S. Foreign Policy: Retrospect and Prospect," *Political Science Quarterly* 105, no. 3 (1990): 435–54.

11. David Halberstam, *War in a Time of Peace* (New York: Scribner's, 2001), 58, 80.

12. Ibid., 58–66. See also Henry Kissinger, *The White House Years* (Boston: Little Brown, 1979).

13. Marc Northern, quoted in Korwa G. Adar, "The Wilsonian Conception of Democracy and Human Rights: A Retrospective and Prospective," *African Studies Quarterly* 2, no. 2; available online at http://www.africa.ufl.edu/asq/v2/v2i2a3.htm.

14. See Lars Schoultz, *Human Rights and United States Policy toward Latin America* (Princeton, N.J.: Princeton University Press, 1981), 121.

15. R. Cohen, "Human Rights Decision-Making in the Executive Branch: Some Proposals for a Coordinated Strategy," in Donald Kommers and Gilbert Loescher, eds. *Human Rights and American Foreign Policy* (Notre Dame, Ind.: University of Notre Dame Press, 1979), 221.

16. Ibid.

17. "Secretary of State Kissinger Appearing on Face the Nation," *Department of State Bulletin* (1976): 608.

18. Jeffrey D. Merritt, "Unilateral Human Rights Intercession: American Practice under Nixon, Ford, and Carter," in *The Diplomacy of Human Rights*, ed. David D. Newsom (Lanham, Md.: University Press of America, 1986), 45.

19. Ibid.; see also John P. Salzberg, "A View from the Hill: U.S. Legislation and Human Rights," in *The Diplomacy of Human Rights*, ed. David. D. Newsom (Lanham, Md.: University Press of America, 1986), 13–20.

20. Salzberg, "View from the Hill," 14.

21. Ibid., 15.

22. Edwin S. Maynard, "The Bureaucracy and Implementation of U.S. Human Rights Policy," *Human Rights Quarterly* 11 (1989): 175–248.

23. Foreign Assistance Act, Pub. L. No. 94-329, 90 Stat. 729 (1982).

24. Merritt, "Intercession," 45.

25. Maynard, "Bureaucracy,"179.

26. Kathryn Sikkink, "The Power of Principled Ideas: Human Rights Policies in the United States and Western Europe," in *Ideas & Foreign Policy: Beliefs, Institutions, and Political Change*, ed. Judith Goldstein and Robert O. Keohane (Ithaca, N.Y.: Cornell University Press, 1993), 151.

27. Jimmy Carter, Inaugural Address, January 20, 1977; available online at http://library.thinkquest.org/5501/caterinaugaddress.html.

28. Cyrus Vance, 1977 address at University of Georgia School of Law, quoted in Sara Steinmetz, *Democratic Transition and Human Rights* (Albany: State University of New York Press, 1994), 14.

29. Steinmetz, *Democratic Transition*, 17.

30. John P. Salzberg, "The Carter Administration and Human Rights," in *The Diplomacy of Human Rights*, ed. David D. Newsom (Lanham, Md.: University Press of America, 1986), 61.

31. Jimmy Carter, *Keeping Faith: Memoirs of a President* (New York: Ballantine, 1982), 150.

32. See Michael Stahl, David Carleton, and Steven E. Johnson, "Human Rights in U.S. Foreign Policy from Nixon to Carter," *Journal of Peace Research* 21 no. 3 (1984): 215–26.

33. Forsythe, "Human Rights," 260.

34. Ibid.

35. David D. Newsom, "The Diplomacy of Human Rights: A Diplomat's View," in *The Diplomacy of Human Rights*, ed. David D. Newsom (Lanham, Md.: University Press of America, 1986), 5.

36. Maynard, "Bureaucracy," 181.

37. Salzberg, "Carter Administration," 62.

38. Forsythe, "Human Rights," 264–65.

39. Maynard, "Bureaucracy,"183.

40. Ibid. citing American Association for the International Commission of Jurists, *Human Rights and United States Foreign Policy, The First Decade, 1973–1983* (1984).

41. Maynard, "Bureaucracy," 183; Sikkink, "Principled Ideas," 155.

42. Maynard, "Bureaucracy," 183.

43. Jeanne Kirkpatrick, quoted in Daniel W. Drezner, "Ideas, Bureaucratic Politics, and the Crafting of Foreign Policy," *American Journal of Political Science* 44, no. 4 (2000): 745.

44. Ibid.

45. David Forsythe, "Human Rights in U.S. Foreign Policy: Two Levels, Two Worlds," *Political Studies* 3 (1995): 123.

46. Drezner, "Ideas," 745.

47. Sikkink, "Principled Ideas," 155.

48. John W. Spanier and Steven W. Hook, *American Foreign Policy Since World War II*, 15th ed. (Washington, D.C.: Congressional Quarterly Press, 2000), 213–17.

49. President Reagan's March Fourteenth Address to Congress (1986), quoted in Spanier and Hook, *American Foreign Policy*, 215.

50. Steven A. Shull, *A Kinder, Gentler Racism?* (Armonk, N.Y.: M.E. Sharpe, 1993); see also Human Rights Watch, "Race and Incarceration in the United States," February 27, 2002; available online at http://hrw.org/backgrounder/usa/race/.

51. Drezner, "Ideas," 746.

52. George [H. W.] Bush, "Remarks at Maxwell Air Force Base War College in Montgomery, Alabama," *Public Papers of the President of the United States 1991*, book 1 (Washington, D.C.: USGPO, 1992), 368; see also Timothy M. Cole, "When Intentions Go Awry: The Bush Administration's Foreign Policy Rhetoric," *Political Communication* 13, no. 1 (1996): 102.

53. Walter Russell Mead, *Special Provenance: American Foreign Policy and How It Changes the World* (New York: Routledge, 2002), 268.

54. Ibid.

55. Forsythe, "Two Levels, Two Worlds," 124.

56. Terry L. Deibel, "Bush's Foreign Policy: Mastery and Inaction," *Foreign Policy* 84 (1991): 3–23; Robert Pastor, "George Bush and Latin America," in *Eagle in a New World: American Grand Strategy in the Post-Cold War Era*, ed. Kennth A. Oye, Donald S. Rothschild, and Robert J. Lieber (New York: Harper Collins, 1992), 361–88.

57. Clair Apodaca and Michael Stohl, "United States Human Rights Policy and Foreign Assistance," *International Studies Quarterly* 43, no. 1 (1999): 185–98.

58. Forsythe, "Two Levels, Two Worlds," 124.

59. Adar, "The Wilsonian Conception."

60. Apodaca and Stohl, "Foreign Assistance," 186.

61. David P. Forsythe, "U.S. Foreign Policy and Human Rights: The Price of Principles after the Cold War," in *Human Rights and Comparative Foreign Policy*, ed. David P. Forsythe (New York: United Nations University Press, 2000), 30.

62. Ibid.

63. Forsythe, "Two Levels, Two Worlds," 125.

64. Ibid.

65. George [H. W.] Bush, "Address to the Nation Announcing Allied Military Action in the Persian Gulf," *Public Papers of the Presidents of the United States 1991*, book 1 (Washington, D.C.: USGPO, 1992) 43; see also Cole, "Intentions," 97.

66. George [H. W.] Bush, "Address before the Forty-Fifth Session of the UN General Assembly in New York, New York," *Public Papers of the Presidents of the United States 1991*, book 1 (Washington, D.C.: USGPO, 1991), 1332; see also Cole, "Intentions," 97.

67. Thomas Omestad, "Why Bush Lost," *American Foreign Policy* 89 (1992): 71.

68. Ibid.

69. Ibid., 72.

70. See William Schabas, "Spare the Rud or Spoil the Treaty," in *The United States and Human Rights: Looking Inward and Outward*, ed. David P. Forsythe (Lincoln: University of Nebraska Press, 2000), 110–25.

71. Louis Henkin, "U.S. Ratification of Human Rights Conventions: The Ghost of Senator Bricker," *American Journal of International Law* 89 (1995): 341–52.

72. M. Christian Green, "The 'Matrioshka' Strategy: U.S. Evasion of the Spirit of the International Convenant on Civil and Political Rights," *South African Journal of Human Rights* 10 (1994): 357–58.

73. See 138 Cong. Rec. 4783, at Reservation I(4) (1992) (ratified); 138 Cong. Rec. 4783, at Reservation I(1), Understanding III(2) (1992) (ratified); see also 140 Cong. Rec. 7634, at Reservation I(1) (1994) (ratified).

74. George [H. W.] Bush, "Address before a Joint Session of the Congress on the State of the Union," *Papers of the Presidents of the United States, 1992–1993*, book 1 (Washington, D.C.: USGPO, 1993), 157; see also Cole, "Intentions," 98; see also George [H. W.] Bush, "Remarks at a Luncheon Hosted by Prime Minister Ruud Lubbers of the Netherlands in the Hague," *Papers of the Presidents of the United States, 1992–1993*, book 1 (Washington, D.C.: USGPO, 1992); George [H. W.] Bush, "Remarks to the American Society of Newspaper Editors," *Papers of the Presidents of the United States, 1992–1993*, book 1 (Washington, D.C.: USGPO 1993), 564–73; and George [H. W.] Bush, "Remarks at Maxwell Air Force Base."

75. Forsythe, "Two Levels, Two Worlds," 111; 136 Cong. Rec. 17,492, at Understanding II (4) (1992) (ratified).

76. See Steven Kull and I. M. Destler, *Misreading the Public: The Myth of a New Isolationism* (Washington D.C.: Brookings Institution Press, 1999).

77. See Human Rights, Summaries of Polling Data, Program on International Policy Attitudes (PIPA); available online at http://www.americans-world.org/digest/ global_issues/ human_rights/HR_Summary.cfm.

78. See Steven Livingston and Todd Eachus, "Humanitarian Crises and U.S. Foreign Policy: Somalia and the CNN Effect Reconsidered," *Political Communication* 12 (1995): 413.

79. Charles William Maynes, "A Workable Clinton Doctrine," *Foreign Policy* 93 (1993): 5.

80. See Jonathan Mermin, "Television News and American Intervention in Somalia," *Political Science Quarterly* 112, no. 2 (1997), 386.

81. For an excellent review of the literature on this point, see Piers Robinson, "The News Media and Intervention: Critical Media Coverage, Political Uncertainty and Air Power Intervention During Humanitarian Crisis," paper presented at the conference of the Political Science Association–UK, April 10–13, 2000, London. Available online at http://www.psa.ac.uk/cps/2000/Robinson%20Piers.pdf.

82. Ibid. See, generally, Larry Minear, Colin Scott, and Robert Weiss, *The News Media, Civil Wars and Humanitarian Action* (Boulder, Colo.: Lynne Rienner, 1997); and Warren Strobel, *Late Breaking Foreign Policy* (Washington, D.C.: United States Institute of Peace, 1997).

83. John Dietrich made this point in "U.S. Human Rights Policy in the Post-Cold War Era," paper presented at the Annual Meeting of the International Studies Association, February 28, 2002.

84. Theodore C. Sorenson made this point in 1992; see Sorenson, "America's First Post-Cold War President," *Foreign Affairs* 71 (1992): 40–44; and, as this book was being written in 2003, "Remarks of Theodore C. Sorenson at the May 2003 American University Commencement," on file with the author.

85. United States Institute of Peace, "United States Human Rights Policy: A 20-Year Assessment," June 16, 1999, 8.

86. Forsythe, "Human Rights," 264, supports the conclusion as do the author's interviews.

87. Douglas C. Foyle, "Public Opinion and Bosnia: Anticipating a Disaster," in *Contemporary Cases in U.S. Foreign Policy: From Terrorism to Trade*, ed. Ralph G. Carter (Washington, D.C.: Congressional Quarterly Press, 2000), 33.

88. Ibid.

89. George [H. W.] Bush, "Address Before a Joint Session of the Congress on the Persian Gulf Crisis and the Federal Budget Deficit." *Public Papers of the Presidents of the United States, 1990*, book 2 (Washington, D.C.: USGPO, 1991), 1219.

90. George [H. W.] Bush, "Remarks to the American Legion National Convention in Chicago Illinois," *Public Papers of the Presidents of the United States, 1992–1993*, book 2 (Washington, D.C.: USGPO, 1993), 1421; see also Cole, "Intentions," 96.

91. George [H. W.] Bush, "Remarks to the American Legion," 1422; see also Cole, "Intentions," 96.

92. See also Jonathan Clarke, "The Conceptual Poverty of U.S. Foreign Policy," *Atlantic Monthly* 272 (1993): 54–66; Charles Krauthammer, "The Unipolar Moment," *Foreign Affairs (America and the World 1990/1)* 70 (1991), 23–33; John Mearsheimer, "Disorder Restored," in *Rethinking America's Security: Beyond Cold War to New World Order*, ed. Graham Allison and Gregory Treverton (New York: W. W. Norton, 1992), 213–37.

93. George [H. W.] Bush, "State of the Union Address: Envisioning One Thousand Points of Light," delivered January 29, 1991.

94. George [H. W.] Bush, "Remarks at Maxwell Air Force Base War College in Montgomery, Alabama," *Public Paper of the Presidents of the United States, 1991*, book 1 (Washington, D.C.: USGOP, 1992): 368.

95. Cole, "Intentions," 101; see also Helmut Sonnenfeldt, "Foreign Policy for the Post-Cold War World," *Brookings Review* 10, no. 4 (1992): 35.

96. Cole, "Intentions," 101.

97. George [H. W.] Bush, "Remarks to the American Society of Newspaper Editors," 567.

98. Sonnenfeldt, "Foreign Policy," 33.

99. Douglas Brinkley, "Democratic Enlargement: The Clinton Doctrine," *Foreign Policy* 106 (1997): 112.

100. Ralph G. Carter, "Conclusion," in *Contemporary Cases in U.S. Foreign Policy: From Terrorism to Trade*, ed. Ralph G. Carter (Washington, D.C.: Congressional Quarterly Press, 2000), 388.

101. James Scott, "Interbranch Policymaking after the End," in *After the End: Making U.S. Foreign Policy in the Post–Cold War World,* ed. James Scott (Durham, N.C.: Duke University Press, 1998), 401.

102. Mead, *Special Provenance*, 269.

103. Ellen Dorsey, "Human Rights and U.S. Foreign Policy: Who Controls the Agenda?" *Journal of Intergroup Relations* 22, no. 1 (1995): 4.

104. Omestad, "Why Bush Lost," 70, 79; Forsythe, "Two Levels, Two Worlds," 126.

105. David C. Hendrickson, "The Recovery of Internationalism," *Foreign Affairs* 73, no. 5 (1994), 27.

106. Omestad, "Why Bush Lost," 81.

107. Ibid.; Dorsey, "Human Rights," 4.

108. For a provocative profile, see Thomas W. Lippman, "Madame Secretary," *National Journal* 3 (2000), 1736–43.

109. Forsythe, "Two Levels, Two Worlds," 126.

110. Anonymous interview with the author, May 2002.

111. William J. Clinton, "State of the Union Address by the President," delivered January 24, 1994; available online at www.washingtonpost.com/wp-srv/politics/special/states/docs/sou94.htm.

112. Neil Hicks, "The Bush Administration and Human Rights," *Foreign Policy in Focus*; available online at www.foreignpolicy-infocus.org/commentary/2001/ 0101humrights.html.

113. Anthony Lake, quoted in Kenneth Anderson, Jean Betulce Elshtain, Kim R. Holmes, Will Marshall and Frank McClosky, "Is there a Doctrine in the House?" *Harper's* 288, no. 17 (1994): 60; see also Brinkley, "Democratic Enlargement," 112.

114. See "President Clinton's Remarks on NATO Enlargement," The White House July 3, 1997; available online at http://www.embusa.es/nato/clinton2.html.

115. Elizabeth Cohn, "U.S. Democratization Assistance," *Foreign Policy in Focus* 4, no. 20 (1999).

116. Brinkley, "Democratic Enlargement," 121.

117. Warren Christopher, "Overview of 1995 Foreign Policy Agenda and the Clinton Administration's Proposed Budget," statement before the Senate Foreign Relations Committee, Washington, D.C., February 14, 1995. *U.S. Department of State Post Dispatch* 6, no. 8 (1995): 113.

118. Stephen Schlessinger, "The End of Idealism: Foreign Policy in the Clinton Years," *World Policy Journal* 15, no. 4 (1998–99): 39.

119. Cohn, "Assistance".

120. Anderson et al., "Doctrine," 60.

121. Richard Falk, "Clinton Doctrine: The Free Marketeers," *The Progressive* 58, no. 1 (1994): 20.

122. Brinkley, "Democratic Enlargement," 116.

123. Richard Falk, "Clinton Doctrine: The Free Marketeers," *Progressive* 58, no. 1 (1994): 20.

124. David P. Forsythe and Barbara Ann Rieffer, "U.S. Foreign Policy and Enlarging the Democratic Community," *Human Rights Quarterly* 22 (2000): 999.

125. Ibid.

126. Thomas Carothers, *Aiding Democracy Aborad: The Learning Curve* (Washington, D.C.: Carnegie Endowment for International Peace, 1999).

127. Dorsey, "Human Rights," 4.

128. Apodaca and Stohl, "Foreign Assistance," 185; see also Forsythe, "Price of Principles," 39–40.

129. Forsythe, "Price of Principles," 40.

130. Margaret Huang, "U.S. Human Rights Policy toward China," *Foreign Policy in Focus* 6, no. 8 (2001).

131. Dorsey, "Human Rights," 5–6; Forsythe, "Two Levels, Two Worlds," 127.

132. Clinton's China policy is defended in Steven M. Walt, "Two Cheers for Clinton's Foreign Policy," *Foreign Affairs* 79, no. 2, (2000): 69.

133. Huang, "China."

134. Forsythe, "Price of Principles," 32.

135. Ralph G. Carter and Donald W. Jackson, "Funding the IMF: Congress vs. The White House," in *Contemporary Cases in U.S. Foreign Policy: From Terrorism to Trade*, ed. Ralph G. Carter (Washington, D.C.: Congressional Quarterly Press, 2000), 339.

136. Forsythe, "Price of Principles," 33–34.

137. Harold Hongju Koh, "1999 Country Reports on Human Rights Practices," *Defense Institute of Security Assistance Journal* 22, no. 3 (2000).

138. Forsythe, "Price of Principles," 34.

139. Ibid., 35.

140. Michael Lund, "What Kind of Peace Is Being Built? Assessing Post-Conflict Peacebuilding, Charting Future Directions" (Ottawa: International Development Research Centre, 2003).

141. George Ward, interview with the author, July 3, 2001.

142. Lund, "What Kind of Peace."

143. Timothy C. Evered, "An International Criminal Court: Recent Proposals and American Concerns," *Pace International Law Review* 6 (1994): 131–34.

144. Foreign Relations Authorization Act, Fiscal Year 1994 and 1995, § 517(b), H.R. 2333, 103rd Cong., 108 Stat. 382, at 469 (1994).

145. Margaret Huang, interview with the author, June 2003.

146. Jack Donnelly, *Universal Human Rights in Theory and Practice* (Ithaca, N.Y.: Cornell University Press, 1989), 135.

147. See Patrick Flood, "Human Rights, UN Institutions and the United States," in *The United States and Human Rights: Looking Inward and Outward*, ed. David P. Forsythe (Lincoln: University of Nebraska Press, 2000), 367.

148. Schlesinger, "Human Rights," 38.

149. Forsythe, "Price of Principles," 29.

150. David Stewart, correspondence with the author, August 2003.

151. For more information on the CERD agreement, see the International Human Rights Law Group, online at http://www.hrlawgroup.org/country_programs/united_states/advocacy.asp.

152. Joe Stork, "Human Rights and U.S. Foreign Policy," *Foreign Policy in Focus*, 4, no. 8 (1999).

153. Ibid.

154. The Clinton Administration "didn't go out on a limb" with its first report on the state of racism in the United States, submitting essentially a long list of U.S. laws against racism. "While this list was impressive, it said little about what actually happens . . . and it missed many issues," said Margaret Huang (interview with the author, June 2003). To address the deficiencies, the International Human Rights Law Group coordinated a series of independently prepared "shadow" reports on racism in the United States. The shadow reports expanded the range of issues which the Committee on the Elimination of Race Discrimination was asked to account for during the oral hearing, and they further informed questions on environmental racism, indigenous peoples, disparities in health and education, affirmative action, and detention and imprisonment.

155. See Sean D. Murphy, "Contemporary Practice in the United States Relating to International Law," *American Journal of International Law* 93 (1999): 479.

156. David Stewart, correspondence with the author, August 2003.

157. Margaret Huang, interview with the author, June 2003.

158. Input from civil society, however, was not permanently institutionalized. The interagency process became far more restrictive during the subsequent presidential administration. Huang (interview with the author, June 2003) says that the administration of George W. Bush has assured her that the working group still exists, but as of June 2003, the Law Group still had not received any communication from it.

159. Observation drawn from interviews with NGOs in connection with this study.

160. Anonymous interview with the author, 2001.

161. Walt, "Two Cheers," 77.

162. "Clinton Wins Some, Loses Some at Summit," *Salt Lake Tribune*, May 11, 1995.

163. Ralph G. Carter, "Conclusion," 389.

164. Ibid., 388–89.

165. Dick Kirschten, "Pinched Pitchmen," *National Journal*, October 14, 1995, p. 2529.

166. Schlesinger, "Human Rights," 39.

167. *Foreign Policy* Editors, "Clinton's Foreign Policy," *Foreign Policy* 121 (2000): 26.

168. Richard N. Haass, "The Squandered Presidency: Demanding More from the Commander-in-Chief," *Foreign Affairs* 79, no. 3 (2000): 139.

169. Lally Weymouth, "Making Hay of Karabakh," *Washington Post*, April 24, 1996.

170. Hendrickson, "Recovery," 27; Dorsey, "Human Rights," 4.

171. Forsythe, "Two Levels, Two Worlds," 128.
172. Chicago Council on Foreign Relations, "American Public Opinion Report—1995" (1995); available online at http://www.uicdocs.lib.uic.edu/ccfr/publications/opinion_1995/2-3html.
173. Ibid.; see also Walt, "Two Cheers," 63–79.
174. Martin Woollacott, "Between Bombs and Bananas," *Guardian* 13, no. 1 (1999): 13.
175. Mortimer B. Zuckerman, "Policies to Comfort a Pariah: Why Has Clinton Backed a Deal that Leaves Saddam Stronger than Ever?" *U.S. News and World Report* 124, no. 11 (1998): 68.
176. Forsythe, "Price of Principles," 25.
177. Dorsey, "Human Rights," 4.
178. Miles A. Pomper, "The Religious Right's Foreign Policy Revival," *Congressional Quarterly Weekly* May 8, 1998: 1209–10.
179. United States Bureau of Democracy, Human Rights, and Labor Affairs, "United States Policies in Support of Religious Freedom: Focus on Christians," July 22, 1997. Report Consistent with the Omnibus Consolidated Appropriations Act, Fiscal Year 1997, House Report 3610.
180. Ibid.
181. *Foreign Policy* Editors, "Clinton's Foreign Policy," 26.
182. Halberstam, *War*, 206–7.
183. Anonymous interview with the author, 2001.
184. Harold Hongju Koh, "A United States Human Rights Policy for the Twenty-first Century," *St. Louis University Law Journal* 46 (2002): 293–332.
185. Bill Clinton, quoted in Brinkley, "Democratic Enlargement," 119.
186. Steven Wagenseil, "Human Rights in U.S. Foreign Policy," *Journal of Intergroup Relations* 26, no. 3 (1999): 4.
187. Ibid.
188. Samuel Berger, "A Foreign Policy for the Global Age," *Foreign Affairs* 79, no. 6 (2000): 24.
189. Wagenseil, "Human Rights," 13.
190. Ibid.; see also *Foreign Policy* Editors, "Clinton's Foreign Policy."
191. The Clinton team made it clear that they rejected the notion that human rights were not universal in nature or scope. At the World Conference on Human Rights in 1993, they stated this position clearly. Christopher in no uncertain terms denounced efforts by Syria, China, Iran, and Cuba to define human rights differently based on "various historical, cultural, and religious backgrounds." Albright maintained this stance in her own term as secretary of state, convening a conference attended by some one hundred countries in Poland to draft a global declaration on the universal principles of democracy. See *Foreign Policy* Editors, "Clinton's Foreign Policy," 19.
192. Walt, "Two Cheers," 78.
193. George Kourous and Tom Berry, "Protecting Human Rights," *Foreign Policy in Focus* 1, no. 1 (1996).
194. Inna Nazarova, "Alienating 'Human' from 'Right': U.S. and U.K. Non-Compliance with Asylum Obligations under International Human Rights Law," *Fordham International Law Journal* 25, no. 5 (2002): 1325–1420.
195. Human Rights Watch, 1994 Annual Report; available online at http://www.hrw.org/reports/1994/WR94/Middle-06.htm.
196. Ibid.
197. Thomas W. Lippman, "Ambassador to the Darkest Areas of Human Conflict," *Washington Post*, November 18, 1997.

198. David J. Scheffer, "Seeking Accountability for War Crimes: Past, Present, and Future," May 13, 1998; available online at http://www.state.gov/www/ policy_remarks/1998/98051_scheffer_war&uscore;crimes.html.

199. Dorsey, "Human Rights," 3.

200. George Ward, interview with the author, July 2001.

201. Dorsey, "Human Rights," 5.

202. Mark Danner, "Clinton, the UN, and the Bosnia Disaster," *New York Review of Books*, December 18, 1997.

203. Ibid.

204. Barbara Crossette, "Bush Finding It Rough Going on U.N. Human Rights Issues," *San Diego Union-Tribune*, April 8, 2001.

205. Hicks, "Bush Administration."

206. See Jarat Chopra, ed., *The Politics of Peace-Maintenance* (Boulder, Colo.: Lynne Rienner, 1998).

207. Oliver P. Richmond, *Maintaining Order, Making Peace* (New York: Palgrave, 2002), 140.

208. Mead, *Special Provenance*, 176.

209. George W. Bush, "Presidential Debate at Wake Forest University," October 11, 2000; available online at www.issues2000.org/Archive_2000.htm.

210. See Human Rights Watch, online at www.humanrightswatch.org.

211. For an interesting assessment of the impact of the neoconservatives in the Bush administration, see Elizabeth Drew, "The Neocons in Power," *New York Review of Books* 50, no. 10 (2003): 20.

212. Jeff Cohen, "The Return of Otto Reich: Will Government Propagandist Join Bush Administration?" *Fairness & Accuracy in Reporting*, June 8, 2001.

213. See Peter Kornbluh and Malcolm Byrne, eds., *The Iran-Contra Scandal: The Declassified History (The National Security Archive Document)* (New York: New Press, 1993). See also Duncan Campbell, "Bush Nominees under Fire for Link with Contras," *Guardian,* April 6, 2001.

214. Peter Kornbluh, "Bush's Contra Buddies," *Nation* 272, no. 18 (2001): 6–9.

215. Michael Dobbs, "Back in Political Forefront: Iran-Contra Figure Plays Key Role on Mideast," *Washington Post*, May 27, 2001.

216. "Reagan's Crying 'Wolf' in Nicaragua: Report," *Chicago Tribune*, May 16, 1985.

217. Joshua Michael Marshall, "Practice to Deceive," *Washington Monthly* 35, no. 4, (2003): 28.

218. Ibid.

219. Dick Proctor, "President Bush's Appointment of Elliot Abrams," August 2001; available online at http://www.dickproctor.ca/ndp.php/columns/21/.

220. Fred Barnes, "Mr. Rice Guy," *Weekly Standard* 8, no. 14 (2002).

221. Jim Lobe, "The Return of Elliott Abrams," December 11, 2002; available online at http://www.tompaine.com/feature2.cfm/ID/6895/view/print.

222. "Wrong Man for the Job," *San Francisco Chronicle*, April 23, 2001.

223. Kornbluh, "Buddies."

224. Campbell. "Nominees."

225. Jonathan Wright, "Senate Panel Backs Negroponte for UN Post," Reuters News Service, September 14, 2001.

226. John R. Bolton, "Unsign the Treaty," *Washington Post*, January 4, 2001; John R. Bolton, "Notebook," *Australian Financial Review*, January 3, 2001; John R. Bolton, "Rule of Law: Why an International Criminal Court Won't Work," *Wall Street Journal*, March 30, 1998; John R. Bolton, "CTBT: Clear Thinking . . ." *Jerusalem Post*, October 18, 1999.

227. Bolton, "Rule of Law," A19.

228. John R. Bolton, "U.S. Money and a U.N. Vote," *Washington Times*, October 16, 1998.

229. John R. Bolton, "Hard Man Who Sits at the Heart of U.S. Foreign Policy," *Financial Times*, December 19, 2002.

230. Earl Ofari Hutchinson, "Ashcroft Poses a Moral Threat to Civil Rights," *San Francisco Chronicle*, December 28, 2000.

231. Ibid.

232. "Ashcroft Quizzed about Southern Partisan Endorsement." *Fairness and Accuracy in Reporting*, January 19, 2001.

233. John Ashcroft, "Path-Breaking Strategies in the Global Fight against Sex Trafficking," paper presented to the U.S. Department of State, February 25, 2003.

234. Lawyers Committee for Human Rights, *Women Asylum Seekers in Jeopardy* (New York: Lawyers Committee for Human Rights, 2003).

235. Jonathan Turley, "Camps for Citizens: Ashcroft's Hellish Vision," *Los Angeles Times*, August 14, 2002.

236. Madeleine Drohan, "Abusive Multinationals Have a Pal in Washington," *Globe and Mail*, May 19, 2003.

237. Steven R. Weisman, "Pre-Emption: Idea with a Lineage Whose Time Has Come," *New York Times* (March 23, 2003).

238. Ralph G. Carter, "Conclusion," 391.

239. Spanier and Hook, *American Foreign Policy*, 316.

240. Jean Edward Smith, "Firefight at the Pentagon," *New York Times*, April 6, 2003.

241. Mead, *Special Provenance*, 307.

242. Jyothi Kancis, "Trafficking in Women," *Foreign Policy in Focus* 3, no. 39 (1998).

243. George W. Bush, "President George W. Bush's Inaugural Address," January 20, 2001; available online at http://www.whitehouse.gov/news/print/inaugural-address.html.

244. Ibid.

245. Ibid.

246. Ibid.

247. Steven Tipton, quoted in "Lawton Interview with Steven Tipton," *Religion and Ethics,* May 9, 2003, PBS; available online at http://www.pbs.org/wnet/religionandethics/week623/news.html.

248. Kenneth D. Wald, *Religion and Politics in the United States*, 2nd ed. (Washington, D.C.: CQ Press, 1992).

249. "President Bush's Religious Rhetoric," *Religion and Ethics,* May 9, 2003, PBS; available online at http://www.pbs.org/wnet/religionandethics/week623/news.html.

250. George W. Bush, "President Bush Address at Fifty-first Annual National Prayer Breakfast," February 6, 2003; available online at http://www.whitehouse.gov/news/releases/2003/02/20030206-1.html.

251. George W. Bush, "President Addresses Nation on Space Shuttle Columbia Tragedy," February 1, 2003; available online at http://www.whitehouse.gov/news/releases/2003/02/20030201-2.html.

252. George W. Bush, "President Delivers State of the Union Address," January 29, 2002; available online at http://www.whitehouse.gov/news/releases/2002/01/20020129-11.html.

253. Lorne Craner, "The Role of Human Rights in Foreign Policy," remarks to the Heritage Foundation, Washington, D.C., October 31, 2001; available online at http://www.state.gov/g/drl/rls/rm/2001/6378.htm.

254. Ibid.

255. Ibid.

256. George W. Bush, "President Bush Delivers State of the Union Address," January 28, 2003; available online at www.whitehouse.gov/news/releases/2003/01/print/2003012819.html.

257. Ibid.

258. White House, *National Security Strategy of the United States of America,* Washington, D.C. (2002): 2–5.

259. Ibid., 4.

260. Ibid., 5.

261. Ibid., 3, 4.

262. John D. Van der Vyver, "American Exceptionalism: Human Rights, International Criminal Justice, and National Self-Righteousness," *Emory Law Journal* 50 (2001): 775–822.

263. Johan Galtung, "Violence, Peace, and Peace Research," *Journal of Peace Research* 6, no. 3 (1969): 109–34.

264. Thomas Buergenthal, "To Respect and to Ensure: State Obligations and Permissible Derogations," in *The International Bill of Human Rights: The Covenant on Civil and Political Rights,* ed. Louis Henkin (New York: United Nations Press 1981), 78–86; Oren Gross, "Once More unto the Breach: The Systemic Failure of Applying the European Convention on Human Rights to Entrenched Emergencies," *Yale Journal of International Law* 23 (1998): 437–501.

265. One good illustration of this phenomenon is President Bush's initiative for Cuba, announced in May 2002, in which he warns Cuba that it must improve its record on civil and political rights, most notably in the areas of freedom of speech and assembly, treatment of prisoners in detention, and open and fair multiparty elections. When it comes to social and economic rights, however, he focuses narrowly on property rights, framing the issue with the interests of large U.S. corporations in mind. He states, "If Cuba wants to attract badly needed investment from abroad, property rights must be respected. If the government wants to improve the daily lives of its people, goods and services produced in Cuba should be made available to all Cuban citizens. Workers employed by foreign companies should be paid directly by their employers, instead of having the government seize their hard-currency wages and pass on a pittance in the form of pesos." George W. Bush, "Remarks by the President on Cuba Policy Review," May 20, 2002; available online at http://www.whitehouse.gov/news/releases/2002/05/20020520-1.html.

266. United Nations General Assembly, *Charter of the United Nations* (1948); available online at http://193.194.138.190/html/menu3/b/ch-pream.html.

267. United Nations General Assembly, *Universal Declaration of Human Rights,* UN General Assembly Resolution 217A (III), December 10, 1948.

268. United Nations General Assembly. *International Covenant on Economic, Social, and Cultural Rights,* UN General Assembly Resolution 2200A (XXI), December 16, 1966.

269. United Nations General Assembly, *International Covenant on Civil and Political Rights,* UN General Assembly Resolution 2200A (XXI), December 16, 1966.

270. United Nations General Assembly, *Vienna Declaration and Programme for Action,* World Conference on Human Rights, Vienna, June 14–25, 1993.

271. Jack Donnelly, "Post-Cold War Reflections on the Study of International Human Rights," in *Ethics and International Affairs*, ed. Joe Rosenthal (Washington D.C.: Georgetown University Press, 1999), 241–70.

272. Donnelly, *Universal Human Rights*, 81.

273. Biku Paarekh, "Non-ethnocentric Universalism," in *Human Rights in Global Politics*, ed. Timothy Dunne and Nicholas J. Wheeler (Cambridge: Cambridge University Press 1999), 128–59.

274. White House, "National Security Strategy," 1.

275. Crossette, "Rough Going."

276. Stephen Zunes, "U.S. Arrogance on Display in UN Human Rights Commission Flap," *Foreign Policy in Focus*; available online at http://www.foreignpolicy-info-cus.org/commentary/0105unhr_body.html.

277. Ibid.

278. "U.S. Eager to Bolster Bioterrorism," *International Herald Tribune*, November 2, 2001.

279. Dan Balz, "Bush's Rights Record Assailed; Democratic Hopefuls Tailor Message to Feminist Audience," *Washington Post*, May 21, 2003.

280. Kenneth Roth, the executive director of Human Rights Watch, has explained that the U.S. opposition to the land mines treaty stems from its desire to continue to use land mines in South Korea, and its rejection of the child soldiers treaty is out of fear that the ban would prevent the U.S. military from recruiting high school students for military service; see Roth, "Sidelined on Human Rights," *Foreign Affairs* 77, no. 2 (1998): 2–6.

281. Hicks, "Bush Administration."

282. Javier Solana, "International Court Signals a New Era," *International Herald Tribune*, April 11, 2002, 9.

283. Tina Rosenberg, "Conference Convocation, War Crimes Tribunals: The Record and the Prospects," *American University International Law Review* 13 (1998): 1406–08.

284. John B. Anderson, "Unsigning the ICC," *Nation,* April 29, 2002.

285. "UN Security Council Renews ICC Exemption for U.S. Peacekeepers," *Voice of America Press Releases and Documents* (2003); accessed through Westlaw, 2003 WL 56391486.

286. Felicity Barringer, "U.S. Renews U.S. Peacekeepers' Exemption from Prosecution," *New York Times*, June 13, 2003.

287. Kofi Annan, quoted in Felicity Barringer, "U.S. Retains World Court Exemptions Germany and France Abstain from UN Vote," *International Herald Tribune*, June 14, 2003.

288. Peter Slevin, "U.S. Renounces Its Support of New Tribunal for War Crimes," *Washington Post,* May 7, 2002.

289. George W. Bush, "Second Presidential Debate," October 11, 2000; available online at www.foreignpolicy2000.org/library/.

290. George W. Bush, "Statement on Defense at Campaign Rally," Kansas City, February 22, 2000; available online at www.foreignpolicy.org/library.

291. Julie Kosterlitz, "Occupational Hazards," *National Journal*, March 22, 2003; accessed through Westlaw, 2003 WL 5140852.

292. Observation drawn from author's interviews with over 120 people for this volume.

293. Kosterlitz, "Hazards."

294. Interview with the author, July 2003.

295. "Rumsfeld Denies Media Reports of Quagmire," *CBS Evening News with Dan Rather*, September 5, 2003.

296. Ibid.
297. Anonymous interview with the author, July 2003.
298. Ibid.
299. George W. Bush, "Remarks on Global Development, Inter-American Bank," March 14, 2001; available online at www.whitehouse.gov/newsreleases/2002/03/2002200314.7.html.
300. Andrew Natsios, quoted in "Natsios: NGOs Must Show Results; Promote Ties to U.S. Or We Will 'Find New Partners,'" Interactions 2003 Forum, "The Challenges of Global Commitments: Advancing Relief and Development Goals through Advocacy and Action," Washington, D.C.: May 12–14, 2003; available online at http://www.interaction.org/forum2003/panels.html.
301. Harold Hongju Koh, "Testimony Before Committee on House International Relations, July 9, 2003," *Federal Documents Clearing House*; available online at http://www.law.yale.edu/outside/html/Public_Affairs/390/070903testimony.pdf.
302. Ibid.
303. George W. Bush, "President Bush Calls for a New Palestinian Leadership," June 24, 2002; available online at http://www.whitehouse.gov/news/releases/2002/06/20020624-3.html.
304. Laura Neack, *The New Foreign Policy: U.S. and Comparative Foreign Policy in the Twenty-first Century* (Lanham, Md.: Rowman and Littlefield, 2003), 149.
305. George W. Bush, "President Delivers State of the Union Address," January 28, 2003; available online at http://www.whitehouse.gov/news/releases/2003/01/print/20030128-19.html.
306. Ibid.
307. Ibid.
308. Human Rights Watch, "State Department Criticism of Torture in Countries to which Detainees Have Allegedly Been Returned," May 11, 2003; available online at www.hrw.org/press/2003/04/torture.htm.
309. Bob Woodward, "CIA-Terror Sweep Nets 360 Suspects Outside the U.S.," *International Herald Tribune*, November 23, 2001.
310. Barton Gellman, "CIA Seeks Rules from Top Leaders on Assassinations," *International Herald Tribune*, October 29, 2001; Bob Woodward, "'Gloves Are Off,' as CIA Pursues bin Laden," *International Herald Tribune*, October 22, 2001.
311. See Mike Allen, "Bush Defends Tribunal Plan," *International Herald Tribune*, November 21, 2001; see also Elisabeth Bumiller and David Johnston, "New Court for Terror Defendants," *International Herald Tribune*, November 15, 2001.
312. Anne-Marie Slaughter, "Secret Trial by Military Commission Is Not Justice," *International Herald Tribune*, November 19, 2001.
313. Tom Malinowski, "Court-Martial Code Offers a Fair Way to Try Terrorist Suspects," *International Herald Tribune*, December 29–30, 2001.
314. Bumiller and Johnston, "New Court," 5.
315. Jim Edwards, "Government Sued over Post–September 11 Detentions," *Legal Intelligencer* 226, no. 79 (2002): 4.
316. Steve Fainaru, "U.S. Jail Is Harsh Place for Terror Detainees," *International Herald Tribune*, April 18, 2002.
317. "Detainees and Disclosure," *Washington Post*, March 18, 2002; see also editorial, "War and Justice," *International Herald Tribune*, December 3, 2002.
318. Walter Pincus, "Silent Suspects: U.S. May Get Tough," *International Herald Tribune*, October 22 , 2001; see also Jim Rutenberg, "Media Stoke Debate on Torture as U.S. Option," *International Herald Tribune*, November 6, 2001.

319. Pincus, "Silent Suspects;" see also Lawyers Committe for Human Rights, "Assessing the New Normal: Liberty and Security for Post–September 11 United States (New York: Lawyers Committee for Human Rights, 2003).

320. Anonymous interview with the author, Washington D.C., 2001.

321. See Brian Knowlton, "Rumsfeld Replies Firmly to Allies on Prisoners' Treatment," *International Herald Tribune,* January 23, 2002.

322. Steven Erlanger, "Europeans Take Aim at U.S. On Detainees," *International Herald Tribune*, January 24, 2002.

323. Michael Richardson, "Asian Regimes Appear to Use War on Terror to Stem Dissent," *International Herald Tribune*, November 21, 2001; Jackson Diehl, "Russia and Israel Want to Hijack the Anti-Terror Campaign," *International Herald Tribune*, October 18, 2001.

324. New recipients included Uzbekistan, Yemen, Jordan, and Oman; restrictions on military aid were lifted from Armenia, Azerbaijan, India, Pakistan, Tajikistan, and Yugoslavia. See Victoria Garcia, "U.S. Military Aid for Allies in a War against Iraq" (Washington, D.C.: Center for Defense Information, 2003).

325. U.S. Agency for International Development (USAID), *Foreign Aid in the National Interest: Freedom, Security, and Opportunity* (Washington D.C.: USGPO, 2002).

326. Karen De Young and Dana Milbank, "Military Plans Informed by Polls; Carefully Chosen Words Prepare Americans for Potential Toll in Ground War," *Washington Post*, October 19, 2001; Robin Toner and Janet Elder, "Broad Support for Terror War in Opinion Poll," *International Herald Tribune*, December 13, 2001.

327. Richard Falk, quoted in Dan Balz, "War Dissent? Don't Look on the (Hawkish) Left," *International Herald Tribune*, November 27, 2001.

328. Harold Meyerson, quoted in Ibid.

329. Ibid.

330. Michael R. Gordon, "Pentagon Limits on the Media Tighter Than in Earlier Wars," *International Herald Tribune*, October 22, 2001.

331. Melanie McAlister, "Saving Private Lynch," *New York Times*, April 6, 2003.

332. E. A. Hugh and Torriero Dellios, "Sorting Fact from Fiction in POW's Gripping Story: Doubts about the Tale of Jessica Lynch's Rescue Aren't Limited to the Details; Questions Also Swirl about Who is to Blame for the Hype," *Chicago Tribune*, May 26, 2003.

333. Ibid.

334. Michael Dobbs, "For Wolfowitz, a Vision May Be Realized; Deputy Defense Secretary's Views on Free Iraq Considered Radical in Ways Good and Bad," *Washington Post*, April 7, 2003.

335. Charlotte Bunch, "Whose Security? Bush's Counterterrorism Efforts Neglect Women and Frustrate Feminists," *Nation*, September 23, 2002.

336. Elizabeth Olson, "UN Rights Panel to Hear Criticism of War on Terror," *International Herald Tribune*, March 18, 2002.

337. Neil A. Lewis, "Aftereffects: Detainees: More Prisoners to Be Released from Guantanamo, Officials Say," *New York Times*, May 6, 2003.

338. Dayton Maxwell, interviews with the author, July 2001 and June 2002.

339. USAID, *Foreign Aid*, 26. See also Dayton Maxwell, interviews with the author, spring 2001 and 2002.

340. Ibid., 26

341. Quotations from former State Department and USAID employees, interviews with the author, July 2001 and July 2003.

342. See United States Institute of Peace, "Whither the Bulldozer? Nonviolent Revolution and the Transition to Democracy in Serbia," Special Report, August 6, 2001.

343. Albert Cevallos, interview with the author, July 2003.

344. Ibid.

345. David Forsythe, *Human Rights and International Relations* (New York: Cambridge University Press, 2000).

346. George Shultz, "Human Rights and the Moral Dimension of U.S. Foreign Policy," address in Peoria, Illinois, February 24, 1984, quoted in *The Diplomacy of Human Rights*, ed. David D. Newsom (Washington D.C.: Institute for the Study of Diplomacy, 1986), 213, 214.

347. George W. Bush, "President Bush on Foreign Affairs," *U.S. Department of State International Information Programs*; available online at http://usinfo.state.gov/prod-ucts/pubs/presbush/foraf.htm.

348. Shultz, "Moral Dimension," 214.

349. Ibid., 215.

350. Ibid., 217.

351. Steven Mufson, "American Foreign Policy Suddenly Shifts Course," *International Herald Tribune*, September 28, 2001.

352. "China and Terrorism," editorial, *Washington Post*, October 19, 2001.

353. Jonathan Mirsky, "Remind Beijing: Human Rights and Arms Control Do Matter," *International Herald Tribune*, October 22, 2001.

354. Joseph Fitchett, "U.S. Policy on Terrorism: Think Globally and Don't Interfere Locally," *International Herald Tribune*, September 28, 2001.

355. Peter Slevin, "New Trade Relations Sought for 8 Countries; Rights Groups Hit War-Aid Reward," *Washington Post,* January 6, 2002, A19.

356. Mufson, "American Foreign Policy."

357. Jackson Diehl, "U.S. Again Supports Unsavory Dictators," *International Herald Tribune*, March 20, 2002.

358. USAID, *Foreign Aid*, 2.

359. Ibid., 13.

360. Ibid., 2.

361. Joe Stork, "Human Rights and U.S. Policy."

362. See Human Rights Watch, online at http://www.hrw.org/us/ usdom.php?theme= Prison%20Conditions.

363. Office of Inspector General, "The September 11 Detainees: A Review of the Treatment of Aliens Held on Immigration Charges in Connection with the Investigation of the September 11 Attacks," U.S. Department of Justice, 2003; see also Human Rights Watch, online at http://www.hrw.org/press/2003/06/us060203.htm.

364. For example, Turkey has long topped the list of U.S. arms importers and recipients of U.S. military aid despite its poor record in human rights. See Tamar Gabelnick, "Turkey: Arms and Human Rights," *Foreign Policy in Focus* 4, no. 16 (1999).

365. Kourous and Berry, "Protecting Human Rights."

THREE

THE NEW MILITARY HUMANISM: HUMAN RIGHTS AND THE U.S. MILITARY[1]

On May 1, 2003, President George W. Bush addressed the nation from aboard the USS *Abraham Lincoln*, concluding with remarks to the servicemen and servicewomen, in which he implored, "All of you—all in this generation of our military—have taken up the highest calling of history. You're defending our country, and protecting the innocent from harm. And wherever you go, you carry a message of hope—a message that is ancient and ever new. In the words of the prophet Isaiah, 'To the captives, 'come out'—and to those in darkness, 'be free.'"[1]

As the commander in chief of the armed forces, President Bush had the job of defining the role of the military in promoting U.S. foreign policy. In statements such as the one above, President Bush has characterized the U.S. military as an embodiment of U.S. values and a tool for promoting those values. He has portrayed the men and women who serve in the armed forces as messengers of hope and of freedom—the value the United States holds most precious. Such comments would seem to bode well for the role of human rights in the president's approach to foreign policy—and to the role of the military therein. However, all of this human rights talk has not necessarily led to human rights behaviors. As was explained in Chapter 2, the exceptionalist manner in which the post–Cold War presidents have treated international human rights norms mitigates and limits the extent to which the human rights framework holds a taken-for-granted or "embedded" place in U.S. foreign policy.

---

[1] This chapter title refers to Noam Chomsky's *The New Military Humanism: Lessons from Kosovo* (Monroe, Me.: Common Courage Press, 1999).

Yet as the world has changed, so has the military changed to satisfy new demands that the modern world has placed upon it, and this has not happened in isolation from the impact of human rights. The military has taken its own approach to the institutionalization of human rights norms, and in so doing it has been more receptive than civilian policy makers. Even as American foreign policy has resisted the application of human rights norms to American behavior, the branches of the armed services military have justified both their identities and behaviors on human rights terms.

This chapter examines changes in the U.S. military—both its operations and its culture—that reflect and in turn influence human rights norms. The discussion is divided into four parts. The first section of the chapter reviews the two most critical developments with respect to the U.S. military and human rights: the emergence of a new military identity and, closely related, military roles that depart from traditional war operations. As Lieutenant Colonel Richard Lacquement Jr. has put it, "The [military] institution is still about war fighting, but it is useful for things other than war fighting, and increasingly these things are being seen as valuable and we are integrating as part of our self-image things that we do for the state."[2] Second, this chapter discusses three relatively new areas of military activity that have proved—sometimes surprisingly—to have an undermining influence on human rights: the training of foreign militaries in "becoming democratic," the use of private military companies, and the development of new, purportedly civilian-friendly weapons and pinpoint targeting. Third, it searches the record of recent U.S. military interventions for evidence of the influence of human rights norms. Finally, the chapter analyzes constraints on the U.S. military's ability to incorporate to a greater degree a human rights perspective into its institutions and practices.

WHAT HAS CHANGED: IDENTITY AND ROLES

I signed up to fight the Cold War and for a while I did . . . but not anymore. I fly aid in and fly wounded kids out . . . and there is nothing abnormal about this. I expect [that I will be called on to do this].

—Anonymous U.S. Air Force officer, in an interview with the author

The U.S. military has long had a sense that American military power could be used for a moral purpose. Members of the armed services have always viewed themselves as "morality promoters." What has changed is the manner in which this sense of identity is linked to human rights norms. These changes are far more pronounced in the military's identity than in civilian policy-making branches of government. This can be explained by the command structure of the military and its culture of obedience to lawful orders. Although soldiers and officers may resist change,[3] once they are made, those changes become solidly embedded in the culture. It took the U.S. military approximately fifteen to twenty years to take up the human rights cause overtly after President Jimmy Carter first publicly wove it into U.S. foreign policy, but human rights are now part of the fabric.

Military training focuses on creating a shared culture and on shaping individual and group identities. While each branch of the service has its own distinct identity, an order to change certain socialization rituals and operational practices may have profound impacts on cultural norms, as well as on individual and group identities and behaviors. "Cultural norms produce consistent patterns of behavior by becoming institutionalized in community rules and routines," Theo Farrell and Terry Terriff explain. "Once institutionalized, norms are either taken for granted or enforced through powerful sanctions."[4] Even elites who disbelieve their own rhetoric and use it to manipulate others may contribute to cultural change. On the one hand they may "stir up beliefs that are genuinely held by community members," while on the other hand they may "end up 'buying into' their own rhetoric."[5] Jack Synder has referred to this process as "blowback."[6]

In reflecting on changes in their organizations, civilian employees and military officers gave extremely different responses in my surveys and interviews with them. When asked how the shift from the administration of Bill Clinton to that of George W. Bush affected their everyday life, career foreign service officers responded with comments such as "We are now told to write shorter memos"; "The garbage is picked up more regularly"; and "The names of things have changed, but little else."[7] Foreign service officers who were active in some manner in the administration of George H. W. Bush or in prior administrations pointed to changes outside the administration that had an impact on their jobs, such as post–Cold War power shifts, the Vienna Conference on Human Rights in 1993 and the growing international consensus on some human rights issues, and the enhanced interest of the U.S. Congress in human rights.

In contrast, U.S. military personnel responses to the same question about how their day-to-day activities have changed in the post–Cold War era were definitive: "Dramatically"; "It's a whole new place;" and "Once we were warriors, now we're feeding refugees."[8] One lieutenant colonel explained, "I joined up to keep America safe from the Soviet Union. I was one of the guys who loaded the bomb every day, just in case we needed to use it. I believed in what I was doing. Man, I did that a long time. . . . Now there is no Soviet Union and we got all these enemies that aren't states. Now, I'm told to protect America by keeping the peace."[9]

In their responses, the military personnel focused on what they perceived to be changes *within* the military, pointing to the projected public image of the military, the recruitment and retention of officers, and changes in military training and military culture. Certainly these changes derive not only from developments within the military but are also reflective of the interplay between outside pressures on the military as an institution and the culture from within the military. An exploration of these areas reveals the military's openness and overall acceptance of human rights rhetoric while simultaneously disclosing the limits, shortcomings, and inconsistencies in the integration of human rights in military interventions.

The Projected Image: The High-Tech, High-Speed Professional

Be "An Army of One," the home page of the Special Forces website promises those who are good enough to join in an extreme adventure. "Warfare today has new rules—and calls for a different type of Soldier—a new warrior. They need to be mentally superior and creative, highly trained and physically tough. They will work in diverse conditions, act as a diplomat, get the job done in hostile situations, and, at times, establish virtual citizenship in a foreign country for months. . . . Right now, the Army is looking for dedicated men with the highest mental and physical capabilities to become An Army of One in the Special Forces."[10] The webpage asking "What is the U.S. Army?" has an answer that could be from a corporate recruitment brochure, although the photo at the top of the page is of soldiers chatting while getting out of a helicopter: "It's having individual strength and the support of an unstoppable team. It's you at your best. With training, technology, and support, you will become stronger, smarter, and better prepared for the challenges you face. You will gain invaluable skills, experience, and the opportunity to use them while working in a challenging environment."[11]

Those who concocted this advertising blitz hope to sell young people on the idea that by joining the military they can improve themselves and do some good in the world. To a great extent this message is getting through. The recruits of the past signed up to "get money for college," but also to "to fight for America" and to prove their manhood—"show my father I could do it."[12] Today's recruits, while still interested in serving the United States, are more career minded.[13] They seek more than just cash for college, including skills and experience that will enhance their career potential in the long term while providing a "cool adventure" in the short term.[14] While the interests of recruits certainly had already shifted in this direction during the Cold War, the post–Cold War recruits who were aware of U.S. engagement in peacekeeping operations had quite different expectations about the nature of the job.

Due to the changing nature and scope of military engagements and the different skills nontraditional missions demand from military personnel, military recruiters have had to reorient their strategy. Charles Moskos, a leading military sociologist, has described the role of the military officer as shifting from combat leader to manager, technician, and, most recently, to soldier-statesman and scholar.[15] Recruiters seek higher-quality prospects to fill these roles.[16] While the quality of recruits may have improved and the military has been successful overall at meeting its recruitment goals, doing so has not been cheap or easy. The 2000 General Accounting Office report states that the Department of Defense is "experiencing a recruiting challenge that has called for an extraordinary increase in the attention and the resources focused on this area." The report continues, "From fiscal year 1993 through 1998, the

Army increased its number of recruiters from 4,368 to 6,331 and increased its advertising expenditures from $34.3 million in FY 1993 to $112.9 million in FY 1999 (in FY 2000 constant dollars)."[17]

In the era of an all-volunteer force, the face of the American military has changed dramatically.[18] Much of this may be attributed to the self-selection of military personnel, as well as the military's broad recruitment strategies, which cut across racial lines. While women had comprised only 2 percent of military personnel in the United States during the years of the Vietnam War, by 1998 women comprised 14 percent of uniformed U.S. military personnel.[19] Studies conducted by military researchers and independent academics demonstrate that women perform well as soldiers and have a positive effect on unit cohesion.[20] Consequently, military policies incorporating women have incrementally become more inclusive.[21] Some researchers have suggested that women soldiers have a particularly strong role to play in today's humanitarian missions. As Kim Field and John Nagl note, "It appears that men are less willing to serve in these [humanitarian] roles than they were to serve in traditional combat roles during the cold war, making it even more important that women fill a larger role in the post–cold war military."[22]

The military has also changed considerably with respect to racial diversity. At the lower ranks, the military is perhaps the most racially diverse institution in the entire country. A 2003 study found that Latinos and African Americans comprised 32 percent of all military personnel.[23] Yet simultaneously, the racial balance (like the gender balance) is far from equal in terms of critical leadership positions; African Americans and Latinos comprised only 12 percent of officer corps in 2003.[24] Demographics from 1999, more specifically, indicated that among the 55,000 active duty navy officers, only 15 percent are women, only 7 percent are black, and a mere 4.5 percent are Latino. In the Air Force, out of 3,500 fighter pilots, fewer than 50 are women, and slightly more than 12 of 800 bomber pilots are women.[25] The military is also unbalanced on the lines of class and ideology, as it draws disproportionately from low-income areas, from the south, and from people with conservative political inclinations.[26] The Triangle Institute five-year surveys of political attitudes among military service war-college students—the soon-to-be general officers—reveal a hugely lopsided political ideology in the senior officer corps. Self-identified "liberals," for example, are such a small group now that they are nearing statistical insignificance.[27] Several observers have expressed concern about this disjuncture between the culture and values of American society and those of the individuals composing the military—particularly the officer corps.[28]

The demographic disparities between the newly enlisted and senior officers are also telling. It helps to explain the disconnection between the leadership of the military and those under their command by analyzing acceptance of the peacekeeping image. While older soldiers prefer more traditional military operations, many younger soldiers view peacekeeping and other nontraditional operations, particularly disaster relief activities, as more desirable than traditional war scenarios.[29] At the same time, Captain Jane Dalton says, "These guys don't want to be bored. They want to really feel like they are doing something."[30] Members of the new generation in the armed services are also more concerned with quality-of-life issues, and are moving away from self-identification as warriors toward a self-image as professional soldiers who may be called upon to engage in a variety of tasks on behalf of the state.[31]

Now, perhaps more than ever before, new military recruits enter with the expectation that they will be called upon to participate in peace operations.[32] In one study, military personnel were enthusiastic about their peacekeeping duties in Bosnia, as indicated by reenlistment rates that were 50 percent higher for those units assigned to Bosnia than they were for other units in Europe in early 1998.[33] As the military becomes increasingly more open to women and many members of minority groups,[34] so too does the military personnel's support change on the whole, increasingly toward favoring humanitarian missions.

Support for the solider-as-peacekeeper identity is particularly strong among younger, female, and minority soldiers. An empirical study found that both African American and female soldiers (and, in particular, female African American soldiers) are more likely to support humanitarian missions than are other soldiers. In Operation Restore Hope in Somalia in March 1993, U.S. Army personnel in these groups held more positive attitudes toward the performance of U.S. troops there—and for humanitarian missions generally—than did white male soldiers in combat specialties.[35] Reports also suggest stark differences in support for peacekeeping missions based on age. "The kind of missions the military is doing is appealing to single, young people who are looking for experience and adventure, but [support for these missions is] less for older enlistees."[36]

The military's public persona as a humanitarian organization has prompted deep debate within the armed services over the traditional role versus nontraditional missions, often referred to as military operations other than war (MOOTW). Some fear that the nontraditional missions "may be chipping away at the [services'] sense of itself.[37] Charles Dunlap worries that "people in the military no longer considered themselves warriors. Instead, they perceive themselves as policemen, relief workers, educators, builders, health care providers, politicians—everything but war fighters."[38] These roles may be better served by civilians, many soldiers and civilians argue.[39]

The military officers who resist U.S. military involvement in humanitarian missions express two main concerns. First, they argue that the military is already overtaxed and thus unable to take on anything else. Indeed, a recent study from the Center for Strategic and International Studies painted a bleak picture of a "stressed and over-committed" institution plagued with morale problems.[40] According to the Pentagon's "Joint Vision 2020,"[41] the U.S. military should be capable of conducting peacekeeping and humanitarian operations (the low end of the conflict spectrum), full-scale nuclear war (the high end), and everything in between. The document makes clear that dominance across the conflict spectrum means superiority in any military operation, at any time or place, and in more than one theater simultaneously, if necessary. This portends even busier days ahead for the U.S. military.

Second, many fear that forces not engaged in combat are compromised in their readiness.[42] They claim that operations such as "nation building, peacekeeping, peacemaking, humanitarian, counter[ing] drugs" are only "a *major distraction* from the battle-focused training needed to fulfill the Army's traditional war fighting role."[43] General Maxwell R. Thurman, for example, testified that after completing peacekeeping missions, "soldiers have to go through an extensive training regime to regain the level of operational proficiency which they held at the outset of that duty."[44]

Yet some military officers agree with General Wesley Clark that those in the military today require "both a war-fighting spirit and a peacekeeping capability."[45] And these high-ranking officers who support nontraditional roles for the military do so under one strict condition: "the servicemen and women sent out to fulfill those [new roles] must be properly trained and rewarded for what they do."[46] If soldiers are not trained properly for the tasks they must perform, the officers warn, they will not only lose competency but also experience a decline in motivation.[47]

Training Professional Soldiers

The nature of the world has changed. It requires someone to [address gross human rights abuses]. We're the ones. We just have to get the men ready. We can do it. We always have.

—John Fishel, professor of national security affairs, Center for Hemispheric Defense Studies, National Defense University, in an interview with the author

Traditional military culture follows from the traditional functional purpose of the military, which is "to fight and win the nation's wars."[48] Recruits internalize this purpose. To take one illustration from the army, the Officer Personnel Management System (OPMS) recognizes that "military culture self-consciously contrasts with civilian culture in order to shape its members' mentality and behavior. [To this end] young officers are trained and developed in their war fighting roles from the outset. Through a series of unit assignments, lieutenants and captains are schooled in the 'muddy boots' heritage: the knowledge that 'soldiering' is a profession driven by technical expertise in the art of war, singleness of purpose, and enduring core values."[49]

"Tradition, morale, esprit, discipline, unity, cohesion, integrity"[50]—these are all asserted to be central military values. At the same time, recruits are taught to accept highly centralized, hierarchical structures and to seek "linear organization, precision of definition, objective values, abstract communication found in low contexts, and factual inductive or axiomatic inductive decision-making structures."[51] Some observers point out that the armed forces are making increased efforts at inspiring the warrior spirit into their service cultures.[52] The dominant belief at top military ranks is that "warfighting still determines the central beliefs, values, and complex symbolic formations that define military culture."[53] Despite increased humanitarian and peacekeeping missions and the different attitudes necessary for such interventions, the warrior ethic is nonetheless the dominant ideological foundation of the military and "what distinguishes soldiers from other government employees is that they are trained to kill on behalf of the state."[54]

Many commentators have urged that this traditional warrior ethic and the specialized training and discipline it entails have been endangered by humanitarian and peacekeeping missions.[55] As Sam Sarkesian writes, "The involvement of the U.S. military in humanitarian crises requires a mind-set [sic] and operational doctrine contrary to the military's traditional raison d'etre and organizational system."[56] Warriors and peacekeepers are said to be almost diametrically opposed to one another when it comes to the three key operational variables in foreign interventions: neutrality, consent, and use of force.[57] In short, warriors take sides, do not ask for permission, and use force; peacekeepers do not take sides, wait for consent, and refrain from using force. The reality in the field, however, is more complex and the distinction between warrior and peacekeeper far more blurred.

In practice, the relationship of soldiers to these three variables is informed by the particular context in which they operate, and this context may indeed change over time. And as stated in *Joint Tactics, Techniques, and Procedures for Peace Operations*, the leading guide for U.S. military policy in this area, "there are no standard peace operations."[58] Although U.S. participation in peace operations are guided by the six principles of MOOTW (objective, security, unity of effort, legitimacy, perseverance, and restraint),[59] officers are explicitly instructed that "the principles of war should be considered in those peace operations where combat actions are possible."[60]

Following the practice of the international community, U.S. military doctrine distinguishes between two types of peace operations: (1) peacekeeping operations (PKOs, or "Chapter VI operations," named after the UN Charter provision said to provide authorization), which are "undertaken with the consent of all major parties to a dispute, are designed to monitor and facilitate implementation of an agreement (ceasefire, truce, or other such agreement), and support diplomatic efforts to reach a long-term settlement;[61] and (2) peace enforcement operations (PEO or "Chapter VII operations") involving "application of military force or the threat of its use, normally pursuant to international authorization, to compel compliance with resolutions or sanctions designed to maintain or restore peace and order."[62] PKO and PEO challenge traditional military doctrine in different ways.

According to the *Joint Tactics, Techniques, and Procedures for Peace Operations*, fundamentals of PKO include "firmness, impartiality, clarity of intention, anticipation, consent, and freedom of movement."[63] The goal of the peacekeeper is "to produce conditions which are conducive to peace and not to the destruction of an enemy."[64] Thus, the joint doctrine also explicitly recognizes that "coordination between peacekeeping and international organizations, nongovernmental organizations, and private military organizations is an important factor of PKO."[65] Out of all of these factors, the requirement of impartiality is perhaps the most challenging for soldiers trained to fight an enemy.

The commanding of troops trained in war fighting in a peacekeeping or peacemaking mission is recognized as a challenge in the new military. "We are trained to go after the bad guys, but in places like Bosnia, the bad guys kept shifting," said one soldier, "It was totally demoralizing. . . . We didn't know who we were supposed to whack."[66] Another soldier who was part of Operation Deliberate Force in Bosnia recalled, "We were all pretty demoralized because we didn't know why we were doing what we were doing. And then the boss comes in one day and says, 'O.K. guys, we are bombing Serbs to the bargaining table.' Then we could operate with righteousness."[67]

U.S. soldiers conducting peacekeeping assignments in Kosovo also spoke of a need for a clear and necessary mission to be conveyed by commanders. As one noted, "When I first got here, I wondered, why are we guarding the [Serbian Orthodox] churches? But then [when a church went unguarded], they blew it up. . . . [Then] I knew that we're here so these guys don't destroy [each other]."[68]

Although PEO are more in line with traditional warfare, they present similar challenges to the traditional warrior mentality. Fundamentals said to "guide the conduct of successful PEO" include "impartiality, restraint in the use of force, a goal of settlement rather than victory, the use of methods of coercion, and the presence of civilians. Peace enforcers generally have full combat capacities and operate without the consent of the parties, but they are told they are not in war. The *Joint Tactics, Techniques, and Procedures for Peace Operations* states, "In PEO, the enemy is the dispute, not the belligerent parties or parties to a dispute. Although PEO may require combat, they are not wars and have more restrictive ROE [rules of engagement] than wars."[69]

How does one prepare for the new nonwar aspects of peace operations? To succeed in peacekeeping, United States Institute of Peace Senior Fellow Graham Day urges, the United States must develop a "new warrior ethos."[70] As General Wesley Clark testified to Congress right after he was relieved as the supreme allied commander in Europe in 2001, "The Army needs to teach its junior officers to find honor in peacekeeping."[71] Soldiers indoctrinated only in the warrior tradition are ill-prepared to undertake roles in peace operations.[72] As the *Joint Tactics, Techniques, and Procedures for Peace Operations* recognizes, though warfighting skills are still necessary, deploying members of a peace operations force requires "negotiation, mediation, and other nonstandard skills."[73]

To help create a "new warrior ethos" more receptive to MOOTW,[74] the armed services have introduced new training requirements, many of which positively affect the upholding of human rights. With the new challenges of peace operations, human rights behaviors are emphasized in specific peace-keeping training centers, where combat units engage in simulation activities to learn how to use their authority—but not deadly force—to monitor communal tensions and resolve interethnic conflict.[75] They also study the history, culture, geography, politics, and economy of the region to which they deploy personnel. In short, they learn "a constabulary ethic, which calls for both impartiality and minimal use of force."[76] The behaviors taught in peacekeeping training, as well as in other combat trainings, strongly emphasize acting in accordance with the laws of war. These behaviors in turn place significant emphasis on acting in accordance with human rights norms.

The Army's Officer Personnel Management System is "superficially unrelated to operations other than war." In practice, however, "it is a system which formalizes and focuses on the non-combat functions of officers" by specifically rewarding performance in these areas.[77] This change, attests Matthew Morgan, represents a "tremendous cultural shift."[78] Peacekeeping trainers recognize that they are requiring soldiers to accept something that is out of sync with the lesson they have already assimilated: the need for overwhelming force to achieve decisive results. The problem, then, is "of changing required mindsets, desired automatic reactions and conditioned responses, with insufficient time and training for reorientation of the soldier who must accomplish the tasks. The required mental transition is significant."[79] The main military joint publication on peacekeeping, the *Doctrine for Joint Operations Other than War,* explicitly admonishes officers to ready troops for transitions from one mindset to the other: "Planning for mission specific training should be part of the force's predeployment activities. Before the peacekeeping mission, training is provided to transition the combat ready individual to one constrained in most if not all, actions. At the conclusion of the peacekeeping mission, certain actions are necessary to return the individual to a combat-oriented mindset."[80]

The goal of this specific training is not just to teach new soldiering skills, but to influence military culture—in the words of one former officer, "to make [the soldiers] able to think like peacekeepers."[81] Only with this thinking can soldiers trained as warriors effectively complete their missions. Experienced military personnel involved in assessing peace operations suggest that in order to develop the frame of mind for peace operations, commanders must be exposed to the way of peace operations thinking and attitudes upon their initial entry into military duty.[82] "When they begin to think differently, they can use the skills they already have to protect civilians," one officer explained.

The "unique Peace Operations skills/tasks span every Army echelon."[83] Military personnel must take courses in human rights as a standard part of their training. The imprint of human rights norms on the behavior of U.S. soldiers is both furthered and evidenced by undergoing mandatory training that the army conducts in peace operations. This training is given to both U.S. and foreign soldiers, and trainings as well as required courses in human rights have increased ever since they were first instituted.

The Army War College's Peacekeeping Institute (PKI) provides a good illustration of the military's changing attitude toward training for nonwarrior roles.[84] The PKI was founded in 1993 to "enable the U.S. Army to better participate in peace operations and other complex humanitarian emergencies" through leadership development, officer training, interagency cooperation, creation of peacekeeping doctrine, and coordination with nongovernmental organizations (NGOs) and multilateral institutions.[85] The PKI had ten original permanent staff and continues to operate on a very a small budget. The institute primarily trains senior officers for one year with a mandatory peacekeeping course. It maintains a reputation as a world leader in peacekeeping strategy and studies.[86] The PKI is involved in planning, training, or deployment of soldiers in conflicts in Bosnia, Haiti, Rwanda/Zaire, Angola, and Peru/Ecuador within the last decade.[87] In the fall of 2003, the institute was slated for closing, but a public outcry offered a last minute reprieve and it continues to operate today.[88]

Meanwhile, at Fort Bragg, midlevel officers in civil affairs training take similar courses for a period of between three months and two years. Through these two programs, hundreds of U.S. soldiers have been trained in the norms and strategies for conducting peace operations since the early 1990s. The peacekeeping and humanitarian assistance course loads have increased in recent years, with courses being taught in negotiation and conflict resolution, property control, and relief assistance.[89]

In addition to regular peacekeeping training, the army also ordered *all* of its fighting units based in the United States to "undergo specialized training intended to prevent the possibility of human rights abuses by soldiers sent overseas on peacekeeping missions" in the year 2000.[90] This new focus on human rights was in response to publicity surrounding the rape and murder of a young girl by a U.S. Army peacekeeper in Kosovo.[91] Military officers based in Kosovo speak proudly of the positive results of this training, which they view as "safeguarding human rights."[92] Each student that attends any course at the U.S. Army School of the Americas receives a minimum eight-hour block of human rights instruction. The trend appears to be one of continually increasing time spent on human rights instruction at all levels at which it is taught.[93]

Along with the many training programs, the attempt to break down the dichotomy between the warrior and peacekeeper is manifest in personnel promotion and recognition policies. Members of the armed forces believe that success in their organization necessarily entails a successful combat record. "There's no way you're going to get anything [in the military] if all you do is feed refugees," said one soldier, expressing the sentiment of many interviewed for this book. "That's nice and all, and it will take you somewhere, but you better have some other career plans—you know what I mean?" To address this concern, military personnel policies and structures have adapted in order to recognize, validate, and even reward the experiences of soldiers who undertake humanitarian missions.

Some of these developments have been quite public, such as offering retention bonuses and promotions in direct connection to the acceptance of peacekeeping posts. According to former Pentagon spokesman Kenneth Bacon, "The importance and complexity of major peacekeeping operations today makes the officers who command them prime candidates for promotion."[94] The vast majority of military personnel interviewed for this book agreed that peacekeeping is a valued service and that a new military self-image was indeed emerging. Still, they felt that opportunities for promotion would be limited unless peacekeeping was accompanied by more traditional service.

THE BEST MILITARY THAT DOESN'T FIGHT

The [U.S.] military has taken steps to reduce casualties when they do fight and to decrease the chance that they will have to fight. They want to be the best military in the world that does not fight.

**—Jim Hooper, director of the Balkan Institute,
in an interview with the author**

What's the point of having this superb military if we can't use it?

**—Secretary of State Madeleine Albright,
quoted in Colin Powell, *My American Journey***

While the identity and culture of the military have changed over the past decade to reflect a closer alignment with human rights, so too has the nature of operations. Three developments with particular relevance for human rights are noted here: (1) the military's continued involvement in training foreign militaries; (2) the increased subcontracting of military tasks to private companies; and (3) the development and use of more technologically advanced weapons designed to mitigate casualties, accompanied by the design of new procedures for employing these weapons that also reduce risk to civilians. Each of these developments is discussed below in turn.

Training Foreign Soldiers

One of the best things we can do is to train foreign soldiers. It's great for them, and great for us. . . . It helps us get out of there.

**—Anonymous U.S. Army officer,
in an interview with the author**

The training of foreign soldiers has been much more controversial from a human rights standpoint than the training of the U.S. military. While the training of foreign military and civilian leaders could potentially improve human rights promotion, it is fraught with challenges. One hurdle for the U.S. military lies in selecting participants to train. In many cases, the U.S. military does not know, or chooses not to know, the background of either their trainees or the local person (often a soldier or former soldier) who selected them.[95] By undergoing a U.S.-conducted or U.S.-sponsored training program, an individual who engaged in grave human rights abuses in the past may gain a new status of respectability. Thus, one unintended result of U.S. military training may be to effectively ensure that soldiers who engaged in grave abuses in the past are never brought to justice. The specific techniques taught may also raise problems. While valid in some contexts, the techniques may serve to "improve the ability of a government or army to repress its own civilian population or to engage in hostilities with its neighbors."[96] Depending on the context, by cooperating with a government or faction accused of human rights abuses, the United States may be viewed as either interfering with or supporting local courts and other mechanisms for truth and reconciliation.

Foremost on the list of controversial foreign training programs is the former Army School of the Americas (SOA) at Fort Benning, Georgia. Human rights groups have organized mass protests in recent years against the SOA for its repeated dealings with dictators, generals, and soldiers who committed human rights abuses against their own people throughout Latin America.[97] In 1996, the SOA was forced to admit through a Freedom of Information Act request that it maintained training manuals that advocated "motivation by fear, payment of bounties for enemy dead, false imprisonment and the use of truth serum."[98] In response, the SOA called this an "oversight" that was apparently corrected in the early 1990s; it subsequently changed its name to the Western Hemisphere Institute for Security Cooperation; and it has added several courses in human rights to the curricula.[99]

Another controversial military training program has been the International Military Education and Training (IMET) program, which trains officers in over one hundred countries in U.S. military doctrine and tactics with an annual budget of around fifty million dollars.[100] Throughout the 1990s, Congress began to limit IMET training to particular countries such as Indonesia (1992), Guatemala (1997), and Zaire (1997) because of the linkage of IMET training to human rights abuses in those countries. Despite these warnings from Congress, the Pentagon instead used the U.S. Army's Special Forces unit to train Indonesian soldiers through the Joint Combined Exercises and Training (JCET) program. The Indonesian army was later linked to human rights abuses in places such as East Timor. While the casual relationship was debated, the incident led Congress to pass a law in 1998 prohibiting any IMET or JCET training to any foreign troops who have committed human rights abuses.[101] The State Department Bureau for Democracy, Human Rights, and Labor now monitors the human rights component of foreign military training. The IMET program, now called the Expanded IMET because of the inclusion of foreign civilian officials in the trainings, includes new courses on democracy building and human rights.[102]

A final foreign military training program to note is the African Crisis Response Initiative, established by the Clinton administration in 1997 to train African soldiers in peacekeeping and rapid response to humanitarian emergencies.[103] The courses are conducted by the Special Forces, who are themselves trained by the U.S. Institute of Peace. The goal of the program, which is budgeted at approximately twenty million dollars annually, is to train up to twelve thousand African soldiers in a "professional program of peacekeeping and humanitarian relief operations."[104] According to the U.S. State Department, "Observance of human rights, issues of humanitarian law, negotiation and mediation, and other humanitarian concerns relevant to peacekeeping are interwoven into the training program."[105]

Foreign military training programs on the balance remain controversial, and the causal relationship between the programs and the domestic human rights situation remains hotly debated. As foreign training programs have frequently been spotlighted by the media and the activist public, they have been subject to ongoing evaluation by U.S. civilian and military officials according to human rights criteria.

Private Military Companies

The U.S. military can't be everywhere. Contracting out to private militaries is a good solution for meeting all of its obligations . . . and it is cost effective too.

—Doug Brooks, president of the International Peace Operations Association, in an interview with the author

The practice of the United States contracting out to private military companies has become increasingly frequent as the nation seeks to exert influence in many conflict areas while simultaneously limiting risks and costs.[106] At least thirty-five private military companies are based in the United States, hired domestically and abroad to do everything from providing cooks, cleaners, and janitors to assisting in military training, logistical support, and security.[107] From 1994 to 2002, the U.S. military entered into more than three thousand contracts with private military companies.[108] Vice President Dick Cheney's former employer, the Halliburton Company, has emerged as the industry leader, now "provid[ing] logistics for every major American military deployment."[109] In the recent campaign against Iraq, private companies like Halliburton had one private military worker in the field for every ten U.S. soldiers, and provided everything from toilets and housing for troops to maintenance of weapons and training for the new Iraqi military.[110] According to private industry projections, revenues from the global international security market are expected to more than triple, increasing from a 1990 total of $55.6 billion up to $202 billion by 2010.[111]

Proponents of privatization argue that subcontracting to private militaries may enrich military capacity and improve efficiency. The argument is that if you take the support functions—cooks, janitors, groundskeepers, truck drivers—away from soldiers, they can concentrate on war-fighting skills and therefore became more professional as warriors. The main drawback, however, which has serious implications for human rights, is that virtually no international laws regulate the private military industry. The United Nations has taken a stand against the use of mercenaries, notably in the International Convention against the Recruitment, Use, Financing, and Training of Mercenaries (1989), but the private military companies that the U.S. military engages mainly supply maintenance and construction workers, not soldiers, and thus this convention does not apply.

The main check on the behavior of private military companies is the threat that their contracts could be terminated for cause. Yet these companies are often out of the spectrum of supervision that might be expected for such significant responsibilities. Further, the lobbying power of these companies is generally very strong in the U.S. political system, as the companies have strong financial foundations and are often associated with retired military officers. A partial explanation for the poor human rights records of some foreign militaries may be explained by the reliance of these private firms in training their soldiers in techniques of warfare and interrogation. Since they are generally out of the radar of the public and international eye because they are privately owned, some private military companies have aided unscrupulous regimes and trained foreign militaries in techniques that violate international human rights standards.[112]

The quality standards in privately run military trainings are harder to enforce, and the ability to obtain information becomes increasingly obscured by protections on private industry.[113] One poignant illustration of the reach and power of private military companies involved American private contractors who were piloting a Central Intelligence Agency plane over Peru during a drug interdiction mission in 2001. The contractors mistakenly identified a missionary plane as belonging to drug smugglers, and when the Peruvian military shot down the plane, an American missionary and her infant were killed.[114]

Objections to private military companies come from within the United States, in the military and in Congress. In a 1998 essay for the Army War College, Colonel Bruce Grant wrote, "Privatization is a way of going around Congress and not telling the public. Foreign policy is made by default by private military consultants motivated by bottom-line profits."[115] Representative Jan Schakowsky of Illinois concurred, stating, "There is little or no accountability in this process of outsourcing. This is a way of funding secret wars with taxpayers' money that could get us into a Vietnam-like conflict."[116] Critics on the other side of the political spectrum point out that the increased reliance on high-tech warfare has led to greatly increased reliance on contractors to support the high-tech hardware. Thus, they contend, using private companies for training as a substantial part of American foreign policy may weaken the military's capacity for engagement, since it leads to expertise development in the private sector rather than from within. The main human rights argument against privatization in the military, however, is that private companies are relatively out of reach of regulative scrutiny.

Advanced Weaponry

An advertisement that is two mouse-clicks after the U.S. Army's home webpage shows photos of the new "Stryker" weaponry, promoting the army's new "Transformation: stealth, speed, and mobility" campaign. Along with music and gunshot-like sounds, the website text reads, "As Transformation unfolds, soldiers increasingly utilize satellite intelligence, robotic weapons, and aerial drones. Today's tech-savvy soldier remains the most important factor in making Army Transformation work. Having the best take up this challenge is more important now more than ever."[117]

The U.S. military has trumpeted its new weapons programs and targeting practices as ushering in an era of high-tech, humane warfare. There is nothing "natural" about the new weaponry chosen as part of this project. The designs chosen are not necessarily the strongest, most efficient, or most humane. Rather, they are the ones that win out through a contested social process. "Social networks develop around rival designs," Theo Farrell and Terry Terriff observe, "each functioning to mobilize resources and build consensus for its own preference. It is this social process, whereby debate closes around a dominant design, and not design efficiency, that shapes technological development."[118] As illustrated below, both claims to accuracy and assertions of nonlethality are socially constructed and informed by human rights ideas.

The Most Accurate: Precision-Guided Munitions

Supporters of precision-guided munitions (PGMs) claim that the new weapons have made war significantly more humane.[119] The development of "smart" weapons and other new technologies, coupled with their marketing portrayal as incorporating humanitarian concerns,[120] further demonstrates the influence of human rights norms in the military.

Production of PGMs is on the rise. Between 1991 and 1998, the U.S. Air Force tripled the number of PGM platforms; increased inventory by 25 percent; and developed several new generations of weapons.[121] The inventory now includes laser-guided and global positioning system–aided bombs and missiles that can be used in any weather conditions, day or night. In the Gulf War, about 9 percent of the tonnage dropped was of PGMs, while in Bosnia, PGMs comprised about 98 percent of the munitions used.[122] Some commentators have gone so far as to suggest that the prevalence of PGM use in urban areas demonstrates the emergence of a customary norm of international law.[123] In other words, consistent state practice of using PGMs in urban areas, coupled with a belief that such use is required, is leading to a customary norm requiring it.

Despite their enhanced accuracy, PGMs are not flawless. Critics assert that evidence from the Federal Republic of Yugoslavia undermines the claim that there were significantly fewer civilian casualties in cities that were bombed exclusively with PGMs than cities that were bombed with cluster bombs or other weapons.[124] The benefit of PGMs for civilians may, in any event, be overstated. Kosovo provides one good illustration that the danger to civilians from air strikes applies to precision bombing, despite rhetoric to the contrary. Air force, navy and marine aircraft flew more than 36,000 sorties in the 11-week campaign.[125] Defense Secretary William Cohen described the air strikes in Kosovo as "the most precise application of air power in history." In the early days of the war, 90 percent of the munitions used were PGMs. Cohen continued, "As a result, NATO forces were able to hold civilian casualties to a very low level while concentrating on the military targets. Of more than 23,000 bombs and missiles used, we have confirmed just twenty incidents of weapons going astray from their targets to cause collateral damage."[126] He later added, "Let me say that we have always taken into account the potential loss of innocent human life. In fact, we have been criticized for the way in which the campaign was executed, that we didn't give enough flexibility to the military, in the judgment of some. . . . The fact of the matter is that we reviewed with great care every recommended target for an examination in terms of what the potential was for harming innocent civilians. I can tell you that I reviewed it with the chairman [of the joint chiefs of staff], even at the White House. We went over in great detail what type of activity was contemplated, what time of day or night, what angle of attack, what was the likely explosive impact, in order to reduce the loss of innocent lives. We don't want to see any innocent people harmed, and we took extraordinary care to achieve those results."[127]

The use of PGMs, although better, does not ensure the avoidance of collateral damage and civilian casualties. As one airman worried, "If you operate too easily in the air, you hit some targets because you can hit them, not because you should."[128] Targets may be selected carelessly or civilian areas targeted. One could point to the example of a bunker that was bombed with precision in Iraq, killing hundreds of civilians taking shelter there, or the Chinese embassy that was mistakenly targeted in Belgrade in 1999. In the Iraqi incident, the air campaign within Baghdad was suspended for ten days to deal with the political ramifications of the civilian deaths;[129] and in Serbia, U.S. officials were compelled to make a public apology for their error. While both the suspension of bombing and the public apology reflect a greater sensitivity with respect to human rights, they also underscore the fact the PGMs cannot eliminate all risks to civilians.

Wholly apart from their accuracy, the manner in which precision-guided munitions are used raises troubling questions. "NATO planes [using precision guided missiles] did not hit as much stuff as they thought in the first sixty-seven days or so," notes one defense department analyst, asserting that the PGMs had little impact on the Serb leadership. "If anything, it bought Milosevic more time . . . [that is] the unintended consequences of hitting targets of dual interest."[130] The scenario changed, however, when the United States began flying low. "When we went in low and started dropping some cluster bombs, the Yugos said 'uncle.'"[131] This raises the question of whether the advanced technology really is better, or rather, if the public perception of its capability is enough to justify its use.[132]

The Least Deadly: Nonlethal Weapons

In addition to developing weapons that kill with greater precision, the Pentagon is also developing weapons that don't kill at all—that is, nonlethal weapons (NLWs) for nontraditional missions. NLWs have a long and controversial history. It was President Dwight Eisenhower who, in a 1960 secret meeting between the National Security Council and Pentagon officials, was presented with a "humane" germ weapon that would temporarily paralyze and cause lethargy to its victims. Eisenhower rejected the idea with skepticism, indicating in a recently declassified memo the "great difficulty" with the weapons given that adversaries might retaliate with full force, thereby creating a cataclysm of global proportions.[133] Research and development on NLWs continued with a National Science Foundation study in 1971, but NLWs really gained ground in 1995 during the U.S. mission to help withdraw UN peacekeepers from Somalia.[134]

Some weapons have been developed for specific peacekeeping operations. For the Somalia mission, for example, the Pentagon consulted with U.S. police to develop NLWs for military use, and Lieutenant General Anthony Zinni deployed several types of NLW technologies for the purpose of controlling hostile crowds without the loss of U.S. or Somali lives.[135] These included firing sticky foam and tiny beanbags in order to immobilize rioters. After some initial success with NLWs, Zinni advocated strongly for their continued development, and by 1996 the Department of Defense had established a Joint Non-lethal Weapons Directorate (JNLWD) within the Marine Corps.[136]

The JNLWD budget was only $34 million in 1998, but it has received wide support from other government agencies and private contractors.[137] A 1999 report of the Council on Foreign Relations praised the weapons as politically important because they are a less violent means of engaging the military, which in political terms makes them more acceptable.[138] NLW technologies are being developed, and include a variety of inventions that can disorient or immobilize people, or affect technologies. Some of these were used in Bosnia and Kosovo, and the list includes loud noises, bright lights, horrendous odors, radio jamming devices, graphite threads that can be dropped to take out power grids, and electromagnetic devices and nets that serve as roadblocks for vehicles.[139]

Weapons with a more direct personal effect, including chemical agents, are also being investigated by the Pentagon. These include nonlethal variants of Claymore mines that temporarily injure rather than kill, and "Stinger" grenades that can be thrown by hand or shot from another device. In March 2001 a weapon was unveiled by the Pentagon that fires microwaves more than a third of a mile, causing a burning sensation. The weapon is said to be useful for dispersing crowds. A group of researchers issued a report on "calmatives" in October 2000 that highlighted Fentanyl, a chemical agent that killed one in seven people when it was used by the Russian government in the fall of 2001 during a hostage incident sparked when Chechnyan rebels took over a theater.[140]

The new weapons and strategic bombing practices are part of the military's "kinder, gentler" identity,[141] but whether they ultimately lead to greater attention to human rights concerns is open to question. In particular, critics question whether the new weapons enhance protection for civilians or simply place civilians in new forms of danger. The availability of NLWs could encourage more military interventions abroad and increased targeting of civilians and, in so doing, threaten international humanitarian law.[142] Human rights advocates also express concern that NLWs are difficult to control. In international treaties and regulation of arms, NLWs fall into a gray area of international regulation, thus potentially damaging the greater good of international law by arguably eroding its ability to limit the design and use of weapons.[143]

Some commentators have said that nonlethal weapons should be better labeled "less than lethal" weapons, because NLWs can often kill their targets, especially if used incorrectly.[144] As the 1999 Council on Foreign Relations report made clear, "It is not the primary purpose of non-lethal weapons to prevent death or major injury to opposing troops. Instead, they are intended to increase the lethality of force used against combatants, while reducing death and injury among noncombatant civilians. For example, NLWs can prevent a crowd from approaching closely enough to be a serious threat to U.S. forces. They can also unmask snipers or other combatants in a crowd of civilians, opening a field for U.S. lethal fire."[145]

What is new is the extent to which the development and use of "smart" weapons and nonlethal weapons is linked to the military's new identity. In short, as the 1999 Council on Foreign Relations study concluded, NLWs are important because they give the appearance of a lower level of violence, "[a]nd in political terms, less violence equals more acceptability."[146]

LAWYERS, DOCTORS, OR SOLDIERS?

U.S. Marine Interrogator: *How many of your soldiers were killed by the air war?*

Iraqi Officer: *To be honest, for the amount of ordnance that was dropped, not very many. Only one soldier was killed and two were wounded. The soldier that was killed did not die as a result of a direct hit, but because the vibrations of the bomb caused a bunker to cave in on top of him.*

Interrogator: *So, then you feel the aerial bombardment was ineffective?*

Officer: *Oh no! Just the opposite! It was extremely effective! The planes hit only vehicles and equipment. Even my personal vehicle, a "Waz" was hit. They hit everything!*

—Exchange quoted in Richard P. Hallion, *Precision Guided Munitions and the New Era of Warfare*

The use of new technology, both in weapons and in targeting, has gone a long way to redefining the nature of war. We talk less about casualties than about surgical strikes. Soldiers are now said to be like highly trained physicians, using skill and technology to remove an ailment. The legality of military operations are subject to public debate, and the U.S. military now presents an argument of legality in advance of its actions, as well as upon conclusion of military campaigns.[147] Military lawyers have long been employed to review and apply international law to military actions, but the extent to which they have recently been employed in the field and the degree to which they review each targeting decision represents a new development.[148]

The wars in the Balkans accelerated the military's concern with humanitarian law,[149] and with it the use of lawyers in the targeting review process.[150] "Every target was reviewed up and down and back again" in a four-step review process, one officer explained. "We had to be able to justify each target under international law, and then again."[151] Military lawyers interviewed for this project expressed frustration at their mandate in Bosnia and Kosovo: "Kosovo went overboard"; "It was a freak show"; "It took so long to decide to review a target that we might have just as well as sent our [target] list to Milosevic." At times, they said, they questioned whether the target in question was related to a legitimate military objective, but were instructed "to find some legal justification—just as long as we don't harm civilians." One explained, "This went totally against what we had been taught as airmen: identify the attackable center of gravity, attack in a reasonable manner and be done." Another officer similarly lamented, "They have us plotting every move. . . microsurgically analyzing targeting. . . . [The targeting process] has gotten totally out of control."

Military lawyers pointed to General Wesley Clark's strategy in Bosnia—that of showing Serbian President Slobodan Milosevic that he could bomb with impunity[152]—as one that "raised eyebrows" among the military attorneys tasked with finding legal justification for the bombing strategy. "After we ran out of targets and there were none left, the military started to bomb them over again. What was the military purpose of that?" They were instructed to find one. The military purpose could not be that striking terror in the heart of the enemy is good for the overall war effort. The use of war to spread terror among civilians is prohibited by the Geneva Conventions. "When I tried to question the rebombing of a bridge," one lawyer confided, "It was sent back to me with instructions to examine the question of civilian casualties."

The focus on the benefits of new technology and improved targeting was taken up by President George W. Bush as he emphasized the safety of civilians in the 2003 war on Iraq. He linked the new technology to a sense of achievement of a moral good. As he told the nation, "With new technology and precision weapons, we can achieve military objectives without directing violence against civilians . . . it is a great moral advance when the guilty have far more to fear from war than the innocent."[153]

The tailoring of weaponry to minimize harm to noncombatants is, of course, not new. As Max Boot observes, the military must always "struggle with the deadly calculus of how many casualties it is willing to incur among its own forces to save civilian lives."[154] Boot is concerned that the pendulum has swung too far on the application of human rights ideas in war time: "Nowadays, the military tries to save not only the civilians, but enemy combatants as well."[155] He suggests that it is immoral to use less force than necessary, because that only prolongs the struggle. Other critics of the new military humanism caution that "the law of armed conflict is not like using a calculator to solve a mathematical equation,"[156] and warn that setting unrealistic standards for combat would prevent the United States from ever deploying troops.[157]

In the final analysis, the net result of new technology and the "lawyerization" of targeting does not provide adequate protection nor necessarily generate consistency with international law. Flying high and using pinpoint strikes in Kosovo protected the U.S. military, but over 500 civilians died.[158] In Afghanistan, estimates of civilian casualties are as high as 3,767,[159] and in the 2003 war on Iraq, the low end of estimates are 5,553 civilian deaths, while the maximum estimates reach 7,236 people.[160]

While legal warfare is more humane than a war without legal controls, these recent military campaigns may indeed reveal that human rights concerns have served as a justification for facilitating violence rather than an obstacle to violence.[161] The next section tests this thesis through an examination of justifications provided for recent military interventions, and in so doing searches for further evidence of incorporation of human rights norms.

THE CHANGING NATURE OF U.S. MILITARY INTERVENTIONS

No nation in human history has done more to avoid civilian casualties than the United States has in this conflict.

—Secretary of Defense Donald Rumsfeld (referring to Afghanistan), quoted in Esther Schrader, "Response to Terror; Pentagon Defends Strikes as Civilian Toll Rises"

Human Rights Watch was saying, "Five hundred civilians killed!" We went, "Not bad for a seventy-seven-day air campaign!" . . . the notion of "collateral damage" is entirely subjective and fact dependent.

—Lieutenant Colonel Jeffrey Walker (referring to Kosovo), in an interview with the author

While the U.S. military was involved in humanitarian activities well before the 1990s, the level of commitment to such missions increased throughout the 1990s.[162] Humanitarian activities comprised about 15 percent of the Pentagon's funding for small-scale contingencies in the 1990s.[163] The 2001 Quadrennial Defense Review, the Pentagon's four-year planning document, makes clear the military's ongoing expectation to be involved in foreign humanitarian operations that do not defend any "vital national interests."[164] The demand for U.S. peacekeeping is likely to mount as violent conflict continues unabated intrastate (through civil conflict between two warring groups) or transstate (through terrorism or other threats to security). The U.S. military remains the strongest force, with a track record of willingness to intervene. When the United States does intervene, the operations are likely to become ever more complex as more actors become involved in the peacebuilding process, and more difficult to resolve as world problems become more interconnected and the root causes of conflict remain unaddressed.

The public sees an inconsistent pattern of engagement and wonders why there have been large-scale military interventions in Haiti, Bosnia, and Kosovo, and not in Rwanda, the Sudan, and Tajikistan. The motivation for interventions has rarely, if ever, been purely humanitarian. Yet throughout the 1990s, the White House increasingly employed humanitarian and human rights justifications for both the decision to deploy troops and for the strategies and tactics employed. Military officers are among the last to advocate use of force: "The military is deeply skeptical of intervention"; "You'll never see us embracing the doctrine of humanitarian intervention"; "We know what war means . . . we want to avoid it."[165] Yet, military personnel complain that their expertise is discounted by government and the private sector alike. The civilian commander in chief has the power to order that the military be deployed in peace operations, even over the objection of military leadership.

In justifying the decision to intervene, to what extent do the civilian command and military spokesmen refer to human rights ideas, such as the protection of civilians or the alleviation of suffering? Is the image of the U.S. military that emerges from recent interventions consistent with the new military identity? With these questions in mind, this section provides an overview of many of the most prominent military interventions undertaken in the last three presidential administrations. Although President George H. W. Bush invoked humanitarian justifications for earlier interventions,[166] this narrative begins with Somalia, the "watershed" case for both governmental and military policy makers and humanitarian NGOs. While many of the human rights implications of the "new war on terror" were examined as part of Chapter 2, this chapter ends with a note on the U.S. military's engagement in what appears to be a new era of warfare.

Operation Restore Hope in Somalia (1992–93) has been described as the first and perhaps only "true case of humanitarian intervention." In the words of Admiral David Jeremiah, then vice chair of the U.S. chiefs of staff, there was "nothing of geopolitical value in Somalia that should engage U.S. interest . . . the intervention had only one motivation—humanitarianism."[167] Somalia was in the midst of a civil war, a drought and food shortage causing nearly a thousand Somalis deaths each week, and a refugee exodus of a thousand people per day. "Somalia was a real turning point," says George Ward, the former ambassador to Nicaragua (1996–99) and now coordinator for humanitarian assistance in the Office of Reconstruction and Humanitarian Assistance in Iraq (appointed 2003). "Somalia made people realize that when human rights violations reached a certain level, some kind of intervention was inevitable. There was an outcry among informed elites—people who knew what was going on—to do something."[168]

The failure to act early on as the Somalia situation developed was in the public spotlight particularly because George H. W. Bush was in the midst of a reelection campaign against Bill Clinton. The issue of intervention in the situation was a key point of confrontation in debates and media questions. The announcement of Operation Provide Relief in Somalia came on the eve of the Republican National Convention, when Bush was behind in the polls.[169] As Bush was leaving office, he was redoubling his efforts to ameliorate the conditions for the Somalis, calling a four-day-long meeting of the Deputies Committee during the lame-duck period of his presidency.

The human rights situation in Somalia had reached an abysmal level well before U.S. and UN involvement. Only reluctantly did the United States decide to intervene. David Jeremiah, Powell's top assistant, stated in a high-level meeting with President Bush, "If you think U.S. forces are needed, we can do the job."[170] Historian David Halberstam attributes this statement of willingness to internal military politics, which perceived an intervention in Somalia as a means of avoiding entering the Bosnian conflict, a complicated knot of tension. Further, the military's readiness to intervene in Somalia came at a time when the Republican administration was being criticized by Democrats, particularly by then presidential candidate Bill Clinton, about overlooking human rights in humanitarian crises throughout the world. As Halberstam observes, "By the summer of 1992, the televised images from Somalia were, if not worse than the images from Bosnia, certainly more plentiful . . . [and] the outcry over the pictures of starving children grew."[171]

The express purpose of Operation Restore Hope, also known as the United Task Force, was to support the United Nations operations already at work in the area (known as UNOSOM I) in providing a secure environment for the safe delivery of humanitarian supplies to vulnerable populations.[172] Operation Restore Hope was to last for four months, until a multinational peace operations unit could be installed (UNOSOM II). The Pentagon issued an official mission statement for Somalia, emphasizing its humanitarian nature.[173] At the same time, Defense Secretary Dick Cheney told a CNN audience that "[t]he mission is very clear indeed, it's a humanitarian mission."[174] Cheney acknowledged that the U.S. role in Somalia could establish a "useful precedent" and suggested that the military would be open to similar requests in the future.[175] On the ground, Field Commander Robert Johnston explained that the deployment of his marines would be strictly humanitarian and that his soldiers "would use only whatever force was necessary to protect themselves and food convoys."[176]

Adding further support for the mission, Colin Powell, then chairman of the joint chiefs of staff, authored an article for *Foreign Affairs* justifying U.S. intervention in Somalia on humanitarian grounds.[177] He asserted that the U.S. forces in Somalia would be a "helpful, supportive, humanitarian army that will take care of human needs."[178] Powell stated what the military was willing to do for the 1.5 million Somalis facing starvation: "If there are those who look to us for sustenance and medical care and dental care and protection, that is something we are prepared to do and are willing to do as part of our mission."[179] In saying this, Powell was supporting a new role for the U.S. military, as willing provider to foreign nations desperately in need of assistance. Powell had earlier enunciated his doctrine of—as Henry Carey terms it—"certain victory cum superior power cum national interests cum U.S. public support."[180] Powell summarized his doctrine this way: "[I]s the national interest at stake? If the answer is yes, go in, and go in to win. Otherwise, stay out."[181] Powell would somehow have to justify humanitarian actions under these criteria.[182]

Operation Restore Hope demonstrated the main limiting principle that the Powell doctrine implicitly placed on humanitarian missions: military casualties must be kept to the minimum. Throughout the summer of 1993, attempts to oust Somali faction leader General Mohamed Farrah Aidid continued, and several foreign journalists and U.S. troops were killed in attacks by Somalis. Officials in Washington became aware of the vulnerability of American troops, and some officials in the new Clinton administration began to argue that the risk was too great for the troops. The Pentagon asserted, as they had all along, that the U.S. public and Congress would not tolerate high numbers (or, for that matter, any number) of casualties among U.S. soldiers unless the mission was absolutely vital to U.S. interests.[183] Zbigniew Brzezinski decried this development as "a new technological racism" based on the premise that the life of "one American service-man is not worth risking in order to save the lives of thousands."[184] Secretary of State Madeleine Albright wrote in a *New York Times* article in August 1993, "The decision we must make is whether to pull up stakes and allow Somalia to fall back into the abyss or to stay the course and help lift the country and its people from the category of a failed state into that of an emerging democracy. For Somalia's sake, and our own, we must persevere."[185]

The disaster that everyone feared took place on October 3, 1993, when eighteen U.S. soldiers and approximately a thousand Somalis died in a Black Hawk air attack on General Aidid's compound. U.S. officials immediately called for the withdrawal of troops. After the well-intentioned humanitarian intervention in Somalia turned into a highly publicized blood bath and an ineffective coup attempt against Aidid, protecting human rights plummeted as a national priority in the United States. Certainly, the UN shared the blame for the disaster in Somalia for many reasons. Karin von Hippel, political affairs officer to the UN Secretary General for Somalia, lists some of them: poor coordination; overconcentration in Mogadishu at the expense of the rest of the country; the special representative of the secretary general of UNOSOM II (Jonathan Howe) offering a $25,000 reward for Aidid's capture, dead or alive; the ramifications of mutual antipathy between Butros Butros-Ghali, then secetary general of the UN, and General Aidid; and the frequent change of the person acting as the special representative of the secretary general and of the humanitarian coordinators.[186] The American public, however, did not continue to support humanitarian intervention in a reformed UN. Instead, it withdrew support for humanitarian missions altogether. While arguably still a component of American "national interests," it appeared that humanitarian missions and upholding human rights in other countries through military actions would be undertaken only in cases that presented minimal risk to American soldiers.

The "trauma of Somalia shook Washington and affected decisively the formulation of policy on peace operations," remembers Ambassador George Ward, then principal deputy of state for international affairs and organizational affairs.[187] After a year of study, in May 1994 President Clinton issued Presidential Directive 25 (PDD-25), which set strict criteria for engagement of U.S. military personnel: (1) there must be minimal risk to U.S. combatants; (2) there must be an identifiable interests at stake; (3) the mission must be clearly defined in size, scope, and duration; (4) there must be sufficient resources and political will to carry out the mission; and (5) there must be an identifiable "exit strategy" for the United States.[188] The terms of PDD-25, however, "did not dictate the outcome of any policy discussion on the wisdom of U.S. involvement." As Eric Schwartz, a former member of the National Security Council during the Clinton administration, points out, PDD-25 "established guidelines to inform decision-making, but left to decision-makers the key responsibility of weighing the various factors in determining the appropriate government response."[189]

The Clinton peacekeeping policy favored the use of the North Atlantic Treaty Organization (NATO) over the United Nations for peacekeeping, and specified that to the extent the United States would participate, U.S. forces would remain under the command and control of U.S. officers. In response to the debacle in Somalia, the U.S. Congress added its own restrictions to the deployment of U.S. forces in peace operations. It required the administration to "report monthly in detail to all commitments of American forces."[190] Furthermore, Congress mandated that it be shown the text of any Security Council resolution authorizing a peace operation before the U.S. permanent representative to the United Nations voted on it.[191]

The 1990s did present numerous other opportunities for engagement in low-risk humanitarian missions and the United States approached each one with great caution. In Operation Support Hope in Rwanda/Zaire (1994), the U.S. military provided humanitarian assistance, including delivering aid supplies, training soldiers in civil and military relations, and conducting demining operations, during a two-month period to refugees fleeing genocide. The intervention came only after the genocide in Rwanda had already occurred,[192] but the United States, still reeling from the painful lessons of Somalia, was unwilling to intervene earlier.[193] "We told the administration that the information coming out of Rwanda put it clearly under the Genocide Convention," said one State Department lawyer, "But they didn't like that because calling it genocide would mean the United States was obligated to act. They told us to come up with a way of describing what was happening without calling it genocide." The original formulation was "acts of genocide" and initial resistance to the intervention placed the issue at a whisper level among U.S. decision makers.[194] It took President Clinton until the end of his term to publicly call the systematic killings in Rwanda genocide.[195]

Critics of the effort in Rwanda point to the great extent that the operation undermined international cooperation. Some human rights advocates criticized Clinton for failing to respond to early signs of impending violence and then for failing to put forth a plan to quell the violence once it began, citing the perceived lack of national interest and pressure as the culprit. Only as the death toll soared and pressure mounted was Clinton moved to respond.[196] Furthermore, the country's efforts to minimize the UN force and to pull out UN troops as the genocide was going on were a great detriment to the international community addressing the situation.[197] When Operation Support Hope finally did enter Rwanda on its humanitarian mission, over two thousand military personnel were involved.[198] This intervention illustrates Americans' willingness to use the military to support human rights norms even when there were no "vital" national interests at stake—but only under the condition that risk to American soldiers be limited to the greatest extent possible.

One international quagmire Clinton inherited from Bush was the crisis in Haiti, which provided a different test for the United States' view of itself and its military moral actors. Three years earlier, after a coup had ousted Jean-Bertrand Aristide, the Bush administration imposed economic sanctions against the country. The sanctions were having no discernible positive impact on the new regime, and were harming the poorest civilians and causing a humanitarian crisis that sent Haitians fleeing for U.S. shores. Despite his campaign speeches condemning Bush's policy of interdicting the boats and summarily sending the civilians back,[199] Clinton reinstated similar interdiction measures shortly after assuming office.[200] The new Clinton policy stated that these Haitians were economic migrants, and thus, the United States had no legal obligation to them and could return them at will.[201]

The backlash to the policy regression was intense as religious groups, human rights organizations, the Congressional Black Caucus, and other Haitian and African American leaders cried foul.[202] One foreign policy scholar noted that "attempting to extend democracy through trade embargoes violates two fundamental norms of the society of states—the prohibitions against intervention in the internal affairs of states and against doing harm to the innocent."[203] Due to growing domestic and foreign pressure and condemnation, Clinton modified this policy several times, and ultimately launched the U.S. military intervention into Haiti with the stated mission of restoring democracy. Operation Uphold Democracy in Haiti (1994) both invoked human rights and raised a new set of human rights concerns.[204]

American military involvement was only seriously contemplated after Haitian refugees began streaming onto U.S. soil. The United States attempted to address the matter in the long negotiations between Aristide and General Raoul Cedras leading up to the Governors Island Accord in July 1993. This agreement stated that the junta would leave and be granted amnesty, and Aristide would return. The accord proved to be a dismal failure, as violence continued against Aristide supporters; by May 1994, comprehensive economic sanctions were put in place.[205]

Another early U.S. humiliation in Haiti was the USS *Harlan County* debacle, named after the U.S. naval vessel sent to Haiti on October 12, 1993, only one week after the Black Hawk incident in Somalia. The troops were met at shore by a jeering, hostile crowd, where many people were heard shouting, "Somalia! Somalia!" The boat waited offshore and turned back home the next day without disembarking.[206] The embarrassment hurt the Clinton administration, and the "Haiti issue" was tabled for nearly a year to let the situation cool.

The Clinton administration's approach to Haiti was influenced by a fear of being overwhelmed by refugees as well as a desire to court the Congressional Black Caucus, which had publicly framed the decision to aid Haiti in racial terms.[207] Along with other factors, however, human rights figured prominently in the Clinton administration's public justifications for intervening in Haiti. Human rights organizations and journalists had already framed the issue in human rights terms through their extensive documentation of cases of murder, rape, torture, and other forms of abuse committed by the ruling regime. Urging that human rights violations could not be tolerated in the Americas, President Clinton stated that the intervention would "help to end human rights violations that we find intolerable everywhere, but are unconscionable on our doorstep."[208] Four days before the intervention, Clinton argued that the United States had an obligation to respond: "In Haiti, we have a case in which the right is clear, in which the country in question is nearby, in which our own interests are plain, in which the mission is achievable and limited, and in which the nations of the world stand with us."[209]

Madeleine Albright, then U.S. ambassador to the UN, sought UN Security Council authorization for military action. Within ten days of Albright's request, in June 1994, the UN Security Council issued Resolution 940 "authorize[ing] Member States to form a multinational force under unified command and control and, in this framework, to use all necessary means to facilitate the departure from Haiti of the military leadership."[210] A total of twenty-seven countries took part in the intervention, which occurred on September 19, 1994. The operation was "unforced" due to the last-minute mediation efforts of former President Jimmy Carter. Backed by the threat of the arriving troops, Carter had managed to reach an agreement with Cedras to leave office within a month.[211]

Once U.S. soldiers were on the ground in Haiti, the role of human rights norms emerged clearly. In September 1994, with U.S. troops watching nearby, Haitian military authorities brutally dispersed a group of Haitians who were engaging in pro-U.S. demonstrations. General John Shalikashvili publicly ordered in response that U.S. troops "may be authorized to intervene by the senior U.S. commander on the scene" if they witnessed "grave abuses that threaten the life of the victim."[212] Over one thousand U.S. military police were deployed and instructed for the first time to use force to protect Haitian citizens from Haitian police.[213] Thus, the mission sought to protect human rights through the provision of security and monitoring of abuses.

President Clinton also inherited the Balkan wars from President George H. W. Bush. Clinton's strategy was always to pursue a diplomatic solution over a military one. In the debates over whether and how intervention should proceed in Bosnia in 1995, Pentagon resistance successfully limited the involvement of U.S. troops to such matters as behind-the-scenes training of local troops, and policing the no-fly zone over Bosnia-Herzegovina. It took the massacre of more than 7,500 Bosnian men in Srebrenica on July 12, 1995, for the United States to engage in airstrikes against Bosnian Serb targets.[214] Then, once the bombing began, the Pentagon did everything it could to end it. In his book reflecting on his experiences as chief negotiator, Richard Holbrooke explains that "the military did not like to put their pilots at risk in pursuit of a limited political objective, hence their desire to end the bombing as soon as possible."[215]

Only after negotiations in Dayton promised to bring an end to the war did Clinton commit to a sizable U.S. presence in Bosnia. As part of the Dayton Peace Accords, he agreed to send some twenty thousand U.S. troops to the NATO Implementation Force in Bosnia-Herzegovina.[216] Their role, however, was limited. The Pentagon obstructed Holbrooke's attempts to make the disarmament of assault weapons an obligatory, rather than optional, part of the Dayton Accords.[217] Thus, without a firmer mandate, U.S. peacekeeping troops rarely attempted to disarm forcibly paramilitary forces. Shalikashvili, chairman of the joint chiefs of staff, told a television audience, "Our terms of engagement do not require police actions or to find arms in homes or clandestine locations."[218]

Kosovo Albanians had been watching the Bosnian peace process from the sidelines, having been excluded from the Dayton negotiation process despite their demands for a comprehensive regional solution.[219] Many Kosovo Albanians grew impatient with their campaign of "passive resistance" to Serb aggression and instead supported a new tactic of more aggressive and armed resistance, with the Kosova Liberation Army (KLA) emerging as the vanguard by the end of 1997. In the hot spring of 1998, fifty-one members of an Albanian family were killed by Serb forces in retaliation for KLA provocation. U.S. Secretary of State Madeleine Albright immediately condemned the attacks, warning, "We are not going to stand by and watch Serbian authorities do in Kosovo what they can no longer get away with in Bosnia."[220]

In June 1998, NATO staged practice bombing raids in Albania and Macedonia in an attempt to induce Milosevic to back down. Milosevic called NATO's bluff: in the summer of 1998, Serb forces began a scorched-earth policy of destroying whole villages.[221] Up to 300,000 people were internally displaced from their homes in this stage of the conflict and several thousand others fled to neighboring Albania and Macedonia, as well as to destinations farther into Europe and abroad.[222]

In October 1998, U.S. Special Envoy Richard Holbrooke negotiated an agreement with Serbian president Slobodan Milosevic to decrease Serb forces in Kosovo and to allow two thousand unarmed "verifiers" into the territory under the control of the Organisation for Security and Cooperation in Europe. The United Nations Security Council issued a resolution "welcoming" the October agreement and "demand[ing] immediate action from the authorities of the Federal Republic of Yugoslavia and the Kosovo Albanian leadership to cooperate with international efforts to improve the humanitarian situation and to avert the impending humanitarian catastrophe."[223] The verifiers were deployed, but Milosevic reneged on his agreement to reduce his forces in Kosovo. Despite the presence of the international verifiers, sporadic fighting continued.[224]

The turning point for many U.S. diplomats was in January 1999, when Serb forces killed forty-one civilians in the Kosovo village of Racak.[225] Over the attempts of Serb authorities to block international war crimes investigators from entering Serbia, the efforts of international forensic specialists managed to investigate the incident. They found that the dead were indeed civilians, not KLA troops as claimed by Serbian officials. The KLA retaliated and the fighting escalated.

In March 1999, a group of nations—"the contact group" (the United States, Britain, France, Germany, Italy, and Russia)—brought Kosovar and Serbian negotiators together in Rambouillet, France. The message was clear: sign the agreement or be bombed. All international verifiers were pulled out of Kosovo in preparation for the threatened bombing. Meanwhile, Serb forces and heavy weapons flooded into Kosovo. U.S. Special Envoy Richard Holbrooke continued to meet with Milosevic, but the Serbian leader refused to sign the Rambouillet agreement. On March 23, 1999, Operation Allied Force in Kosovo began as NATO war planes commenced military air operations and missile strikes against targets in Serbia proper, Montenegro, and Kosovo.

The Clinton administration considered but refused to base its actions in Kosovo solely on humanitarian grounds. Instead, the administration, like other international leaders who have intervened in nation states in the past,[226] offered an array of justifications. Although humanitarian concerns were included "because we care about saving innocent lives,"[227] they were rolled together with other factors, most prominently: (1) the need for regional stabilization, or in Clinton's words, "because our children need and deserve a peaceful, stable, free Europe";[228] (2) national security concerns relating to a long war and a large refugee flow, "because we have an interest in avoiding an even crueler and costlier war;"[229] and (3) the need to protect NATO's reputation, because looking the other way "would discredit NATO, the cornerstone on which our security has rested for 50 years."[230] As Clinton explained these factors to the nation in his first public address on NATO intervention in Kosovo, he emphasized the United States' economic and security concerns, not humanitarianism: "[I]f America is going to be prosperous and secure, we need a Europe that is prosperous, secure undivided and free. . . . That is why I have supported the political and economic unification of Europe. That is why we brought Poland, Hungary and the Czech Republic into NATO, and redefined its missions."[231]

One Clinton staffer who helped craft the "mutually reinforcing factors for intervention" in Kosovo explained that the president was deliberately vague: "We tried to make sure that any [intervention] decision was as narrow as possible. We did not want to establish a new doctrine."[232] The idea, said another Clinton staffer, was to craft such a long and specific list of reasons for the intervention that no case in the future could possibly meet the criteria.[233] By framing the problem partially in human rights terms,[234] the administration made human rights solutions part of the range of available policy options. Although human rights were one set of concerns out of many motivating the U.S. military action in Kosovo, they were prominent in the rhetoric surrounding the initial decision to become involved,[235] as well as the decision to stay on as peacekeepers afterward.[236] After the strikes began, Defense Secretary William Cohen and Chairman of the Joint Chiefs of Staff General

Hugh Shelton went on the major television networks to justify the military action in human rights terms.[237] During the Kosovo bombing, military spokespersons similarly went out of their way to stress that they were doing all they could to limit injury to civilians, and thus to stay within the bounds of international humanitarian law.[238] For her part, Secretary of State Madeleine Albright championed human rights as the major motivator of intervention: "Developing a real democracy in the Federal Republic of Yugoslavia is crucial. And America has a fundamental interest in seeing the rule of law upheld, human rights protected and justice done."[239] In Clinton's speech announcing the beginning of the bombing of Kosovo, the primary justifications he cited included protecting innocent lives, avoiding an even crueler and more costly war on NATO's doorstep, and ensuring peace and stability in a free Europe.[240] Significant evidence exists, however, that the United States was also thinking about protecting its investment in Bosnia.[241]

The military was initially reluctant to intervene to protect ethnic Albanians from Serb oppression.[242] Pentagon officials argued that intervention was not in the United States' "vital" interests because, unlike in Bosnia five years earlier, these developments were occurring within Serbia's sovereign borders and did not threaten NATO stability.[243] They also doubted the efficacy of air strikes in achieving U.S. political objectives.[244] Although not successful in preventing the war entirely, the Pentagon was successful in convincing Clinton to refrain from any use of ground troops.[245]

The decision of the allied air forces to bomb from high enough to be out of range of Serbian antiaircraft weapons while also refraining from mounting a ground campaign for fear of casualties came under attack from critics inside and outside the military. In one provocative critique, West Point professors Don Snider and Major John Nagl wrote, "To our understanding these [high flying] tactics, driven by Alliance and domestic political considerations, were more designed to preserve soldiers' and aviators' lives than to rapidly and effectively accomplish the mission, thus allowing more civilian casualties than would have otherwise been the case."[246] Snider and Nagl contend that "[b]y not using Apache helicopters, A-10's or NATO ground troops to destroy Serbian military capacity, NATO forces failed to take risks they should have taken." The failure to take risks prolonged the war, and improperly shifted the risk to civilians, increasing civilian casualties. "By not taking the risks necessary to destroy Serb tanks and other military and paramilitary forces," Snider and Nagl argue, "NATO forces did not diminish the Serb capability to carry out their brutal policies. By aiming at Serbian infrastructure and military bases (resorting to the WWII strategy of attrition), NATO forces failed to stop the continued slaughter of innocent civilians, and, as some have argued, might have accelerated it."[247]

The general public was unaware that the military was having its own internal debate on the legality and morality of the Kosovo tactic of flying high. During the Kosovo bombing, military spokespersons stressed that they were doing all they could to limit injury to civilians, and thus to stay within the bounds of international humanitarian law.[248] And after the campaign ended,

Defense Secretary Cohen justified the action by reference to the humanitarian crisis: "We knew that to stand on the sidelines as a witness to the unspeakable horror that was about to take place, affect the peace and stability of NATO countries was simply unacceptable."[249] He added, "This was a fight over values. It's a fight against ethnic and religious hatred, lack of tolerance for others, and the right to live in peace. The United States and NATO used force as a last resort and only after Milosevic refused to respond to diplomatic initiatives."[250]

The Kosovo campaign gave shape to what military commentators have identified as the Clinton Doctrine on intervention: "morals and values as much as geopolitics play a key role [in decision making surrounding intervention]." David Jablonsky asserts that in the Kosovo campaign "every cruise missile and bomb in that conflict [was] aimed not only at destroying the Serbian national will, but also at demolishing the idea that leaders could commit criminal acts so long as they acted in their country."[251] At the conclusion of the Kosovo bombing, President Clinton, appearing before victorious NATO troops in Macedonia, announced that the universal condemnation of gross human rights abuses would be applied in the future "whether within or beyond" the borders of a state.[252]

A NEW ERA OF WAR

The new millennium not only heralded a new American presidential administration but a new kind of war. With the attacks on the World Trade Center and the Pentagon, American foreign policy took on a new direction: preemptive deployment. The idea that the United States can act militarily against perceived threats preserves a role,[253] albeit a contorted one, for a humanitarian intervention.[254] As the administration of George W. Bush discovered, reference to "human rights" could provide moral justifications for new military engagements that were on questionable legal footing. Thus, although remaining true to his reluctance to invoke the term *human rights*, the administration did instrumentally use human rights ideas in both Afghanistan and Iraq.

For example, in explaining the goals behind bombing Afghanistan in October 2001, Defense Secretary Rumsfeld explained that the U.S. military action in Afghanistan was part of a long tradition of U.S. humanitarianism: "The United States has organized armed coalitions on several occasions since the cold war for the purpose of denying hostile regimes the opportunity to oppress their own people and other people," explained Rumsfeld. "In Kuwait, in Northern Iraq, in Somalia, Bosnia, and Kosovo the United States took action on behalf of Muslim populations against outside invaders and oppressive regimes. The same is true today. We stand with those Afghans who are being oppressed by a regime that abuses the very people it purports to lead and that harbors terrorists who have attacked and killed thousands of innocents around the world of all religions, of all races, and of all nationalities."[255]

Just prior to the beginning of operations in Afghanistan, Powell held open the possibility of the Taliban receiving humanitarian aid if they handed over Osama bin Laden.[256] The White House expressed a deep interest in the human rights of women and children as it commenced bombing, purportedly in their name. "As we strike military targets, we'll also drop food, medicine and supplies to the starving and suffering men and women and children of Afghanistan."[257] President Bush promised to create "[a]n Afghanistan that is prosperous, democratic, self-governing, market-friendly, and respectful of human rights."[258]

As the bombing in Afghanistan began, General Richard Myers, chairman of the joint chiefs of staff, invoked humanitarian concerns, declaring that "these efforts are designed to disrupt and destroy terrorist activities in Afghanistan and to set the conditions for future military action as well as to bring much-needed food and medical supplies to the people of Afghanistan."[259] The campaign was trumpeted as evidence that "pinpoint airpower had come of age."[260] Responding to criticisms over civilian deaths from the U.S. bombing, Defense Secretary Rumsfeld suggested that any harm done to civilians was more than outweighed by the harm committed by the Taliban against its own people, which he described in humanitarian terms. In an interview on CNN, Rumsfeld commented that "what [the Taliban and al Qaeda] have done to the people of Afghanistan is a tragedy. . . . It is truly a tragedy. And our hope is that it can end soon and that the Afghan people can be cared for and assisted. It's not an accident that the United States of America [had given] something like $170 million for food assistance to Afghanistan well before September 11th. We do care about the people of that country."[261] In a speech shortly after the attacks and food drops began, U.S. Undersecretary of State for Global Affairs Paula Dobriansky explained the policy in human rights terms, urging that "[c]ompassion is an integral component of President George W. Bush's foreign policy, and it motivates America, even in these trying times, to continue to lead the international effort to provide humanitarian relief to those most vulnerable." She credited the policy of feeding the hungry with advancing U.S. interests: "The provision of food and medical supplies will reduce illness and mortality. Stabilizing the situation and facilitating a return to normal life will create the conditions under which longer-term development problems can at last be addressed. That process will remove openings that extremist groups otherwise would exploit. So humanitarian assistance to Afghanistan also serves as a vital tool in our overall fight against terrorism."[262]

This instrumentalist motivation for providing humanitarian relief was further elucidated by Colin Powell. As Patrick Tyler has noted, "A decision to occupy Kabul and perhaps other cities liberated from the Taliban would serve a twofold purpose of blunting a humanitarian disaster that Secretary Powell said was already in the making [in] the drought- and war-stricken nation, but would also serve to show the rest of the country, still under Taliban control, that the overthrow of the current regime would bring immediate rewards in the form of food supplies, reconstruction aid and stability."[263]

The air drops of food were criticized on a number of grounds. They were widely viewed as merely symbolic and therefore making little progress toward feeding an estimated 7.5 million hungry Afghans.[264] A related concern was that the U.S. operation was damaging the effectiveness of humanitarian aid delivery in Afghanistan while jeopardizing future relief efforts. The president of Medicins sans Frontieres, Morten Rostrup, charged: "Those food drops are a superficial and misleading gesture. Decisions on humanitarian intervention should be based on needs alone, independent of military or political objectives. Otherwise those Afghans in greatest need of food and medical assistance will go without. If the military is involved in delivering humanitarian assistance, the aid can be regarded by opponents as an act of war. If humanitarian action is seen as partisan, aid and aid workers can be denied access to people in need."[265]

When the color of the air-dropped food packs—yellow—was discovered to lure Afghanis toward unexploded bomblets from cluster bombs that were also, tragically, yellow in color, human rights advocates and the press howled. Human Rights Watch demanded a halt to the use of cluster bombs altogether, claiming, "They have proven to be a serious and long-lasting threat to civilians, soldiers, peacekeepers and even clearance experts.[266] While General Myers quickly acknowledged the potential for human disaster—"Unfortunately, they get used to running to yellow"—both he and Defense Secretary Rumsfeld said they had no intention to stop dropping cluster bombs due to their usefulness in attacking masses of troops. As a conciliatory measure, they pledged to change the food packaging color from yellow to blue.[267]

With respect to Iraq, the Bush administration also used the human rights card as it suited U.S. objectives. Before the conflict began, Bush framed the conflict in human rights terms, attesting, "America believes that all people are entitled to hope and human rights, to the non-negotiable demands of human dignity. People everywhere prefer freedom to slavery; prosperity to squalor; self-government to the rule of terror and torture. America is a friend to the people of Iraq. Our demands are directed only at the regime that enslaves them and threatens us. When these demands are met, the first and greatest benefit will come to Iraqi men, women and children. The oppression of Kurds, Assyrians, Turkomans, Shi'a, Sunnis and others will be lifted. The long captivity of Iraq will end, and an era of new hope will begin."[268]

When the bombing in Iraq began, the main justification for it was the existence of weapons of mass destruction.[269] When no weapons of mass destruction were found, emphasis was placed on both the "freedom" given to Iraq and the oppression of the Iraqi people under Saddam Hussein's leadership. "Every day Iraqis are moving toward democracy and embracing the responsibilities of active citizenship," Bush proclaimed. "Every day life in Iraq improves as coalition troops work to secure unsafe areas and bring food and medical care to those in need. America pledged to rid Iraq of an oppressive regime, and we kept our word."[270]

This instrumental and partial commitment to human rights was joined by an equally halfhearted commitment to peacekeeping in Afghanistan and Iraq.

Bush's antipeacekeeping inclinations were made clear from the beginning of his administration, in his withdrawal of American NATO troops from southeastern Europe.[271] In 2000, National Security Adviser Condoleeza Rice had called for a "new division of labor" between the U.S. and European militaries, in which the United States would fight wars and the Europeans would take care of the postconflict peace operations. The Bush administration has largely tried to stick to this arrangement even as the engagement in Afghanistan and Iraq poses new challenges to Rice's original plan. Ivo Daalder and James Lindsay have observed, "Nothing in the events of Sept. 11 appear to have diminished the White House's hostility toward using U.S. troops as peacekeepers." Key officials have acknowledged that the United States must not repeat the mistake it made in 1989 when it walked away from Afghanistan after the Soviet Union's defeat. However, they have steadfastly opposed committing any U.S. forces to help stabilize Afghanistan. As Rice said, "There's nothing wrong with nation-building, but not when it's done by the American military."[272]

The Bush administration's "hit and run" nation building has been accomplished on a shoestring. The administration budgeted absolutely nothing for the rebuilding of Afghanistan in the January 2003 budget submitted to Congress,[273] though ultimately Congress appropriated $295 million and estimates in 2003 by experts involved in Afghanistan's nation-building efforts felt that $14 billion might be more of an appropriate figure.[274] The Iraq rebuilding effort is well financed, though equally controversial. The Bush administration awarded a ten-year contract to the Halliburton Company,[275] with no lid on the costs (estimates are upwards of $8 billion) to put out the fires on oil fields in Iraq and to repair them to their pre-1991 functioning conditions. The United States was instrumental in "unfreezing" Iraqi assets and gaining UN approval for lifting sanctions against Iraq, all of which are contributions to the rebuilding of the country.

A LITTLE FINGER-POINTING?

The problem is not the military, it is the civilians. The military does not act [in response to human rights abuses] because the civilians have not decided what they want.

—Dana Priest, *Washington Post* correspondent on military and national security issues, in an interviw with the author

What matters in all these interventions is what will it cost me in terms of time, resources and risk. These are all civilian decisions. But I am the one who has to make it work.

—Anonymous U.S. military officer, in an interview with the author

This overview of recent U.S. military actions shows the prevalence of human rights rhetoric as justification for deployment. It also reveals the many influences over the way the military goes about its business. Civilians determine when and where, and to some extent how, the military should act. Ultimately, of course, the decision of when to go to war is not in the hands of the military, but rather is the responsibility of the president of the United States, in his capacity as commander in chief. Struggles between the White House and the Pentagon on intervention decisions are common. In the post–Cold War era, this has most often involved a cautious military trying to hold back a more interventionist-minded president.

Congress also plays a tremendous role in constraining military decision making through its war powers as well as its "power of the purse."[276] The military must gain budgetary approval from the Congress for all of their programs. This process often leads to extensive argumentation to prove the need and legitimacy for humanitarian programs. In recent years, one scholar of congressional–executive interactions finds, "The executive branch has largely become the voice in favor of international engagement, at some expense to national sovereignty and free, domestic, democratic decision-making."[277] Congress has alternated between being the "voice against such engagement" and the "voice of ambivalence."[278]

Kosovo illustrates the recent pattern of congressional votes that partially, but incompletely, addresses the issue of authorizing war.[279] Before the bombings began, the House of Representatives approved a proposal to send U.S. troops to Kosovo as part of a peace accord.[280] After negotiations broke down and the bombing began, the Senate adopted a resolution in support of the action.[281] Then when U.S. public opinion continued to be ambivalent about the bombing, House Republicans invoked the War Powers Resolution to compel votes on whether to remove U.S. armed forces from the NATO operations.[282] Eventually, the House would approve appropriations for the U.S. role in the bombing.[283] Then, after the bombing concluded, the Department of Defense would submit a report to Congress justifying its actions.[284]

Once funding has been allocated for a particular purpose, the funding itself becomes a constraint. Budgets are difficult to refuse once they have become established. Examples of such programs include the Non-Lethal Weapons program, the Army's Peacekeeping Institute, and the African Crisis Response Initiative. The United States is now obligated to contribute roughly three hundred million dollars per year to UN peacekeeping activities, an amount that the United States has negotiated successfully with the UN to reduce. Congress may relinquish this amount begrudgingly and only after accumulating large debts, but nonetheless it cannot find the way to remove it entirely.[285] Similarly, once set in motion, civilian and military leadership have found it difficult to abandon new weapons programs, funding mechanisms, and training courses created for humanitarian purposes. The military's budget is equal to 40 to 45 percent of the defense spending of all nations on earth, totaling more than three hundred billion dollars per year.[286] To their credit, the military's requests for and use of congressionally approved funding has maintained significant budgetary support of programs that promote human rights through their outcomes.

Institutional reversals are difficult, but not impossible, as evidenced by the fate of the Pentagon's Office for Democracy and Human Rights. The office was created by Defense Secretary Les Aspin in 1993 to address issues of military assistance, training of foreign soldiers, U.S. peacekeeping policy, humanitarian aid, and human rights criteria for military cooperation with other countries.[287] However, Aspin's proposed director, Mort Halperin, was never confirmed by Congress, and when William Perry succeeded Aspin as defense secretary he quickly dismantled the "little State Department" that Aspin had created.[288] While some tension in gathering intelligence data may encourage national security, critics suggest that the analyses are based on seeking particular information to support political objectives, and that the announcements of particular information by political leaders (such as Defense Secretary Rumsfeld, in this case) undermines and neutralizes other information and throws off the public discourse.[289]

While often competition between the military and the executive branches of government and Congress can be a detriment to the overall functioning and achievement of the military, the trend in recent years has been more on the side of cooperation. Interagency and multilateral governmental cooperation is particularly significant on missions of humanitarian assistance and peacekeeping, where the trend in the past decade has been increasingly a group effort at problem solving. For successful peacemaking operations, the United States depends upon international agreements and needs plans that will maximize economic gains and minimize personnel and material losses.[290]

One institution that both influences and competes with the military is the Central Intelligence Agency. Senator Bob Graham, the chairman of the Senate Intelligence Committee, pointed out that while the Pentagon and the CIA often push different agendas, it is the duty of the CIA director, rather than a Pentagon official, to present a unified assessment of all views to the committee. In a recent example, the Pentagon competed with the CIA in information gathering in order to influence military actions. Through the encouragement of Secretary of Defense Rumsfeld, the military, in the fall of 2002, encouraged the Defense Intelligence Agency in the fall of 2002 to establish connections between al-Qaeda and the Iraqi government.[291] Questions arose from the general public as to the legitimacy of this information, though the public stir caused by Rumsfeld's announcement that al-Qaeda officials had recently held a meeting in Iraq was enough to swing the issue away from deep skepticism.[292] Still, critics of the maneuver questioned the integrity of the CIA for its potential secreting of the information when Rumsfeld had originally requested it, and further, they questioned the method as an information-gathering process that selects information based on desired outcomes.[293]

The general public may also act as a constraint on the military. When the U.S. public does support intervention, its support is contingent on U.S. command of the operation.[294] Although it is typically the job of the civilian leadership to justify intervention decisions, representatives of the U.S. military increasingly take the stage to explain their own motivations and rationales for specific actions. Through invoking the language of human rights and humanitarianism, they seek to shape the public image of "humanitarians" who are "in touch with America's desire to help" and "on the side of human rights."[295] Time and time again, military commanders testify about being overwhelmed by the magnitude of humanitarian crises and their compulsion to "do something" in response.[296] For example, the commander of U.S. Marines in Somalia, Lieutenant General Anthony Zinni, remembered, "On the Hill, I was challenged a few times about why we ever got involved in [Somalia]. Well, we get involved with this because we get asked to do it. . . . [But] I'll tell you what—I've walked the ground and seen a lot of dead children. I've seen a lot of people who have starved to death or have been brutally massacred alongside a road. And something inside me says, 'Maybe I shouldn't be doing this, but . . . I *want* to do it.'"[297]

The media's images portraying humanitarian disasters and foreign assistance in these situations has frequently been used to influence the way the public interprets a military action, and thus the popularity of the endeavor. In the United States, the public support for the Afghanistan war was enormously positive, not only because it was portrayed as a response to the September 11, 2001 attacks but particularly because of the media's highlighting of humanitarian issues.[298]

CONCLUSION

The U.S. military, like other bureaucratic organizations is traditionally resistant to change and resilient to outside pressures. But when its leaders want to change, or when outside pressures make change inevitable, they can do so with relative speed and efficiency. Table 2 summarizes some of this chapter's main conclusions with respect to the military's incorporation of human rights. There is substantial evidence of both the influence of human rights as well as the absence of influence.

On the positive side, the military is integrating into its identity the new roles it has been called upon to play in peacekeeping and humanitarian operations. While the military has always framed its mission in moral terms, these new roles lend themselves more readily to the incorporation of human rights as a standard feature in the way the military conducts its work, views itself, and presents itself to others. Military operations are often described in human rights terms and there has been a concerted public relations effort to project an image of a new, high tech, career oriented, and professional soldier—as opposed to the traditional and more one-dimensional warrior. In terms of operations, there is much emphasis on new training for peace and humanitarian operations and changes in the nature of missions to incorporate a host of new ways in which the military can serve the state, as well as a noticeable increase in the degree to which the military values service in peace operations.[299] Even in more traditional operations involving armed interventions and the use of force—whether purported to be for humanitarian or other reasons—much attention is focused on the use of new technologies that provide

TABLE 2

The U.S. Military's Incorporation of Human Rights

EVIDENCE OF HUMAN RIGHTS INFLUENCE		COUNTEREVIDENCE: LACK OF HUMAN RIGHTS INFLUENCE	
Representation of itself to itself has changed	Professional specialist Technical expertise Humanitarian Peacekeeper	Ambivalence about humanitarian missions	Lack of consensus among leaders on military involvement in humanitarian activities during wartime and in postconflict stages
Representation of itself to others has changed	Operations described in humanitarian and human rights terms Public relations presents image of new warrior	Operational limitations	Difficulty working multilaterally Technological limitations Risk aversion limits acceptable strategies
Military business has changed to leave an opening for human rights concerns	New technology—revolution in military affairs is restructuring military force to confront asymmetrical threats New weapons—precision-guided munitions—allow for carefully chosen targets while avoiding excessive collateral damage and civilian casualties New training for peacekeeping and other nonwarrior tasks and more attention to humanitarian and human rights law Nature of mission changed—the military is more involved in traditional policing activities and in postagreement reconstruction activities	Military resources used counter to human rights and humanitarian norms	Military training for human rights–abusing governments Arms sales to human rights–abusing governments Military opposition to International Criminal Court and Landmines Treaty Military opposition to nondiscrimination based on sexual orientation

weapons of greater precision, decreasing risk to civilians. All of these areas provide evidence of the influence on human rights.

Just as human rights norms have had an impact on military identity and behavior, so too have changes in the military had an impact on human rights. The military has indirectly bolstered human rights norms by framing their operations in human rights terms. The military has also supported human rights norms directly. From Bosnia to Iraq, the military now often plays a role in the direct on-the-ground work of upholding human rights. Military training programs and weapons have become increasingly important for military personnel to undertake nontraditional operations in line with international human rights standards.

Despite these shifts, several challenges to deep institutional and cultural change remain. Within the military there is a lack of consensus on many aspects of peacekeeping and humanitarian operations. Many military officers express concern that the military is already overburdened and that forces not engaged in combat lose critical combat readiness. Operational difficulties creating resistance to peace operations include historical difficulty working multilaterally, a more risk-averse attitude when it comes to humanitarian missions (which may arguably cause more risk to civilians) and technological limitations on weaponry such that even peacekeeping and humanitarian missions carry a risk for civilians. (After all, even the most high-tech weapons designed to limit civilian casualties still do cause civilian deaths.) "We do this peacekeeping stuff," one soldier on a peacekeeping mission in Bosnia confided, "but when it comes right down to it our mission is to protect ourselves and hurt the enemy."[300]

The changes in the military with respect to human rights should not be overstated. Nonetheless, by using human rights terms—at least sometimes—to define purpose or guide actions, the military does indeed play an important role in framing the debate about international problems and in making human rights arguments more socially available. It is clear that human rights ideas, to some extent, have been institutionalized in the U.S. military. This progress notwithstanding, as long as the civilians in command of the military use human rights norms in an exceptionalist manner, human rights will still have a way to go before they can be said to be "embedded," that is, having a taken-for-granted power of influence in the U.S. military.

ENDNOTES

1. George W. Bush, "President Bush Announces Combat Operations in Iraq Have Ended" May 1, 2003; available online at http://www.whitehouse.gov/new/releases/2003/05/iraq/20030501-15.html
2. Lieutenant Colonel Richard Lacquement, Jr., interview with the author, August 2003.
3. See Williamson Murray, "Does Military Culture Matter?" *Orbis* 43, no. 3 (1999): 28.
4. Theo Farrell and Terry Terriff, "Introduction," in *The Sources of Military Change: Culture, Politics and Technology*, ed. Theo Farrell and Terry Teriff (Boulder, Colo.: Lynne Rienner, 2002).

5. Ibid., citing Jack Snyder, *Myths of Empire: Domestic Politics and International Ambitions* (Ithaca, N.Y.: Cornell University Press, 1991).

6. See Snyder, *Myths of Empire*.

7. Anonymous interviews with the author.

8. Anonymous interviews with the author.

9. Anonymous interview with the author.

10. U.S. Army Special Forces homepage, http://www.goarmy.com/sf/flindex.htm.

11. U.S. Army website, http://www.goarmy.com/army101/index.htm.

12. For an excellent analysis of military policies and recruiting, see David R. Segal, *Recruiting for Uncle Sam: Citizenship and Military Manpower* (Lawrence: University of Kansas, 1989).

13. William Nash, interview with the author, August 2001; Jane Dalton, interview with the author, June 2001.

14. Soldiers in Kosovo, interviews with the author, spring 2002.

15. Michael Noonan and John Hillen, "The Coming Transformation of the U.S. Military?" *Foreign Policy Research Institute e-notes*, 2002; available online at www.fpif.org/enotes/military.20020204.noonanhillen.comingtransformationsmilitary.html.

16. Matthew J. Morgan, "Army Recruiting and the Civil-Military Gap," *Parameters* 31, no. 2 (2001): 101–17.

17. U.S. General Accounting Office report, quoted in Morgan, "Army Recruiting," 101.

18. Compare Samuel A. Stouffer, *The American Soldier* (Princeton, N.J.: Princeton University Press, 1949); and Martin Binkin, *Who Will Fight in the Next War? The Changing Face of the American Military* (Washington, D.C.: Brookings Institution, 1993).

19. Cynthia Enloe, *Maneuvers* (Berkeley and Los Angeles: University of California Press, 2000).

20. See Leoran N. Rosen, Kathryn H. Knudson, and Peggy Fancher, "Cohesion and the Culture of Hypermasculinity in U.S. Army Units," *Armed Forces and Society* 29, no. 3 (2003): 325–51.

21. Kim Field and John Nagl, "Combat Roles for Women: A Modest Proposal, "*Parameters* 31, no. 2 (2001): 74–88.

22. Ibid, 77.

23. Frank Del Olmo, "In War, Diversity Can Be a Lifesaver," *Los Angeles Times*, May 11, 2003.

24. Ibid.

25. Mark Saur, "Today's Recruits Reflect Brighter, Leaner Military," *San Diego Union-Tribune*, January 21, 2002.

26. Tim Collie, "The Civilian-Military Divide: Poorer Classes Serve Their Country While America's Elite Have Other Dreams," *Toronto Star*, November 27, 2001.

27. See, e.g., Adam J. Schiffer, "I'm Not *That* Liberal: Explaining Conservative Democratic Identification," *Political Behavior* 22, no. 4 (2000): 293–310.

28. See Ole R. Holsti, "A Widening Gap between the U.S. Military and Civilian Society: Some Evidence, 1976–96," *International Security* 23, no. 3 (1998–99): 5–42.

29. Volker C. Franke, "Generation X and the Military: A Comparison of Attitudes and Values between West Point Cadets and College Students," *Journal of Political and Military Sociology* 29, no. 1 (2001): 92–119.

30. Dalton interview.

31. Lacquement interview. Lacquement stressed that he disagreed warrior characteriza-
tion of the U.S. military: "Historically, warriors have been identified with fighting
simply for the sake of fighting." "This is not a manhood test," he said, "We are
professional soldiers—service members are also concerned with quality of life issues
and are moving toward a self-image as professional soldiers who may be called upon
to engage in a variety of tasks on behalf of the state." See also Captain Rosemary
Mariner, "Public Attitudes towards the U.S. Military," paper presented at the conference The Roles and Responsibilities of the U.S. Military in the New Millennium,
Women in Internatioanl Security Conference, Chicago, September 14–15, 2000; and
Franke, "Generation X."

32. Ronald Halverson and Paul Bliese, "Determinants of Soldier Support for Operation
Uphold Democracy," *Armed Forces and Society* 23 (fall 1996): 81, Laura Miller, "Do
Soldiers Hate Peacekeeping? The Case of Preventive Diplomacy Operations in Macedonia," *Armed Forces and Society* 23 (spring 1997); David Segal, "Constabulary
Attitudes of National Guard and Regular Soldiers in the U.S. Army," *Armed Forces
and Society* 24, no. 2 (1998): 535. Interviews by the author with peacekeepers in
2002 also support this conclusion.

33. Michael O'Connor, "GI Disinterest Is a Casualty in Bosnia," *New York Times*, January
4, 1998.

34. Openly gay men and lesbians still are not welcome. For the debate on homosexuality
in the military, see Elizabeth Kerr, "Homosexuals in the U.S. Military: Open Integration and Combat Effectiveness," *International Security* 23, no. 2 (1999): 5–39;
Charles C. Moskos, "From Citizen's Army to Social Laboratory," *Wilson Quarterly*
17, no. 1 (1993): 83–94; U.S. Senate Committee on Armed Services, Policy Concerning Homosexuality in the Armed Forces, July 20, 1993 (Washington, D.C.:
Government Printing Office, 1995).

35. Laura Miller and Charles Moskos, "Humanitarians or Warriors? Race, Gender, and
Combat Status in Operation Restore Hope," *Armed Forces and Society* 21, (1995):
615–37.

36. Tom Gjelton, interview with the author, June 2001.

37. Thomas E. Ricks, "The Great Society in Camouflage," *Atlantic Monthly* 278, no. 6
(1996): 24–29.

38. Charles J. Dunlap Jr., "The Origins of the American Military Coup of 2012," *Parameters* 22, no. 4 (1993): 2–20.

39. Peter Karsten, "The U.S. Citizen-Soldier's Past, Present, and Likely Future," *Parameters* 31, no. 2 (2001): 61–73; see also Eliot Cohen, "Twilight of the Citizen Soldier,"
Parameters 31, no. 2 (2001): 23–28, and the response to the same article in "Commentary and Reply" *Parameters* 31, no. 3 (2001): 1–23. See also John Hillen, "Must
U.S. Military Culture Reform?" *Parameters* 29, no. 3 (1999): 9–23.

40. American Military Culture in the Twenty-first Century (Washington, D.C.: Center
for Strategic and International Studies, January 2000).

41. Joint Vision 2020 (Washington, D.C.: U.S. Government Printing Office, June 2000), 8.

42. Sam C. Sarkesian, "The U.S. Military Must Find Its Voice," *Orbis* 42, no. 3 (1998):
423–37. See also John G. Ross, "The Perils of Peacekeeping: Tallying the Costs in
Blood, Coin, Prestige, and Readiness," *Armed Forces Journal International* 131
(December 1993): 13–17; James Warren, "Small Wars and Military Culture," *Society*
36, no. 6 (1999): 56–63; Major Mark L. Kimmey, "After the Deployment: The Impact
of Peacekeeping on Readiness," *Army*, (July 1999): 11.

43. Lieutenant General James H. Johnson, letter to Ancell R. Manning, August 10, 1993, quoted in Edward C. Meyer and Ancell R. Manning with Jane Mahaffey, *Who Will Lead? Senior Leadership in the United States Army* (Westport, Conn.: Praeger, 1995), 224; emphasis added. See also David Callahan, *Unwinnable Wars: American Power and Ethnic Conflict* (New York: Hill and Wang, 1997), 177.

44. General Maxwell R. Thurman, quoted in Ross, "The Perils of Peacekeeping," 17.

45. Vince Crawley, "What's Wrong with Keeping the Peace?" *Army Times*, May 22, 2000. Notably, many of those who agree are, like Clark, retired.

46. Nash interview.

47. The classic study on the American soldier and motivations to fight is Samuel A. Stouffer, *The American Soldier* (Princeton, N.J.: Princeton University Press, 1949). See also Charles C. Moskos Jr., *The American Enlisted Man* (New York: Russell Sage, 1970).

48. Earl H. Tilford, "Reviewing the Future," *Parameters* 30, no. 3 (2000): 148–52; Kim Field and John Nagl, "Combat Roles for Women: A Modest Proposal;" Eric S. Krauss and Mike O'Leary, "Utilitarian vs. Humanitarian: The Battle over the Law of War," *Parameters* 32, no. 2 (2002): 73–85.

49. Officer Personnel Management System Task Force, Officer Personnel Management System XXI Study, (July 1997), as quoted in Mathew J. Morgan, "Army Officer Personnel Management and Trends in Warfighting," *Journal of Political and Military Sociology* 29, no. 1 (2001): 119.

50. Abigail Gray-Briggs and Michael MacIver, "Preparing the War Fighter for the Sojourn to Peacekeeping," *Airpower Journal* 13, no. 2 (1999).

51. Ibid.

52. John C. Bahnsen and Robert W. Cone, "Defining the American Warrior Leader," *Parameters* 20 (1990): 24–28.

53. James Burk, "Military Culture," in *Encyclopedia of Violence, Peace and Conflict*, ed. Lester Kurtz (San Diego: Academic Press, 1999), 413–24.

54. Lacquement interview.

55. Brigadier General Morris J. Boyd, "Peace Operations: A Capstone Doctrine," *Military Review* 75 (1995): 22.

56. Sam C. Sarkesian, "Humanitarian Intervention: The Price Paid by the Military," *ORBIS* 45, no. 4 (2001): 557–68.

57. F.T. Liu, *United Nations Peacekeeping and the Non-Use of Force*, Occasional Paper Series (New York: International Peace Academy, 1992), 11.

58. Joint Chiefs of Staff, *JP 3-07.3*, Joint Tactics, Techniques, and Procedures for Peace Operations, February 12, 1999.

59. Joint Chiefs of Staff, *JP 3-07*, Joint Doctrine for Military Operations Other Than War, June 16, 1995.

60. Joint Chiefs of Staff, *JP 3-07.3*.

61. Ibid.

62. Ibid.

63. Ibid.

64. Boyd, "Peace Operations," 25.

65. Ibid.

66. Anonymous interview with the author, 2001.

67. Anonymous interview with the author, 2001.

68. Anonymous interview with the author, Kosovo, 2001.

69. Joint Chiefs of Staff, *JP 3-07.3*.

70. Graham Day, interview with the author, June 2001.

71. General Wesley Clark, "Testimony Before the U.S. Senate Armed Services Committee," Federal Document Clearing House [FDCH] Political Transcripts, October 21, 1999; see also Howard Olsen and John Davis, "Training U.S. Army Officers for Peace Operations: Lessons from Bosnia," United States Institute of Peace Special Report, October 29, 1999.

72. Tony Pfaff, *Peacekeeping and the Just War Tradition* (Carlisle Barracks, Penn.: Strategic Studies Institute, U.S. Army War College, 2000), 21–22.

73. *JP 3-07.3.*

74. See *JP 3.07.*

75. Matthew Cox, "Keeping the Peace Is No Easy Task: U.S Soldiers Try to Gain Control in Kosovo," *Army Times*, July 5, 1999; Dane L. Rota, "Combat Decision Making in Operations Other Than War," *Military Review* 76, no. 2 (1996): 24–6.

76. David T. Fautua, "Transforming the Reserve Components," *Military Review* 80, no. 5 (2000): 63.

77. Morgan, "Army Recruiting," 130.

78. Ibid.

79. Lieutenant Colonel N. Winn Noyes, "Peacekeepers and Warfighters: Same Force, Different Mindset" (Newport, R.I.: Naval War College, 1995), 1.

80. *JP 3-07.*

81. Anonymous member of the U.S. military, interview with the author, April 2001.

82. Brent C. Bankus, "Training the Military for Peace Operations: A Past, Present, and Future View," paper presented at the United States Institute of Peace Symposium on Best Practices for Training for Humanitarian and Peace Operations, June 25–26, 2001.

83. Ibid., 18.

84. Jim Lobe, *Army Peacekeeping Institute Sent Packing* (2002); available online at http://www.tompaine.com/feature.cfm/ID/5799.

85. Center for Strategic Leadership, Peacekeeping Institute; U.S. Army, March 23, 2001; available online at http://carlisle-www.army.mil/asacsl/divisions/pki/pki.htm.

86. Elizabeth Becker, "U.S. War Colleges Hone Peacekeeping Skills along with Fighting Reflexes," *New York Times*, August 6, 1999; see also Lobe, *Sent Packing.*

87. Center for Strategic Leadership, Peacekeeping Institute.

88. Lacquement interview.

89. Becker, "War Colleges."

90. James Dao, "Army Orders Peacekeepers to Sessions on Rights," *New York Times*, December 2, 2000.

91. Ibid.

92. Officers at Camp Bondsteel and Camp McGrath, interviews with author, April 2002.

93. See Glenn R. Weidner, "Obligatory Training in International Humanitarian Law in the United States Army," Memorandum, U.S. Army (2001); See also Brent C. Bankus, "Training the Military."

94. Kenneth Bacon, quoted in Becker, "War Colleges."

95. Anonymous interview with the author, 2003. It is important to note here that the entrants into the trainings are not directly be chosen by U.S. military officers but rather may come to the program by the invitation of their own countries. U.S. policy decisions, rather than direct decisions by the military on which countries to invite into the programs, are likely to play a significant role in the resulting candidates.

96. Federation of American Scientists, *U.S. International Security Assistance and Training* (2001); available online at http://www.fas.org/asmp/campaigns/training.html. This publication quotes Senator Tom Harkin as saying that he has seen "no evidence in my 24 years in Congress of one instance where because of American military involvement with another military that the Americans have stopped that foreign army from carrying out atrocities against their own people."

97. See School of the Americas Watch, http://www.soaw.org for more information.

98. Ibid.

99. Ibid.

100. Federation of American Scientists, *Security Assistance and Training*.

101. John M. Miller, "Congress Bans Military Training for Human Rights Violators," *East Timor Action,* press release, September 29, 1998; available online at http://www.etan.org/et/1998/september/sep22-30/29congre.htm.

102. Federation of American Scientists, *Security Assistance and Training*.

103. Project on Peacekeeping and the United Nations, *African Crisis Response Initiative: A Peacekeeping Alliance in Africa*, Council for a Livable World Education Fund, 2001; available online at http://www.clw.org/pub/clw/un/acri.html.

104. U.S. Department of State Office of International Information Programs, *Summary of the African Crisis Response Initiative*, 2001; available online at http://usinfo.state.gov/regional/af/acri/acrisumm.html.

105. Ibid.

106. Thomas K. Adams, "The New Mercenaries and the Privatization of Conflict," *Parameters* 29, no. 2 (1999): 103–16.

107. Ibid.

108. P. W. Singer, "Have Guns, Will Travel," *New York Times*, July 21, 2003. See also P. W. Singer, *Corporate Warriors: The Rise of the Privatized Military Industry* (Ithaca, N.Y.: Cornell University Press, 2003).

109. Singer, "Have Guns."

110. Ibid.

111. Deborah Avant, "Privatizing Military Training," *Foreign Policy in Focus* 7, no. 6 (2002).

112. Ibid.

113. Ibid.

114. Ibid.

115. Bruce Grant, quoted in Juan O. Tamayo, "Private Firms Take On U.S. Military Role in Drug War," *Miami Herald,* May 22, 2001.

116. Representative Jan Schakowsky, quoted in Avant, "Privatizing Military Training."

117. U.S. Army Website, http://www.goarmy.com.

118. Farrell and Terriff, "Introduction," 13.

119. Richard P. Hallion, *Precision Guided Munitions and the New Era of Warfare* (Australia: Air Power Studies Centre, 1995).

120. Ibid.; See also David Phinney, "Less Than Deadly Force: New World of Military Conflict Calls for 'Non-Lethal' Weapons," *ABC News*, May 10, 1999.

121. John Pike, "What's New with Smart Weapons," Federation of American Scientists, March 4, 2000; available online at http://www.fas.org/man/dod-101/sys/smart/new.htm.

122. Ibid.

123. For military points of view, see Stuart W. Bett, "Missiles over Kosovo: Emergence, Lex Lataof Customary Norm Requiring Use of Precision Munitions in Urban Areas," *Naval Law Review* 47 (2000): 115–75; see also Frederich Borch, "Targeting after Kosovo: How the Law Changed for Strike Planners," *Naval War College Review* 56, no. 2 (2002): 64–81.

124. Human Rights Watch, *Civilian Deaths in the NATO Air Campaign*, vol. 12, February (New York: Human Rights Watch, 2000), 2. For an endorsement of the air strategy in Kosovo, see Ivo H. Daalder and Michael E. O'Hanlon, *Winning Ugly: NATO's War to Save Kosovo* (Washington, D.C.: Brookings Institution, 2000).

125. David Jablonsky, "Army Transformation: A Tale of Two Doctrines," *Parameters* 31, no. 3 (2001): 43–62.

126. William Cohen, Hugh Shelton, and Chuck Wald, Department of Defense press briefing, June 10, 1999.

127. William Cohen, Department of Defense press briefing, February 7, 2000.

128. Anonymous interview with the author, Bosnia, April 2002.

129. Hallion, *Precision Guided Munitions*.

130. Anonymous interview with the author. For an interesting account of why Milosevic settled when he did, see Stephen T. Hosmer, *The Conflict over Kosovo: Why Milosevic Decided to Settle When He Did*, MR-1351-AF, prepared for the United States Air Force by the Rand Corporation, 2001; available online at www.rand.org/publications/MR/MR1351. For the military's assessment of the war, see Bruce R. Nardulli, *Disjointed War: Military Operations in Kosovo*, MR-1406 (Washington, D.C.: Rand Corporation, 2002); Benjamin S. Lambeth, *NATO's War over Kosovo: A Strategic and Operational Assessment*, MR-1365-AF (Washington, D.C.: Rand Corporation, 2001); and Scott A. Vickery, "Strategic Coercion in the Kosovo Air Campaign," (Washington, D.C.: Joint Military Intelligence College, 2000).

131. Anonymous e-mail correspondence with author, June 2003.

132. See also the issues raised in Eric Schmitt, "It Costs a Lot More to Kill Fewer People," *New York Times*, May 2, 1999; Michael Ignatieff, "The Virtual Commander: How Nato Invented a New Kind of War," *New Yorker*, August 2, 1999, 30–36; Stephen Biddle, "The New Way of War? Debating the Kosovo Model," *Foreign Affairs* 81, no. 3 (2002): 138–44.

133. William Broad, "Oh, What a Lovely War. If No One Dies," *New York Times*, November 3, 2002. Broad states that the earliest origins of NLWs go back to 1953, when the Central Intelligence Agency administered LSD to an employee, who met his death by subsequently falling out of a tenth-story window.

134. Center for Defense Information, "Non-Lethal Weapons: War without Death?" (Washington, D.C.: Center for Defense Information, 1995).

135. Anonymous senior military official, "Department of Defense Background Briefing on Non-Lethal Weapons," Defense Link, February 17, 1995; available online at http://www.defenselink.mil/news/Feb1995/x021795_x0217nlw.html.

136. See *Joint Non-Lethal Weapons Program History* on the JNLWD website, http://www.jnlwd.usmc.mil/Programs/History.htm.

137. Phinney, "Less Than Deadly Force."

138. Broad, "Lovely War."

139. See Center for Defense Information, "Non-Lethal Weapons"; also Phinney, "Less Than Deadly Force"; and Broad, "Lovely War." This last so-called soft-kill technology was used effectively in the airstrikes over Serbia in 1999 to cut off power for a few hours at a time to Belgrade. It was enough to disorient the Yugoslav military, but it posed minimal harm to civilians or the environment.

140. Center for Defense Information, "Non-Lethal Weapons"; Phinney, "Less Than Deadly Force"; see also Broad, "Lovely War."

141. Stephanie Gutmann, *The Kinder, Gentler Military* (San Francisco: Encounter, 2000).

142. See Center for Defense Information, "Non-Lethal Weapons"; and Jane's Information Group, *'Non-Lethal' Weapons May Have Significant Impact on International Law*, December 14, 2000; available online at http://www.janes.com/press/pc001214.shtml.

143. Broad, "Lovely War."

144. Center for Defense Information, "Non-Lethal Weapons."

145. Richard Garwin, *Nonlethal Weapons: Progress and Prospects* (New York: Council on Foreign Relations, 1999); available online at http://www.cfr.org/publication.php?id=3326.

146. Ibid.

147. See, e.g., U.S. Department of Defense, "Report to Congress: Kosovo/Operation Allied Force: After Action Report" (Newport, R.I.: Naval War College, 2000).

148. Interview with Lieutenant Colonel Jeff Walker, U.S. Air Force, May 2002.

149. See Nardulli, *Disjointed War*, and Lambeth, *NATO's War*.

150. The need to maintain cohesion within the alliance also added layers of review to the process. See U.S. Department of Defense, "Report to Congress: Kosovo."

151. Anonymous interview with the author. All anonymous interviews in this section took place in the spring and fall of 2001.

152. See Wesley K. Clark, *Waging Modern War: Bosnia, Kosovo and the Future of Combat* (New York: Public Affairs, 2001).

153. Bush, "Combat Operations in Iraq Have Ended."

154. Max Boot, "Sparing Civilians, Buildings and Even the Enemy," *New York Times*, March 30, 2003; see also Jeffrey L. Gingras and Tomoslav Rudy, "Morality and Modern Air War," *Joint Forces Quarterly* 25 (2000): 109.

155. Boot, "Sparing Civilians," 5.

156. Borch, "Targeting after Kosovo," 75.

157. Ibid, 75–76.

158. Human Rights Watch, "The Crisis in Kosovo: Civilian Deaths in the NATO Air War Campaign." (New York: Human Rights Watch, 2000); Amnesty International, "'Collateral Damage' or Unlawful Killings? Violations of the Laws of War by NATO During Operation Allied Force" (Washington, D.C.: Amnesty International, 2000).

159. Marc W. Herold, *A Dossier on Civilian Victims of United States' Aerial Bombing of Afghanistan: A Comprehensive Accounting [Revised]* (2002); available online at http://www.cursor.org/stories/civilian_deaths.htm.; see also "Afghanistan's Civilian Deaths Mount," *BBC News*, January 3, 2002. Mainstream media in the United States, however, cited civilian casualty estimates at just over one thousand in Afghanistan.

160. A comprehensive listing of civilian casualty count projects is available online at http://www.iraqbodycount.org.

161. Thomas W. Smith, "The New Law of War: Legitimizing Hi-Tech and Infrastructural Violence," paper presented at the International Studies Association Conference, February 20–24, 2001.

162. John J. Spinelli, "Peacetime Operations: Reducing Friction," in *QDR 2001: Strategy-Driven Choices for America's Security* (Washington, D.C.: National Defense University, 2001).

163. Ibid.

164. Ibid.

165. Quotes are all from various interviews with the author in Washington, D.C., 2001.

166. In December 1989 President Bush pointed to humanitarian concerns in justifying sending military troops to Panama, asserting, "General Manuel Noriega had declared a state of war with the United States and publicly threatened the lives of Americans in Panama." See Ved P. Nanda, "U.S. Forces in Panama: Defenders, Aggressors or Human Rights Activists? The Validity of United States Intervention in Panama Under International Law," *American Journal of International Law* 84 (1990): 494, quoting a statement by the president, December 20, 1989, Office of the Press Secretary, the White House.

167. Admiral David Jeremiah, quoted in Andrew S. Natsios, "Humanitarian Relief Intervention in Somalia," in *Learning from Somalia*, ed. Walter Clarke and Jeffrey Herbst (Boulder, Colo.: Westview Press, 1997), 78.

168. George Ward, interview with the author, July 2001.

169. Robert C. Di Prizio, *Armed Humanitarians* (Baltimore: Johns Hopkins University Press, 2002).

170. David Jeremiah, quoted in Di Prizio, *Armed Humanitarians*, 51, and in David Halberstam, *War in a Time of Peace* (New York: Scribner's, 2001), 251.

171. Halberstam, *War,* 251.

172. See, for example, "Pentagon Speaks about Operation Restore Hope," television interview, CNN, 1992.

173. Michael R. Gordon, "Mission to Somalia: U.S. Is Sending Large Forces as Warning to Somali Clans," *New York Times*, December 5, 1992.

174. CNN, "Pentagon Speaks."

175. Mark Thompson, "Mission Underlines New Scope of U.S. Military after Cold War," *Houston Chronicle*, December 5, 1992.

176. Robert Johnston, quoted in John Drysdale, "Foreign Military Intervention in Somalia: The Root Cause of the Shift from U.N. Peacekeeping to Peacemaking and Its Consequences," in *Learning from Somalia: The Lessons of Armed Humanitarian Intervention*, ed. Walter Clarke and Jeffrey Herbst (Boulder, Colo.: Westview Press, 1997).

177. Colin Powell, "U.S. Forces: Challenges Ahead," *Foreign Affairs* 71, no. 5 (1992/1993): 36, 39.

178. Thompson, "New Scope."

179. Ibid.

180. Henry F. Carey, "U.S. Domestic Politics and the Emerging Humanitarian Intervention Policy: Haiti, Bosnia, and Kosovo," *World Affairs,* 164, no. 2 (2001): 72–82.

181. Lawrence F. Kaplan, "Colin Powell's Out-of-Date Doctrine," *New Republic*, January 7, 2001.

182. Di Prizio, *Armed Humanitarians*, 50–51.

183. Michael R. Gordon, "Mission to Haiti: Military Analysis; Pentagon's Haiti Policy Focuses on Casualties," *New York Times*, October 6, 1994.

184. Statement by Zbigniew Brzezinski, reported on *The News Hour with Jim Lehrer*, PBS; quoted in R. W. Apple Jr., "A Domestic Sort with Global Worries," *New York Times*, August 25, 1999.

185. Madeleine K. Albright, "Yes, There Is a Reason to Be in Somalia," *New York Times*, August 10, 1993.

186. Karin von Hippel, *Democracy by Force: U.S. Military Intervention in the Post–Cold War World* (New York: Cambridge University Press, 2000), 70.

187. Ward interview.

188. See John A. Ausink, *Watershed in Rwanda: The Evolution of President Clinton's Humanitarian Intervention Policy,* (Washington, D.C.: Institute for the Study of Diplomacy, Georgetown University, 1997).

189. Eric P. Schwartz, "Tools of Engagement: Saving Lives, Restoring Community, and the Challenge of Humanitarian Response in U.S. Foreign Policy," United States Institute of Peace, September 24, 2002, 7; Eric Schwartz, interview with the author, 2001. Schwartz notes that the Clinton administration built on PDD-25 with two directives, Managing Complex Contingency Operations (PDD-56) and Strengthening Criminal Justice Systems in Support of Peace Operations and Other Complex Contingencies (PDD-71).
190. Albright, "There Is a Reason."
191. Ibid.
192. See Samantha Power, "Bystanders to Genocide," *Atlantic Monthly* 288, no. 2 (2001): 84–108.
193. Halberstam, *War*, 276.
194. Ibid. The UN had a small force in Rwanda before the United States became involved in the effort, and the UN commanders had information on the coordinated genocidal acts even before they occurred. Yet they did not get permission from their supervisors in New York to act preventively, primarily because of their fear, too, that Rwanda would turn out to be a situation akin to that of Somalia.
195. Ibid., 277.
196. Ellen Dorsey, "Human Rights and U.S. Foreign Policy: Who Controls the Agenda?" *Journal of Intergroup Relations* 22, no. 1 (1995): 5; see also Stephen Schlesinger, "The End of Idealism: Foreign Policy in the Clinton Years," *World Policy Journal* 15, no. 4 (1998–99): 37.
197. Di Prizio, *Armed Humanitarians*, 71–72.
198. Steve Vogel, "Rwanda Mission's Timing Vague; U.S. Task Force in Uganda Delays First Kigali Deployment," *Washington Post*, July 29, 1994.
199. Halberstam, *War*, 278–82.
200. Ibid.
201. David C. Hendrickson, "The Recovery of Internationalism," *Foreign Affairs* 73, no. 5 (1994): 28–29; see also David P. Forsythe, "Human Rights and US Foreign Policy: Two Levels, Two Worlds," *Political Studies* 43 (1995): 126–27.
202. Dorsey, "Human Rights," 6.
203. Hendrickson, "Recovery," 30.
204. Dorsey, "Human Rights," 6; see also Richard Haass, "The Squandered Presidency: Demanding More from the Commander-in-Chief," *Foreign Affairs* 79, no. 3 (2000): 136–40.
205. Von Hippel, *Democracy by Force*, 100; Robert C. Di Prizio, "Post-Cold War Humanitarian Interventions: What Motivated the Bush and Clinton Administrations?" paper presented at the International Studies Association 42nd Annual Convention, Chicago, February 20–24, 2001; see also Di Prizio, *Armed Humanitarians*.
206. Halberstam, *War*, 280–82.
207. Di Prizio, "Post-Cold War Humanitarian Interventions."
208. Von Hippel, *Democracy by Force*, 101 (citing *International Herald Tribune*, September 14, 1994).
209. Ibid., 103.
210. UN Security Council Resolution 940, 31 July 1994; available online at http://www.un.org/Docs/scres/1994/scres94.htm.
211. Von Hippel, *Democracy by Force*, 104.
212. Paul Hoversten and Judy Keen, "Troops Learn 'Specifics' on Intervention: Rules of Engagement Still a Case-by-Case Basis," *USA Today*, September 23, 1994.

213. John Marcus and Ruth Harris, "U.S. Sends Military Police; Aristide Thanks Clinton, Carter; Scenes of Violence Prompt a Shift in Troop Policy," *Washington Post*, September 22, 1994.

214. Anthony Deutsch, "Ex-Yugoslav President Backs Milosevic," *Miami Herald*, June 17, 2003.

215. Richard Holbrooke, *To End a War* (New York: Random House, 1998), 145.

216. "Bosnia and Herzegovina-Croatia-Yugoslavia: General Framework Agreement for Peace in Bosnia and Herzegovina with Annexes," *International Legal Materials* 35 (1995): 75; and "Annex 1-A, Agreement on the Military Aspects of the Peace Settlement," *International Legal Materials* 35 (1996): 92.

217. Holbrooke, *To End a War*, 222. One anonymous Department of Defense analyst contends that removing assault weapons has never really worked, and that it is nearly impossible to remove assault weapons without a full and intrusive occupation. E-mail correspondence with author.

218. ABC Sunday Morning News, September 24, 1994.

219. One could argue that because Kosovo was at that time part of Yugoslavia, it was part of the negotiations. Yet no one could assert with a straight face that Kosovar Albanian claims were or could be represented by the Serb negotiators in Dayton.

220. Michael Peter Smith and Luis Eduardo Guarnizo, *Transnationalism from Below* (New Brunswick, N.J.: Transaction, 1998).

221. See Human Rights Watch, "Federal Republic of Yugoslavia: Humanitarian Law Violations in Kosovo," October 1998; available online at http://www.hrw.org/reports98/kosovo/; see also Physicians for Human Rights, "Action Alert: Kosovo Crisis; Aid in the Balkans," August 1998; available online at http://www.phrusa.org/campaigns/kosovo.html (reporting extensively about the "intensive systematic destruction and ethnic cleansing of villages by Serb police"); and Physicians for Human Rights, "Medical Group Recounts Individual Testimonies of Human Rights Abuses in Kosovo," June 24, 1998; available online at http://www.phrusa.org/research/kosovo2.html (reporting "serious human rights violations, including detentions, arbitrary arrests, violent beatings and rape, throughout Kosovo during the past six months").

222. This is the estimate of the UN Office for the Coordination of Humanitarian Affairs; see Relief Web, 1999; available online at www.reliefweb.int/w/rwb.nsf.

223. United Nations Security Council, Resolution 1203.

224. Human Rights Watch, "Federal Republic of Yugoslavia: Humanitarian Law Violations in Kosovo," October 1998; available online at http://www.hrw.org/reports98/kosovo/.

225. Human Rights Watch, "Human Rights Watch Investigation Finds: Yugoslav Forces Guilty of War Crimes in Racak, Kosovo," January 29, 1999; available online at http://www.hrw.org/hrw/press/1999/jan/yugo-prs.htm; see also Human Rights Watch, "A Week of Terror in Drenica," 1999; available online at http://www.hrw.org/hrw/reports/1999/kosovo/ (documenting violations of international humanitarian law during the last week of September 1998).

226. Sean D. Murphy's review of incidents of intervention demonstrates that "government officials of the intervening state (rightly or wrongly) based the legality of that state's action on one or more other reasons." See Murphy, *Humanitarian Intervention: The United Nations in an Evolving World Order* (Philadelphia: University of Pennsylvania Press, 1996).

227. "Address to the Nation on Airstrikes against Serbian Targets in the Federal Republic of Yugoslavia (Serbia and Montenegro)," *Weekly Compilation of Presidential Documents* 35 (1999): 516, 518.

228. Ibid.
229. Ibid.
230. Ibid.
231. Ibid.
232. Anonymous interview with the author, spring 2001.
233. Anonymous interview with the author, spring 2001.
234. Dana Priest, interview with the author, June 2001.
235. Some critics, both outside and within the military establishment, have questioned Secretary Cohen's assertions about the primacy of protecting innocent life, particularly with regard to relying solely upon air strikes rather than sending ground troops in to protect Kosovar Albanians. See, for example, Ancell and Manning with Mahaffey, *Who Will Lead?* and Chomsky, *The New Military Humanism*, 81. In response, General Shelton has argued that even if the United States had used ground troops in Kosovo, it still would have required several days of air strikes at the beginning of the campaign, and would therefore have allowed the Serb atrocities to continue. See Cohen, Shelton, and Wald, Department of Defense press briefing.
236. See "Interview by Cheryl Martin and Others," an interview with Colin Powell, BET, June 3, 2001; and Nicole Winfield, "Report on Rights Hails Kosovo, Trial of Pinochet," *Salt Lake City Tribune*, December 10, 1999.
237. Mary Dejevsky, "Assault on the Serbs: Clinton Team Launches a TV Offensive; Persuades America," *Independent*, March 29, 1999.
238. See Linda D. Kozaryn, *No Silver Bullet to Stop Serb Aggression*; available online at http://www.defenselink.mil/news/Mar1999/n03311999_9903311.html.
239. Madeleine K. Albright, "Remarks by Secretary of State Madeleine K. Albright at the U.S. Institute for Peace," 1999, 140.
240. "President Clinton's Speech from Wednesday Night" (regarding the onset of airstrikes over Yugoslavia). For the complete text of this speech, see http://www.s-t.com/daily/03-99/03-25-99/d08wn132.htm.
241. In 1995, for example, Secretary of State Warren Christopher testified before the House Committee on International Relations, "It is in our absolute national interest to maintain our leadership in the world by following through on the agreement that we reached in Dayton." See "Fiscal Year 2000 National Defense Authorization Act-United States Policy in the Balkans: Hearings on Authorization and Oversight before the House Armed Services Committee," 106th Cong. 722 (1999).
242. Bradley Graham, "Joint Chiefs Doubted Air Strategy," *Washington Post*, April 5, 1999.
243. Ibid.
244. Ibid.
245. John Barry and Christopher Dickey, "Warrior's Rewards," *Newsweek*, August 9, 1999, 40–41.
246. Don Snider and John Nagl, "Army Professionalism, the Military Ethic, and Officership in the Twenty-first Century" (West Point, N.Y.: United States Military Academy), available online at http://arlisle–www.army.mil/ssi/pubs/1999/ethic/ethic/pdf. citing "Foreign Policy: The ABC Club," *Economist*, May 22, 1999, 30–31; Michael Debbs, "Post-Mortem on NATO's Bombing Campaign," *Washington Post National Weekly Edition*, July 19–26, 1999, 23; and Paul Kahn, "War and Sacrifice in Kosovo," *Philosophy and Public Policy* 19, no. 43 (1999): 1–6.
247. Snider and Nagl, "Army Professionalism."
248. See Kozaryn, "No Silver Bullet"; see also U.S. Department of Defense, "Report to Congress: Kosovo."

249. William Cohen, speech at Norfolk Naval Air Station, April 1, 1999; available online at www.defenselink.mil/speeches/1999/s19990401-secdef.html.

250. Cohen, Shelton, and Wald, Department of Defense press briefing.

251. Jablonsky, "Army Transformation," 51.

252. Ibid.

253. Mary Ellen O'Connell, *The Myth of Preemptive Self-Defense* (Washington, D.C.: American Society of International Law Task Force on Terror, 2002). See also Nico Krisch, "Legality, Morality, and the Dilemma of Humanitarian Intervention after Kosovo," *European Journal of International Law* 13, no. 1 (2002): 323–35; and Michael J. Glennon, "The New Interventionism: The Search for a Just International Law," *Foreign Affairs* 78, no. 2 (1999): 2–7.

254. Kevin Murray, "Iraq: The Challenge of Humanitarian Response," *Foreign Policy in Focus* 3, no. 6 (2003).

255. Donald Rumsfeld, "Briefing on Enduring Freedom," Public Affairs Office Press Release, October 7, 2001, Embassy of the United States, Caracas, Venezuela; available online at http://embejadusa.org/ve/wwwh671.html

256. Steven Mufson, "Many Members of President's Crisis Squad Have Been There Before," *International Herald Tribune*, October 2, 2001.

257. George W. Bush, "Presidential Address to the Nation," October 7, 2001; available online at http://www.whitehouse.gov/news/releases/2001/10/20011007-8.html.

258. Jake Tapper, "The Last Place We Liberated," *Salon* April 10, 2003; quoting directly from "Rebuilding Afghanistan Fact Sheet," available online at http://www.whitehouse.gov/ovc/rebuild_afghan_factsheet.html.

259. Department of Defense press briefing given by Donald Rumsfeld and Richard Myers, October 7, 2001; available online at http://www.defenselink.mil/news/Oct2001/t10072001_t1007sd.html.

260. Eric Schmitt and James Dao, "Use of Pinpoint Air Power Comes of Age in New War," *New York Times*, December 24, 2001.

261. "Rumsfeld: U.S. Encouraging Taliban to 'Surrender or Change Sides,'" interview with Christiane Amanpour, *CNN Live*; available online at www.cnn.com/2001/US/10/18/ret.rumsfeld.interview/.

262. Paula Dobriansky, *Washington Post* editorial, October 17, 2001. See also "Feeding Vulnerable Afghanistan Is Major Part of Strategy," *International Herald Tribune*, October 18, 2001.

263. Patrick E. Tyler, "Taliban Power Ebbs in North," *International Herald Tribune*, November 13, 2001.

264. Marc Kaufman and Peter Finn, "Aid Experts Skeptical On U.S. Food Airdrops," *International Herald Tribune*, October 10, 2001.

265. Morten Rostrup, "'Humanitarian' and 'Military' Don't Go Together," *International Herald Tribune*, October 18, 2001.

266. Steven Mufson, "U.S. to Alter Color of Air-Dropped Food Packs," *International Herald Tribune*, November 3–4, 2001.

267. Ibid.

268. George W. Bush, "President Bush Outlines Iraqi Threat," October 7, 2002; available online at http://www.whitehouse.gov/news/releases/2002/10/20021007-8.html.

269. George W. Bush, "Remarks by the President at the United Nations General Assembly," September 12, 2002 (http://www.state.gov/p/nea/rls/rm/13434.htm); George W. Bush, "President Delivers State of the Union," January 28, 2003 (http://www.whitehouse.gov/news/releases/2003/01/20030128–19.html); see also Dick Cheney, "Vice President Speaks at VFW 103rd Convention," August 26, 2002 (http://www.white-

house.gov/news/releases/2002/08/20020826.html); and Paul Wolfowitz, "Deputy Secretary Wolfowitz Interview with Karen DeYoung, Washington Post," May 28, 2003 (http://www.defenselink.mil/transcripts/2003/tr20030528-depsecdef0222.html).

270. George W. Bush, "President Discusses the Future of Iraq," April 28, 2003; available online at http://www.whitehouse.gov/news/releases/2003/04/iraq/20030428-3.html.

271. Laura Neack, *The New Foreign Policy: U.S. and Comparative Foreign Policy in the Twenty-first Century* (Lanham, Md.: Rowman and Littlefield, 2003).

272. Condoleeza Rice, quoted in Ivo Daalder and James M. Lindsay, "Bush has an Obligation to Build an Afghan Peace," *International Herald Tribune*, November 24–25, 2001.

273. Tapper, "The Last Place."

274. R. Nolan and Michael Ignatieff, "'Nation Building Lite' in Afghanistan: A Conversation with Michael Ignatieff," *Foreign Policy Association*, October 24, 2002; available online at http://www.fpa.org/topics_info2414/topics_info_ show.htm?doc_id=126829.

275. Donald Rumsfeld, "Secretary Rumsfeld Interview with CNBC," July 15, 2002; available online at http://www.dod.mil/news/Jul2002/t07152002_t15cnbca.html.; Mark Gongloff, "Iraq Rebuilding Contracts Awarded," *CNN Money*, March 25, 2003; available online at http://money.cnn.com/2003/03/25/news/companies/ war_contracts/.

276. Gregory Fox and Brad Roth, eds., *Democratic Governance and International Law* (Cambridge: Cambridge University Press 2000).

277. Charles Tiefer, "Justing Sovereignty: Contemporary Congressional-Executive Controversies about International Organizations," *Texas International Law Journal* 35 (2000): 239–70.

278. Ibid.

279. See, generally, John J. Kavanaugh, "U.S. War Powers and the United Nations Security Council," *B.C. International and Comparative Law Review* 20 (1997): 159. For a detailed account of presidential–congressional interactions over the Bosnia deployment, see Charles Tiefer, "War Decisions in the Late 1990s by Partial Congressional Declaration," *San Diego Law Review* 36 (1999): 1, 9–16; see also Louis Fisher, "Congressional Abdication: War and Spending Powers," *St. Louis University Law Journal* 43 (1999): 931, 972–76 (noting Congress's failure to grant affirmative authorization for military activities in Bosnia).

280. 145 Cong. Rec. H1214, H1249 (daily ed. Mar. 11, 1999); Juliet Eiperin and William Claiborne, "Troop Deployment Narrowly Approved: With Clinton Away and Peace Talks Unresolved, House Debates U.S. Plan for Kosovo," *Washington Post*, March 12, 1999; Alison Mitchell, "In Vote Clinton Sought to Avoid, House Backs a Force for Kosovo," *New York Times*, March 12, 1999.

281. 145 Cong. Rec. S3118 (daily ed. Mar. 23, 1999); Miles A. Pomper, "Members Rally around Kosovo Mission Despite Misgivings about Strategy," *Congressional Quarterly Weekly*, March 27, 1999, 763; Eric Schmitt, "Conflict in the Balkans: On Capitol Hill, a Wary Senate Gives Support for Air Strikes," *New York Times*, March 24, 1999.

282. The resolutions pursuant to the War Powers Resolution were reported unfavorably to the House floor by the Committee on International Relations. See H.R. Rep. Nos. 115 and 116, 106th Cong., 1st Sess. (1999).

283. Pat Towell, "Congress Set to Provide Money, But No Guidance, for Kosovo Mission," *Congressional Quarterly Weekly*, May 1, 1999, 1036.

284. U.S. Department of Defense, "Kosovo/Operation Allied Force: After Action Report" (Newport, R.I.: Naval War College, 2000).

285. Brett D. Schaefer, *Keep the Cap on U.S. Contributions to the UN Peacekeeping Budget* (Washington, D.C.: Heritage Foundation, 2001). See also Stimson Center, "U.S. Funding for Peace Operations: A Look at the FY 03 Budget Request and Selected State Department Programs" (Washington, D.C.: Stimson Center, 2002).

286. These figures are based on a quote from historian Paul Kennedy, in Niall Ferguson, "Power," *Foreign Policy* no. 134 (January/February 2003): 18–24.

287. Michael R. Gordon, "Aspin Overhauls Pentagon to Bolster Policy Role," *New York Times*, January 28, 1993.

288. Art Pine, "On the Offensive: New Pentagon Boss Makes Big Changes," *Chicago Sun-Times*, March 13, 1994.

289. Patrick E. Tyler, "Spy Wars Begin at Home," *New York Times*, November 3, 2002.

290. W. Michael Reisman, "Preparing to Wage Peace: Toward the Creation of an International Peacemaking Command and Staff College," *American Journal of International Law* 88, no. 1 (1994): 70–79.

291. Tyler, "Spy Wars."

292. "In the Crossfire: Questioning Bush's Motives on Iraq," *CNN*, March 10, 2003 (http://www.cnn.com/2003/ALLPOLITICS/03/10/cf.opinion.garofalo/); Donald H. Rumsfeld, "Briefing by Donald H. Rumsfeld, Defense Secretary," September 26, 2002 (http://www.defenselink.mil/today/2002/to20020926.html); Iraq News Agency, "President Says Iraq Has Neither MWD or Links to al-Qaeda," February 6, 2003; (http://www.iraqwatch.org/government/iraq/ina/iraq-ina-hussein-020603.htm).

293. Tyler, "Spy Wars."

294. David Kaye, "Are There Limits to Military Alliance? Presidential Power to Place American Troops under Non-American Commanders," *Transnational Law and Contemporary Problems* 5 (1995): 399, 440–43.

295. Quotes are from members of U.S. military interviews with author, June–July 2001.

296. When military members were interiewed about their involvement in intervention, one of the most common phrases they used was *do something*, as in "We wanted to *do something* to help them." (Observation from the author's interviews with members of the U.S. military, June–July 2001.)

297. Anthony Zinni, quoted in Michael O'Hanlon, *Saving Lives with Force: Military Criteria for Humanitarian Intervention* (Washington, D.C.: Brookings Institution Press, 1997).

298. The Institute for War and Peace Reporting has an excellent archive of such news reports available online at www.iwpr.net/afghan_index1.html.

299. As Don Snider and John Nagl observe, "The decision in 1997 by Chief of Staff of the Army, General Dennis Reimer, to deploy one of the Army's premier heavy divisions, the 1st Cavalry Division, to peacekeeping duty in Bosnia can be seen as evidence that the senior leadership of the Army eventually accepted the importance of performing [peacekeeping] missions." See Snider and Nagl, "Army Professionalism."

300. Anonymous U.S. Armed Services member, interview with the author, spring 2001.

FOUR

RAISING EXPECTATIONS: CIVIL SOCIETY'S INFLUENCE ON HUMAN RIGHTS AND U.S. FOREIGN POLICY

A nongovernmental organization is any non-profit voluntary citizens' group which is organized on a local, national or international level, task-oriented and driven by people with a common interest. We are able to reach out to these groups for advice and my sense is that they have a very significant impact on foreign policy. Because we are a democracy, foreign policy decision-makers solicit the views and ideas of NGO representatives to help ensure that U.S. foreign policy represents a broad spectrum in the interests of the American people.

—Julia Taft, Assistant Administrator and Director of the Bureau for Crisis Prevention and Recovery in the UN Development Programme, in "An Interview with Assistant Secretary of State Julia Taft"

A new and unprecedented force has been created in world politics—the nongovernmental organization. NGOs have joined nation-states, central banks and international agencies as institutions authorized to define the world's problems and propose policy fixes.

—James Sheehan of the Competitive Enterprise Institute, in "Global Greens: Inside the International Environmental Establishment"

The young school teacher from rural Serbia was a bit afraid to venture into the university auditorium where the conference on the war in Bosnia was being held. She passed a small group of women wearing all black, standing on the side of the road, holding daisies and antiwar signs. Three "witches for peace" and a muddle of college boys in dreadlocks playing hacky sack were standing nearby. A former State Department employee in a dark suit, a Quaker in Birkenstocks, and a Gulf War veteran in sweatpants chatted near the coffee machine. A professor was running about trying to persuade everyone to go into the auditorium where a human rights worker was giving her report on Bosnia. "Who are these people?" the school teacher whispered to her companion. "This," the companion gestured with a wave of her arm, "is civil society."

The third group of actors influencing the treatment of human rights in U.S. foreign policy fits into the realm known as "civil society." Nongovernmental organizations (NGOs) are a part of civil society working on human rights issues, but other parts of civil society trying to shape the U.S. human rights agenda may be organized as for-profit consultancy groups, think tanks,[1] lobbyists, foundations, education programs, and academic institutions.[2] During the post–Cold War era, the agendas and strategies of organizations working on human rights issues have become increasingly sophisticated and diverse. And, as this chapter illustrates, civil society organizations influence U.S. foreign policy in ways that are often subtle, yet significant for the shaping and implementation of human rights. By framing issues in human rights terms, NGOs and other civil society actors seek to shape public opinion and influence policy options, ensuring that the human rights dimension of policy options are addressed. This chapter highlights cases in which civil society actors have had an impact on a range of U.S. foreign policy decision making related to human rights. It begins by surveying trends in the way U.S. civil society advances human rights and then turns to more specific illustrations. Finally, the chapter concludes with an acknowledgment that the influence of civil society actors on human rights and U.S. foreign policy remains inconsistent and incomplete.

WHO ARE THESE PEOPLE?

The members of civil society working on human rights issues are not so very different from the individuals, discussed earlier in this book, who work for the government and the military. In many cases, they are the same people, as individuals move frequently between posts in government and civil society, and increasingly retired military leaders find themselves joining think tanks and advocacy groups. Civilian and military leaders read the same books, debate the same issues, and increasingly meet in the same classrooms, where they often obtain the same advanced degrees from the same institutions. Although the culture of the armed services branches differs from that of government and civil society, the individuals involved in these groups share common motivations.[3] According to a survey of over 140 members of government, the military, and civil society conducted as background preparation for this book, the top 3 reasons military officers seek a post within the military are (1) to serve their country; (2) to gain professional training and expertise; and (3) to help people. Individuals in government and civil society list other motivating factors, but also among their top 3 motivators is a desire to help people (see Figure 1).

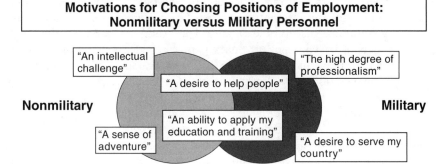

FIGURE 1 Survey respondents were asked, "What is the main factor that influenced you to take this position?" Respondents were asked to circle one of the following: (a) a desire to serve my country; (b) a sense of volunteerism; (c) my religious convictions; (d) a desire to help people; (e) a sense of adventure; (f) the salary and benefits; (g) the intellectual challenge; (h) the high degree of professionalism; (i) an ability to apply my education and training; (j) other. The above chart indicates the top 4 responses for military and nonmilitary personnel who responded to the survey. The data are based upon a total of 120 surveys.

The main factors that distinguish civil society from its peers in the military and government are not motivations or expectations—all of these groups hope to "do good"—but rather, perceptions and techniques. While each presidential administration has its own cast of civil society foes and friends, for the most part civil society organizations remain outsiders to policy making and implementation. The outsider positions permit them to see problems differently and encourage them to adopt different strategic politics.

CIVIL SOCIETY STRATEGIES

The strategic politics of nongovernmental actors, as Margaret Keck and Kathryn Sikkink have observed, is "rooted in values and aimed at changing values."[4] In the language of social movement literature, advocacy groups in civil society frame our ways of understanding and presenting the world that "underscore and embellish the seriousness and injustice of a social condition or redefine as unjust and immoral what was previously seen as unfortunate but perhaps tolerable."[5] Through the use of "specific metaphors, symbolic representations, and cognitive clues" civil society organizations "cast behavior and events in an evaluative mode and . . . suggest alternative modes of action."[6] While some organizations seek to frame issues to fit into existing policy agendas, others seek to prompt the creation of new agendas.[7] Some organizations thus create issues, while others interpret issues. The same organizations may also be involved in domestic or international human rights litigation as well as the direct drafting of legal instruments related to human rights, including international human rights treaties, peace agreements, and domestic legislation.

Strategies and tactics vary considerably among organizations. Gareth Evans, president of the International Crisis Group, has suggested three types of activity: thinking, acting, and doing.[8] The "thinking" organizations help focus the debate by engaging in "data gathering, idea generating, network building, paper publishing and conference organizing."[9] The "talking" or advocacy organizations also "engage in research and analysis, but their primary emphasis is on spotlighting governmental abuses and engaging in tom-tom beating advocacy accordingly."[10] The "doing" organizations address the problem even more directly, through such activities as training and general capacity-building programs, mediation and conflict resolution projects, and other peacebuilding endeavors. While some organizations today are a hybrid of these three activities (the International Crisis Group being the most prominent case in point), today these categories are generally maintained.

The most well-known tactic of human rights civil society has been that of "naming, blaming and shaming"—that is, naming human rights violations, publicly identifying the violators (traditionally a state, but increasingly a corporation or other actor), and shaming them into compliance by employing a public campaign (involving letter writing and other public acts of condemnation).[11] The "bedrock" of all human rights activity thus has involved the collection of credible information and its timely dissemination.[12] By investigating and publicizing human rights norms and, where possible,[13] advocating before treaty-monitoring bodies, human rights NGOs have been extremely influential in shaping domestic and international agendas on such matters as the environment,[14] land mines,[15] women's rights,[16] and human rights in general.[17]

This "watch" role of civil society, popularized by Amnesty International's letter-writing campaigns and Human Rights Watch's various "watch groups" for regions and topics, remains significant today. The efficacy of this tactic has improved as the technical expertise of the "watchers" has been strengthened and as communication technology has advanced.[18] Illustrating the enduring popularity of the "watch" template, the most recent entrant to the human rights civil society scene is a new watchdog group, NGO Watch, a conservative group watching progressive NGOs for their transgressions.[19] As will be explained further in this chapter, NGO Watch caused a stir when, in June 2003, it unveiled a new webpage publicizing the tax records and policy platforms of over two hundred NGOs.

Even as the "watch" campaigns have remained popular, civil-society actors have engaged in policy analysis and advocacy activities in addition to atrocity reporting. Early on, human rights organizations focused on "standard setting," that is, the establishment of the human rights standards by which the conduct of states could be judged.[20] They also began serving as ombudsmen intervening on behalf of "prisoners of conscience" and providing legal services and other support for victims and families of victims of gross human rights abuses.[21] They have advocated for the creation of systems and mechanisms to enforce human rights, at the international, national, and regional levels, and have pressed for greater NGO access to the working of those systems.[22] All of these efforts have had an impact on U.S. foreign policy, but it is the new strategies of more recent years that have targeted U.S. foreign policy specifically. These efforts have moved beyond public shamming techniques focused singularly on human rights to advocacy approaches that integrate human rights into broader public policy agendas and suggest long-term solutions to the roots of human rights violations as well as addressing the impact of their ongoing manifestation.

GREATER EXPERTISE/GREATER INFLUENCE

The ability of civil society to influence U.S. foreign policy has been advanced by the professionalization of the field and the increased mobility of individuals from the government sector to civil society. Today individuals working on human rights issues are likely to be former members of the Clinton administration or of other previous administrations, former State Department employees who quit in protest over U.S. policies, and former ambassadors and military officers, as well as individuals who cut their teeth working on humanitarian projects in Afghanistan, election monitoring in Bosnia, or the founding of the Truth Commission in South Africa. And the organizations they join are more likely to be highly sophisticated, and staffed with lawyers, area experts, lobbyists, advocacy teams, and recent graduates of new programs offering specific training in human rights. "Before, human rights NGOs were a conglomerate of the elite, but with grassroots and idealism as their guide," notes Martina Vandenberg, a former Human Rights Watch researcher. "Now they are a community of elite voyeurs with a few wild haired exceptions."[23] The age of e-mail and websites makes it even more possible for individuals or a small cadre of folks hunched over computers to have an impact on a human rights issue.[24] But even these individuals are likely to have elite training, and over time even they are likely to either join larger organizations or collapse.

One could think of three chronologically distinct generations of individuals in the United States working on human rights. Paul Wapner explains, "The first generation is comprised of people from the peace movement, who opposed what the U.S. was doing in Latin America, as well as some people working on political prisoners in the Soviet Union, general cold war stuff. The second generation is comprised of people who began doing civil rights work and other social justice work in the U.S. and then they crossed over to the international sphere and began working on their issues there. The third generation comprises people who don't know what human rights are, but they want to study the topic nevertheless."[25]

The resources of NGOs have ebbed and flowed along with the financial fortunes of the individuals and foundations that support their operations, leading to new projects and new personnel in good times, and belt-tightening layoffs and program cutbacks when the domestic and global financial picture soured. Yet throughout these three generations of human rights work, the training and expertise of individuals has steadily improved.

Tapping this expertise, human rights organizations now reach deeper into the U.S. foreign policy establishment and make new demands on the behavior of the U.S. government and military. In contrast to the technique of public shaming, these new efforts often involve private meetings and cooperative information sharing, the provision of concrete policy proposals, and the offer of technical assistance. The new generation of human rights advocates target their advocacy more precisely and work deeper within government structures, turning to particularly sympathetic ears wherever they may be—as long as they have influence over policy makers.[26] During the Clinton administration, for example, the ability of certain highly credible NGOs to obtain the ear of the Department of Defense, for example, increased. "They [the DOD] needed our information and we wanted to influence them," said one human rights advocate working on a sensitive military maneuver.[27] Another NGO employee who also spoke on the condition of anonymity added, "Our [the NGO's] ability to have access [to the DOD and other parts of government] collapsed with the [George W.] Bush administration, but we had already left an impression on them."[28]

NEW CHALLENGES

Even as greater acceptance within the foreign policy establishment presents new opportunities for human rights advocates, it also offers new challenges. "The question now for the human rights movement is how to deal with being part of the dominant discourse," observes Martina Vandenberg, "We see ourselves being spun [by the White House for their own advantage]."[29] As an illustration, she points to Human Rights Watch's report on civilian casualties caused by North Atlantic Treaty Organization (NATO) forces bombing in Kosovo. "We said there were 548 deaths and urged that this was way too many, and the Pentagon seized on this figure and said it was perfectly acceptable."[30]

Apart from the danger of being "spun" or otherwise used by an administration for its own ends, today's professional human rights organizations may be so far removed from human rights abuses that they can no longer identify with them. Catholic Relief Services' Jonathan Evans worries that "human rights has become so businesslike that it is losing its passion . . . we are emphasizing hiring young people who are well trained and interested in making a career out of this work."[31] To force everything into the narrow frame of one's profession blunts other understandings of the problem and often eclipses the original motivations for signing on to human rights and humanitarian work. This is particularly true with respect to the legal framing of human rights, Harvard Law School professor David Kennedy urges. "To come into experience of oneself as a benevolent and pragmatic actor through the professional vocabulary of legal representation has costs for the human rights advocate, compared with other vocabularies of political engagement and social solidarity." Kennedy explains, "Coming into awareness of oneself as representative of something else—heroic agent for an authentic suffering somewhere else—mutes one's capacity for solidarity with those cast as victims, violators, bystanders, and stills the habit of understanding the world one seeks to affect."[32]

Professionalism within the human rights field privileges lawyers "at the expense of priests, engineers, politicians, soothsayers and others who might play a more central role."[33] The greater expertise of the new generation of human rights staff tilts many organizations even further toward working only with other highly trained elites, ignoring parallel grassroots efforts to advance human rights. As a result, they deprioritize human rights education and other activities aimed at building a human rights culture.[34] Patrick Coy, a Kent State University political science professor who specializes in social movements, has found that new information technologies have made little difference in this regard. "Although technological changes have expanded human rights information campaigns to a general audience [primarily through e-mail]," Coy writes, "most information that human rights [organizations] gather is still aimed at policy elites, including governmental and intergovernmental officials, and the diplomatic community."[35] While human rights education projects like Human Rights Education Associates and the People's Movement for Human Rights Education have grown over the past decade,[36] they remain disconnected from mainstream human rights organizations and have little influence on U.S. foreign policy. The U.S. government may indirectly support human rights education as part of a postconflict peacebuilding and democratization effort, but "human rights education *per se* is never a top priority—and always among the first things to be cut [from government projects]."[37]

While human rights NGOs continue to target states for criticism, they often seek to work in partnership with states instead of against them. "In the past, U.S. [human rights] activists were concerned about preventing the U.S. from doing harm," Tom Malinowski, Human Rights Watch's Washington, D.C., advocacy director, observes. "Now, they are concerned about keeping the U.S. engaged and trying to construct nationally based international arguments to justify humanitarian activities."[38] The human rights implications of the "war on terror" (see Chapter 3) have "brought many human rights people back to criticizing government more," but still, human rights advocates seek to locate allies within government wherever and whenever possible.[39]

While *partnership* may be a buzz word in many human rights circles, whether and how the U.S. military should be viewed as a partner in advancing human rights concerns remains hotly debated.[40] Amnesty International has taken the position that human rights NGOs need not or should not involve themselves in debates about military interventions, because these are primarily political questions that are properly in the domain of governments and the United Nations.[41] The Geneva-based International Council on Human Rights Policy observes that "Amnesty's own position has been criticized from within the organization. . . . In cases of genocide—such as Rwanda, where influential governments refused to act—critics say that Amnesty's silence affects its credibility with activists and victims and may be used by governments to justify inaction."[42] In contrast to Amnesty's approach, Human Rights Watch determines on a case-by-case basis its position on whether to support military intervention on human rights grounds, considering the scale of abuses, whether nonmilitary means have been exhausted, and whether the intervention is likely to do more good than harm.[43] Based on these criteria, Human Rights Watch spoke out in favor of military intervention in Bosnia, Rwanda, and Somalia, but criticized NATO's intervention in Kosovo on the grounds that nonmilitary options had not been exhausted. Physicians for Human Rights, however, advocated for military intervention in Kosovo, leading the call for ground troops and a larger civilian monitoring contingent.[44]

Another challenge facing human rights NGOs in recent years is one of coordination with other nongovernmental actors. Increasingly, the mission and mandate of human rights NGOs overlaps with other nongovernmental and governmental organizations with humanitarian, development, and reconstruction mandates. In places such as Afghanistan in 2002–03, where the end of war was declared even as fighting continued, a host of human rights, humanitarian, development, conflict-resolution, and civil-society-building organizations crowded the field, at times with complementary, but often with contradictory mandates. This has led to duplication of efforts (for example, with most organizations working in the same urban areas to the neglect of rural areas) as well as heated disputes as to the sequencing and prioritization of efforts (for example, with some organizations claiming that human rights issues should be put on hold until other matters are accomplished, such as the true cessation of conflict, provision of emergency humanitarian assistance, or accomplishment of basic democratic institution building).[45]

To take one illustration of this challenge, humanitarian organizations, such as Mercy Corps and Catholic Relief Services,[46] address the provision of social and economic rights, and to the extent that they are committed to the protection of human life, they address civil and political rights as well.[47] Many humanitarian organizations work increasingly closely with governments—sometimes too closely, opening themselves up to criticism by human rights NGOs and other critics that they have become "cheap service providers" for the U.S. government.[48] "The more money they take from government, the more they lose their voice," worries veteran humanitarian aid analyst Ian Smillie.[49] At the same time, humanitarian aid workers, along with the democratizers, conflict resolvers, and peacebuilders crowding postconflict areas, are taken to task for prolonging the conflicts they seek to ameliorate.[50] The division of aid commodities to warring parties may fuel conflict and, though this result is not inevitable, it is fostered by the prevalence of "technical approaches" to humanitarian action. Fiona Terry, director of research for Medecins sans Frontieres, Paris, explains that where the focus of many humanitarians is on delivery of a certain amount of foodstuffs, "issues of a political or ethical nature are suppressed."[51] The provision of assistance in the postwar stage may also prolong conflict when the intervening organizations undertake functions typically reserved to the state, thus undermining the ability of local people to build their own government institutions to address their own priorities.[52]

Humanitarian organizations present another challenge to human rights NGOs wholly apart from funding. Because many of the organizations involved in humanitarian and postconflict activities are funded by and/or are perceived to be closely associated with the U.S. government, their activities shape the image of U.S. foreign policy and circumscribe its effectiveness in many conflict areas. When they ignore human rights issues, by themselves operating in a manner contrary to human rights standards (e.g., by discriminating in employment) or by overlooking local abuses, they undercut U.S. rhetorical demands for respect for international human rights standards.

U.S.-based humanitarian NGOs are increasingly dependent on U.S. government support. Thus, they face the challenge of fitting their plans into the agenda of the U.S. government, compromising just enough to get the money, but not too much so as to lose sight of their mission. Critics of this process, including many NGO staff members engaged in it, feel that they often fail to strike the right balance. "It's not the NGOs driving the government's agenda; it's the U.S. government driving the NGO agenda," attests one NGO staff member who preferred to remain anonymous.[53] The point that donor dollars shape NGO programs is well taken, but the influence runs in the other direction as well. NGOs are the idea people; as Ken Anderson notes, "In today's world, in matters from human rights to the environment to population policy to adventures in humanitarian intervention, the leadership and driving force behind policy often comes from international NGOs."[54] Once a government agency agrees to fund the project, it may be influenced in the long run by the type of project it begins to fund and the personal relationships those projects engender.

Individuals may move in and out of jobs, frequently transiting from civil society to government and back again, but the relationships remain. It is all about relationships, explains Search for Common Ground's Andy Loomis. "The real thing that needs to happen . . . is to build relationships between the various communities that often tend to be very skeptical of one another (e.g., policymakers, NGOs, academics, etc.)."[55] It is through the work in the field, Loomis notes, that such relationships are built. Because in recent years the leadership and staff of human rights organizations is comprised of people with prior experience in another field and/or sector,[56] they have the kind of extensive networks and relationships that can make them effective in influencing U.S. human rights foreign policy.

The remainder of this chapter turns to nine short case studies to explain how civil society organizations impact U.S. foreign policy with respect to human rights. The examples were chosen based on three criteria: (1) the issue profiled involves specific organizations who have some discernable impact on the application or formation of U.S. foreign policy (in Kathryn Sikkink and Martha Finnemore's terminology, they are "norm entrepreneurs"),[57] despite the difficulties of gauging the exact impact of civil society organizations;[58] (2) the example occurred during the time period under study in this book, with greater preference for more contemporary examples and unfinished campaigns; (3) examples were chosen from activities that generally have less information available, contributing a wider portrayal of civil society actions than has been available about their activities (and thus, the traditional "naming, shaming, blaming" campaigns, and well-publicized NGO activities such as those involving the International Criminal Court and the Landmines Treaty,[59] are excluded).[60] While this account omits several important developments in civil society—including participation in UN conferences, advocacy for truth commissions and tribunals, and developments within the humanitarian and conflict resolution fields, it does provide a range of illustrations of influence over human rights foreign policy. The first three case studies illustrate the role of civil society in framing policy choices in human rights terms and, specifically, in their influence over the creation, ratification, and implementation of international treaties; the second three examine activities related to the role of civil society in the framing of domestic perceptions of human rights policy choices and the development of domestic human rights legislation; and the last three suggest ways in which civil society influences the larger foreign policy agenda.

A TALE OF THREE TREATIES

Civil society organizations play vital roles in influencing the stance of the United States toward international human rights treaties. As a recent white paper on "The Role of an International Convention on the Human Rights of People with Disabilities" notes, the advantages of pursuing an international treaty include: (1) providing an immediate statement of international legal accountability; (2) providing an authoritative and global reference point for domestic law and policy initiatives; (3) providing mechanisms for more effective monitoring, including reporting on the enforcement of the convention by governments and nongovernmental organizations, supervision by a body of experts mandated by the convention, and possibly the consideration of individual or group complaints under a mechanism to be created by the convention; (4) establishing a useful framework for international cooperation; and (5) providing transformative educative benefits for all participants engaged in the preparatory and formal negotiation phases.[61]

The benefits of pursuing a treaty, however, must be weighed against competing arguments against multilateral treaty efforts. As the white paper notes, treaty strategies are often blocked by "well-worn and oddly unquestioned justifications for U.S. non-participation in human rights treaties based on the complexities of our federal system, the notion that human rights are an exclusive concern of domestic jurisdiction and the U.S. Constitution does not permit the use of the treaty power for regulation of such matters, the potential for conflict between treaty obligations and the Constitution, and the like."[62]

Nonetheless, despite the odds against them—or perhaps because of these odds—civil society continues to press for the adoption of new treaties. The following examples illustrate how in some cases, key individuals act as norm entrepreneurs by playing a persistent role in bringing certain concerns to the negotiating table and in shaping how they are discussed and ultimately reflected in the resulting treaty.[63] Throughout treaty negotiations, human rights advocates may be partners with or opponents of the U.S. government and, as these examples suggest, the nature of the relationship between government and NGO is likely to change over time. The cases also demonstrate that the creation of a treaty sets in motion a new set of tasks for civil society, as the treaty must be ratified by a sufficient number of governments before it comes into force, which entails not only persuading the president to sign on, but enlisting support of two-thirds of the Senate as well. Ratification of a treaty sets in motion a host of tasks concerned with the monitoring and implementation of the treaty. But also, when the United States refuses to ratify a treaty, civil society organizations may play a role in persuading the United States to refrain from obstructing other states' adherence to the treaty. No matter what happens, civil society has a role to play.

Shaping Treaty Language: Pea Soup and Children's Rights

Tired from another day's work on proposed treaty language for a new convention on the rights of children, governmental and nongovernmental delegates slipped into blue jeans and sweaters and headed out for some pea soup. For five years, Simmone Ek of Sweden's Save the Children had been opening the doors of her Geneva flat each Thursday evening of the treaty negotiations for pea soup parties. Governmental officials and NGO representatives would ladle their own soup into Chinese porcelain bowels, spread a little orange Swedish caviar on crackers, and help themselves to some Swedish wine. Then they would informally drift off into little groups of two or three, sitting on the floor together with their shoes off. David Balton, the U.S. representative in 1988, might show off some of his juggling tricks,[64] or Adam Lopatka, the Polish delegate, might tell some jokes, but most of the time the room was filled with parallel conversations about the latest controversy on the treaty.[65]

Debate over the children's rights convention had been ongoing since 1978, when a working group of the UN Commission on Human Rights began to meet each year, for one week, to discuss and draft the convention.[66] No records were kept for the first two years of the working group's existence, and it was not until 1981 that even a list of attendees was kept. In that year, there were representatives from only twenty-seven governments, four NGOs, and one UN body in attendance. Momentum for the treaty did not really build until participation picked up in 1983 and NGOs created a more formal working group, the ad hoc group on drafting of the Convention on the Rights of the Child (the "Ad Hoc NGO Committee").[67] The Convention process got another boost in 1996 when, under Anwarul Chowdhury's leadership, the United Nations International Children's Emergency Fund (UNICEF) board accepted a series of decisions that made them more actively engaged in the drafting process.[68] By 1988, NGO and government representatives had developed a strong rapport over the years of pea soup gatherings, and they were ready to settle the final controversies on international standards for children's rights.

Most of the controversial issues reflected the underlying East–West tensions at the time. Cynthia Price Cohen, an American international child rights authority who participated in the negotiations, remembers, "The Western countries tended to look at the Convention on the Rights of the Child as an Eastern Bloc initiative with an Eastern Bloc concept of rights. The original emphasis of the Convention was heavily weighted toward that group in the form of economic, social and cultural rights, instead of emphasizing the Western view of human rights, which puts a high value on civil and political rights that protect the individual from the power of the State. As a consequence, many proposals reflected these political differences and gave rise to the possibility of ideological conflicts."[69]

In 1988, much of the conversation at the pea soup parties reflected these ideological differences. At the forefront of discussion were the U.S. proposals to the treaty which centered on civil and political rights. The Polish government submitted two draft versions of the Convention to the Commission on Human Rights. The first version was simply the Declaration of the Rights of the Child with a weak implementation mechanism attached. The second version contained one article that gave a hint that the child might have civil and political rights.[70] It read, "The States Parties to the present Convention shall enable the child who is capable of forming his own views the right to express his opinion in matters concerning his own person, and in particular, marriage, choice of occupation, medical treatment, education and recreation."

This article was used by the United States as the basis for an expanded version, dividing the single article into more specific separate articles.[71] The U.S. proposal, which had been written based largely on NGO suggestions, contained five paragraphs that covered the panoply of civil and political rights recognized (at least to some degree) in American law, including freedom of expression, freedom of association and assembly, the right to privacy, and a prohibition against imprisoning children for exercising their rights.[72] Not surprisingly, China and the USSR led the opposition to the American plan.

The Polish chairman of the working group, Adam Lopatka, relied heavily on NGOs to draft proposals on key issues and to break deadlocks between the government representatives.[73] Specifically, when a dispute did arise among government representatives, if a parallel proposal from the ad hoc NGO Committee existed he would turn to NGOs as a source of compromise. If this did not work, he would charge a small drafting party composed of the disagreeing delegations to come up with an alternative text. If the drafting party returned to the working group with no consensus, Lopatka would suggest that the controversial provision be muted through the addition of a limitation clause, which permitted the government to place restrictions on the protected right by the claiming of national security or similar purposes.[74]

In 1988, Lopatka faced the task of somehow prompting consensus on several of the American suggestions pertaining to civil and political rights. Perhaps it was a particularly good year for pea soup, the keen negotiating skills of Adam Lopatka, or sheer impatience to get on with the treaty process, but whatever the reason, 1988 proved to be a breakthrough year. The delegates reached consensus on controversial American proposals on freedom of religion and freedom of association and assembly. The final version of the free association article, Cohen points out, "basically duplicated a two paragraph proposal from the NGO Group."[75] In addition the delegates reached consensus on a very broad freedom of expression provision that went beyond the typical American version of free speech as a "negative right" against which the government could not intrude. The provision not only protected children from interference with their free expression, but also included the "right to receive and impart information," an inclusion for which NGOs had pushed based on its presence in other international human rights treaties (such as the International Covenant on Civil and Political Rights).

Finally, the delegates also approved a privacy provision: "The States Parties to the present Convention recognize the right of the child not to be subjected to arbitrary or unlawful interference with his or her right to privacy, family, home or correspondence, nor to unlawful attacks on his or her honor or reputation."[76] In the final crafting of the privacy article, at the suggestion of the Federal Republic of Germany, the first eleven words would be deleted and rephrased with the stronger phrasing of "No child shall be subjected to. . . ." As Cohen observes, "this produced a very strange result. The United States, which has a somewhat fragile constitutional right to privacy, was responsible for an article that uses the strongest obligatory language in the human rights lexicon to protect the child's privacy rights." Ironically, the attempts of the United States to thwart the Soviet Union with American-style political rights ended up setting international standards for children that in some cases went far beyond those guaranteed by American law.[77]

After a decade of drafting the standards, the NGOs and governments involved prepared for a long battle for treaty adoption and ratification. However, when the Convention on the Rights of the Child (CRC)[78] came before the UN General Assembly in 1989, it was adopted without a vote—a gesture similar to a unanimous decision. The CRC soon became the treaty ratified by a great number of countries in the shortest period of time.[79] By 1995, only two countries were outstanding in not making the treaty legally binding: the United States and Somalia. In February 1995, President Clinton did sign the treaty based on the deathbed request of James Grant, the former head of UNICEF, but he did not send the treaty to Congress for consideration.[80] In signing the treaty,[81] Clinton emphasized that the United States would likely not agree to ratify the treaty without a detailed statement of reservations, which would effectively exempt the United States from compliance with provisions that were not compatible with U.S. law.[82]

The United States today is thus in the strange position of being outside a convention that it actively helped to create. The United States was by far the most active of all the participating countries, making proposals and textual recommendations for thirty-eight of the forty substantive articles.[83] The U.S.-based NGOs were at odds with their government on some aspects of the negotiations (most notably, on the U.S. intransigence on raising the minimum age for soldiers from fifteen to eighteen, and on elimination of the death penalty for children).[84] Nonetheless, both NGO and U.S. government representatives remember their relationship throughout the negotiations as congenial and cooperative.[85] In the end, the U.S. delegates were responsible for proposing five new articles: Article 10 (family reunification), Article 13 (freedom of expression), Article 14 (freedom of religion), Article 15 (freedom of association and assembly), Article 16 (right to privacy), Article 19 (protection from abuse), and Article 25 (periodic review of treatment). All of these articles reflected significant NGO input. [86]

Both the U.S. negotiators and NGO activists were dissatisfied with the outcome of having influenced a treaty that the United States would never ratify. As David Balton put it, "my hope was to negotiate a treaty the U.S. could sign."[87] Balton and the other American negotiators moved on to new assignments far removed from children's rights; many NGO activists did the same. Others turned their attention to different human rights agreements that protect children—for example, pushing the United States to become one of the first states to adopt the International Labor Organization Convention on the Worst Forms of Child Labor.[88] In 2003, however, the child rights movement began gearing up for a new round of the struggle to push U.S. ratification.[89] Spearheaded by the Child Welfare League of America, this new movement has vowed to "raise the issue, everywhere."[90] In doing so, it faces a new array of allies and opponents.

Opposition to the CRC is well organized and active. According to Senate staff in the United States, the advocacy against the CRC far outweighs the support for the treaty in terms of the sheer numbers of advocacy letters: they receive one hundred letters against the CRC for every one letter in support of it.[91] Those on the far right describe the convention as "the most insidious document ever signed by an American president,"[92] warning that parents will lose all authority over their children.[93] They worry that granting children "rights" is fundamentally incompatible with "protection" of children.[94] Others claim that participation in the convention would undermine U.S. sovereignty and states' rights,[95] or that the convention is simply unworkable in the American system—due to what David Stewart terms "the compatibility gap."[96] Parental rights advocates warn that the Convention "will limit the ability of United States parents to act in the best interests of their children, as only they are qualified to do, by granting children freedoms which clash with the duty of parents to direct the lives of their children."[97]

Meanwhile, the coalition in favor of the treaty continues to grow. Advocates for children's rights increasingly frame the issue broadly, reaching out to parents whose children have been incarcerated, parents with kids on death row, parents denied health services for their children, and parents with children injured or killed by gun violence. "These issues cross race and class," comments Cohen. "If there is any hope for international human rights for kids in the U.S., organizing must start here."[98] Advocates agree that ratifying the CRC would not automatically solve the issues facing American children, but they do assert that it could be a tool for influencing the domestic agenda to improve conditions for youth. Furthermore, they assert that ratification would allow the United States to participate in the work of the committee, in establishing international standards for such concerns and providing the country with a means of measurement of these issues.[99]

Mitigating Damage on Treaty Negotiations: Tobacco Control

The World Health Organization (WHO) had never negotiated an international treaty before, but the new WHO director general, Dr. Gro Harlem Brundtland, thought it was worth a try. The idea for an international treaty on tobacco control had been circulating ever since Professor Ruth Roemer, at the University of California–Los Angeles, and her then student Allyn Taylor (who, by 1998, was a well-established WHO legal consultant) wrote about the idea in the early 1980s and 1990s.[100] But it was not until Brundtland took the helm that the WHO started the "Tobacco Free Initiative" and made international tobacco control a top priority for that organization.[101]

In a move that surprised those who expected the WHO to maintain its nonactivist tradition, its 191 member countries, meeting at the 1999 World Health Assembly, voted to support opening negotiations for the Framework Convention on Tobacco Control (FCTC).[102] The goal of the convention was to place legally binding obligations on countries to protect the public from tobacco-related deaths and disease by addressing such issues as the method of taxation for tobacco-related products, smoking prevention, illicit trade, tobacco advertising, and product regulation.[103] Formal talks on the convention commenced in 2000, with the first session of the FCTC Intergovernmental Negotiating Body.[104]

From the outset, the WHO turned to nongovernmental organizations for expertise and assistance. The London-based organization Action on Smoking and Health (ASH) was one of the NGOs working closely with the WHO from the beginning, and a host of public health and human rights organizations soon joined on the effort. But they needed a strong U.S. partner. ASH turned to the American-based Campaign for Tobacco-Free Kids, a privately funded antismoking organization, to fill the void. While Tobacco-Free Kids had no experience with international standard setting, it had a reputation for impeccable research, creative advocacy, and unflagging energy. To spearhead the American side of the campaign, Tobacco-Free Kids hired attorney Judy Wilkenfeld as director of international programs. Having served as special advisor for tobacco policy in the U.S. Food and Drug Administration (1994–99) and as assistant director of the Division of Advertising Practices in the U.S. Federal Trade Commission (1980–94), Wilkenfeld not only knew the issues, but also enjoyed congenial relations with many in the Clinton administration who would work on the proposed treaty.

Support for the treaty among NGOs grew rapidly. In March 2000, eight groups set out to "inquire and induce and cajole more groups to join."[105] The coalition-building effort included groups from all over the spectrum of activism and issues pertaining to tobacco, including not only public health and human rights groups but also labor rights groups, women's organizations, and environmental groups. Within the course of 3 years, the coalition grew from the original eight to more than 120 partners.

Over this course of time, the sophistication of the advocacy, which began at a high level, improved even more as participation widened and deepened and advocacy campaigns became more targeted. For example, in places where social problems and health issues were viewed as human rights issues (for example, in South Africa), tobacco usage was viewed as raising human rights concerns. Just as AIDS was framed as a human rights issue in Africa, so were the negative health consequences from cigarette smoking in the United States. By contrast, in tobacco-growing regions, anything associated with tobacco tended to be framed as a labor issue, local labor organizations were involved, and the subject was argued with local examples. And in places where tobacco was treated as a public health issue, as in the United States and much of Europe, the advocates drew from larger public health debates. Despite (or perhaps because of) the variety of localized approaches to the same problem, the NGOs were able to present a united front.

For those from the United States, the negotiation process involved a different cast of characters than that present in the usual treaty negotiation. Because the treaty was developed under the auspices of the WHO, the State Department took a backseat to the Department of Health and Human Services—that is, they did not head the delegation. The NGOs enjoyed a cooperative partnership with the delegation under the Clinton administration headed by Thomas Novotny. "The administration was in general supportive of the treaty and working against companies like Phillip Morris," Wilkenfeld states. "We didn't always agree with them, but we were able to deal with them and to tell them our disappointments. But then prior to the second session, there was a radical change in how the delegation behaved."[106]

The early work which the Campaign for Tobacco-Free Kids conducted was mostly as a collaborative partner of the U.S. government. Initially there were "major questions [of] whether the United States and other tobacco-exporting nations will support a strong treaty."[107] Once the first round of negotiations was completed, however, there was a feeling of "cautious optimism about the progress of the discussions" on the part of NGOs.[108] On the fifth day of the first meeting, the U.S. delegate gave a statement calling for "a robust statement restricting advertising, sponsorship and promotion of tobacco, to the extent permitted under domestic law, with a special emphasis on eliminating those messages that have special appeal to children and adolescents."[109] With such strong support from the Clinton administration, the American NGOs focused less on the passage of a treaty, which appeared to be within grasp, and more on working with the government representatives to make the treaty a strong one.

The new presidential administration of George W. Bush brought an abrupt change in the relationship between NGOs and the U.S. government. To ease the transition before the second international meeting on the convention, active NGO groups and the outgoing U.S. delegates convened a meeting with the incoming U.S. delegates. According to Wilkenfeld, who attended the meeting, "prior to the second session, there was a radical change in how the delegation behaved . . . it became quite painful . . . they were backing away on secondhand smoke—all of the provisions they had taken a decent stance on they were backing away from. Not to mention they were becoming more unilateral."[110] Other people in the United States who were closely involved with the issue, such as Congressman Henry Waxman (Democrat—California), accused the United States of taking cues from Phillip Morris in their international negotiations.[111] Even at this early stage of the new administration's involvement on the tobacco treaty issue, the lines were being drawn.

Throughout the rest of the negotiations, NGOs perceived the U.S. government as "no longer an ally, but an obstacle."[112] The lead official of the U.S. delegation, Thomas Novotny, resigned after the second round of negotiations "rather than argue the case of the new [Bush] administration on tobacco issues," including U.S. proposals that would make certain mandatory steps voluntary and soften restrictions on advertising aimed at children and smoking in public places.[113] Tensions mounted, and by the fifth session of negotiations of the tobacco treaty, American NGOs attempting to influence foreign policy were at a point of collision with the delegation. "As their behavior became worse and worse, more intransigent, more unilateral—so did our rhetoric,"[114] remembers Wilkenfeld. The first press release on the U.S. behavior came during the fifth meeting. Headlined "U.S. Continues Obstructionist Behavior as Negotiations Resume on Proposed Tobacco Treaty," the statement accused the delegation of taking positions protecting industry interests rather than public health.[115]

The leading American NGOs working on public health issues, many of whom have Republican reputations, were among those galvanized into taking the strongest stand yet on the negotiations. In a joint statement in February 2003, the American Cancer Society, American Heart Association, American Lung Association, and Campaign for Tobacco-Free Kids called on the United States to withdraw from the negotiations on the proposed international tobacco treaty. Dr. Alfred Munzer, past president and spokesman for the American Lung Association at the negotiations, explained, in a joint press release, that "the U.S. government has squandered an opportunity to lead the efforts to develop a strong Framework Convention on Tobacco Control. It has instead chosen to be the handmaiden of the tobacco industry and to use its power to sabotage and to weaken the treaty. The most honorable thing the U.S. can do now to ensure a strong Framework Convention is to be forthright and honest in its opposition to an effective convention and to tell its delegation to go home."[116] This statement "sent a message to the world community that U.S. NGOs did not stand by the actions of their government."[117] The relationship of the NGOs toward the U.S. delegation thus evolved from a cooperative partnership in the Clinton era, to being combative in the beginning of the Bush administration, to one of outright dismissal later in the Bush administration.

The openly confrontational tactics of the U.S. representatives eventually gave way to a quieter "poison pill" policy. On March 1, 2003, 171 nations reached agreement on a strong treaty. The United States agreed to sign the treaty, but only if the convention were substantially changed. The United States issued a new statement of position on the FCTC that was generally supportive but still complained that "our ability to sign and ratify the Convention is undermined by the current prohibition on reservations." The U.S. proposal was essentially to allow any nation to opt out of any of the treaty's substantive provisions.[118] When the nongovernmental community received information regarding this development, it signaled a virtual call to arms in their activism and rhetoric. It launched a media blitz that yielded stories in all of the major U.S. newspapers.

In another abrupt about-face, on May 18, 2003, Health and Human Services Secretary Tommy Thompson declared that the United States would join the other members of the WHO in supporting the Framework Convention on Tobacco Control. "This is an outstanding day when you can stand up and make a step forward for public health," Thompson said, adding, "It is no exaggeration to state that the United States is a world leader in anti-smoking efforts." It appeared as if the Bush administration's fight against the treaty was forgotten: "Let me say that again: there can be no questioning the profound dedication of the United States to controlling the public health threat from smoking. I am very proud of that, and we look forward to working with partners from around the world to prevent future death and disease through effective and sustainable global prevention and control efforts."[119] Thompson did not specify whether the United States would sign the treaty, but said the United States is "carefully reviewing the text."

Adoption of the treaty by the WHO assembly cleared the way for the FCTC to be opened for signature on June 16, 2003. The treaty commits nations to banning all tobacco advertising, promotion, and sponsorship (with an exception for nations with constitutional constraints). It also commits them to requiring large warning labels covering at least 30 percent of the principal display areas of the cigarette pack. The treaty provides nations with a roadmap for enacting strong, science-based policies in other areas such as secondhand smoke protections, tobacco taxation, tobacco product regulation, combating cigarette smuggling, public education, and tobacco cessation treatment.

As of June 19, 2003, the treaty had been signed by over forty countries.[120] The NGOs claimed an initial victory, but immediately began preparing for the hard work that lay ahead. "The key now is for nations to quickly sign and ratify the treaty and fully implement its important public health measures," urged Tobacco-Free Kids, warning, "As they have done throughout the treaty negotiations, the tobacco companies will undoubtedly work to delay and weaken the implementation process in individual nations."[121] Tobacco-Free Kids vowed to continue to demand that states reject tobacco industry pressure and put the health of their citizens first. They believed that framing the issue as a public health matter ultimately would have more influence over policy makers than the alternative framing of the debate as one of free enterprise versus regulation.

Initiating a Treaty: Disability Rights

"Nothing about us without us"[122]—so goes the familiar refrain of the disability rights movement. When, in the last month of 2001 the U.S. State Department began sizing up its position on a prospective international convention on disability rights, leaders in the disabled community wanted to make sure they had input from the outset. While the presidency of George W. Bush was unlikely to recommend that the United States sign an international treaty on disability rights, the State Department had a variety of options, none of which the disability community considered constructive: it could use its powerful voice to obstruct the progress of a treaty desired by other countries; it could ignore the process; or it could indirectly support the process while still asserting its irrelevance to the United States. No matter how it acted, the State Department would leave its mark on the way disability issues are understood. Knowing this, the disability movement in the United States geared up to try to work with government actors on framing the issues and initiating the treaty process.

The first step the disability movement took was to eliminate the chance that the United States could ignore the growing momentum for an international treaty on disability rights and thus signal its irrelevance to the rest of the world. Once dead, a treaty process is hard to revive. The advocates needed to send a clear message to the U.S. government that an international convention on disability rights was of great importance to disabled people in America and throughout the world. But disability rights advocates are an extremely diverse lot, and very few at that time were thinking in terms of international human rights. They had been a bit taken by surprise when Mexico raised the issue of an international disability rights convention as part of the Platform of Action adopted at the World Conference against Racism in Durban, South Africa.[123] The speed with which the United Nations took up the issue was indeed breathtaking. On November 28, 2001, the UN General Assembly adopted by consensus a resolution calling for the establishment of an ad hoc committee to elaborate "a comprehensive and integral international convention to promote and protect the rights and dignity of persons with disabilities, based on the holistic approach in the work done in the field of social development, human rights and non-discrimination."[124]

The establishment of the ad hoc committee created a new focus and source of energy for disability activists. The small pockets of the disability community that were versed in human rights and international treaties suddenly found themselves in demand. Mainstream human rights movement had demonstrated little interest in disability issues,[125] and the people in the disability movement viewed international human rights organizations with distrust.[126]

Historically, the human rights community had dismissed disability as a medical issue to be "handled" by the medical establishment or as a personal tragedy best "dealt with" by charitable groups.[127] It was up to those activists serving as a bridge between the disability and human rights communities to introduce human rights advocates to a new way of thinking. The disability community urged an understanding of disability in terms of a social construction. Under this socially constructed model of disability, emphasis is placed on how *society* requires adaptation, and *not* the person with a disability.[128] For those working on the new treaty process this meant the understanding that "full participation of people with disabilities will be achieved not by focusing on disability itself as the problem or 'fixing' people, but by a conscious effort to eliminate the social, cultural, physical and ideological barriers that prevent people with disabilities from claiming their human rights."[129] It was with this view of disability, drawn from the experience of people with disabilities and disability activists, that advocates began approaching a host of Washington, D.C., actors: congressmen, State Department attorneys, the National Council on Disability, domestic policy advisors on disability in the White House and National Security Council, as well as other relevant agencies with some link to disability policy.

In planning their advocacy strategy, disability leaders tried to ensure that it was inclusive of the disability community as a whole and not dominated by European or North American members of the network or by any particular sector of the disability community. The framing of the issue in legal and human rights terms posed great challenges to inclusiveness. As Janet Lord, legal counsel and advocacy director for Landmine Survivors Network, has observed, "human rights framing will necessarily, in the short term at least, privilege a certain elite group of disability advocates and organizations unless and until the [disability community] succeeds in equipping and supporting its members to engage in human rights advocacy at many levels."[130]

To avoid privileging elites, the National Council on Disability embarked on an extensive capacity-building campaign. Significant publications included the National Council on Disability's "A Reference Tool: Understanding the Potential Content and Structure of an International Convention on the Human Rights of People with Disabilities."[131] Most significant was the white paper publication titled "Understanding the Role of an International Convention on the Human Rights of People with Disabilities,"[132] which was published by the council and around which two historical events took place. One event brought together leaders of the American disability community and leaders of the international human rights movement for the first time. Another brought together leaders of the American grassroots disability community for a day long conference on international disability rights, and the convention process in particular. To further enhance participation of people with disabilities in the decision-making process, a coalition of nine American-based disability organizations wrote a "rough guide" to participation in the ad hoc committee to help on-site participants influence the negotiations.[133] Landmine Survivors Network followed up the first edition with revisions and five regional editions of the rough guide (Inter-American, African, European, Asia-Pacific, and Middle Eastern) in anticipation of the meeting of the second ad hoc committee at the UN in 2003.

In the months leading up to the first ad hoc committee meeting, disability organizations lobbied hard to achieve access to the meeting at the United Nations. The participation of NGOs was far from decided. Only seven membership-based international disability groups comprising the International Disability Alliance (IDA) held Economic and Social Council (ECOSOC) consultative status, while many of the organizations taking leadership roles in the new treaty process were excluded from the IDA group, making coordination among NGOs a challenge.[134] An additional obstacle was presented by the UN, which kept disability organizations in limbo, refusing to commit on procedures for NGO participation. Just one week before the meeting was to commence, the UN General Assembly adopted a resolution that allowed all organizations enjoying consultative status with the ECOSOC to participate in ad hoc sessions and to speak in the general debate and provided that other, nonaccredited organizations could apply for accreditation for the meeting.[135]

For people with disabilities, however, real "access" was still denied. The facilities of the United Nations posed major barriers. As Janet Lord explains, "the gallery space was inaccessible for people using wheelchairs and a move to an alternative conference room with equally inaccessible space for observers forced disability activists onto the floor of the committee itself (the unintended advantage being that NGOs found themselves sitting alongside delegates and IGO representatives). Participants with hearing impairments discovered conference facilities designed with [dated] technology. . . . No sign language interpretation or real-time transcription services were provided by the United Nations, and no documents were available in alternative formats appropriate for people with visual impairments."[136]

Although many of the problems would be addressed by the second meeting, they did pose significant obstacles at the outset.

While the building conditions started to improve, the State Department became more and more of an obstacle. By the time of the first ad hoc meeting in July 2002, the State Department had come around from being apathetic to the treaty process to being obstructionist. The State Department's original stance was classic American exceptionalism: the United States did not need the treaty because it had the much stronger Americans with Disabilities Act (ADA). In so doing they implied that human rights treaties are for other people. At the 2002 ad hoc meeting, however, the U.S. representatives stalled the process, poking technical holes in the document, asserting that the time was not ripe for a disability treaty.

Avraham Rabby, U.S. advisor for economic and social affairs, told the UN delegates that the American experience (through the ADA) "proves that, when crafted correctly, legislation can have real and lasting effects on the promotion of the rights of persons with disabilities and have a positive effect on the population as a whole." However, he warned, "A new treaty, hurriedly conceived and formulated, will not necessarily change the practice of states. Indeed, experience has shown that the human rights instruments that have resulted in the most profound change in state practice have been those instruments which were carefully considered over a substantial period of time and which were adopted by consensus among states, after significant discussions and debate."[137]

In issuing his remarks, the U.S. representative indicated the Americans' displeasure at the amount and intensity of NGO participation at the meeting. While Rabby did state, "We are pleased with the participation of NGOs in the meetings of this Working Group," he went on to say, "We would note, however, that it is normally the practice in the UN General Assembly to allow all Member States to speak in the General Debate prior to the commencement of NGO speeches. Although we adopted a different format yesterday to allow for maximum NGO participation in the General Debate, we would stress that this format should not be viewed as a precedent for purposes of other negotiations in the UN General Assembly or its subsidiary bodies. Rather, it should be viewed as an exception to the general rule, because of the unique expertise that the NGOs can bring to our discussions."[138]

Disability advocates and human rights activists fought back by publicizing America's recalcitrant stance and by framing America's opposition in terms of hostility toward the disabled. Throughout the two weeks of the first ad hoc committee meeting in 2002 in New York, meetings of a spontaneously created Disability Caucus were held adjacent to the ad hoc committee conference room. This tactic was successful in terms of presenting, at various points, a unified voice of NGOs before the ad hoc committee.[139] The NGOs agreed to use the Internet and other mechanisms to expose the United States' obstructionist behavior.[140]

A variety of tools adopted by the NGOs helped spread information on meetings, draft resolutions, and statements by delegations as the news unfolded. At the first ad hoc committee meeting (and continuing at the second), the Landmines Survivors Network provided daily editions of the *Disability Negotiations Daily Summary*, which provided detailed overviews of statements made on the floor of the ad hoc committee that were then electronically transmitted to local partners around the world for further dispersion among local and national partners.[141] The content and process for daily preparation of these summaries models that of *Earth Negotiations Bulletin*, the long-established international environmental reporting service for intergovernmental meetings.[142]

Still another helpful tool adopted at the ad hoc committee by the disability community was the preparation of a daily *Disability Negotiations Bulletin*, providing a political and informational platform for members of the community to convey their message to delegates. To prod states into reexamining their behavior, the bulletin awarded states with a "Disability Awareness Badge of Honor" or "Disability Awareness Badge of Dishonor." The *Disability Negotiations Bulletin* was credited on the floor of the ad hoc committee when Denmark, speaking on behalf of the European Union, noted that it "appreciated one of the more creative means of communication of the ad hoc committee, namely, the *Disability Negotiations Bulletin*," and stated further that "none of us have at any point been in doubt of the engagement of the entire group of NGOs in this meeting and in the future process."[143]

Before the close of the first ad hoc committee, an urgent action alert was sent out to mobilize American disability activists to demand that the United

States withdraw its objection to the treaty.[144] Under intense pressure, the U.S. delegation stepped aside and allowed the process to continue. While the end result of the meeting was only a decision to continue deliberations,[145] NGOs could claim victory.[146]

The conclusion of the first ad hoc committee meeting stepped up the domestic momentum for the disability community and its supporters. Four developments are particularly noteworthy.[147] First, Senator Tom Harkin (Democrat–Iowa) established a working group after the first ad hoc committee that, on a monthly basis, brought together disability activists and members of the National Council on Disability to discuss developments in relation to the convention. Activists worked with staffers from the officers of Senator Harkin, and Representatives James Langevin (Democrat–Rhode Island), and Tom Lantos (Democrat–California) to develop a draft congressional resolution which would call on the United States to support the new convention effort. Activists also used the "New Freedom Initiative" of President Bush to build an argument for support of the convention effort.[148] Finally, the National Council on Disability's International Watch, a federal advisory group established to follow international disability issues began to focus extensively on the new convention effort and discussed ways in which to build awareness of the effort in its monthly teleconferences.

At the next major United Nations meeting on the proposed convention, in June 2003, the United States agreed to neither support nor obstruct the treaty process. The American representatives still insisted that American law was far superior and that, although some countries might need a treaty, the United States did not.[149] In marked contrast to the Tobacco Control Treaty negotiations, however, the United States would take a stance that was very close to what NGOs were calling for from them—namely, a nonobstructionist position.

What explains the U.S. adoption of a more congenial position? According to some human rights activists in Europe, the American UN Mission in Geneva was telling Washington to support this treaty effort, given the backlash about U.S. action in Iraq and positions on other treaties.[150] Some activists in Washington, D.C., assert that individual personalities in government were genuinely in support of the treaty, and others speculate that the United States made a simple instrumental calculation that it had more to gain than to lose by a "non-position position."[151] In any event, the American position paved the way for a remarkable outcome: the ad hoc committee's decision to put the drafting of the initial treaty text in the hands of a working group consisting of twenty-five governments, twelve NGO representatives, and one representative of a national human rights institution. While this group is reminiscent of earlier treaty drafting processes (such as the Rights of the Child convention development process), it is completely unprecedented in according twelve NGOs a formal place at the negotiating table via the drafting working group. In previous UN multilateral treaty negotiations in the human rights and other spheres, the most that could be hoped for in the way of participation was informal observer status. By the close of the two-week working group meeting in January 2004, a draft text to serve as the basis for formal negotiations had emerged.

THE TURN TOWARD U.S. LEGISLATION AND COURTS

Civil society has also had a tremendous impact on the shaping and implementation of domestic human rights legislation. The oldest legislative strategies have involved linking foreign assistance to improvements in human rights.[152] As noted in Chapter 2, beginning in the 1970s, the U.S. government began tying military and economic aid to countries' human rights records, rewarding good human rights performances and restricting or eliminating aid as punishment for human rights abuses. More recently NGOs have pushed for such measures as the Lautenberg and Leahy-McConnell bills on aid conditionality to the former Yugoslavia. The Coalition for International Justice, for example, helped shape the Lautenberg Amendment to the Foreign Assistance Act of 1997,[153] which links bilateral aid and multilateral loans to evidence of cooperation with International Criminal Tribunal for the Former Yugoslavia. Among its provisions, the law also stipulates that Congress consult with human rights organizations prior to awarding aid.[154]

At the level of local government, human rights advocates have passed laws and regulations on human rights, thus testing the ability of local governments to shape foreign affairs. The Free Burma Campaign, for example, succeeded in persuading the state of Massachusetts to pass a law forbidding purchases from any corporation doing business in Burma. The U.S. Supreme Court struck down the law in June 2000 on the grounds that it was preempted by a federal law imposing sanctions on Burma. However, because the decision did not comment directly on the foreign affairs question, some commentators argue, it left open the possibility of locally imposed sanctions.[155] The campaign of human rights activists in Massachusetts served to spur a new effort for legislation addressing Burma at the federal level.[156]

This section provides illustrations of three contemporary examples of the role NGOs play in shaping the content and implementation of federal legislation related to human rights. As these cases demonstrate, foreign aid conditionality can be used in creative ways to further a variety of human rights goals. The decision to push for new domestic legislation, like the decision to pursue a treaty strategy, may be the product of a small set of "norm entrepreneurs" who design and execute a concerted strategy to draw congressional support for the adoption of new legislation. The content of these strategies may be ideologically conservative or liberal, but they all share a faith in the power of domestic human rights legislation to effect change. These cases also demonstrate that the creation of new legislation marks only the beginning of monitoring efforts as civil society remains vigilant to the legislation's implementation. Finally, the last case in this series examines the question of the role of human rights attorneys in raising claims in U.S. courts.

Shaping Legislation: The International Religious Freedom Act

Sometimes, ideas for social change initiatives come in a flash of inspiration and at other times, they are carried around in a briefcase for years until the right opportunity presents itself. For the Reverend Richard Cizik, vice president for governmental affairs of the National Association of Evangelicals (NAE), the umbrella association for Evangelical churches in the United States and around the world, accomplishing his dreams was a matter of long-term persistence. In 1992, Cizik read an article by Darryl Hart in the *Christian Century* discussing the Evangelical "midlife crisis." The article argued that the movement suffered from an identity problem and in order to be political relevant, it had to change its strategy away from "eliminating individual sins" to focusing on the "broader structural problems that often breed the evils they oppose."[157] Cizik couldn't have agreed more, but he did not know how to frame the issues differently.[158] While he mulled over these ideas, the article went into his briefcase, where it stayed for a few more years.

The right moment to act on the ideas in the article came a few years later when, in 1995, Cizik and four others similarly concerned with broadening the evangelical agenda met and, in his words, "decided to change the status quo."[159] By then, Cizik was using human rights discourse to engage U.S. policy makers on issues of religious freedom internationally. So he sat down with Nina Shea of Freedom House's Center on Religious Freedom, Diane Knippers of the Institute of Religion and Democracy, Mike Horowitz of the Hudson Institute, and Dwight Gibson of the World Evangelical Alliance and began discussing a plan of action.[160]

This initial meeting produced the text for the NAE Statement of Conscience Concerning Worldwide Religious Persecution.[161] In a section titled "Facts," persecution of religious believers, and in particular Christians, is characterized as "an increasingly tragic fact in today's world."[162] Citing such countries as China, Cuba, Laos, North Korea, and Vietnam, specifically, as well as "Islamic countries," generally, the statement outlines threats, persecution, and intimidation against Evangelical Protestants and Catholics seeking freedom from repressive regimes. It calls on the U.S. government to take a leadership role on these issues and outlines four action areas for government: (1) public acknowledgement of anti-Christian persecution through international and national agencies; (2) State Department reporting of incidents of religious persecution; (3) reform of Immigration and Naturalization Service policies for refugee and asylum petitions of those fleeing anti-Christian persecution; and (4) its most controversial provision, the "termination of non-humanitarian foreign assistance to governments of countries that fail to take vigorous action to end anti-Christian or other religious persecution."[163]

To advance this agenda, NAE embarked upon a highly coordinated campaign that included a strong media component, a large, well-publicized public gathering in Washington, D.C., and smaller private meetings bringing together leaders in the evangelical community with White House officials, congressmen, and other political leaders. Their strategy was to present the statement as a fait accompli at the meeting and to request that conservative religious organizations sign on and support the initiative. To raise the stakes, NAE succeeded in getting an article about the statement and the event in the *New York Times* to coincide with the start of the public meeting.[164] The timing of the event and the targeted publicity around it was intended to maintain momentum on this issue.[165]

While the publicity was welcome and indeed desired, it brought the movement to the public eye and in so doing invited criticism as well as praise. Some detractors worried about the lack of democratic process in the drafting of the NAE agenda and expressed concern that it "disproportionately represents the interests of the so-called 'missionary religions' that have evangelicalism, particularly international evangelicalism, at the heart of their mission."[166] Supporters of the NAE insisted, however, that the bill, while prompted by the concerns of Christians, was not privileging any particular faith. Pragmatic reasons, Cizik contends, explain the drafting process, rather than any desire to exclude any group. Cizik explains that it would have been impossible to craft a document with a larger group. In his opinion, having the smaller group undertake the initial drafting and then heavily promoting the final language was more effective.[167] He argues that they "had to start with the most aggressive, highest and best, most assertive language knowing full well that with everyone opposing us, it was going to be watered down."[168]

In May 1997, the text of the NAE Statement served as the basis for a bill introduced by Congressman Frank Wolf (Republican–Virginia). It immediately set off intense debate.[169] While strongly endorsed by the Christian Coalition and other conservative religious groups in the United States, the proposed law was viewed with skepticism by moderate and liberal religious groups.[170]

Mainstream and liberal religious NGOs expressed concern with the language of the proposed law and pressed for a final product that would reflect a more ecumenical approach. Prominent among the opposition was the National Council of Churches (NCC), a group that, according to its self-description, is "the leading force for ecumenical cooperation among Christians in the United States."[171] As the representative coalition of thirty-six Protestant, Anglican, and Orthodox member denominations in the United States, the NCC advocated for a multilateral approach to human rights violations abroad, drawing on established human rights instruments and mechanisms instead of creating new unilateral measures. The NCC was particularly concerned about the provisions of the proposed law that required sanctions against countries that violated religious freedom. Instead of sanctions, the NCC also suggested training for government officials in investigating human rights violations, reserving sanctions as a "thoughtful last resort, not automatic first resort," language that respected cultures and traditions of other nations, and measures to ensure that the issue of religious freedom would not be further politicized.[172]

The sanctions provisions also troubled the Clinton administration. John Shattuck, assistant secretary for democracy, human rights, and labor, expressed the Clinton administration's concerns about these provisions in a statement before the Senate Committee on Foreign Relations. He pointed to four problems that echoed the NCC's concerns:

> We are concerned that the bill's sanctions-oriented approach fails to recognize the value of incentives and dialogue in promoting religious freedom and encouraging further improvements in some countries. . . .

> We also believe that the sanctions provisions will be counterproductive. In particular, while the imposition of sanctions is likely to have little direct impact on most governments engaged in abuses, it runs the risk of strengthening the hand of those governments and extremists who seek to incite religious intolerance.

> We fear that the sanctions could result in greater pressures—and even reprisals—against minority religious communities. . . .

> We also believe that sanctions could have an adverse impact on our diplomacy in places like the Middle East and South Asia, undercutting Administration efforts to promote the very regional peace and reconciliation that can foster religious tolerance and respect for human rights.[173]

While "public condemnation—and even sanctions—may be appropriate in many instances," Shattuck urged that the United States maintain the flexibility to determine when and how to condemn violators.[174]

Some of the administration's concerns about the need for flexibility were addressed in the revised version that was passed by both Houses of Congress. Senator Orrin Hatch (Republican–Utah) noted that the Congressional consensus on the bill came "at a time that was in other respects highly polarized politically—the House of Representatives was determining whether to go forward with impeachment proceedings against President Bill Clinton."[175]

On October 27, 1988, President Clinton signed the International Religious Freedom Act into law.[176] In doing so, he tried to downplay its significance, suggesting that it did not represent a great change of policy: "Section 401 of this Act calls for the President to take diplomatic and other appropriate action with respect to any country that engages in or tolerates violations of religious freedom. This is consistent with my Administration's policy of protecting and promoting religious freedom vigorously throughout the world. We frequently raise religious freedom issues with other governments at the highest levels."[177]

The president also emphasized the flexible nature of the new law, commenting, "I commend the Congress for incorporating flexibility in the several provisions concerning the imposition of economic measures. Although I am concerned that such measures could result in even greater pressures—and possibly reprisals—against minority religious communities that the bill is intended to help, I note that section 402 mandates these measures only in the most extreme and egregious cases of religious persecution. The imposition of economic measures or commensurate actions is required only when a country has engaged in systematic, ongoing, egregious violations of religious freedom accompanied by flagrant denials of the right to life, liberty, or the security of persons—such as torture, enforced and arbitrary disappearances, or arbitrary prolonged detention. I also note that section 405 allows me to choose from a range of measures, including some actions of limited duration." The act provides additional flexibility by allowing the president to waive the imposition of economic measures if violations cease, if a waiver would further the purpose of the act, or if required by important national interests.[178]

The provisions of the act that lack flexibility, the president contended, infringe on the authority vested by the Constitution solely with the president. For example, Section 403(b) continued to contain mandatory language ordering the president to undertake negotiations with foreign governments for specified foreign policy purposes. In signing the treaty, Clinton also vowed, "I shall treat the language of this provision as precatory and construe the provision in light of my constitutional responsibilities to conduct foreign affairs, including, where appropriate, the protection of diplomatic communications."[179]

The White House's attempts to downplay the impact of the International Religious Freedom Act (IRFA) were soon eclipsed by the many real and substantial changes the new law required. The president was required to consider taking action against countries named by the State Department to be violators of religious freedom.[180] The IRFA created three government bodies to monitor and respond to issues of religious freedom: the State Department Office on International Religious Freedom, directed by an ambassador at large;[181] the Commission on Religious Freedom, an independent body with nine members with the ambassador at large serving as an ex-officio member; and the office of the special adviser on international religious freedom in the National Security Council. The Office on International Religious Freedom was assigned the responsibility of issuing annual reports on the status of religious freedom for all foreign countries, advising the president and the secretary of state on the issues, and representing the United States with foreign governments on issues of religious freedom.[182]

The Office on International Religious Freedom country reports, issued yearly since the IRFA's enactment, provide human rights organizations with information about violations of freedom of belief and conscience in countries around the world.[183] By providing a certain amount of leverage for human rights organizations to request that the U.S. government take specific actions in religious freedom cases, the Office on International Religious Freedom has changed the way many human rights organizations approach the issue. Human Rights Watch, for example, created "The Religious Freedom Program of Human Rights Watch" in order to "press the U.S. government to identify nations engaged in serious violations of religious freedom as countries of particular concern and enforce the restrictions called for in the International Religious Freedom Act." In August 2002, for example, the Europe and Central Asia Division of Human Rights Watch wrote a letter to Secretary of State Colin Powell asking him to designate Uzbekistan and Turkmenistan as countries of particular concern for religious freedom under provisions of the IRFA. As the letter states, designating these countries would not trigger sanctions, but would "strengthen the U.S. government's hand in that dialogue and give the administration a broad range of policy tools that it could use to prod both governments toward better practices in the area of religious freedom."[184]

There is little doubt that the small group of NGOs meeting at Cizik's request had an enormous impact in shaping legislation dealing with human rights concerns and U.S. foreign policy. While the IRFA's strategy for confronting serious concerns of religious persecution remains controversial in the human rights and religious community, the NAE did succeed, to use President Clinton's words, in making religious freedom a "central element of U.S. foreign policy."[185] Some critics argue that IRFA seeks to impose Western notions of separation of church and state and is particularly imperialistic in Muslim countries,[186] that the law promotes "a hierarchy of human rights in which religion is placed at the top, above secular concerns such as due process of law or freedom of speech."[187] Another criticism is that "the United States acts unilaterally and ignores international mechanisms for addressing human rights issues, and that the International Religious Freedom Act is just the latest example of American indifference to international institutions and norms."[188] The IRFA's strategy for furthering religious freedom is also controversial. On the one hand, some suggest that the private, diplomatic pressure by U.S. leaders is more effective than public shaming and threats of sanctions. On the other hand, other critics suggest that the IRFA is too weak and that the United States should always adopt a zero-tolerance policy toward offender nations with the full application of sanctions.[189] While the various sides argue, the work of the bodies established by IRFA continues.

Monitoring Legislation: Human Trafficking

"Well, it could be a lot worse," said Martina Vandenberg, a human rights attorney with years of experience working on human trafficking, as she ruffled through the U.S. State Department's third annual Trafficking in Persons Report. She looked up with a shrug and smiled, "You know, they still have a lot to learn." Through the efforts of human rights, women's rights, and antislavery organizations, the U.S. government had already come a long way on the issue of human trafficking. By enlisting the help of some sympathetic Congressmen, most notably Senator Paul Wellstone (Democrat–Minnesota), NGOs pressured Congress in July 2000 to require the Department of State to increase and improve its reporting on trafficking in its annual *Country Reports on Human Rights Practices*.[190] In 1998, President Clinton identified trafficking in women and girls as a "fundamental human rights violation," and tasked the President's Interagency Council on Women with coordinating government policy on this issue.[191] This led to several important initiatives including the holding of congressional hearings and implementation of foreign aid policies related to trafficking.

For some observers it appeared as if the antitrafficking advocates reached the pinnacle of success in October 2000, when Congress enacted comprehensive federal legislation with the stated purpose of "combat[ing] trafficking, ensur[ing] the just and effective punishment of traffickers and protect[ing] victims."[192] Among other measures, the Trafficking Victims Protection Act (TVPA) mandated that the State Department monitor the status of trafficking in other countries and government responses and, with this ranking at hand, adjust foreign aid allotments, in some cases eventually denying aid entirely.[193]

Far from settling the issue, the TVPA created new controversies and challenges for antitrafficking advocates. The TVPA's three-tier system for ranking countries is particularly open to scrutiny. The TVPA requires reporting on only those countries worldwide with a "significant number" of trafficking victims, thus excluding countries with low numbers of gross human rights abuses. Each country that is included is judged on how well its domestic efforts meet the legislation's minimum standards for the elimination of trafficking and are classified as to whether they (1) fully comply with such standards; (2) do not yet fully comply but are making significant efforts to comply; and (3) do not fully comply and are not making significant efforts to do so. Countries that fail to improve their ranking may face the withholding of nonhumanitarian, non–trade-related assistance. Section 111 of the act authorizes the president to impose sanctions under the International Emergency Economic Powers Act, including the freezing of assets located in the United States.[194]

This process is only as good as the accuracy and completeness of information upon which it relies. NGOs have tried to supplement the information through their own field work, but ultimately the end result depends on the willingness and ability of the reviewer to analyze it in a fair and methodologically sound manner.

The first report, for example, was criticized for glossing over the problems of state complicity and corruption, and for concentrating too much on trafficking for "sexual exploitation," to the exclusion of trafficking into other forms of forced labor, among them sweatshop labor, domestic servitude, and forced agricultural and construction work.[195] The second report was criticized for not adequately evaluating antitrafficking measures. In 2002, LaShawn Jefferson, the director of the Women's Rights Project of Human Rights Watch, wrote Secretary of State Colin Powell a letter asserting, among other complaints, that the "Trafficking Report cites 'actions' taken by governments to combat trafficking, such as setting up victim service programs, establishing inter-ministerial working groups, and proposing draft legislation, but does not evaluate the content or effectiveness of such measures."[196] Human Rights Watch continued to voice similar complaints in 2003, asserting that "the report gives undue credit for minimal effort and ignores government practices, such as summary deportation and incarceration, that effectively punish trafficking victims."[197] Moreover, the report in 2003, like the previous two reports, was lacking in specifics and was almost entirely devoid of statistics.[198]

The ranking component of the reports is also a subject of controversy. Tier 2 so broadly encompasses countries of disparate trafficking records that it renders the ranking system almost meaningless. Moreover, human rights advocates note with suspicion that some governments have moved up a tier once they became an ally in the war on terror. For example, in 2002 Pakistan moved from Tier 3 to Tier 2, even though the State Department's latest human rights report indicated that Pakistan "has done little to stem the flow of women trafficked into the country or to help victims of trafficking."[199]

NGOs working on trafficking debate the methodology and usefulness of the tier reporting system and the adoption of sanctions. They often argue about how to address and approach the issue of prostitution—or "sex work." In general, however, they do agree that the TVPA holds great potential for improving programs that work with victims of trafficking to ensure their rehabilitation and reintegration into society. For example, the act directs the secretaries of the Departments of Health and Human Services and Labor, the board of directors of the Legal Services Corporation (LSC), and the heads of other federal agencies to expand benefits and services to victims of severe forms of trafficking in persons within the United States "without regard to the immigration status of such victims."[200]

"Sometimes, in a rush to accomplish other goals, such as prosecuting the traffickers, states focus on victims for the information they can provide or their usefulness to the criminal justice system," Widney Brown, Human Rights Watch advocacy director explains. "The danger is that states treat the victims as merely a pawn in a struggle between the state and the trafficker, not as a human being in need of services and deserving of respect. We must reject the practice of criminalizing victims of trafficking and placing their lives at risk through summary deportations or their psychological well being at risk though detention or imprisonment. . . . Any program must first and foremost return control to the victims. It is only when we have created the space for the trafficking victim to see her or himself again as a person, not an object, whose agency we respect and whose value is inherent, that she or he becomes a survivor."[201]

Several aspects of the TVPA are designed to address the potentially damaging aspects of the American criminal justice and immigration systems. Significantly, the act amends the Immigration and Nationality Act (INA) to create a new nonimmigrant "T" visa for "an alien who the Attorney General determines is a victim of a severe form of trafficking in persons."[202] Under limited conditions, the "T" status can be converted into a more permanent status.[203] These provisions must be monitored as well, and, where social services or advocacy support for victims are lacking, some organization must fill the void.

Single-issue NGOs that focus on antitrafficking often fill this role. The Protection Project, for example, advises policy makers, legislative bodies, governmental agencies, and international organizations on the status of domestic and international trafficking, advocates for the protection and rights of victims, increases public awareness, and provides training for law enforcement personnel. "We play a vital role, not only in providing assistance to victims and playing a role in the prosecution of traffickers, but also in lobbying and assisting the government in the formulation of U.S. foreign policy,"[204] asserts Mohamed Mattar, Protection Project codirector. Mattar is resolute in his conviction that NGO activities have contributed successfully to changes in U.S. foreign policy and the establishment of the Trafficking in Persons report. He states the evidence is found by comparing the 2001, 2002, and 2003 reports and the progressive record of improvement signified by changes in status of governments with regard to trafficking, prevention, and protection. More optimistic about the ability of the State Department reports to influence governments, Mattar credits the reports with prompting governments to adopt new antitrafficking laws and improve practices related to trafficking.[205]

Despite the progress of the TVPA, a looming issue of concern is how to hold international peacekeepers accountable for their involvement in trafficking. In Bosnia and Herzegovina, work by Human Rights Watch revealed that International Police Task Force members were complicit in, and in some cases actively supportive of, the trafficking of women and girls. Investigation into their actions remains minimal, and the action taken against officers in the past was merely limited to repatriation.[206] The organization is pressing the European Union for antitrafficking legislation. Information and concern continues to mount as the issue is highlighted by NGOs working on education and public information campaigns in the United States. The U.S. government estimates that 45,000 to 50,000 people are trafficked into the country every year, and these people become trapped in slave-like situations, such as forced prostitution.[207]

While the NGOs achieved successful passage of the TVPA in October 2000, the legislation was only a beginning for the work to be done on the trafficking issue. Enforcement, implementation, and encouraging the U.S. government to raise its reporting standards are the next steps for improving the situation for victims of trafficking. In this arena, the TVPA was a significant first step.

Human Rights Claims in U.S. Courts: The Alien Tort Claims Act

Amnesty International had a problem.[208] A former Paraguayan police inspector suspected of torturing and killing the teenage son of a political dissident was discovered in Brooklyn, New York, and was about to be deported. The dissident, Dr. Joel Filartiga, and his daughter Dolly wanted to hold Amerigo Peña-Irala accountable for Joelito Filartiga's slaying and keep him in the United States to face trial. If Peña-Irala were returned home, he would likely never face trial for the atrocities. The year was 1979, and very few lawyers had experience in international human rights, but some had carved a niche for themselves as civil rights lawyers. So Amnesty turned for help to Peter Weiss, a New York attorney with experience crafting creative civil rights litigation.[209] Weiss faced an enormous stumbling block. How could he convince U.S. courts they had legal authority to hear cases in which the parties were foreign nationals and the scene of the crime was beyond U.S. borders? Weiss called together lawyers from the Center for Constitutional Rights, where he served as an officer, to brainstorm a solution.

Weiss remembered an idea he had when contemplating a suit against U.S. military commanders on behalf of a survivor of the 1968 My Lai massacre in Vietnam.[210] Why not use the Alien Tort Claims Act (ATCA) to pry open the U.S. courts to foreign litigants? [211] The law would take some dusting off: it had been rarely used in the 190 years since its enactment.[212] But the same kinds of goals driving its enactment during George Washington's era were moving Amnesty to seek its application in 1979.[213] When written in 1789, the ATCA was designed to bring justice to piracy victims, who were subjected to horrendous crimes nearly impossible to address because they were usually committed on the high seas by foreign citizens and, often, against foreign citizens. In the Filartiga case, the murdered teenager's family, foreign nationals, sought justice in the United States, where their son's torturer had fled, because a fair trial was highly unlikely back home.

Weiss persuaded the Second Circuit Court of Appeals to hold that the ATCA permitted victims to pursue claims in U.S. federal courts based on serious violations of international human rights law.[214] The ATCA allows federal courts to hear complaints by foreign nationals for civil wrongs in violation of the "law of nations" or a treaty of the United States.[215] The torture involved in the Filartiga case, Weiss argued, was clearly against the "law of nations." Subsequent ATCA cases have named as violations of the law of nations: genocide, crimes against humanity, war crimes, "disappearances," extrajudicial executions, forced labor, and prolonged arbitrary detention.[216]

The strategy of using domestic courts as a stage for the hearing of international human rights claims makes sense in the United States, where legal culture supports the notion that individuals with claims should have an opportunity to prove their claims in court. The cases have caught on among liberal lawyers and been embraced by grassroots human rights advocates seeking to hold accountable those who have committed grave abuses against individuals. While expert attorneys are needed to bring the cases to court, nonlawyers can work with the facts of the cases in their own human rights campaigns. "These cases have wide appeal," says Sandra Coliver, the executive director of the Center for Justice and Accountability. "They can act as a bridge between human rights communities . . . bringing in labor and religious freedom groups."[217]

ATCA courts may award damages to victims and families of victims, but collection is nearly impossible. The goal of the cases, however, is not to collect money but to raise awareness and to honor victims. The cases provide public acknowledgement that the crimes occurred and offer a warning to potential perpetrators that they cannot commit gross human rights abuses with impunity.

Alien Tort Claim cases have been brought against perpetrators of widespread torture and other human rights abuses in Latin America and the Balkans.[218] Starting in 1993, as the human rights movement became more involved in monitoring corporate activity,[219] human rights attorneys began using the ATCA to file suits against multinational corporations accused of direct complicity in crimes committed by foreign governments and their security forces.[220] The first corporate case, brought by Cristobal Bonifaz, a Massachusetts attorney and native of Ecuador, accused Texaco of poisoning the Ecuador Amazon rain forest and endangering the health of its inhabitants. The company succeeded in convincing the court to send the suit to an Ecuadorian village for trial. This case was reintroduced into U.S. courts in May 2003, and as yet a decision has not been determined.[221] Undeterred, human rights attorneys have continued to bring suits, filing over twenty-five cases against such companies as Chevron, Shell Oil, Fresh Del Monte Produce, Coca-Cola, and Bank of America for acts committed on foreign soil.[222] Although most courts flatly dismissed these cases, one issued a judgment against a company and, even when they failed to bring a favorable verdict, the cases still served to draw public attention to the gross abuses of corporations.

The Justice Department has never openly opposed the use of the ATCA to raise human rights concerns. The State Department attorneys handling the Filartiga case during the Jimmy Carter era—energized by such talent as Stefan Riesenfeld, Joan Fitzpatrick, and Drew Days—"submitted a legal brief stating that refusing to recognize a private cause of action under the law 'might seriously damage the credibility of our nation's commitment to the protection of human rights.' The department stated that when the stringent conditions of the law are satisfied, 'there is little danger that judicial enforcement will impair our foreign policy efforts.'"[223]

The election of George W. Bush had many of the lawyers worried that the State Department would begin obstructing ACTA cases. Yet, when after the administration was installed, the State Department indicated it would not bring new challenges to the ATCA, human rights lawyers thought they were in the clear. The struggles, they thought, would be with the courts, not with the administration. Thus, many human rights advocates were blindsided when, on May 8, 2003, Attorney General John Ashcroft launched an assault against the law which, in the words of Professor Harold Hongju Koh, "seeks to upend almost 25 years of court rulings and contradicts previous government interpretations."[224]

The Justice Department filed an amicus curiae ("friend of the court") brief in support of the oil company Unocal in an ATCA case brought by Earthrights International.[225] The case, known as *Doe* v. *Unocal*,[226] alleges that the oil company was complicit in forced labor and other abuses committed by the Burmese military during the construction of the Yadana gas pipeline. The company maintains that no forced labor was used on the pipeline and denies responsibility for any alleged abuses by troops guarding the project, saying it had no control over the military. In September 2002, a federal appeals court overturned a trial court judge and ruled that Unocal could be sued for human rights abuses committed by Burmese soldiers, provided that the company knew about and benefited from the troops' conduct.[227] The legal claim is straightforward. "While charging an American company with slavery is controversial, there's nothing unusual in American courts holding a company responsible for the acts of its business partner."[228]

Wholly apart from the factual dispute, the Justice Department argued for a radical reinterpretation of the 1789 Alien Tort Claims Act, asserting that the ATCA could not be used as a basis to file civil cases. The Justice Department contended that victims should sue under other laws; that the "law of nations" covered by the ATCA did not include international human rights treaties, and that abuses committed outside of the United States would not be covered under the law. Their argument essentially minimizes any role for the applicability of the ATCA and thus thwarts torture victims in their search for justice.

The Justice Department brief warned that ATCA cases were taking the United States down a slippery slope to the point where federal courts were making foreign policy decisions. "Although it may be tempting to open our courts to fight every wrong all over the world," the Justice Department brief stated, "that function has not been assigned to the federal courts."[229] Attorney General Ashcroft's opinion that the Unocal suit interfered with U.S. foreign policy contradicted the State Department's view that it did not. If the State Department had perceived a conflict with U.S. foreign policy, it would have initiated the brief or, at the very least, would have signed the Ashcroft brief. In off the record conversations, State Department attorneys confided to the author that the opinions of State Department attorneys on the merits of the Ashcroft objections were mixed, with many career service members fearful that he was undermining "good law for political reasons."

Why do John Ashcroft and President Bush want to take away the ability of torture survivors to pursue human rights abusers? Sandra Coliver is "concerned that the answer has less to do with the law than with the Bush administration's interest in protecting the unfettered discretion of companies operating overseas to use whatever means they choose,"[230] and safeguarding "the ability of the administration to use whatever means necessary in the war on terrorism."[231] The countries named in many of the ACTA suits, such as Indonesia and Burma, could potentially cooperate in the war on terrorism and, thus, the Bush administration doesn't want to do anything to antagonize them, including interfering with lucrative business contracts,[232] by permitting the hearing of human rights allegations that implicate government officials. Tom Malinowski, director of Human Rights Watch's Washington, D.C., office, offered another explanation for Ashcroft's obstruction of Alien Tort Claims suits: "I don't think this has anything to do with the war on terror," he says, "I think this is motivated by a very hard-core ideological resistance within the Justice Department to the whole concept of international law being enforced. The notion that international norms are enforceable by anyone is repugnant to some in the Justice Department."[233]

As of this writing, the federal judges hearing the Unocal case have yet to decide what weight to give Ashcroft's arguments. A ruling in Ashcroft's favor may have grave implications for other suits, such as the one filed by the Presbyterian Church against Talisman Energy in Sudan, and another filed by the family of Ken Saro-Wiwa against Royal Dutch/Shell in Nigeria.[234] Human rights lawyers will not give up the Alien Tort Claims Act easily. They are already creating new arguments to get around Ashcroft's objections, should he succeed. Also, they are urging utilization of existing legislation that enables the Department of Justice (DOJ) to criminally prosecute people who committed torture anywhere in the world, so long as they are physically present within the United States.[235] To date, the DOJ has not completed a single prosecution. Some human rights advocates are also urging that DOJ prosecute the human rights abusers now in this country for perjury on their immigration forms, a crime that carries a penalty of up to five years of imprisonment.

Senators Patrick Leahy, Russell Feingold, and Orrin Hatch and Congressmen Gary Ackerman and Mark Foley have sponsored parallel bills that, if passed, would expand the grounds for exclusion or deportation to include participation in torture or extrajudicial killing.[236] The legislation also would direct the attorney general to consider prosecution or extradition of human rights abusers. "Deportation, though undoubtedly a penalty of sorts, is not a penalty that fits the crime," Coliver says, "Most abusers simply return to their home countries where they remain at large."[237] New law is needed instead, she says. Coliver is part of a group of lawyers working on new legislation that would make it easier for U.S. federal courts to hear criminal cases involving torture or extrajudicial killing. This does not mean, however, that she has given up on Alien Tort Claims suits. That battle is only beginning.[238]

SHAPING THE FOREIGN POLICY AGENDA

Civil society organizations have found creative ways to shape policy options far beyond participation in treaty processes, human rights litigation, and legislative initiatives. While these activities may be described as "lobbying," David Forsythe observes that "in order to preserve their non-political and tax-free status . . . the groups tend to refer to these activities as education."[239] In recent years, examples of the civil society influencing the U.S. foreign policy agenda can be claimed by both liberals and conservatives. For example, just as Ken Roth, the executive director of Human Rights Watch, convinced President Clinton to end his term by signing onto the treaty on the International Criminal Court (ICC), the conservative think tanks that provided President George W. Bush with his anti-ICC platform persuaded the new president to begin his term by "unsigning" the treaty.

The cases discussed in this section only begin to illustrate the ways in which civil society has an impact on foreign policy. At times, in entering the political fray, a group has a specific foreign policy goal in mind—for example, lifting an embargo or imposing sanctions. Yet for other advocates, the goal is much broader. Some advocates try to change the structure of decision making, support the inclusion of a group that has been traditionally excluded, or advocate for a set of issues that has gone unaddressed. Alternatively, their emphasis may be encouraging foreign policy makers to favor certain groups or ideas that have long been part of establishment thinking, but which are in danger of being sidelined. As these examples illustrate, the members of civil society come from all political and ideological vantage points. In seeking to influence the philosophy and operation of U.S. foreign policy, they forge unusual alliances and test new political strategies.

Mr. Smith Goes to Washington: The "Lift and Strike" Campaign

On August 23, 1993, Stephen Walker became the third person that month to quit the U.S. Foreign Service in response to American policy in the Balkans. "When I quit, I was under this delusion that no one outside the Beltway knew about or cared about Bosnia, and I would slink off and try to find a life doing something else," Walker recalls.[240] His work on Bosnia, however, had only just begun.

Walker, like many of his colleagues, believed that the war in Bosnia was resulting in widespread atrocities that would likely continue to escalate unless a third party intervened or until the United Nations arms embargo, in place on all parts of former Yugoslavia, was lifted against Bosnia "so that the [Bosnian] Muslims could defend themselves."[241] President George H. W. Bush had supported the arms embargo in September 1991, when the Serb-controlled Yugoslav National Army was using its immense weapons stash against Croatia. A lot had changed "on the ground in Bosnia" since 1991. The United Nations had recognized Bosnia as a separate state, war raged, and well-documented reports of mass rape and forced expulsions of civilians had drawn public sympathy to the plight of the most victimized group, the Bosnian Muslims. Walker had had good reason for pinning his hopes on the newly elected President Clinton turning U.S. policy on Bosnia around. After all, throughout his campaign and his early presidency, Clinton had talked as if he would support the lifting of the arms embargo and the commencement of air strikes.[242] Specifically, Clinton had declared that the United Nations, supported by the United States, must do "whatever it takes to stop the slaughter of civilians and we may have to use military force. I would begin with air power against the Serbs."[243] It was the Clinton administration's refusal to follow through with this pledge that led to Walker's resignation.

One of Walker's first speaking engagements as an ex–Foreign Service officer was with Friends of Bosnia at Amherst College. "I went out up there to find standing room only, with all these people who knew about [Bosnia] and cared about it and felt frustrated with the policy and wanted to do something about it," remembers Walker.[244] The audience was united in its concern over Bosnia, not by any ideological platform. This is not to say that all views were represented. The Left remained—in the words of Aryeh Neier, former head of Human Rights Watch and now president of the Soros foundations network and the Soros-funded Open Society Institute—"fundamentally antagonistic to the idea of U.S. military intervention."[245] At the same time certain members of the Right opposed U.S. military intervention in the absence of a direct threat to American security. But between the Right and the Left was a broad middle of both political conservatives and liberals, including many who had long activist careers opposing U.S. intervention abroad, but who believed in the necessity of intervention in Bosnia.

Looking back at that time, Glenn Ruga, cofounder of the prointervention advocacy group Friends of Bosnia, sighs, "Sometimes I feel it was a brief moment in human existence where people with a genuine commitment to human rights came together."[246] The diversity of the movement "led to some strange bedfellows: Richard Perle, Wolfowitz, Jeane Kirkpatrick, Dick Cheney, Anthony Lewis, and Susan Sontag."[247] This provoked some soul searching, particularly among the more left-leaning adherents to the cause. "Generally, there was not much discomfort over the issue of human rights," remembered Ruga.[248] "There was a general agreement on lifting the arms embargo. But some people had a very aggressive military agenda, talking about military hardware and strategy" and it took some of the activists a long time to "understand that this is what we were calling for."[249]

Human rights activists supporting the "lift and strike" campaign, remembering the failure of the United States to act to prevent genocide in Rwanda, focused on the precedent that American failure to act was setting. What did it mean for the United States to have the power to act to stop genocide but to instead do nothing? What kind of people were we becoming? Many supporters of "lift and strike" wondered if animosity toward people of Muslim faith were preventing many Americans from sympathizing more with their plight. "Imagine if Sarajevo were a 'Christian-led' city and the forces doing the raping and shelling were Muslim," Susan Sontag said, "It would have stopped in a month."[250]

"If Americans don't care about what is happening in Bosnia, what will they ever care about?" wondered Aryeh Neier.[251] Financier-philanthropist George Soros was already funneling a tremendous amount of money into humanitarian assistance, but this was not enough. Both Soros and Neier had a personal commitment to Bosnia, and they wanted to do more to put an end to the human rights abuses that were causing people to flee.

Earlier that year, Soros had taken out a large newspaper ad urging the lifting of the arms embargo and the commencement of air strikes against Serbian targets. Soros had also begun funding a lobbyist group led by Marshall Harris, another former State Department officer who had quit over the U.S. policy on Bosnia.[252] The missing element in the campaign was a coordinated grassroots campaign. Thus, under the name American Committee to Save Bosnia, Walker began to organize grassroots support for a more aggressive U.S. foreign policy in the Balkans.[253]

The "lift and strike" campaign garnered the support of Senators Bob Dole (Republican–Kansas) and Joe Lieberman (Democrat–Connecticut), who had sponsored a Senate resolution that called on Clinton to lift the arms embargo. But at that time there were few other allies for their proposal. "We were told by one former member of Congress . . . 'you guys are crazy . . . they are never going to go for it,'"[254] Walker remembers. He had low expectations. "We thought, we'll give it our best effort and a year from now, at least we'll be able to say, we tried." So he set off to take the "lift and strike" campaign "to the people."

As it turned out, Walker had little difficulty getting his message across. The "lift and strike" message resonated surprisingly well with both the general public and Congress. Mark Danner explains its popularity: "[T]he arms embargo had come to seem the most blatantly and incomprehensibly unfair.

Under what rationale could the international community prevent a member state of the United Nations from defending itself—which was, after all, its explicit right under Article 51 of the UN Charter? To even the least informed voter, this seemed clearly wrong, and giving Bosnians 'the means to defend themselves' not only seemed clearly right, it had a reassuringly American, pull-yourself-up-by-your-bootstraps sound to it. As for the 'strike,' protecting Bosnians with NATO fighters and bombers until they could absorb their new weapons and use them to fight for themselves sounded like the sort of low-cost, middle-of-the-road help Americans should be willing to supply."[255]

The debate between Congress and the administration centered on whether there should be a unilateral lifting of the arms embargo. Anthony Lake explains that President Clinton was reluctant to do anything unilaterally with respect to Bosnia: "The president's clear position throughout had been we didn't like the arms embargo. We thought it had been a mistake to put it in place earlier. But that to lift it unilaterally would split NATO, destroy UNPROFOR [United Nations Protection Force, the UN troops in Bosnia supporting delivery of humanitarian aid and monitoring "no fly zones" and "safe areas"] and face us with a terrible choice of having to replace UNPROFOR with American troops or see the collapse of Bosnia. And we didn't want to do either."[256]

In testimony before the Senate, Lake would later contend that, in fact, the White House reached a compromise on the embargo which amounted to a de facto lifting. "The United States would continue itself to implement the arms embargo, but we would no longer enforce it," Lake said. In other words, the U.S. policy of "no instructions" amounted to looking the other way when Bosnian Muslims did import arms. The only mistake with this approach, Lake asserted, was that Congress was "not informed of the no-instructions policy." On the other hand, "Congress knew, as [the administration] did, that there were Iranian arms going in. . . . That had been briefed to the Congress in a variety of ways from the intelligence community. It was in the press. There was no secret about it."[257]

The "no instructions" approach, however, did not satisfy the activists who pushed for an open endorsement of the lifting of the embargo. Richard Perle captures the sentiments of the "lift and strike" advocates when he asserts that "Clinton's well-meaning attempt to end the shameful, unprecedented embargo that kept a member state of the United Nations from exercising its fundamental right of self-defense, was half-hearted and ineptly presented."[258] At times, the Clinton administration appeared extremely receptive to the "lift and strike" campaign. Indeed, in May 1993 Clinton had sent Warren Christopher to Europe to urge the United States' NATO allies to lift the arms embargo on Bosnia and to join in air strikes to suppress Serb forces. However, as soon as Christopher encountered resistance from the European allies, he urged Clinton to drop his demands and from then on the support of the administration for a more assertive policy in Bosnia would waiver.

So it was over the vacillation of the Clinton administration that the "lift and strike" campaign pushed for several pieces of legislation mandating increased U.S. involvement in Bosnia. One of the greatest successes came on

July 27, 1995, when, in a "stinging rebuke" to President Clinton's handling of the Bosnia crisis, the Senate voted 69–29 to lift unilaterally the arms embargo on Bosnia's government.[259] The bill specified, however, that the embargo be lifted only after the United Nations peacekeeping force withdrew from Bosnia, or twelve weeks after the Bosnian government asked the UN to leave.

The bill still faced a fight in the House and a likely presidential veto, but the "lift and strike" activists saw it as an enormous victory. "It was like Civics 101 and *Mr. Smith Goes to Washington,*" exclaimed Walker, "I said, 'My God, it worked! The system worked!' There were votes that we got because grassroots people faxed and called and lobbied and influenced their representatives to change their votes."[260] Indeed, James O'Brien, a senior adviser to then Secretary of State Madeleine Albright, agrees that the activists were a major factor in the congressional debate over Bosnia.[261] But according to O'Brien, the activists' influence went far beyond these debates. "Mostly they created issues and an agenda to which the administration had to respond," he explained, "They helped those of us [within the administration] arguing for U.S. engagement in Bosnia and certainly kept human rights issues front and center."[262]

The Ambassador Goes to Civil Society: Women Waging Peace

Ambassador Swanee Hunt recalls walking into a room in her Vienna embassy and seeing a blurry-eyed Bosnian hunched over a computer. "Do you have any material that would be good for a constitution?" he asked. It was the spring of 1994 and the height of the American-brokered negotiations between Bosnian Croats and Muslims. Hunt's staff quickly phoned up the Swiss embassy and obtained a copy of their constitution on disk. "That might be why the Federation of Bosnia is carved into cantons," she sighs, remembering the somewhat quirky and extremely personal nature of diplomacy. One thing that really stood out in Hunt's experience was the absence of women. "Out of all of the negotiators that came through Vienna while I was ambassador, zero were women," she remembers. "With Yugoslavia having the highest percentage of women Ph.D.s in central and eastern Europe, I wondered, how is this possible?"[263]

In her four years (1993–97) as ambassador to Vienna, Hunt would sponsor numerous meetings and projects to strengthen forces of reconciliation in the Balkans, all the while trying to support the voices of women from the region. After the Bosnian war ended, she spearheaded the establishment of a major reconstruction fund targeting women, the Bosnian Women's Initiative, and organized a global campaign for refugee women in northern Bosnia, mobilizing efforts valued at millions of dollars. As Hunt continued to draw more attention to women's experiences in war, she grew more troubled by their absence in the peace process.[264] As she remembers, "On the ground, in the middle of the war, there were over forty women's associations, multiethnic, working on trying to stop the war. I would go and meet with them. Were they invited to the Dayton peace talks? No. Why were they not invited? Well, they weren't invited because they were not the warmakers. You figure that one out—why we think that the people who are best at planning the peace are the ones who have been waging the war. Second, they weren't invited because, as I was told, they should have organized. I told you there were forty women's associations. They had actually come together in an organization called the Union of Women's Organizations. Who was not organized?"[265]

The solution to the problem, Hunt says, rests with policy makers. "We didn't have any conduit to reach into those communities, to engage them in what we wanted to do. . . . That is what needed to change."[266]

After her ambassadorship ended in 1997, Hunt moved from Vienna to the Kennedy School of Government at Harvard, where she started a center on women and public policy and began teaching on related topics. The transition from the world of politics to academia was bumpy at first. A State Department official threatened to initiate criminal proceedings against Hunt for continuing to work with the women of Srebrenica—women whose husbands, sons, and fathers were killed by Serb forces in the 1995 slaughter. Hunt was trying to help the women to discover more information about their loved ones and, if possible, to return to their homes. The official accused Hunt of violating a law prohibiting former ambassadors from continuing activities that they began as ambassadors. He applied the law, which was intended to prohibit ambassadors from benefiting from business dealings, to NGO activities. The official sent a cable to every embassy in Europe telling them not to work with Hunt and not to support any NGO that did, thus forcing her to give up that particular initiative.[267] Instead, however, Hunt threw herself into designing a program at the Kennedy School to advance the role of women in peace processes throughout the world.

When Hunt started inviting women from war regions to come to campus, and the women began exchanging their stories, she was "totally unprepared" for the impact the gatherings would have on her life and work. "Listening to them was a life changing experience," she says, "They had been so isolated in their work . . . these were not just NGO activists, but also women from government and the military, all women . . . there was a tremendous outpouring of ideas."[268] To tap and support this synergy, Hunt began holding regular networking meetings of women from war regions and designed other projects to support the inclusion of women in formal and informal peace processes, under the rubric Women Waging Peace. Eventually Waging became too large for the Kennedy School and, although the Kennedy School still hosts many of their events, Hunt moved a large portion of Waging's work to her foundation, Hunt Alternatives Fund.

Through a series of meetings, briefings, presentations, events, roundtables, and consultations, the staff of Waging "connect traditional decision makers and policy shapers with the women who are affected by their mandates and provide essential feedback on how these decisions are received and implemented," says Ambassador Hattie Babbitt, director of the Waging office in Washington, D.C., and former deputy administrator of the U.S. Agency for International Development.[269] A primary example of such a connection was the Waging-hosted G8, NEPAD, Women, Peace and Security Meeting, held in November 2002, which brought together eleven African women leaders from Burundi, the Democratic Republic of Congo, Nigeria, Rwanda, Sierra Leone, South Africa, and Sudan; representatives from the U.S. government; and representatives from relevant Canadian and U.K. government agencies and multilateral organizations. A matrix of recommendations for donors, African governments, and African women peacebuilders was formulated from the consultation, and was distributed widely.[270]

Yet, perhaps the most powerful example of Waging's influence on the policy community is Colin Powell's support for the inclusion of women in peace activities. In January 2002, the principal deputy assistant secretary of the Bureau for Democracy, Human Rights, and Labor (DHRL) Michael Parmly requested that Waging submit a proposal with suggestions on how the DHRL could encourage the work of women peacebuilders in conflict areas. This proposal memo, along with continued advocacy efforts by Waging staff, eventually led to a "best practices" cable, sent by Secretary Powell in February 2003 to all U.S. embassies abroad, highlighting ways those institutions can include women peacebuilders in their work. The cable clearly states the department's support for women: "As we engage in peace processes, it is essential that those who suffer, including women, have a voice in decision making. The Department urges posts to involve women in conflict prevention, peace-making, and post-conflict reconstruction."[271] Much of Waging's list of "best practices" made it into the cable, calling on embassies to identify and train women to be involved in the peace process and providing examples of successful programs.[272]

Not all of Waging's efforts were so successful. The letter they sent to John Negroponte, the U.S. ambassador to the UN, requesting that the United States affirm its willingness to pursue implementation of the UN Resolution calling for greater inclusion of women in peacemaking (Resolution 1325)[273] did not result in any immediate changes in U.S. practices.[274] However, for the most part, Waging believes that they are making headway. "The various policy instruments that have emerged in recent years are indicative of the growing awareness of women's roles in peace building," stated Sanam Anderlini, Director of the Waging Policy Commission.[275] Indeed, it appears as if women's organizations have been so successful that U.S. policy makers have begun adopting the agenda as their own. A clear example is the March 2003 speech of Ambassador Donald Steinberg, principal deputy director of policy planning at the U.S. Department of State. In remarks to the Council on Foreign Relations, Steinberg presented an entire address on the importance of women's involvement in all phases of the peace process. He closed with a recommendation for his colleagues: "We must elevate the issue of women in conflict within our foreign policy establishment. This issue still suffers from second-class citizenship . . . you still hear advancement of women's interests described as the 'soft side' of foreign policy. . . . There is nothing 'soft' about insisting that women have a seat at the table in peace negotiations and post-conflict governments."[276]

These kinds of statements please Hunt, but she notes that "policy proclamations are but a beginning; implementation is the key to advancing women in the peace process."[277] Women have made it into the rhetoric of the foreign policy establishment, but in far too many cases not to the negotiation table.

The Federalists Take on the NGOs: NGOWatch.org

It all started with some conservative lawyers at the Federalist Society discovering the scholarly literature on the ways in which NGOs influence international law.[278] John McGinnis and Mark Movesian's article in the *Harvard Law Review* stood out in particular.[279] The authors warn of the dark side of NGOs in influencing the World Trade Organization.[280] Reading this, Leonard Leo, a lawyer with the Federalist Society, was struck by the similarities with Federalist Paper No. 10. In this passage, James Madison warns of the "mischief's of factions," that is the danger posed where "a number of citizens . . . are united . . . by some common impulse of passion, or of interest, adverse to the rights of other citizens, or to the permanent aggregate interests of the community."[281] NGOs present similar dangers, Leo realized. "They play a similar role to nation-states, and, of course, they are not nation-states . . . they do not have the same mechanisms for control or transparency."[282]

Having decided that the debate on NGOs was a significant one with "great impact on U.S. policies on international law" and on "whether the U.S. gives up sovereignty to international institutions,"[283] the Federalists decided to enter the fray. They teamed up with the influential Washington, D.C., think tank, the American Enterprise Institute (AEI), best known as President Bush's shadow "Central Command in Iraq."[284] Leo stresses that in formulating their plans, they had "no conversations with the Bush administration" and, in fact, sought to weigh in on the debate "wholly independently."[285]

Blending eighteenth-century Madisonian inspiration with twenty-first-century computer technology, the Federalist Society and AEI project launched NGOWatch.org. Announced on June 11, 2003, the Internet-based project was intended to fill a void in information on NGOs. The purpose of the project was stated on its website: "While it is true that many NGOs remain true to grassroots authenticity conjured up in images of protest and sacrifice, it is also true that non-governmental organizations are now serious business. NGO officials and their activities are widely cited in the media and relied upon in congressional testimony; corporations regularly consult with NGOs prior to major investments. Many groups have strayed beyond their original mandates and assumed quasi-governmental roles. Increasingly, non-governmental organizations are not just accredited observers at international organizations, they are full-fledged decision-makers."[286]

NGO Watch conceded that tax forms provide transparency about NGO resources, and it provided links to these forms on its page. However, NGO Watch asked, "[W]here is the rest of the story? Do NGOs influence international organizations like the World Trade Organization? What is their agenda? Who runs these groups? Who funds them? And to whom are they accountable?"[287] NGO Watch intends to expose NGO connections to controversial issues and influence over international organizations that are, as NGO Watch asserts, themselves not accountable and transparent. Supporters of NGO Watch like Jarol Manheim, a George Washington University political science professor, worries about NGOs pursuing "a new and pervasive form of conflict" against multinational corporations. Thus, NGO Watch was also designed to expose—to use Manheim's term—"Biz-War" in the form of shareholder resolutions, consumer boycotts, and other efforts to influence corporate behavior.[288]

To these ends, the NGOWatch.org website promises to "without prejudice, compile factual data about non-governmental organizations" and "include analysis of relevant issues, treaties, and international organizations where NGOs are active." The early postings on the site, however, were directed almost entirely at blasting NGOs for supporting abortion or homosexuality, or for crippling free market enterprise. The tone was combative and much of the information misleading. For example, NGOWatch.org stated that "Human Rights Watch, in a report promoting sexual confusion among students in public schools, recommends groups that promote same-sex marriage, and have been associated with NAMBLA (North American Man Boy Love Association)." The Human Rights Watch website, however, said no such thing. Instead, it called on school districts to "prohibit harassment and discrimination based on sexual orientation and gender identity."[289] Human Rights Watch also listed many resources for information on gender identity and sexual orientation, but did not include nor make any reference to the North American Man Boy Love Association.

Leo defended the content of the website, pointing out that the entries on homosexuality and abortion are merely links to news stories. This was just the beginning of NGO Watch, he contended, and over time a "wide spectrum of views" will be added. "I don't think we could be all that much more objective," he said.[290]

NGO Watch set off a wave of criticism in the NGO community. Critics of NGO Watch contended that it was just another example of the conservatives' war on NGOs.[291] The tense relationship between NGOs and the Bush administration had come to a head shortly before the launch of NGO Watch, when the head of the U.S. Agency for International Development (USAID), Andrew Natsios, called NGOs "an arm of the government."[292] Interaction, a coordination network of 160 humanitarian relief and development NGOs, reported on Natsios's chastisement of humanitarians working in Afghanistan and Iraq for failing to give sufficient credit to the U.S. government as the source of the aid.[293]

The American Enterprise Institute and the Federalist Society do have an unusually close connection to the George W. Bush White House—which has recruited no less than forty-two senior administration foreign policy and justice officials from AEI and the Federalist Society.[294] Given this background, NGO Watch has frequently been linked to an emerging Bush doctrine hostile to NGOs. As journalist Naomi Klein notes, "Taken together with Mr. Natsios' statements, this attack on the non-profit sector marks the emergence of a new Bush doctrine: NGOs should be nothing more than the good-hearted charity wing of the military, silently mopping up after wars and famines."[295] Critics of NGO Watch also pointed out that AEI, supported by such corporations as Motorola, American Express, and Exxon-Mobil,[296] did not list itself on the NGOWatch.org website. While a link to the AEI website is present on the site, there is no comparable exposure of media articles on AEI nor are the organization's tax forms available.

The ability of NGOs to influence policy has generated a backlash within conservative political circles. Klein describes a "war on NGOs" being fought on two clear fronts: "One buys the silence and complicity of mainstream humanitarian and religious groups by offering lucrative reconstruction contracts. The other marginalizes and criminalizes more independent-minded NGOs by claiming that their work is a threat to democracy."[297] By favoring organizations that agree with it, the U.S. Agency for International Development is said to be in charge of handing out the carrots, while the American Enterprise Institute wields the sticks through use of the traditional NGO tactic of "naming, shaming and blaming."

A new UN study on the relationship of NGOs and government seems to challenge the growing anti-NGO sentiment in Washington. The study, released in June 2003 at the World Bank by the United Nations and SustainAbility, a consultancy firm that has followed the evolution of NGOs for some fifteen years, concludes that northern-based NGOs and corporations have become much closer in their support for globalization. "[M]any NGOs now argue for more globalization, not less," the report states. "However, they stress that it needs to be focused on 'globalizing' human rights, justice and accountability for those that abuse those rights."[298]

The charge that NGOs are pursuing a "liberal" agenda at the global level that threatens both U.S. sovereignty and free-market capitalism "seem[s] almost quaint . . . as many civil society organizations (CSOs) go mainstream," according to the SustainAbility report."[299] John Elkington, the chair of SustainAbility, noted that "[t]he good news for NGOs is that they are emerging as vital ingredients in the health and vitality of markets," and that "they are also highly trusted, far more so than business or governments." The bad news, he added, "is that unless they recognize and address growing financial, competitive and accountability pressures, their impact will be significantly reduced."[300]

NGOs have not solved the accountability question. "But who has?" asks Paul Wapner, a professor at American University who has studied NGOs throughout his career.[301] NGO Watch itself is proof of the accountability mechanisms that exist in civil society. "The currency of civil society has always been the provision of information and reputation for accuracy." Wapner points out that the mere existence of NGO Watch is evidence that "the robustness and democratic sensitivities of civil society are alive and well." That AEI has put considerable resources into NGO Watch demonstrates that it shares a belief in the power of NGOs to influence policy.

CONCLUSION

Human rights NGOs and other actors in civil society have changed considerably in the post–Cold War era. Table 3 shows some of the trends discussed in this chapter. For each identifiable trend, however, an identifiable exception exists. On the one hand, the kind of human rights organizations that influence policy makers are larger and better funded, with staff better trained and professionally specialized and tactics broader and more sophisticated. But on the other hand, policy makers may be influenced by a single, well-networked person, with little formal training in either human rights issues or advocacy campaigns. Civil society actors have become more adept at providing influential information on human rights issues. Some have enhanced their effectiveness within the traditional documentation of abuses framework. Others are now directing their advocacy to a broader range of government bodies and including not only documentation of abuses, but also analysis of their root causes and suggestions for their redress. Along with creating and interpreting issues in human rights terms, civil society actors are increasingly directly involved in domestic or international human rights litigation or in the drafting of legal instruments. Many human rights organizations have been drawn into the debate on the use of military force for human rights purposes, with some organizations endorsing such actions on limited grounds. Others still steer clear of the debate or vigorously denounce the use of force in all cases.

Today, civil society is equally likely to act as a partner with the U.S. government as it is to take on an adversarial position with the government.

TABLE 3
Characteristic Trends of "Human Rights Civil Society"

IDENTIFIABLE TRENDS	BUT . . .
Bigger organizations, which are better funded	A single computer can make a substantial difference
Professional, highly trained, specialized	Wider field, open to all despite qualifications
More emphasis on "doing"	"Thinking" and "talking" remain central
Sophisticated advocacy	Older techniques of "naming, shaming, blaming" important
Closer relationship with government	Still challenges to government
Key activities include institution-building	Critics of human rights institution building urge other approaches
Increased networking	Non-elites establish own networks
More accurate information is available, (not only documentation of abuses, but also analysis of their root causes and suggestions for their redress).	Information limited to describing abuses
Policy changes on the use of military force for human rights purposes	Many remain against the use of force

While groups like NGO Watch strive for NGO transparency in order to expose their interests in participating in U.S. foreign policy, the increasingly prominent roles that civil society may take are evident to critics and participants alike. Many NGOs assume functions that were once the province of states, for example, social service delivery and humanitarian relief.[302] These NGOs must actively promote, or at least not contravene, the agenda of their donor. Once they become a sort of "public service sub-contractor,"[303] NGOs remain at risk of having their agendas and ethical principles compromised by the financial control of states.[304] Civil society must remain strong enough to resist subordination by the state. At the same time, civil society must maintain open accountability and transparency in order to be considered legitimate in its role as a participant in the democratic processes of shaping of U.S. foreign policy.[305]

This chapter features what some people would call "success stories." It demonstrates that civil society organizations can and do make substantial differences in shaping human rights discourse, initiating and monitoring treaties, and raising the domestic conscience toward human rights issues. Nonetheless, as the other chapters in this book demonstrate, these successes are often modest and are frequently offset by inconsistencies and outright failures. In the final foreign policy decision making, human rights norms often lose out to competing demands.

In reviewing the record of human rights activism as a whole, one is reminded of Sisyphus, the figure from Greek mythology charged with rolling a great boulder up a steep cliff. Every time he made progress, the boulder would slide back down and he was forever finding himself back where he started. Thus, day in and day out, he struggled up and tumbled down the cliff. Human rights advocacy groups also face a Sisyphean struggle. While they have proven influential by framing policy choices in human rights terms, human rights is only one of a range of arguments that are socially available. Human rights groups have yet to figure out a way to ensure that their approach prevails with any consistency, finding all too often that the power of competing frameworks pushes them back down to the bottom of the hill. But, as in all matters of weight and gravity, leverage can prove just as important a factor as sheer strength. For human rights organizations to truly succeed, perhaps the straightforward "shoulder to the boulder" approach should be rethought. The final chapter in this book suggests a significant departure from the current focus on changing the interests and expectations of decision-making elites.

ENDNOTES

1. Robert Hunter, "Think Tanks: Helping to Shape U.S. Foreign and Security Policy," *U.S. Foreign Policy Agenda* 5, no. 1 (2000): 33–36.
2. Stephen J. Wayne, "The Multiple Influences on U.S. Foreign Policy-Making," *U.S. Foreign Policy Agenda* 5, no. 1 (2000): 25–27.
3. See, in particular, the findings of the Research Triangle Institute, available online at http://www.rti.org/index.cfm.

4. Margaret E. Keck and Kathryn Sikkink, *Activists beyond Borders* (Ithaca, N.Y.: Cornell University Press, 1998). See also Audie Klotz, *Norms in International Relations: The Struggle against Apartheid* (Ithaca, N.Y.: Cornell University Press, 1995).

5. Sidney Tarrow, *Power in Movement: Social Movements and Contentious Politics* (Cambridge: Cambridge University Press, 1998), 110.

6. Mayer Zaid, "Culture, Ideology and Strategic Framing," in *Comparative Perspectives on Social Movements*, ed. Doug McAdam, John D. McCarthy, and Mayer Zaid (New York: Cambridge University Press, 1996), 262.

7. S. L. Weldon, "Inclusion, Solidarity and Social Movements: The Global Movement against Gender Violence," paper presented at the Annual Meeting of the International Studies Association, Portland, Oregon, 2003.

8. Gareth Evans, "Preventing Deadly Conflict: The Role and Responsibility of Governments and NGOs," lecture at the Centre for Study of Human Rights, London School of Economics, February 2, 2001; available online at http://www.lse.ac.uk/Depts/human-rights/Documents/PreventingDeadlyConflict.doc. Gareth Evans, interview with the author, May 2003.

9. Ibid.

10. Ibid.

11. The techniques of human NGOs include: the monitoring and surveillance of human rights problems; notification of emergency situations; the dissemination of information about human rights norms and their violations to the general public; the exchange of such information with other nonstate actors in transnational civil society; the reporting of human rights problems to state and international bodies; and ongoing or ad hoc consultation with governments or international human rights bodies. See Peter J. Spiro, "New Global Communities: Nongovernmental Organizations in International Decision Making Institutions," *Washington Quarterly* 18 (1995): 45.

12. David Forsythe, *Human Rights in International Relations* (Cambridge: Cambridge University Press, 2000), 166.

13. Title 71 of the UN Charter grants NGOs consultative status with the Economic and Social Council. In recent years, this provision has been read broadly, and an increasing number of NGOs now are involved in the work of UN bodies. See Peter Willetts, "Consultative Status for NGOs at the United Nations," in *The Conscience of the World: The Influence of Nongovernmental Organizations in the UN System*, ed. Peter Willetts (Washington, D.C.: Brookings Institution 1996), 31.

14. Kal Raustiala, "States NGOs, and International Environmental Institutions," *International Studies Quarterly* 41 (1997): 710; see also Thomas Princen and Matthias Finger, *Environmental NGOs in World Politics* (London: Routledge, 1994).

15. Richard Price, "Reversing the Gun Sights: Transnational Civil Society Targets Land Mines," *International Organization* 42, no. 3 (1998): 613. See also Kenneth Anderson, "The Ottawa Convention Banning Landmines: The Role of International Non-Governmental Organizations and the Idea of International Civil Society," *European Journal of International Law* 11 (2000): 91–120.

16. Martha Alter Chen, "Engendering World Conferences: The International Women's Movement and the UN," in *NGOs, the UN and Global Governance*, ed. Thomas G. Weiss and Leon Gordenker (Boulder, Colo.: Lynne Rienner, 1996).

17. Felice D. Gaer, "Reality Check: Human Rights NGOs Confront Governments at the UN," in *NGOs, the UN and Global Governance*, ed. Thomas G. Weiss and Leon Gordenker (Boulder, Colo.: Lynne Reinner, 1996).

18. Martina Vandenberg, interview with the author, June 2001.

19. NGO Watch: A Project of the American Enterprise Institute and the Federalist Society, http://www.ngowatch.org/.
20. William Korey, *NGOs and the Universal Declaration of Human Rights* (New York: St. Martin's Press, 2001), 3.
21. Ibid.
22. Ibid., 139, 229
23. Vandenberg interview.
24. See Paul Wapner, "Introductory Essay: Paradise Lost? NGOs and Global Accountability," *Chicago Journal of International Law* 3, no. 1 (2002): 157.
25. Ibid.
26. Ibid.
27. Anonymous interview with the author, spring 2001.
28. Anonymous interview with the author, spring 2001.
29. Vandenberg interview.
30. Ibid.
31. Jonathan Evans, interview with the author, May 2001.
32. David Kennedy, "The International Human Rights Movement: Part of the Problem?" *Harvard Human Rights Journal* 15 (2002): 112.
33. Ibid., 120.
34. The Landmine Survivors Network human rights education campaign is an important exception.
35. Patrick Coy, "Cooperative Accompaniment and Peace Brigades International in Sri Lanka," in *Transnational Social Movements and Global Politics*, ed. Jackie Smith, Charles Chatfield, and Ron Pagnucco (Syracuse, N.Y.: Syracuse University Press, 1997), 94.
36. For more information on Human Rights Education Associates, see http://www.hrea.org. More information on the People's Movement on Human Rights Education is available from http://www.pdhr.org. See also the UNCHCR website on human rights education and training, http://www.unhchr.ch/education/main.htm.
37. Nancy Flowers, interview with the author, June 2003.
38. Tom Malinowski, interview with the author, July 2001.
39. Glenn Ruga, interview with the author, June 2003.
40. Ken Roth, "A Dangerous Security," *Worldlink,* January 17, 2002.
41. Stephanie Farrior, interview with the author, March 2001.
42. International Council on Human Rights Policy, *Human Rights Crises: NGO Responses to Military Interventions* (Versoix: International Council on Human Rights Policy, 2002), 39.
43. Ibid. See also Human Rights Watch website, http://www.hrw.org/about/whoweare.html.
44. International Council on Human Rights Policy, *Human Rights Crises.* See also Physicians for Human Rights website, http://www.phrusa.org.
45. This is the subject of a forthcoming edited collection; see Julie Mertus and Jeffrey Helsing, eds., *Human Rights and Conflict* (Washington D.C.: United States Institute of Peace, 2004).
46. Nancy Lindborg of Mercy Corps, interview with the author, July 2001 and July 2003. Jonathan Evans, interview with the author, May 2001.

47. The International Council on Human Rights Policy, *Human Rights Crises*, page 21, offers this helpful explanation of the relationship between human rights and humanitarian organizations: "Most human rights NGOs are intensely loyal to international human rights law, which provides a key foundation of bare legitimacy. Though their loyalty is to the *values* that human rights law claims to represent, they rely heavily on legal principles in judging the performance of governments. Some humanitarian agencies, most obviously the ICRC [International Committee of the Red Cross], whose mandate is to implement international human rights law, share this legal approach. The great majority of relief agencies, however, are far more pragmatic both in the way they develop policy and in the way they draw upon international human rights standards and humanitarian law. They consider the latter to be useful rather than defining instruments: the purpose is to assist those in need."

48. Ian Smillie, interview with the author, June 2001.

49. Ibid.

50. Fiona Terry, *Condemned to Repeat? The Paradox of Humanitarian Action* (Ithaca, N.Y.: Cornell University Press, 2002).

51. Ibid., 220.

52. Julie Mertus, "Improving Post-Agreement Intervention: The Role of Human Rights Culture in Kosovo," *Global Governance*, forthcoming, 2004.

53. Anonymous interview with the author, 2001.

54. Kenneth Anderson, "The Limits of Pragmatism in American Foreign Policy: Unsolicited Advice to the Bush Administration on Relations with International Nongovernmental Organizations," *Chicago Journal of International Law* 2 (2001): 371.

55. Andrew Loomis, interview with the author, June 2003.

56. While not a sample survey, it is significant that more than a third of the people interviewed for this study from human rights organizations or think tanks had been employed in government and/or the U.S. military. Nearly all respondents had worked in at least two other fields, including private industry, high technology start-up companies, philanthropy, education, the arts, banking, law, and advertising.

57. Martha Finnemore and Kathryn Sikkink, "International Norm Dynamics and Political Change," *International Organization* 52, no. 4 (1998): 887, 909–12.

58. Don Hubert, "Inferring Influence: Gauging the Impact of NGOs," in *Toward Understanding Global Governance: The International Law and International Relations Toolbox*, ed. Charlotte Ku and Thomas G. Weiss, ACUNS Reports and Papers no. 2 (Providence, R.I.: ACUNS, 1998).

59. On the International Criminal Court, see, for example, David H. Martin, "Haste, Gaps, and Some Possible Cures for the ICC: An Introduction to the Panel," *Virginia Journal of International Law* 41 (2000): 152. On the Landmines Treaty see Maxwell A. Cameron, Robert J. Lawson, and Brian W. Tomlin, eds., *To Walk without Fear: The Global Movement to Ban Landmines* (N.Y.: Oxford University Press, 1999); and Don Hubert, *The Landmine Treaty: A Case Study in Humanitarian Advocacy,* Occasional Paper no. 42, Watson Institute for International Studies, 2000. A discussion of NGO roles in information-gathering and dispersal is available in Richard R. Murray and Kellye L. Fabian, "Compensating the World's Landmine Victims: Legal Liability and Anti-Personnel Landmine Procedures," *Seton Hall Law Review* 33 (2003): 303.

60. Ivan Simonovic, "Relative Sovereignty of the Twenty-First Century," *Hastings International and Comparative Law Review* 25 (2002): 378.

61. National Council on Disability, *Understanding the Role of an International Convention on the Human Rights of People with Disabilities: A White Paper* (Washington D.C.: National Council on Disability, 2002); available online at http://www.ncd.gov/newsroom/publications/unwhitepaper_05-23-02.html.

62. Ibid. (Citing, among others, Louis Henkin, "The Constitution, Treaties and International Human Rights," *University of Pennsylvania Law Review* 1012 (1968); remarks of Professor Louis B. Sohn before the 1979 Senate Hearings on International Human Rights Treaties (Senate Committee on Foreign Relations, 96th Congress, 1st Session), wherein Sohn stated that the "fears [of the US regarding human rights treaties] have been exaggerated and that it is simply part of the general feeling that the United States knows better about various things and therefore should not be subject to other peoples' judgments." Henry J. Steiner and Philip Alston, *International Human Rights in Context: Law, Politics, Morals* (New York: Oxford University Press, 2000), 1037.

63. See, e.g., David Lumsdaine, *Moral Vision in International Politics* (Princeton, N.J.: Princeton University Press, 1993).

64. David Balton, interview with the author, June 2003.

65. Cynthia Price Cohen, interview with the author, June 2003.

66. For a record of the Polish proposal to the Commission on Human Rights, see U.N. Doc. E/1978/34 (1978). See also Marjorie Newman-Williams, "How Things Changed," *UN Chronicle* 36, no. 2 (1999).

67. Cynthia Price Cohen, "Implementing the U.N. Convention on the Rights of the Child," *Whittier Law Review* 23, no. 1 (1999): 95–105.

68. Newman-Williams, "How Things Changed."

69. Cynthia Price Cohen, "The Role of the United States in Drafting the Convention on the Rights of the Child: Creating a New World for Children," *Loyola Poverty Law Journal* 4 (1998): 25–26.

70. U.N. Doc. E/CN.4/1349.

71. See Sharon Detrick, Nigel Cantwell, and Jaap Doek, eds., *The United Nations Convention on the Rights of the Child: A Guide to the "Travaux Preparatoires"* (New York: Martinus Nijhoff; 1992); Cynthia Price Cohen, e-mail correspondence with the author, August–September 2003.

72. For an overview of the activities of NGOs in drafting the Convention, see Cynthia Price Cohen, "The Role of Non-governmental Organizations in the Drafting of the Convention on the Rights of the Child," *Human Rights Quarterly* 12 (1990): 137.

73. Cohen, "The Role of the United States," 26.

74. Adam Lopatka, "An Introduction to the United Nations Convention on the Rights of the Child," *Transnational Law and Contemporary Problems* 6 (1996): 251.

75. Cohen, "Role of the United States," 33, citing U.N. Doc. E/CN.4/1988/WG.1/WP. 2 (1988), at 15. It did not include the paragraph on parental rights which the American representative had proposed, but instead included a broad limitation clause permitting restrictions on the right to assembly on several bases, including "public health or morals."

76. Legislative History of the Convention on the Rights of the Child (1978–1989), U.N. Doc. HR/1996/Ser.1.

77. Cohen interview.

78. Convention on the Rights of the Child, G.A. Res. 44/25, 44 U.N. GAOR Supp. No. 49, U.N. Doc. A/44/736 (1989).

79. Rebecca Rios Kohn, "The Convention on the Rights of the Child: Progress and Challenges," *Georgetown Journal on Fighting Poverty* 5 (1998): 146.

80. Cohen interview.

81. Signature of a treaty does obligate the signatory to refrain from taking action which would defeat the object and purpose of the treaty, while signing does not entail a legal commitment to ratify. *Vienna Convention on the Law of Treaties*, art. 18, 1155 U.N.T.S. 332,336 (23 May 1969); see also Detrick, Cantwell, and Doek, eds., *"Travaux Preparatoires."*

82. "White House Statement on U.S. Decision to Sign U.N. Convention on the Rights of the Child," White House Press Office, February 10, 1995.

83. Cohen, "Role of the United States," 26.

84. Balton interview.

85. Ibid. This is not to suggest that they agreed on everything, or that NGOs were a homogenous group. While in the beginning the NGOs were "like-minded," toward the end of the negotiations more NGOs participated that shared different views on abortion and other controversial issues.

86. Ibid.

87. Ibid.

88. Michael J. Dennis, "Newly Adopted Protocols to the Convention on the Rights of the Child," *American Journal of International Law* 94, no. 3(2000): 796.

89. A complete listing of the U.S. organizations and local governments supporting the Convention can be found at the UNICEF website, http://www.unicef.org/crc/updates/usendorse.html; information on new organizing and the revival of the movement may be found at www.hrea.org/lists/child-rights/markup/msg00160.html.

90. Martin L. Scherr, "Convention on the Rights of the Child," speech, Kansas City, Missouri, September 12, 2002; available online at http://www.kcglobalconcepts.org/martin%20scherr.pdf.

91. Susan Kilbourne, "Placing the Convention on the Rights of the Child in an American Context," *Human Rights* 26, no. 2 (1999): 25–31. Cynthia Price Cohen (interview with the author, June 2003) estimated that the ratio of letters against versus in support of the convention received by congressional offices were more like 5,000 to 1. Stephen Walker stated in an interview with the author (June 2003) that most Congressional offices consider every original letter to be representative of 5,000 constituents.

92. John Rosemond, *A Family of Value* (Kansas City, Mo.: Andrews McMeel Publishing 1995) 116.

93. Barbara J. Nauck, "Implications of the United States Ratification of the United Nations Convention on the Rights of the Child: Civil Rights, the Constitution and the Family," *Cleveland State Law Review* 42 (1994): 675, 686–88.

94. Bruce C. Hafen and Jonathan O. Hafen, "Abandoning Children to their Autonomy: The United Nations Convention on the Rights of the Child," *Harvard International Law Journal* 37 (1996): 449.

95. Elizabeth M. Calciano, "United Nations Convention on the Rights of the Child: Will it Help Children in the United States?" *Hastings International and Comparative Law Review* 15 (1992): 515, 521–22.

96. David Stewart, "Ratification of the Convention on the Rights of the Child," *Georgetown Journal on Fighting Poverty* (1998): 173–76. For a view of one of the U.S. representatives taking part in the treaty negotiations, see David A. Balton, "The Convention on the Rights of the Child: Prospects for International Enforcement," *Human Rights Quarterly* 12 (1990): 120.

97. Kevin Mark Smith, "The United Nations Convention on the Rights of the Child: The Sacrifice of American Children on the Altar of Third-World Activism," *Washburn Law Journal* (1998): 124.

98. Cohen interview.

99. Kilbourne, "American Context," 27–31.
100. See Allyn L. Taylor and Ruth Roemer, "International Strategy for Tobacco Control," WHO Doc. WHO/PSA/96.6 (1996); available online athttp://www5.who.int/tobacco/repository/stp41/Taylor.pdf. See also Allyn L. Taylor, "An International Regulatory Strategy for Global Tobacco Control," *Yale Journal of International Law* 21 (1996): 257; David J. Malcolm, "Tobacco, Global Public Health, and Non-governmental Organizations: An Eminent Pandemic or Just Another Legal Product?" *Denver Journal of International Law and Policy* 28, no. 1 (1999): 1.
101. Gro Harlem Brundtland, Response of the Director General to the Report of the Committee of Experts on Tobacco Industry Documents, WHO Doc. WHO/DG/SP, October 6, 2000; available online at http://tobacco.who.int/repository/stp58/inquiryDGres1.pdf; Committee of Experts on Tobacco Industry Documents, "Tobacco Industry Strategies to Undermine Tobacco Control Activities at the World Health Organization," July 2000; available online at http://tobacco.who.int/repository/stp58/who_inquiry.pdf.
102. C. W. Henderson, "Health Letter on CDC World Health Assembly Gives Support to WHO Technical Programs," July 26, 1999.
103. International Framework Convention for Tobacco Control, WHA Res. 49.17, 49th Ass., 6th Plen. mtg., WHO Doc. A49/VR/6 (1996). See also WHO Tobacco Free Initiative, "The Framework Convention on Tobacco Control: A Primer," WHO Doc. WHO/NCD/TFI/99.8 Rev. 3; available online at http://tobacco.who.int/repository/stp41/Primeren.pdf.
104. Bulletin of the Word Health Organization 81, no.4 (2003): 311; available online at http://www.who.int/bulletin/volumes/81/4/WHONews0403.pdf.
105. Judith Wilkenfeld, interview with the author, June 2003.
106. Ibid.
107. Campaign for Tobacco-Free Kids, "Memo on Tobacco Trends in the Twenty-First Century: Domestic and Global Outlook," *U.S. Newswire*, December 16, 1999.
108. "NGOs Urge Strong Action on WHO Tobacco Treaty," *U.S. Newswire*, October 29, 1999.
109. "Framework Convention on Tobacco Control," *Alliance Bulletin* (Geneva) no. 5, October 20, 2000; available online at http://www.fctc.org/Issue_5.pdf.
110. Wilkenfeld interview.
111. Associated Press, "White House is Accused of Deferring to Big Tobacco," *St. Louis Post-Dispatch*, November 20, 2001.
112. Wilkenfeld interview.
113. Marc Kaufman, "Negotiator in Global Tobacco Talks Quits, Official Said to Chafe at Softer U.S. Stands," *Washington Post*, August 2, 2001.
114. Wilkenfeld interview.
115. Judith Wilkenfeld, "U.S. Continues Obstructionist Behavior As Negotiations Resume on Proposed Tobacco Treaty," October 17, 2002; available online at http://tobaccofreekids.org/Script/DisplayPressRelease.php3?Display=559.
116. Alfred Munzer, quoted in "Leading U.S. Public Health Groups Tell U.S. Delegation to Tobacco Treaty Negotiations: Go Home," press release, February 25, 2003; available online at http://tobaccofreekids.org/Script/DisplayPressRelease.php3?Display=607.
117. Wilkenfeld interview.
118. A copy of the U.S. position is available at www.tobaccofreekids.org/pressoffice/release633/convention.pdf.

119. U.S. Department of State, "International Health Officials Adopt Convention on Tobacco Control," press release, May 21, 2003; available online at http://usinfo.state.gov/topical/global/drugs/03052103.htm.

120. Framework Convention Alliance, FCA Scorecard; available online at http://www.fctc.org/FCTC_scorecard.xls.

121. See communications available online at http://www.tobaccofreekids.org.

122. J. I. Charlton, *Nothing about Us without Us: Disability, Oppression and Empowerment* (Berkeley and Los Angeles: University of California Press, 1998).

123. There were two early efforts within the United Nations to build support for the drafting of an international treaty on the rights of people with disabilities. In 1987, the Global Meeting of Experts to review the Implementation of the World Programme of Action concerning Disabled Persons was convened at the midpoint of the UN Decade of Disabled Persons and recommended that the UN General Assembly convene a conference to draft an international convention on the elimination of all forms of discrimination against persons with disabilities. Draft agreements were in fact prepared by Italy (U.N. Doc. A/C.3/42/SR.16 (1987)) and Sweden (U. A/C.3/44/SR.16 (1989)) but were rejected by the UN General Assembly at its forty-second and forty-fourth sessions. See Bengt Lindqvist, "Standard Rules in the Disability Field," in *Human Rights and Disabled Persons: Essays and Relevant Human Rights Instruments*, ed. Theresia Degener and Yolan Koster-Dreese (Dordrecht, Netherlands: Kluwer Academic, 1995).

124. Comprehensive and Integral International Convention to Promote and Protect the Rights and Dignity of Persons with Disabilities, Third Committee, 56 Sess., Agenda Item 119(b), U.N. Doc. A/C.3/56/L.67/Rev.1 (November 28, 2001).

125. National Council on Disability, *A White Paper*, 41–43, 58.

126. In this regard, Mental Disability Rights International has highlighted the impact of "charity" programs that serve to reinforce segregated and discriminatory practices against people with disabilities, drawing particular attention to funding used to rebuild or repair inappropriate institutions instead of community-based alternatives. Eric Rosenthal, et al., "Implementing the Rights to Community Integration for Children with Disabilities in Russia: A Human Rights Framework for International Action," *Health and Human Rights* 4 (1999): 83, 89.

127. For more on traditional models of disability, see Gareth Williams, "Theorizing Disability," in *Disability Studies*, ed. Gary L. Albrecht, Katherine D. Seelman, and Michael Bury (Thousand Oaks, Cal.: Sage, 2001), 123.

128. For some of the leading work in the field of disability studies reflecting the social model of disability, see especially, Michael Oliver, *The Politics of Disablement* (1990); Simi Linton, *Claiming Disability: Knowledge and Identity* (New York: New York University Press, 1998); Benedicte Ingstad and Susan Reynolds Whyte, eds., *Disability and Culture* (Berkeley, Cal.: University of California Press, 1995).

129. Joelle Balfe, National Council on Disabilities, interview with the author, September 2003.

130. Janet E. Lord, "International Disability Rights: Challenging Traditional Theory in the Emergence of a New Transitional Advocacy Network," paper presented at the Annual Meeting of the International Studies Association, Portland, Oregon, February 26–March 1, 2003, 16.

131. National Council on Disability, *A Reference Tool: Understanding the Potential Content and Structure of an International Convention on the Human Rights of People with Disabilities* (Washington, D.C.: National Council on Disability, 2002); available online at http://www.ncd.gov/newsroom/publications/understanding_7-30-02.html

132. National Council on Disability, *A White Paper*, 41–43, 58.
133. Campaign Development Group, *Navigating the Ad Hoc Committee: A "Rough" Guide to NGO Participation in the Development of a Treaty on the Rights of People with Disabilities* (Washington, D.C.: Landmine Survirors Network, 2002). The guide draws heavily on the experience of other movements and activist networks. See, e.g., Sharyle Patton and Karen Perry, *A Manual for NGO Participants in the Persistent Organic Pollutants (POPS) Intergovernmental Negotiating Committee (INC) Process* (Washington, D.C.: The International Persistent Organic Pollutants Elimination Network, 1999); International Women's Tribune Centre, "Get Ready! Connecting Beijing to Action at Home," *The Tribune—A Women and Development Quarterly* 52 (1994); International Women's Tribune Centre, "Get Set! NGO's Worldwide Prepare for Beijing," *The Tribune—A Women and Development Quarterly* 53 (1995).
134. Disabled persons organizations (DPOs) with ECOSOC consultative status include: Disabled Peoples' International, Rehabilitation International, World Blind Union, World Federation of the Deaf, World Federation of the Deafblind, Inclusion International, and World Network of Users and Survivors of Psychiatry. The international DPO with roster status is Support Coalition International.
135. Accreditation and Participation of Non-governmental Organizations in the Ad Hoc Committee to Consider proposals for a Comprehensive and Integral International Convention to Promote and Protect the Rights and Dignity of Persons with Disabilities, U.N. GA Res. A/RES/56/510; available online at http://www.un.org/esa/socdev/enable/rights/adhocngo82e.htm.
136. Lord, "International Disability Rights," 24.
137. Avraham Rabby, "The Rights and Dignity of Persons With Disabilities," statement at the Ad Hoc Committee on a Comprehensive and Integral International Convention on Protection and Promotion of the Rights and Dignity of Persons with Disabilities, UN General Assembly, July 30, 2002; available online at http://www.state.gov/p/io/rls/rm/2002/12365.htm.
138. Ibid.
139. The final report adopted by the ad hoc committee and subsequently adopted by the UN General Assembly contains many of the points advocated by NGOs in their Disability Caucus Platform. For a copy of the Final Report of the Ad Hoc Committee that was subsequently adopted by the UN General Assembly, see http://www.un.org/esa/socdev/enable/rights/adhocngos.htm.
140. Interviews with members of NGOs present at meeting, June 2003.
141. For copies of the *Daily Disability Negotiations Summary*, vol. 1, 1–10, see http://www.rightsforall.org.htm.
142. Earth Negotiations Bulletin; available online at http://www.iisd.ca/enbvol/enb-background.htm.
143. Daily Disability Negotiations Summary, 1, no. 10; available online at http://www.rightsforall.org.htm.
144. Richard Light, Steve Estey, Janet Lord, and Rosangela Berman-Beiler, "Disability Negotiations Extra," August 8, 2002; available online at http://www.worldenable.net/rights/adhocmeetsumm08a.htm.
145. Report of the Ad Hoc Committee on a Comprehensive and Integral International Convention on Protection and Promotion of the Rights and Dignity of Persons with Disabilities, United Nations, A/57/357; available online at http://www.un.org/esa/socdev/enable/rights/adhoca57357e.htm.

146. Meeting of the Ad Hoc Committee, July 29–August 9, 2002; *NGO Daily Summaries: Disability Negotiations Daily Summary* 1, no. 10 (August 9, 2002); available online at http://www.worldenable.net/rights/adhocmeetsumm10.htm.

147. All four developments are from Janet Lord, interview with the author, June 2003.

148. The New Freedom Initiative text is available online at http://www.whitehouse.gov/news/freedominitiative/freedominitiative.html.

149. Ralph F. Boyd, Statement, Agenda item 5: "Review of progress in the elaboration of a comprehensive and integral international convention on the protection and promotion of the rights and dignity of persons with disabilities," *Second Session of the Ad Hoc Committee on a Comprehensive and Integral International Convention on Protection and Promotion of the Rights of Persons with Disabilities,* June 18, 2003; available online at http://www.un.org/esa/socdev/enable/rights/contrib-us.htm.

150. Anonymous interview with the author, June 2003.

151. Lord interview.

152. Sandy Vogelsang, *American Dream, Global Nightmare: The Dilemma of U.S. Human Rights Policy* (New York: W. W. Norton, 1980).

153. Foreign Operations, Export Financing, and Related Programs Appropriations Act of 1990, Pub. L. No. 101-167, § 599D, 103 Stat. 1195 (1989) [commonly known as the Lautenberg Amendment] (codified as amended at 8 U.S.C. § 1157 (1994)).

154. The Leahy-McConnell bill was stricter than the Lautenberg bill in that it linked many types of foreign aid (democratization and humanitarian assistance was excluded) to the Secretary of State certifying that Serbia had met certain conditions evidencing cooperation and progress on human rights. See Patrick Leahy, "Statement of Sen. Patrick Leahy on Secretary Powell's Certification that Serbia has Met Leahy-McConnell Conditions for Release of U.S. Aid," May 21, 2002; available online at http://www.leahy.senate.gov/press/200205/052102a.html; see also *Congressional Record Daily Digest* (June 20, 1999), S7847, S7852.

155. Terrence Guay, "Local Government and Global Politics: The Implications of Massechusetts' 'Burma Law,'" *Political Science Quarterly* 115, no. 3 (2000): 353–76.

156. Sarah Jackson-Han, "Burma Sanctions Garner Qualified Support," *Agence France-Presse,* June 29, 2002; see also "Anti-Myanmar Campaigners 'Clothes In' on Victory," *Agence France-Presse,* June 6, 2002; "U.S. Activists Continue Fight against Junta," *Nation* June 21, 2000, accessed through Westlaw 2000 WL 19047623.

157. D. G. Hart, "The Mid-life Crisis of American Evangelicalism: Identity Problems," *Christian Century* 109, no. 33 (1992): 1028–31.

158. The Reverend Richard Cizik, interview with the author, June 2003.

159. Ibid.

160. The individuals represented centrist and conservative organizations who had expressed concerned about religious persecution around the world. For example, Freedom House started a freestanding division called the Center for Religious Freedom in 1986. According to its website, the center "defends against religious persecution of all groups throughout the world"; see http://www.freedomhouse.org/religion/about/about.htm. The World Evangelical Alliance is a membership organization of evangelical churches around the world, and supports the International Day of Prayer for the Persecuted Church. The Hudson Institute, a policy think tank, lists "respect for the importance of culture and religion in human affairs" among its core values. The Institute of Religion and Democracy supports democratizing efforts under the belief that "democratic principles best embody Christian notions of human freedom, and that religious liberty is a right for all people throughout the world"; see http://www.ird-renew.org/Feedback/FeedbackList.cfm?c=1.

161. "Statement of Conscience of the National Association of Evangelicals Concerning Worldwide Religious Persecution," January 23, 1996; available online at http://images.mychurchesimages.com/4469/pdf/statementofconscience.pdf.
162. Ibid.
163. Ibid.
164. Peter Steinfels, "Evangelicals Ask Government to Fight Persecution of Christians," *New York Times*, January 23, 1996.
165. Cizik interview.
166. Ibid. See also a brief history of the National Association of Evangelicals, available online at http://www.nae.net/index.cfm/method/content.3973D71E-FC09-4A9D-A28A4C28CE2067F4.
167. Cizik interview.
168. Ibid.
169. Jeremy T. Gunn, "A Preliminary Response to Criticisms of the International Religious Freedom Act of 1998," *Brigham Young University Law Review* 2000, no. 3 (2000): 841–65.
170. See Eric Schmitt, "Bill to Punish Nations Limiting Religious Beliefs Passes Senate," *New York Times*, October 10, 1998.
171. National Council of Churches, http://www.ncccusa.org/about/about_ncc.htm.
172. National Council of Churches, "NCC Public Policy Office Offers Qualified Support for Nickles-Lieberman Bill on Religious Persecution," press release, October 6, 1998; available online at http://www.ncccusa.org/news/news90.html.
173. John Shattuck, assistant secretary of state for democracy, human rights, and labor, "S. 1868: The International Religious Freedom Act of 1998: Hearings Before the Senate Comm. on Foreign Relations," statement, 105th Cong. 87 (May 12 and June 17, 1998), 94.
174. Ibid.
175. Orrin G. Hatch, "Religious Liberty at Home and Abroad: Reflections on Protecting this Fundamental Freedom," *Brigham Young University Law Review* 2001, no. 2 (2001): 413–28.
176. Public Law No. 105-292, 112 Stat. 2787 (1998).
177. William J. Clinton, "Statement by the President on Signing the International Religious Freedom Act of 1998," *Weekly Compilation of Presidential Documents* 34 (October 27, 1998): 2149.
178. Ibid.
179. Ibid.
180. The final version of the IRFA had a menu of fifteen different actions from which to choose, ranging from withdrawal of foreign aid to more limited actions such as private demarche. Gunn, "A Preliminary Response," 857.
181. Robert A. Seiple, the first ambassador at large for international religious freedom, favored a quiet diplomacy approach to the issues, which has largely set the tone for the State Department's work in the area.
182. Gunn, "A Preliminary Response," 843.
183. The reports are available online at http://www.state.gov/g/drl/irf/rpt/.
184. "Uzbekistan, Turkmenistan, and the International Religious Freedom Act: Letter to U.S. Secretary of State Colin L. Powell"; available online at http://www.hrw.org/press/2002/08/religious-freedom-ltr.htm
185. Clinton, "Statement on Signing," 2149.

186. Matthew L. Fore, "And You Shall Weigh Your God: Assessing the Imperialistic Implications of the International Religious Freedom Act in Muslim Countries," *Duke Law Journal* 52, no. 2 (2002): 424.

187. John Shattuck, "Religion, Rights, and Terrorism," *Harvard Human Rights Journal* 16 (2003): 185. In reviewing this objection to the IRFA, Shattuck writes, "This is not an entirely invalid concern. While the law does not explicitly give religion a special status in human rights, it does provide the U.S. government with greater powers to deal with violations of religious freedom abroad than other human rights." See also Kristin N. Wuerffel, "Discrimination among Rights? A Nation's Legislating a Hierarchy of Human Rights in the Context of International Human Rights Customary Law," *Valparaiso University Law Review* 33 (1998): 369.

188. Shattuck, "Religion, Rights, and Terrorism," 185. In reviewing this objection to IRFA, Shattuck writes, "Since the United States has yet to ratify a number of international human rights treaties, this criticism tends to stick, and barring a major national policy shift, it is likely to endure."

189. A fascinating exchange of these two divergent approaches are two opinion pieces in *Christianity Today*: Michael Horowitz's "Cry Freedom: Forget 'Quiet Diplomacy'—It Doesn't Work," and the response by T. Jeremy Gunn, "Full of Sound and Fury: Polemics at Home and Abroad Does Not Prevent Religious Persecution." Both articles are available online at http://www.christianitytoday.com.

190. U.S. Department of State, International Information Programs, "Sen. Paul Wellstone on Senate Passage of Anti-Sex Trafficking Bill," August 1, 2000; available online at http://usinfo.state.gov/topical/global/traffic/00080101.htm; see also Regan E. Ralph, Background Briefing, International Trafficking of Women and Children Testimony before the Senate Committee on Foreign Relations Subcommittee on Near Eastern and South Asian Affairs, February 22, 2000; available online at http://www.hrw.org/backgrounder/wrd/trafficking.htm.

191. Ralph, Background Briefing.

192. U.S. Department of State, "Trafficking in Persons Report," Office to Monitor and Combat Trafficking in Persons, June 5, 2002; available online at http://www.state.gov/g/tip/.

193. Trafficking Victims Protection Act of 2000, Public Law No. 106-386.

194. 50 U.S.C. 1701.

195. Human Rights Watch, "U.S. State Department Trafficking Report a "Mixed Bag," press release, Washington, D.C., July 12, 2002; available online at www.hrw.org/press/2001/07/traffick-0712.htm.

196. LaShawn Jefferson, letter to Secretary Powell regarding the U.S. State Department's Trafficking Report, June 18, 2002. Jefferson suggested, "The Trafficking Report should set forth qualitative information: Are the victim service programs appropriately designed and funded, and are they effectively assisting victims in practice? What are the inter-ministerial task forces mandated to do, and have they succeeded? Does draft legislation cover trafficking into all forms of forced labor and provide adequate victim services and witness protections?"

197. Human Rights Watch, "U.S. State Department Trafficking Report Undercut by Lack of Analysis," press release, Washington, D.C., June 11, 2003; available online at http://www.hrw.org/press/2003/06/trafficking report.htm.

198. The 2003 Trafficking in Persons Report can be found at http://www.state.gov/g/tip/rls/tiprpt/2003/. Human Rights Watch has urged that disaggregated statistics (victims' gender, age, and nationality, and the type of forced labor they endure), to the extent available, should be provided on the victims, as well as on prosecutions for trafficking-

related offenses (arrests, conviction rates, and sentencing). Where such information is not available, the Trafficking Report should note governments' failure to compile and publish disaggregated statistics and urge them to do so.

199. Human Rights Watch, "U.S. State Department Trafficking Report Missing Key Data, Credits Uneven Efforts," press release, New York, June 6, 2002; available online at http://www.hrw.org/press/2002/06/us-report0606.htm; see also U.S. Department of State, *Victims of Trafficking and Violence Protection Act of 2000: Trafficking in Persons Report*, 2002; available online at http://www.state.gov/g/tip/rls/tiprpt/2002/.

200. Trafficking Victims Protection Act of 2000, Public Law No. 106-386, Division A – Section 107 (B); available online at http://www.ojp.usdoj.gov/vawo/laws/vawo2000/stitle_a.htm#protection.

201. Widney Brown, Human Rights Watch, "Twenty-first Century Slavery—The Human Rights Dimension to Trafficking in Human Beings," paper presented at A Human Rights Approach to the Rehabilitation and Reintegration into Society of Trafficked Victims, conference in Rome, May 15–16, 2002; available online at http://www.hrw.org/backgrounder/wrd/trafficked-victims.htm.

202. This implements section 107(C) of the TVPA. U.S. Department of Justice, "Department of Justice Issues T Visas to Protect Women, Children, and All Victims of Human Trafficking," January 24, 2002, #038; available online at http://www.usdoj.gov/opa/pr/2002/January/02_crt_038.htm.

203. Trafficking Victims Protection Act of 2000, Public Law No. 106-386, Division A – Section 107 (C); available online at http://www.ojp.usdoj.gov/vawo/laws/vawo2000/stitle_a.htm#protection.

204. Mohamed Mattar, interview with the author, June 2003.

205. Ibid.

206. Human Rights Watch, "Bosnia and Herzegovina: Traffickers Walk Free; Local Corruption and Presence of Internationals Exacerbate Abuses," November 26, 2002; available online at www.hrw.org/press/2002/11/bosnia1126.htm.

207. U.S. Department of Justice, "Department of Justice Issues T Visas."

208. Lisa Girion, "1789 Law Acquires Human Rights Role," *Los Angeles Times*, June 16, 2003.

209. Ibid.

210. Ibid.

211. 28 U.S.C. § 1350 (1994) (originally enacted as part of the Judiciary Act of 1789, ch. 20, § 12, 1 Stat. 73, 79 (1789)).

212. American Society of International Law, "Alien Tort Claims and Business Liability," paper presented at the Ninety-Fifth Annual Meeting of the American Society of International Law, April 4–7, 2001.

213. For more information on international law applied to U.S. courts, see also Jordan J. Paust, *International Law as Law of the United States* (Durham, N.C.: Carolina Academic Press, 1996); Ralph Steinhardt, "Recovering the Charming Betsy Principle," *American Society of International Law Proceedings* 94 (2000): 49; Ralph Steinhardt, "Fulfilling the Promise of Filartiga: Litigating Human Rights Claims against the Estate of Ferdinand Marcos," *Yale Journal of International Law* 20 (1995): 65.

214. See *Filartiga v. Peña-Irala*, 630 F.2d 876 (2d Cir. 1980).

215. Human Rights Watch, "Background on the Alien Tort Claims Act," May 14, 2003; available online at http://hrw.org/campaigns/atca/.

216. See, e.g., *Forti v. Suarez-Mason*, 694 F. Supp. 707 (N.D. Cal. 1988) (Argentine plaintiffs sued Argentine general for abuses committed against their relatives by Argentine soldiers); *Xuncax v. Gramajo*, 886 F. Supp. 162 (D. Mass. 1995) (Guatemalan former Minister of Defense sued for abuses committed by soldiers under his command); *In Estate of Ferdinand Marcos Human Rights Litig.*, 25 F. 3d 1467 (9th Cir. 1994) (Class of plaintiffs including everyone who suffered under the Marcos regime sued for abuses by soldiers and government authorities of the Philippines in the 1970s and 1980s); and *Abebe-Jira v. Negewo*, 72 F. 3d 844 (11th Cir. 1996) (Local Ethiopian leader sued for torture). See also Kathryn L. Boyd, "Collective Rights Adjudication in U.S. Courts: Enforcing Human Rights at the Corporate Level," *Brigham Young University Law Review* vol.1999: 1139–1206; Richard L. Herz, "Litigating Environmental Abuses Under the Alien Tort Claims Act," *Virginia Journal of International Law* (2000): 545.
217. Sandra Coliver, interview with the author, June 2003.
218. Sandra Coliver, "The U.S. Can Still Play a Role in Bringing War Criminals to Justice" *Legal Times*, May 13, 2002.
219. See Robin Broad and John Cavanagh, "The Corporate Accountability Movement: Lessons and Opportunities," *Fletcher Forum World Affairs* 23 (1999): 151.
220. See, e.g., Juan Forero, "Rights Groups Fight U.S. Concerns in U.S. Courts," *New York Times*, June 12, 2003.
221. Abby Ellin, "Suit Says Chevron Texaco Dumped Poisons in Ecuador," *New York Times*, May 8, 2003.
222. David Corn, "Corporate Human Rights," *Nation* 275 (2002): 31.
223. Sandra Coliver, "Centuries-Old Law is Critical for Torture Survivors," *San Francisco Chronicle*, June 11, 2003.
224. Harold Hongju Koh, quoted in Girion, "1789 Law."
225. Daphne Eviatar, "Profits and Gunpoint: Unocal's Pipeline in Burma Becomes a Test Case in Corporate Accountability," *Nation* 276 (2003): 16.
226. Doe v. Unocal Corp., 110 F. Supp. 2d 1294 (C.D. Cal. 2000), aff'd, 248 F.3d 915 (9th Cir. 2001).
227. Ibid.
228. Eviatar, "Profits," 16–17.
229. Brief for the United States of America as *Amicus Curiae, John Doe I, et al., v. Unocal Corporation,* 9th Cir. Court of Appeals, May 8, 2003.
230. Coliver, "Centuries-Old Law."
231. Coliver interview.
232. "The Bush Administration has been dubbed the 'oil and gas cabinet' because of the close financial ties between Cabinet members, including the President and Vice-President, and the energy industry." See Katty Kay, "Nervous Bush Defends Links to Failed Firm," *Times* (London), January 11, 2002.
233. Malinowski, quoted in Jim Lobe, "Rights—U.S.: Ashcroft Attempts to End Victims' Rights Law," *Inter Press Service*, May 15, 2003; accessed on Westlaw (2003 WL 6915334).
234. Madeleine Drohan, "Abusive Multinationals Have a Pal in Washington," *Globe and Mail*, May 19, 2003.
235. Coliver, "The U.S. Can Still Play."
236. Ibid.
237. Coliver interview.
238. Ibid.
239. Forsythe, *Human Rights,* 157.

240. Stephen Walker, interview with the author, June 2003.

241. Ibid.

242. See Max R. Berdal, "Fateful Encounter: The United States and UN Peacekeeping," *Survival* 36, no. 1 (1994): 30, 35–36.

243. Bill Clinton, quoted in Mark Danner and David Gelber with Peter Jennings, "While America Watched: The Bosnia Tragedy," *Peter Jennings Reporting*, ABC News, March 17, 1994.

244. Walker interview.

245. Aryeh Neier, quoted in Carla Anne Robbins, "A Faraway War: Inaction on Bosnia Stirs Critics to Debate and Despair," *Wall Street Journal*, March 18, 1994.

246. Glenn Ruga, interview with the author, June 2003.

247. Ibid.

248. Ibid.

249. Ibid.

250. Susan Sontag, quoted in Robbins, "Faraway War."

251. Neier, quoted in Robbins, "Faraway War."

252. Robbins, "Faraway War."

253. See "The Abdication," *New Republic*, February 28, 1994, 7.

254. Walker interview.

255. Danner and Gelber with Jennings, "While America Watched."

256. "Senate Select Committee on Intelligence Holds Day Two of Hearings on the Nomination of Anthony Lake as Director of Central Intelligence," CNN, March 11, 1997; transcript available online at http://images.cnn.com/ALLPOLITICS/1997/03/12/fdch.lake/.

257. Ibid.

258. Richard Perle, "Statement of Richard Perle before the Committee on International Relations," *House of Representatives Congressional Testimony*, Washington, D.C., May 2, 1996.

259. Carla Anne Robbins, "Senate Votes to Allow Arms for Bosnia," *Wall Street Journal*, July 27, 1995.

260. Walker interview.

261. James O'Brien, interview with the author, June 2003.

262. Ibid.

263. Swanee Hunt, interview with the author, June 2003.

264. Swanee Hunt and Cristina Posa, "Women Waging Peace," *Foreign Policy* 124 (2001): 38–47.

265. Swanee Hunt, "Gender and the American Experience," address before the IPI World Congress; available online at http://www.freemedia.at/Boston%20Congress%20Report/boston32.htm.

266. Ibid.

267. Ibid.

268. Hunt interview.

269. Hattie Babbitt, e-mail correspondence with the author, June 27, 2003.

270. Camille Pampell, Women Waging Peace, "Recommendations from the G8, NEPAD, Women, Peace and Security Meeting," November 2002; available online at http://www.womenwagingpeace.net.

271. Ibid.

272. Ibid.

273. S.C. Res. 1325, U.N. SCOR, 55th Sess., 4213th mtg., U.N. Doc. S/RES/1325 (2000). See also Hilary Charlesworth and Mary Wood, "Mainstreaming Gender in International Peace and Security," *Yale Journal of International Law* 26 (2001): 313–17.
274. Letter from Hattie Babbitt to John Negroponte, July 9, 2002.
275. Sanam Anderlini, e-mail correspondence with the author, June, 2003.
276. Donald Steinberg, "The Role of Women in Peace Building and Reconstruction: More than Victims," address before the Council on Foreign Relations, New York, March 6, 2003; available online at http://www.state.gov/s/p/rem/2003/18759.htm.
277. Swanee Hunt, "Peacemakers, Peacekeepers and Peacebuilders: The Importance of Women in Conflict Prevention," address at the Waging–Wilson Center conference, More than Victims: Women's Role in Conflict Prevention, Washington, D.C., September 12, 2002.
278. Leonard Leo, interview with the author, June 2003.
279. John O. McGinnis and Mark L. Movesian, "The World Trade Constitution," *Harvard International Law Journal* 114 (2000): 511–86.
280. Ibid., 581: "We do not agree that the WTO should allow NGOs a direct role in the dispute settlement process. Such a role would give NGOs—groups that are sometimes unaccountable even to their own memberships—too great a measure of influence. Moreover, conferring standing on NGOs would inevitably aggrandize the WTO's bureaucracy, which would acquire power to designate which of the many NGOs with an interest in a dispute could appear."
281. James Madison, *The Federalist Papers,* no. 10 (1787; reprint New York: New American Library, 1976), 78.
282. Leo interview.
283. Ibid.
284. See, e.g., Robert Dreyfuss, "More Missing Intelligence," *Nation* 277 (2001): 4–5.
285. Leo interview.
286. NGO Watch website, http://www.ngowatch.org.
287. Ibid.
288. Jarol Manheim, "Biz-War: Origins, Structure and Strategy of Foundation-NGO Network Warfare on Corporations in the United States," paper presented at the American Enterprise Institute, Washington, D.C., June 11, 2003.
289. Profile on Human Rights Watch, available online at http://www.ngowatch.org.
290. Leo interview.
291. Karen Tumulty, "I Want My Al TV, Liberals Look to Break the Stranglehold on Talk Radio and TV," *Time,* June 30, 2003.
292. Andrew Natsios, quoted in "Natsios: NGOs Must Show Results; Promote Ties to U.S. Or We Will 'Find New Partners,'" Interactions 2003 Forum "The Challenges of Global Commitments: Advancing Relief and Development Goals through Advocacy and Action," Washington, D.C.: May 12–14, 2003; available online at http://www.interaction.org/forum2003/panels.html.
293. Ibid.
294. See Jim Lobe, "Bringing the War Home: Right Wing Think Tank Turns Wrath on NGOs," *Foreign Policy in Focus,* June 13, 2003; available online at http://www.foreignpolicy-infocus.org/commentary/2003/0306antingo.htm.
295. Naomi Klein, "Bush to NGOs: Watch Your Mouths," *Globe and Mail,* June 20, 2003.
296. Ibid.
297. Ibid.
298. Jim Lobe, "Development: From Confrontation to Collaboration—A Look at NGOs," *Inter Press Service,* June 26, 2003.

299. SustainAbility, "The 21st Century NGO: In the Market for Change," report, June 2003; available online at http://www.sustainability.com/publications/latest/21C-ngo.asp.
300. John Elkington, "More NGOs Are Shifting from Confrontation to Collaboration, Study Shows," Greenbiz.com, London, July 1, 2003.
301. Paul Wapner, interview with the author, June 2003. Paul Wapner, "The Democratic Accountability of Non-governmental Organizations. Paradise Lost? NGOs and Global Accountability," *Chicago Journal of International Law* 3 (2002): 155.
302. See Antonio Donini, "The Bureaucracy and the Free Spirits: Stagnation and Innovation in the Relationship between the UN and NGOs," in *NGOs, the UN and Global Governance*, ed. Thomas G. Weiss and Leon Gordenker (Boulder, Colo.: Lynne Rienner, 1996).
303. See Thomas G. Weiss, ed., *Beyond UN Subcontracting: Task Sharing with Regional Security Arrangements and Security Arrangements and Service-Providing NGOs* (New York: St. Martin's Press, 1998).
304. I expand upon this in Julie Mertus, "Human Rights and the Promise of Transnational Civil Society," in *The Future of International Human Rights*, eds. Burns H. Houston and Stephen P. Marks (Ardsley, N.Y.: Transnational, 1999).
305. See Paul Wapner, "Defending Accountability in NGOs," *Chicago Journal of International Law* 3, no. 1 (2002): 197–205.

FIVE

CONCLUSION:
BAIT AND SWITCH?

Human rights has become the "bait and switch" tool of choice of U.S. foreign policy. Just like the car dealer who publicizes an amazing but often nonexistent deal in order to get people into the showroom and to boost their reputation as preferred dealers, politicians promise human rights in order to induce desired behaviors in others and to support their positive self-image. Then, as soon as the desired behavior happens, a poor substitute is made in place of the original offer.

This book has shown that human rights advocates have reached considerable success in framing policy choices in human rights terms and in influencing the discourse of U.S. foreign policy. Human rights is indeed the lingua franca of diplomacy, and to some extent human rights have become institutionalized. For the White House, however, human rights talk is not supported by consistent human rights behavior. On the contrary, the United States applies a double standard for human rights norms: one that applies to the United States and one that applies to the rest of the world. Where human rights framings of policy choices can so easily lose out to competing interests, one cannot say that human rights have the kind of taken-for-granted quality that comes along with norm embeddedness. Nor can human rights be said to be embedded in the U.S. military, which has adapted more than the civilian sector to accommodate human rights norms. Yet, it is still civilian controlled and, moreover, as in the civilian sector competing interests frequently trump human rights considerations.

What's going wrong with rights?

TOWARD A NEW THEORY OF NORM DIFFUSION

I would assert that there is nothing wrong with human rights. Human rights has become the best available choice for framing arguments and making policy choices. Other options, which may not be intrinsically bad, become less favorable when compared to the better option of human rights. What is wrong is that human rights remains only an option and has not achieved the status of an imperative. Furthermore, in interplay with other options, human rights are vulnerable to misuse by powerful states to their own benefit.[1] To extend the car dealer analogy: the car is a desired commodity promised by the dealer in an attractive package. When the customer arrives, he or she finds that the option actually offered is not the same as the advertised special. The car dealer misleads people through his power of influence, created by both the fact that he has something someone else wants and that his wealth gives him a magnified voice (i.e., his ability to advertise). Like the car dealer, the United States can use its wealth and influence to mislead other states about its commitment to the human rights framework, appearing as universalist when actually it is applying double standards.

Recognizing the ethical problems with "bait and switch" car dealers, consumer protection laws seek to set advertising requirements that diminish the possibility for such behavior. Perhaps even more influential is the limit to the amount of nonsense and trickery that the American consumer is willing to tolerate. What is needed with respect to human rights is some kind of similar safety—the consumer protection of human rights and limits to what is socially acceptable—to eliminate or at least highly restrict the possibility that they will be trumped by lesser competing norms.

This gets to the heart of academic theories about how norms become diffused—that is, how they spread and gain influence. This book began with the insight of Martha Finnemore and Kathryn Sikkink that dialogue, communication, and argumentation are essential mechanisms for the socialization of norms.[2] Arguing the rightness of human rights may not only shame states into action in an individual instances but also, as human rights norm are internalized provoke a shift in identity, interest and expectations.[3] Adopting the socialization and persuasion theory of norms diffusion entails focusing on the relative persuasive force of a convincing or skillful argument advanced in favor of one norm over another.[4] The study of civil society actors in this book demonstrates that human rights arguments are indeed powerful tools for framing policy issues and can influence behavior. But in the cases in which human rights advocates are successful, have they really persuaded anyone in a broad or transformative sense or have they only managed to convince someone to apply their approach to a specific, isolated case? Are we witnessing case-specific persuasion, or will the particular human rights victory carry over to other decisions faced by whomever was successfully persuaded? Given all the double standards and bait and switch behavior manifest in U.S. human rights policy, can we really point to a shift in the identity, interests and expectations of U.S. government and, in particular, of the individuals who occupy influential seats in the White House? Even when the administration appears to take one step toward human rights, the potential remains for arguments based on American exceptionalism to require two steps back.

To put this problem in perspective, we need to consider a new theoretical model. One interesting theory of norm diffusion does not require an explicit showing of a philosophical shift; rather, just enough "rhetorical coercion" to compel the endorsement of a normative stance. Under the model proposed by Patrick Jackson and Ronald Krebs, "[c]laimants deploy arguments less in the hope of naïve persuasion than in the realistic expectation that they can, thorough skillful framing, leave their opponents without access to the rhetorical materials needed to craft a sustained rebuttal."[5] The public nature of the rhetoric plays a key role in rhetorical coercion. Jackson and Krebs explain that "the relevant audiences impose limits on the arguments that can be possibly advanced" and this makes it possible to back an opponent into a "rhetorical corner."[6]

According to this new theory of norm diffusion, human rights advocates who focus on persuasion and target primarily decision makers have it all wrong. Richard Rorty suggests that human rights provide a "sentimental education" that generates openness and awareness to the oppression of others.[7] This may work in some cases, but to divert all resources in this direction is misplaced. Instead of trying to change minds in government, advocates should focus on creating the conditions that compel human rights policy choices. To the extent that advocates concentrate on changing perspectives, the perspectives that matter most are those of the general public, not those of policy-making elites. Back to the car salesman analogy: they should create consumer protection conditions and raise the expectations of consumers in order to limit the range of ways in which the deal can be closed. For human rights advocates, the creation of a human rights culture would serve such a function by providing an environment in which human rights double standards are not tolerated.[8]

TOWARD A HUMAN RIGHTS CULTURE

"We live now in a human rights culture," law professor Helen Stacy triumphantly declares in a 2003 Stanford law review article.[9] She observes, "Increasingly in the second half of the twentieth century, human rights have become the language with which people, groups, and even nation states, frame their requests for better treatment from others—whether those others are citizens, governments, international capital, or neighbors. Human rights have, in short, become the lingua franca of request; the language of human rights has become the language of demand by citizens pressing their government for better treatment at the hands of the police, for cleaner air and fairer distribution of environmental harms, or for universal health care or the special educational needs of a minority group."[10] This is all true, but to claim that Americans live in a human rights culture is a gross overstatement. The level of awareness of human rights is extremely low. According to one study by Amnesty

International, 94 percent of American adults and 96 percent of American youth have no awareness of the Universal Declaration of Human Rights (UDHR).[11] Even if they were aware of it, however, they are far too willing to tolerate their government's abridgement of international human rights standards.

As Renato Rosaldo succinctly explains, "[Culture] refers broadly to the forms through which people make sense of their lives."[12] For each group or society, culture incorporates the shared beliefs and understandings, mediated by and constituted by symbols and language.[13] Two components of culture are particularly relevant for our discussion here. First, cultures are not unidimensional and static; they are multidimensional and dynamic. In the accounts of human rights and U.S. foreign policy provided in this book, it is impossible to define and describe a specific American culture since culture is "interactive and process-like (rather than static and essence-like)."[14] Second, culture is not *natural*, not *inevitable*, not *predetermined*. Rather, it is socially constructed according to an ideological and/or political purpose.[15]

A *human rights culture* is the vehicle through which a particular set of shared beliefs and understandings—human rights norms—take root in and influence a population.[16] The adoption of human rights language is an essential step in building a human rights culture, but this alone is insufficient.[17] Human rights concepts enter culture slowly as a population develops its own shared (although often contested) understanding of the prominence and importance of the norms. Incrementally, they become part of the "'frame' in which people derive a sense of who they are and where they are going."[18] As Tom Malinowski, the advocacy director for Human Rights Watch, has noted, human rights advocates "'win' not only when they get international institutions to do something, but when they get people to see issues in a certain way."[19] Only when people throughout society deploy a human rights lens when they try to make sense of events does a human rights culture exist.

Since the adoption of the UDHR in 1948, the United States has never taken seriously its mandate that "every individual and every organ of society . . . shall strive by teaching and education to promote respect for these rights and freedoms." To do so in 1948 would have been to acknowledge the legal discrimination of racial segregation. To do so in 2002 would be to acknowledge that as a matter of policy every U.S. administration has refused to acknowledge social and economic rights as human rights. Today, "although generally well informed about their civil and political rights under the U.S. Constitution, most people in the United States would be astounded to learn that they have a human rights to health care, housing, or a living wage," says Nancy Flowers, an American educator who pioneered human rights education programs for Amnesty International and other groups.[20] "Rather than cultivating a culture of human rights," Flowers explains, "the U.S. government has consistently found it advantageous to suppress human rights awareness at home while using human rights abuses abroad as a grounds for sanctions and even invasions."[21] Only recently have U.S.-based human rights groups challenged this stance by directing their efforts to human rights culture building activities at home.

Among the most dynamic of the new groups is the National Center for Human Rights Education (NCHRE) in Atlanta, Georgia,[22] which "seeks to catalyze a human rights movement in the United States by integrating a human rights framework into existing social movements."[23] Founder and executive director Loretta Ross views human rights as a key to empowerment. "Like teaching slaves to read in 19th-century America," she says, "teaching human rights in 21st-century America is a far-reaching act that offers a rich vision of human possibilities. Human rights education trains us in a new way of relating to each other—not through opposition, but through uniting us for the sake of our mutual destiny."[24] Activists trained by the NCHRE who work on a multitude of issues—combating racism, homophobia, poverty and discrimination against people with disabilities; promoting women's rights; protecting the environment; defending reproductive rights—identify themselves as part of the global human rights movement.

Other attempts to infuse human rights thinking into existing social movements include the International Human Rights Law Group's efforts to promote the implementation of the Convention on the Elimination of All Forms of Race Discrimination in the U.S. by assisting U.S. civil rights and social justice groups in integrating the language, techniques, and procedures of international human rights law in their efforts to combat racial discrimination.[25] Amnesty International has focused attention on building a human rights culture in the U.S. since 1999 when, in cities across the country, it held hearings on the international human rights dimensions of police brutality.[26] This led to the creation in 2002 of Amnesty USA's first full-scale domestic human rights program. "We've continued to hold public hearings because storytelling by the community is a very important," says Cosette Thompson, Amnesty International's western regional coordinator, pointing to hearings on racial profiling held in 2003 as the most recent such examples.[27]

Outside of human rights education, one of the few advocacy organizations to focus on building a human rights culture is the Center for Economic and Social Rights (CESR). Beyond human rights education, the CESR has employed four additional strategies for building a human rights culture: (1) supporting emerging human rights movements by providing them with capacity building and linking them to UN mechanisms; (2) developing human rights–based advocacy models and policy proposals to effect social change and generate new methodologies for domestic human rights work; (3) building networks of groups working on human rights in the United States; and (4) developing U.S. human rights jurisprudence through legal submissions in courts, commissions, and tribunals, as well as broader analysis of U.S. legal accountability.[28]

The infusion of international norms into the law and policy of state and local communities serves to foster greater participation in the development and enforcement of human rights. Cathy Powell, director of Columbia University School of Law's Human Rights Clinic, explains that by "cultivating and amplifying the voices of state and local governments in the adoption and implementation of human rights, dialogic federalism assists in widening the base of support for and increasing the legitimacy of these norms."[29] Among the several examples of the infusion of international norms at the local level is San Francisco's decision to become the first city in the United States to pass a law instituting the principles that underlie the UN Convention on the Elimination of all forms of Discrimination against Women (CEDAW).[30] This law, which was spearheaded by the Women's Institute for Leadership Development (WILD), requires city departments to use a gender and human rights analysis to review city policy in employment, funding allocations, and delivery of direct and indirect services.

Other local human rights laws have been directed at human rights abuses outside the United States. For example, the Massachusetts General Assembly passed legislation in 1996 that prohibited its state and any of its agencies from contracting with any person doing business with Myanmar.[31] Twenty-six cities, including Santa Monica, San Francisco, Berkeley, Oakland, Boulder, and Ann Arbor, have passed similar ordinances limiting business with Myanmar.[32] Other local ordinances have targeted Nigeria, China, Indonesia, and Cuba for their record of human rights abuses.[33] While still extremely rare, these kind of local efforts have served to enhanced local awareness of human rights norms. Nonetheless, despite the effort expended and progress made, America still does not have a human rights culture.

The culture of American foreign policy is not one of human rights because the American deployment of human rights double standards is perceived as a choice that Americans can make. This is incompatible with the central tenet of human rights that they should be applied to all equally. As Andrew Hurrell reminds us, the most pressing ethical dilemmas of advancing universal human rights concern practice and power.[34] American double standards in human rights policy weakens the United States' claim to lead globally through moral authority and undermines the legitimacy of human rights norms."[35] As long as there is space for the interest in American exceptionalism to trump human rights, it will continue to do so. The building of a strong human rights culture within American society may provide the only antidote.

ENDNOTES

1. For how power distorts speech, see Roger Payne, "Persuasion, Frames and Norm Construction," *European Journal of International Relations* 7, no. 1 (2001): 37–61.
2. See also Thomas Risse and Kathryn Sikkink, *The Power of Principles: The Socialization of Human Rights Norms in Domestic Practice* (New York: Cambridge University Press, 1999).
3. Martha Finnemore and Kathryn Sikkink, "International Norm Dynamics and Political Change," *International Organization* 52, no. 4 (1998): 914.

4. See Joshua Busby, "Listen! Pay Attention! Transnational Social Movements and the Diffusion of International Norms," paper presented at the Annual Meeting of the American Political Science Association, August 2003. See also Neta Crawford, *Argument and Change in World Politics* (New York: Cambridge University Press, 2001); Jeffrey Checkel, "Why Comply? Social Learning and European Identity Change," *International Organization* 55, no. 3 (2001): 553–88.

5. Patrick Thaddeus Jackson and Ronald R. Krebs, "Twisting Tongues and Twisting Arms: The Power of Political Rhetoric," paper presented at the Annual Meeting of the American Political Science Association, August 28–31, 2003.

6. Ibid. Claire R. Kelly proposes a different yet related theory that she terms "modified constructivism and the normative feedback loop," defining the latter as "a mechanism by which states consult national values in their international interactions"; see Kelly, "The Value Vacuum: Self-Enforcing Regimes and the Dilution of the Normative Feedback Loop," *Michigan Journal of International Law* 22 (2001): 673–731.

7. Richard Rorty, "Human Rights, Rationality and Sentimentality," in *On Human Rights: The Oxford Amnesty Lectures*, ed. Stephen Shute and Susan L. Hurley (New York: Basic, 1993), 114.

8. Resources for creating this kind of environment already exist, in that hypocrisy is generally considered a bad thing in most realms.

9. Helen Stacy, "Relational Sovereignty," *Stanford Law Review* 55 (2003): 2048.

10. Ibid.

11. See http://www.hrusa.org/features.shtm. The survey was commissioned in 1997 by Human Rights USA Partners—Amnesty International USA, the National Center for Human Rights Education, Street Law, Inc., and the University of Minnesota Human Rights Center.

12. Renato Rosaldo, *Culture and Truth: The Remaking of Social Analysis* (Boston: Beacon Press, 1993), 26.

13. Mayer Zaid, "Culture, Ideology and Strategic Framing," in *Comparative Perspectives on Social Movements: Political Opportunities, Mobilizing Structures, and Cultural Framings*, ed. Doug McAdam et al. (London: Cambridge University Press, 1996), 262.

14. Yosef Lapid, "Culture's Ship: Returns and Departures in International Relations Theory," in *The Return of Culture in International Relations Theory*, ed. Yosef Lapid and Fredrich Kratochwil (Boulder, Colo.: Lynne Rienner, 1997), 8.

15. Richard Handlet, "Is 'Identity' a Useful Cross-Cultural Concept?" in *Commemorations: The Politics of National Identity*, ed. John R. Gillis (Princeton, N.J.: Princeton University Press, 1994), 29.

16. John Witte, "A Dickensian Era of Religious Rights: An Update on Religious Human Rights in Global Perspective," *William and Mary Law Review* 42 (2001): 707, 712. Witte states that human rights norms "need a human rights culture to be effective."

17. Richard A. Wilson, "Human Rights, Culture and Context: An Introduction," in *Human Rights, Culture and Context: Anthropological Perspectives*, ed. Richard A. Wilson (New York: Pluto Press, 1997), 1, 16–17.

18. Thomas Fitzgerald, *Metaphors of Identity* (Albany: State University of New York Press, 1993), 186.

19. Tom Malinowski, interview with the author, July 2001.

20. Nancy Flowers, interview with the author, September 2003.

21. Ibid.

22. For the National Center for Human Rights Education, see http://www.nchre.org/.

23. See http://www.nchre.org/about/bhrh.shtml.

24. Loretta Ross, quote din Nancy Flowers, "Human Rights Education In The USA," *Issues of Democracy* (electronic publication of the U.S. State Department); available online at http://Usinfo.State.Gov/Journals/Itdhr/0302/Ijde/Flowers.Htm.

25. International Human Rights Law Group, "Combating Racial Discrimination in the U.S."; available online at http://www.hrlawgroup.org/country_programs/ united_states/default.asp.

26. Cosette Thompson, Amnesty International, interview with the author, September 2003.

27. Ibid.

28. For the Center for Economic and Social and Cultural Rights, see http://www.cesr.org/ PROGRAMS/usprogram.htm.

29. Catherine Powell, "Dialogic Federalism: Constitutional Possibilities for Incorporation of Human Rights Law in the United States," *University of Pennsylvania Law Review* 150 (2001): 245–91.

30. See WILD for Human Rights, http://www.wildforhumanrights.org/ human_rights_advocacy.html.

31. The Massachusetts Burma Law is codified at Mass. Gen. Laws Ann. chapter 7 sections 22G-22M.

32. Erin E. Milliken, "*National Foreign Trade Council v. Natsios*: Massachusetts as a Participant or a Regulator in the International Market," *Journal of Law and Commerce* 19 (1999): 188.

33. Ibid.

34. See Andrew Hurrell, "Power, Principles and Prudence: Protecting Human Rights in a Deeply Divided World," in *Human Rights in Global Politics*, ed. Tim Dunne and Nicholas J. Wheeler (New York: Cambridge University Press, 1999), 277, 278.

35. Harold Hongju Koh, "On American Exceptionalism," *Stanford Law Review* 55 (2003): 1487.

SELECTED LIST OF PERSONS INTERVIEWED

Some interviewees chose not to be named, including a large number of military officers. Many other people were consulted more informally for the project. Affiliations are listed as current at the time of the interviews.

Abramowitz, Morton, senior fellow, Century Foundation. Interviewed on July 3, 2001.

Anderson, Elizabeth, executive director, Human Rights Watch. Interviewed on July 18, 2001.

Awad, Mubarak, executive director, Nonviolence International. Interviewed on July 10, 2001.

Balfe, Joelle, consultant, National Council on Disabilities. Interviewed in September 2003.

Balton, David, attorney, U.S. State Department. Interviewed in June 2003.

Bang-Jensen, Nina, executive director and general counsel, Coalition for International Justice. Interviewed on July 20, 2001.

Bassuener, Kurt, former program officer, Balkans Initiative, U.S. Institute of Peace. Interviewed in June 2001.

Bishop, Jim, director, Disaster Response Committee, Interaction. Interviewed on July 19, 2001.

Blank, Laurie, program officer, Rule of Law Program, U.S. Institute of Peace. Interviewed on May 1, 2001.

Boegli, Urs, head of media services, International Committee of the Red Cross. Interviewed on June 8, 2001.

Brooks, Doug, president, International Peace Operations Association. Interviewed on July 2, 2001.

Bugajski, Janusz, director, Eastern Europe Project, Center for Strategic and International Studies. Interviewed on July 26, 2001.

Carothers, Thomas, vice president for studies (in democracy and the rule of law), Carnegie Endowment for International Peace. Interviewed on June 18, 2001.

Cevallos, Albert, senior fellow, U.S. Institute of Peace, Office of Transition Initiatives, U.S. Agency for International Development. Interviewed on June 1, 2001 and in July 2003.

Charny, Joel, vice president for policy, Refugees International. Interviewed on July 10, 2001.

Chin, Sally, project coordinator for Burundi and Angola, Search for Common Ground. Interviewed in May 2001.

Chopra, Jarat, research associate, Global Security Program, Watson Institute for International Studies, Brown University. Formerly with the United Nations Transitional Administration in East Timor. Interviewed in March 2001.

Cilliers, Jaco, senior adviser, Catholic Relief Services. Interviewed in March 2001.

Cohen, Cynthia Price, president, ChildRights International. Interviewed on June 21, 2003.

Cook, Tonja, formerly with the Organization for Security and Cooperation in Europe in Bosnia-Herzegovina. Interviewed on June 27, 2001.

Cooper, Ann, executive director, Committee to Project Journalists. Interviewed on August 9, 2001.

Countryman, Tom, director for southeastern Europe, U.S. Department of State. Interviewed on July 25, 2001.

Crocker, Chester, chairman of the board of directors, U.S. Institute of Peace; James R. Schlesinger Professor of Strategic Studies, School of Foreign Service, Georgetown University. Interviewed on August 16, 2001.

Dalton, Capt. Jane, primary counselor, Legal Office of the Joint Chiefs of Staff. Interviewed on June 14, 2001.

Day, Graham, senior fellow, U.S. Institute of Peace. Former district administrator for the UN Transitional Administration in East Timor, and formerly also a political and field officer with the UN mission in Bosnia. Interviewed in March and June 2001.

Deeks, Ashley, attorney, U.S. Department of State. Interviewed in April 2001.

DeGrasse, Beth, executive director, Peace through Law Education Fund. Interviewed on June 28, 2001.

Dempsey, Gary, foreign policy analyst, CATO Institute. Interviewed on July 18, 2001.

Dragnich, Alexander, professor (retired), George Washington University. Interviewed on July 18, 2001.

Dziedzic, Mike, program officer for the Balkans Initiative, U.S. Institute of Peace. Former peace operations analyst, Institute for National Security Studies, National Defense University. Interviewed on June 12, 2001.

Evans, Gareth, executive director, International Crisis Group. Interviewed in May 2003.

Evans, Jonathan, director of Indonesia office, Catholic Relief Services. Interviewed in May 2001.

Fabian, Greg, human rights trainer, Organization for Security and Cooperation in Europe mission in Kosovo. Interviewed in November 2000.

Falk, Richard, professor, Princeton University; member, Kosovo Committee. Interviewed on March 23, 2001.

Farkas, Evelyn, staff member, Senate Armed Services Committee. Interviewed in March 2001.

Farrior, Stephanie, professor of law, Pennsylvania State University–Dickinson. Former legal counsel to Amnesty International. Interviewed in March 2001.

Fishel, John, professor of national security affairs, Center for Hemispheric Defense Studies, National Defense University. Interviewed on July 2, 2001.

Flowers, Nancy, human rights trainer, Amnesty International (and other groups). Interviewed in August 2003.

Gjelten, Tom, journalist, National Public Radio. Interviewed on June 6, 2001.

Gorove, Katherine, attorney, U.S. Department of State. Interviewed in April 2001.

Greene, Marilyn, executive director, World Press Freedom Committee. Interviewed on April 1, 2001.

Gregorian, Hrach, president, Institute of World Affairs. Interviewed on August 14, 2001.

Gutman, Roy, diplomatic correspondent, *Newsweek*. Interviewed on June 12, 2001.

Halperin, Morton H., senior fellow, Council on Foreign Relations. Interviewed on June 20, 2001.

Hawley, Len (Colonel), former deputy assistant secretary for peacekeeping and humanitarian assistance, U.S. Department of Defense. Interviewed on July 2 and July 26, 2001.

Hilleboe, Amy, emergency response team liaison, Catholic Relief Services. Interviewed in March 2001.

Hilterman, Joost, director, Arms Division, Human Rights Watch. Interviewed on May 31, 2001.

Holtzapple, Rick, foreign service officer, former program director for Montenegro and Serbia at the National Democratic Institute. Former adviser for the National Security Council, U.S. Department of State, and UN mission in Croatia. Interviewed on August 7, 2001.

Hooper, Jim, managing director, Public International Law and Policy Group. Former director of the Balkan Action Council. Interviewed on July 1, 2001.

Huang, Margaret, project director, International Advocacy/U.S. Racial Discrimination Program, International Human Rights Law Group. Interviewed in June 2003.

Hunt, Swanee, founder, Women Waging Peace. Former Ambassador to Austria. Interviewed on June 27, 2003.

Jendrzejczyk, Mike, Washington, D.C., director for Southeast Asia, Human Rights Watch. Interviewed on June 28, 2001.

Jenkins, Rob, program manager, Office of Transition Initiatives, U.S. Agency for International Development. Interviewed on July 6, 2001.

Kritz, Neil, director, Rule of Law Program, U.S. Institute of Peace. Interviewed on May 1, 2001.

Kuhar, Ivana, officer, Croatian desk, Voice of America. Interviewed in April 2001.

Kulick, Gilbert, director of communications, Search for Common Ground. Interviewed in May 2001.

Kuperman, Alan, senior fellow, U.S. Institute of Peace; fellow, Kennedy School of Government, Harvard University. Interviewed in April 2001.

Lacquement, Richard, lieutenant colonel, U.S. Army; professor, U.S. Naval War College. Interviewed in August 2003.

Lagon, Mark, staff member, Senate Committee on Foreign Relations. Interviewed on July 27, 2001.

Leo, Leonard, attorney and division director, Federalist Society. Interviewed on July 1, 2003.

Light, Carol, professor of international law, George Washington University; attorney, U.S. Department of State. Interviewed in April 2001.

Lindberg, Nancy, executive vice president, Mercy Corps, Washington, D.C. Interviewed in July 2001 and July 2003.

Locke, Mary, director, Program on Regional Responses to Internal War, Fund for Peace. Interviewed on July 20, 2001.

Loomis, Andrew, Macedonia project manager, Search for Common Ground. Interviewed in May 2001 and June 2003.

Lund, Michael, senior associate, Management Systems International, and Center for Strategic and International Studies. Interviewed on August 16, 2001.

Malin, Mary Catherine, attorney and adviser, U.S. Department of State; cochair, Washington Steering Committee, Women in International Law Interest Group.

Malinowski, Tom, Washington, D.C., advocacy director, Human Rights Watch. Interviewed on July 17, 2001.

Mataya, Chrissy, program associate for Montenegro and Romania, National Democratic Institute for International Affairs. Interviewed on August 1, 2001.

Matheson, Mike, senior fellow, U.S. Institute of Peace; acting director of International Law Program, School of Advanced International Studies, Johns Hopkins University. Interviewed on June 27, 2001.

Maxwell, Dayton, senior adviser, U.S. Agency for International Development. Interviewed on July 20, 2001 and in June 2002.

Maynard, Kim, consultant on postconflict reintegration, UN Development Program and the U.S. Agency for International Development. Interviewed on July 27, 2001.

McCall, Dick, chief of staff to the administrator, U.S. Agency for International Development. Interviewed on August 14, 2001.

McCarthy, Paul, program officer for Central and Eastern Europe, National Endowment for Democracy. Interviewed on July 26, 2001.

McClymont, Mary, executive director, Interaction. Interviewed on July 3, 2001.

McDonald, John, executive director, Institute for Multi-Track Diplomacy. Interviewed on July 18, 2001 and in June 2003.

Mendelson-Furman, Johanna, consultant and adjunct professor, Association of the U.S. Army, World Bank, U.S. Agency for International Development, and American University. Interviewed on July 24, 2001.

Minear, Larry, director, Humanitarianism and War Project. Interviewed in June 2002 and January 2003.

Muna, Maha, deputy director, Women's Coalition for Refugee Women and Children. Interviewed in July 2001.

Murphy, Sean, author and professor, George Washington University School of Law. Interviewed in May 2001.

Newland, Kathleen, codirector of the International Migration Policy Program and Moscow Program, Carnegie Endowment for International Peace. Interviewed on July 25, 2001.

O'Brien, Jim, principal, the Albright Group; former special adviser to the president and the U.S. Department of State for Democracy in the Balkans. Interviewed in April 2001 and June 2003.

Pittmann, Howard, former member, National Security Council. Interviewed on July 17, 2001.

Priest, Dana, journalist, *Washington Post*; senior fellow, U.S. Institute of Peace. Interviewed on June 6, 2001.

Puljic, Ivica, journalist, Bosnian desk, Voice of America. Interviewed in April 2001.

Richards, Nancy, lieutenant colonel, U.S. Air Force, the Pentagon. Interviewed in May 2001.

Rosen, Laura, freelance journalist and consultant, U.S. Institute of Peace. Interviewed in February 2001.

Ruga, Glenn, cofounder, Friends of Bosnia. Interviewed on June 23, 2003.

Sampler, Larry, consultant, Institute for Defense Analysis. Interviewed on August 1, 2001.

Schear, Jim, director of research and professor, Institute for National Strategic Studies, National Defense University. Interviewed on June 27, 2001.

Scheffer, David, senior fellow, U.S. Institute of Peace. Former ambassador for war crimes, U.S. Department of State. Interviewed on June 4, 2001.

Schwarz, Eric, senior fellow, U.S. Institute of Peace. Former senior director for multilateral and humanitarian affairs, National Security Council. Interviewed on June 28, 2001.

Serwer, Daniel, director, Balkans Initiative, U.S. Institute of Peace. Interviewed in June 2001.

Shea, Dorothy, National Security Council. Interviewed on July 17, 2001.

Shochat, Lisa, coordinator for common grounds production, Search for Common Ground. Interviewed in May 2001.

Smillie, Ian, author and consultant, Humanitarianism and War Project. Interviewed in June 2001.

Smith, Barbara, former spokeswoman, United Nations High Commissioner for Refugees in Bosnia. Interviewed in May 2001.

Smith, Stephanie, major, U.S. Marine Corps, the Pentagon. Interviewed in April and May 2001.

Stewart, David, assistant legal adviser, U.S. Department of State. Interviewed in April 2001.

Stromseth, Jane, author and professor, Georgetown University School of Law. Interviewed in March 2001.

Stuebner, William, director, United Nations Association in Washington, D.C. Interviewed on June 8, 2001.

Taft, Julia, former director and undersecretary for Humanitarian Affairs, U.S. Department of State. Interviewed on August 16, 2001.

Tanovic, Semir, program specialist, International Rescue Committee. Interviewed in July 2001.

Thompson, Cossette, western regional director, Amnesty International. Interviewed in September 2003.

Vaccaro, Matt, Peacekeeping Department, U.S. Department of State. Interviewed on June 4, 2001.

Vandenberg, Martina, senior researcher, Human Rights Watch. Interviewed on June 18, 2001 and June 2003.

Wagenseil, Steve, member, U.S. delegation to the UN Commission on Human Rights, U.S. Department of State. Interviewed on July 19, 2001.

Walker, Jeff, lieutenant colonel, U.S. Air Force, the Pentagon. Interviewed in March 2001 and June 2003.

Walker, Stephen, cofounder and director, American Committee to Save Bosnia. Former State Department employee. Interviewed on June 25, 2003.

Ward, George, director of training, U.S. Institute of Peace. Interviewed on July 3, 2001.

Warrick, Thomas, deputy for war crimes issues, U.S. Department of State. Interviewed on June 12, 2001.

Weiss, Thomas, professor and author, City University of New York Graduate School and Humanitarianism and War Project. Interviewed May 2002.

Wheeler, Nicholas, senior lecturer in international politics, University of Wales. Interviewed in April 2001.

Wingate, Patrick, program manager, Office of Transition Initiatives, U.S. Agency for International Development. Formerly with the Organization for Security and Cooperation in Europe mission in Bosnia. Interviewed on July 6, 2001.

Witte, Eric, former analyst, Coalition for International Justice. Interviewed on June 8, 2001.

BIBLIOGRAPHY

Aall, Pamela, Lt. Col. Daniel Miltenberger, and Thomas Weiss. *Guide to IGOs, NGOs and the Military in Peace and Relief Operations*. Washington, D.C.: USIP Press, 2000.

Abrams, Eliot, ed., *Honor Among Nations: Intangible Interests and Foreign Policy* (Washington, D.C.: Ethics and Policy Center, 1998).

Adams, Thomas K. "The New Mercenaries and the Privatization of Conflict." *Parameters* 29, no. 2 (1999): 103–16.

Adar, Korwa G. "The Wilsonian Conception of Democracy and Human Rights: A Retrospective and Prospective." *African Studies Quarterly* 2, no. 2 (1998).

"Afghanistan's Civilian Deaths Mount." *BBC News*, 3 January 2002.

Albright, Madeleine K. "Remarks by Secretary of State Madeleine K. Albright at the U.S. Institute for Peace." 1999. Available online at www.usip.org/events/pre2002/Albright_02044.html.

_____. "Speech before the U.S. Senate Foreign Relations Committee." Washington, D.C.: United States Information Service, 1999.

_____. "The Testing of American Foreign Policy." *Foreign Affairs* 77, no. 6 (1998): 50–64.

_____. "Yes, There Is a Reason to be in Somalia." *New York Times*, 10 August 1993.

Alcorn, Gay. "Civilian Deaths No Cause for Concern." *Sydney Morning Herald*, 12 January 2002.

Allen, Mike. "Bush Defends Tribunal Plan." *International Herald Tribune*, 21 November 2001.

Allen, Mike and Karen DeYoung. "Bush: U.S. Will Strike First at Enemies: In West Point Speech, President Lays Out Broader U.S. Policy." *Washington Post*, 2 June 2002.

Allott, Phillip. *Eunomia: New Order for a New World*. New York: Oxford University Press, 1990.

American Association for the International Commission of Jurists. *Human Rights and United States Foreign Policy, the First Decade, 1973–1983*. Washington, D.C.: American Association for the International Commission of Jurists, 1984.

Amnesty International. "'Collateral Damage' or Unlawful Killings? Violations of the Laws of War by NATO During Operation Allied Force." Washington, D.C.: Amnesty International, 2000.

Anderson, John B. "Unsigning the ICC." *Nation,* 29 April 2002.

Anderson, Kenneth. "The Limits of Pragmatism in American Foreign Policy: Unsolicited Advice to the Bush Administration on Relations with International Nongovernmental Organizations." *Chicago Journal of International Law* 2 (2001): 371–86.

———. "The Ottawa Convention Banning Landmines: The Role of International Non-Governmental Organizations and the Idea of International Civil Society." *European Journal of International Law* 11 (2000): 91–120.

Anderson, Kenneth, Jean Betulce Elshtain, Kim R. Holmes, Will Marshall, and Frank McClosky. "Is There a Doctrine in the House?" *Harper's* 288, no. 17 (1994): 57–64.

Anderson, Terry and J. Bishop Grewell. "It Isn't Easy Being Green: Environmental Policy Implications for Foreign Policy, International Law, and Sovereignty." *Chicago Journal of International Law* 11 (2001).

"Annex 1-a, Agreement on the Military Aspects of the Peace Settlement." *International Legal Materials* 35 (1996): 92–100.

Anonymous senior military official. *Department of Defense Background Briefing on Non-Lethal Weapons.* Office of Assistant Secretary of Defense, 17 February 1995. Available online at http://www.defenselink.mil/news/Feb1995/x021795_x0217nlw.html.

"Another Target for the American Right." *The Herald,* 16 June 2003.

Apodaca, Clair and Michael Stohl. "United States Human Rights Policy and Foreign Assistance." *International Studies Quarterly* 43, no. 1 (1999): 185–98.

Apple, R. W., Jr. "Preaching to Skeptics." *New York Times*, 16 September 1994.

———. "A Domestic Sort with Global Worries." *New York Times*, 25 August 1999.

Arend, Anthony Clark. "Do Legal Rules Matter? International Law and International Politics." *Virginia Journal of International Law* 38 (1998): 107–29.

Arquilla, John. "Louder Than Words: Tacit Communication in International Crises." *Political Communication* 9 (1992): 155–72.

Ashcroft, John. "Path-Breaking Strategies in the Global Fight against Sex Trafficking." Paper presented at the Department of State, 25 February 2003. Available online at www.state.gov/g/tip/rls/rm/17987.html.

Ausink, John A. *Watershed in Rwanda: The Evolution of President Clinton's Humanitarian Intervention Policy.* Washington, D.C.: Institute for the Study of Diplomacy, Georgetown University, 1997.

Avant, Deborah. "Privatizing Military Training." *Foreign Policy in Focus* 7, no. 6 (2002).

Bacevich, Andrew J. and Eliot A. Cohen, eds. *War over Kosovo.* New York: Columbia University Press, 2001.

Badner, Jenny. "UN Security Council Renews ICC Exemption for U.S. Peacekeepers." In *Voice of America Press Releases and Documents*, 2003. Available online at www.globalsecurity.org/military/library/news/2003/06/mil0306/12–32e4b7cb.html.

Bahnsen, John C. and Robert W Cone. "Defining the American Warrior Leader." *Parameters* 20 (1990): 24–28.

Baker, Peter. "New Criticism Signals Tension between U.S. And Russia." *International Herald Tribune*, 16 January 2002.

Balton, David A. "The Convention on the Rights of the Child: Prospects for International Enforcement." *Human Rights Quarterly* 12, no. 1 (1990): 120–29.

Balz, Dan. "Bush's Rights Record Assailed; Democratic Hopefuls Tailor Message to Feminist Audience." *Washington Post*, 21 May 2003.

———. "War Dissent? Don't Look on the (Hawkish) Left." *International Herald Tribune*, 27 November 2001.

Bankus, Brent C. "Training the Military for Peace Operations: A Past, Present, and Future View." Paper presented at the United States Institute of Peace Symposium on Best Practices for Training for Humanitarian and Peace Operations, 25–26 June 2001.

Baritz, Loren. *Backfire: A History of How American Culture Led Us into Vietnam and Made Us Fight the Way We Did.* New York: William Morrow, 1985.

Barnes, Fred. "Mr. Rice Guy." *Weekly Standard* 8 , no. 14 (2002): 12–13.

Barringer, Felicity. "U.N. Renews U.S. Peacekeepers' Exemption from Prosecution." *New York Times*, 13 June 2003.

Barry, John and Christopher Dickey, "Warrior's Rewards." *Newsweek,* 9 August 1999, 40–41.

Bartley, Robert L. "At Dawn in a New Diplomatic Era." *Wall Street Journal*, 17 June 2002, 19.

Baxi, Uprenda. "Voices of the Suffering, Fragmented Universality and the Future of Human Rights." In *The Future of International Human Rights.* Edited by Burns H. Weston and Stephen P. Marks, 101–56. Ardsley, N.Y.: Transnational, 1999.

Bayne, Nicholas. "Reviews: U.S. Foreign Policy under Clinton. Warren Christopher: In the Stream of History: Shaping Foreign Policy for a New Era." *Government and Opposition* 34, no. 2 (1999): 263–68.

Becker, Elizabeth. "U.S. Suspends Aid to 35 Countries over New International Court." *New York Times*, 2 July 2003.

_____. "U.S. War Colleges Hone Peacekeeping Skills along with Fighting Reflexes." *New York Times*, 6 August 1999.

Bennett, W. Lance. "Political Scenarios and the Nature of Politics." *Philosophy and Rhetoric*, no. 8 (1975): 23–42.

Berdel, Max. "Fateful Encounter." *Survival* 36, no. 1 (1994): 30–50.

Berger, Samuel R. "A Foreign Policy for the Global Age." *Foreign Affairs* 79, no. 6 (2000): 22–39.

Bett, Stuart W. "Missiles over Kosovo: Emergence, Lex Lata of Customary Norm Requiring Use of Precision Munitions in Urban Areas." *Naval Law Review* 47 (2000): 115–75.

Beyers, Michael. *Custom, Power and the Power of Rules: International Relations and Customary International Law.* New York: Cambridge University Press, 1998.

Biddle, Stephen. "The New Way of War? Debating the Kosovo Model." *Foreign Affairs* 81, no. 2 (2002): 138–44.

Binkin, Martin. *Who Will Fight in the Next War? The Changing Face of the American Military.* Washington, D.C.: Brookings Institution, 1993.

Bishara, Marwan. "With Its New Muslim Alliance, U.S. Risks Further Instability." *International Herald Tribune*, 24–25 November 2001.

Bitzer, Lloyd. "The Rhetorical Situation." *Philosophy and Rhetoric* 1 (1968): 1–14.

Bolton, John R. "CTBT: Clear Thinking . . . " *Jerusalem Post*, 18 October 1999.

_____. "Hard Man Who Sits at the Heart of U.S. Foreign Policy." *Financial Times*, 19 December 2002.

_____. "Notebook." *Australian Financial Review*, 3 January 2001.

_____. "Rule of Law: Clinton Meets International Law in Kosovo." *Wall Street Journal*, 5 April 1999.

_____. "Rule of Law: Why an International Criminal Court Won't Work." *Wall Street Journal*, 30 March 1998.

_____. "U.S. Money and a U.N. Vote." *Washington Times*, 16 October 1998.

_____. "Unsign the Treaty." *Washington Post*, 4 January 2001.

Boot, Max. "Sparing Civilians, Buildings and Even the Enemy." *New York Times*, 30 March 2003.

Booth, Ken. "Three Tyrannies." In *Human Rights in Global Politics*, Edited by Tim Dunne and Nicholas J. Wheeler, 31–70. New York: Cambridge University Press, 1999.

Booth, Ken and Tim Dunne. *Worlds in Collision: Terror and the Future of Global Order.* New York: Palgrave, 2002.

Borch, Frederich. "Targeting after Kosovo: How the Law Changed for Strike Planners." *Naval War College Review* 56, no. 2 (2002).

"Bosnia and Herzegovina-Croatia-Yugoslavia: General Framework Agreement for Peace in Bosnia and Herzegovina with Annexes." *International Legal Materials* 35 (1996): 75–169.

Bouchet-Saulnier, Francoise. *The Practical Guide to Humanitarian Law*. Lanham, Md.: Rowman and Littlefield, 2002.

Boyd, Brig. Gen Morris J. "Peace Operations: A Capstone Doctrine." *Military Review* 75 (1995): 22–29.

Boyle, Joseph. "Natural Law and International Ethics." In *Traditions of International Ethics*, edited by Terry Nardin and David R. Mapel, 112–35. New York: Cambridge University Press, 1992.

Brinkley, Douglas. "Democratic Enlargement: The Clinton Doctrine." *Foreign Policy*, no. 106 (1997): 111–27.

Broad, Robin and John Cavanagh. "The Corporate Accountability Movement: Lessons and Opportunities." *Fletcher Forum World Affairs* 23 (1999): 151–66.

Broad, William J. "Oh What a Lovely War, If No One Dies." *New York Times*, 18 March 2002.

Brooks, Doug. "Hope for the 'Hopeless' Continent: Mercenaries." *Traders: Journal for the Southern African Region* 3 (2000).

_____. "Write a Check, End a War: Using Private Military Companies to End African Conflicts." *ACCORD: Conflict Trends*, no. 1 (2000).

Brown, Chris. "Universal Human Rights: A Critique." In *Human Rights in Global Politics*, edited by Tim Dunne and Nicholas J. Wheeler. New York: Cambridge University Press, 1999.

Brown, Widney. "A Human Rights Aproach to the Rehabilitation and Reintegration into Society of Trafficked Victims." Paper presented at 21st Century Slavery — The Human Rights Dimension to Trafficking in Human Beings, conference, Rome, Italy, 15–16 May 2002. Available online at http://www.hrw.org/sbackgrounder/wrd/trafficked-victims.htm.

Brunnee, Jutta, and Stephen J. Toope. "International Law and Contructivism: Elements of an Interactional Theory of International Law." *Columbia Journal of Transnational Law* 39 (2001): 19–79.

Bull, Hedley. *The Anarchical Society: A Study of Order in World Politics*. New York: Columbia University Press, 2002.

_____. *International Theory: The Three Traditions*, New York: Holmes and Meier, 1994.

Bumiller, Elisabeth and David Johnston. "New Court for Terror Defendants." *International Herald Tribune*, 15 November 2001.

Bunch, Charlotte. "Whose Security? Bush's Counterterrorism Efforts Neglect Women and Frustrate Feminists." *Nation* 23 (2002): 36–38.

Burk, James. "Military Culture." In *Encyclopedia of Violence, Peace and Conflict*. Vol. 2, edited by Lester Kurtz and Jennifer Turpin. San Diego: Academic Press, 1999.

Bush, George H. W. "Address before a Joint Session of the Congress on the Persian Gulf Crisis and the Federal Budget Deficit." In *Public Papers of the Presidents of the United States, 1990*, book 1, 1218–22. Washington, D.C.: U.S. Government Printing Office, 1991.

_____. "Address before a Joint Session of the Congress on the State of the Union." In *Public Papers of the Presidents of the United States, 1992–1993*, book 1, 156–63. Washington, D.C.: U.S. Government Printing Office, 1993.

_____. "Address before the Forty-fifth Session of the UN General Assembly in New York, New York." In *Public Papers of the Presidents of the United States, 1990*, book 2, 1330–34. Washington, D.C.: U.S. Government Printing Office, 1991.

_____. "Address to the Forty-sixth Session of the United Nations General Assembly in New York, New York." In *Public Papers of the Presidents of the United States, 1991*, book 2, 1199–203. Washington, D.C.: U.S. Government Printing Office, 1992.

_____. "Address to the Nation Announcing Allied Military Action in the Persian Gulf." In *Public Papers of the Presidents of the United States, 1991*, book 1, 42–44. Washington, D.C.: U.S. Government Printing Office, 1992.

_____. "Address to the Nation Announcing the Deployment of United States Armed Forces to Saudi Arabia." In *Public Papers of the Presidents of the United States, 1990*, book 2, 1107–9. Washington, D.C.: U.S. Government Printing Office, 1991.

_____. "Remarks Accepting the Presidential Nomination at the Republican National Convention in Houston, Texas." In *Public Papers of the Presidents of the United States, 1992–1993*, book 2, 1380–86. Washington, D.C.: U.S. Government Printing Office, 1993.

_____. "Remarks and a Question-and-Answer Session at a Meeting of the Economic Club in New York, New York." In *Public Papers of the Presidents of the United States, 1991*, book 1, 117–27. Washington, D.C.: U.S. Government Printing Office, 1992.

_____. "Remarks at a Luncheon Hosted by Prime Minister Ruud Lubbers of the Netherlands in the Hague." In *Public Papers of the Presidents of the United States, 1991*, book 1, 1426–29. Washington, D.C.: U.S. Government Printing Office, 1992.

_____. "Remarks at Maxwell Air Force Base War College in Montgomery, Alabama." In *Public Papers of the Presidents of the United States, 1991*, book 1, 364–68. Washington, D.C.: U.S. Government Printing Office, 1992.

_____. "Remarks to the American Legion National Convention in Chicago, Illinois, August 25, 1992." In *Public Papers of the Presidents of the United States, 1992–1993*, book 2, 1419–23. Washington, D.C.: U.S. Government Printing Office, 1993.

_____. "Remarks to the American Society of Newspaper Editors." In *Public Papers of the Presidents of the United States, 1992–1993*, book 1, 564–73. Washington, D.C.: U.S. Government Printing Office, 1993.

_____. "State of the Union Address: Envisioning One Thousand Points of Light." Washington, D.C., 1991. Available online at www.c-span.org/executive/transcript.asp?ca=current.event6code=bush.adminByear=1991.

Bush, George W. "President Bush Address at Fifty-first[t] Annual National Prayer Breakfast," 6 February 2003. Available online at http://www.whitehouse.gov/news/releases/2003/02/20030206-1.html.

_____. "President Bush Addresses Nation on Space Shuttle Columbia Tragedy," 1 February 2003. Available online at http://www.whitehouse.gov/news/releases/2003/02/20030201-2.html.

_____. "President Bush Calls for a New Palestinian Leadership," 24 June 2002. Available online at http://www.whitehouse.gov/news/releases/2002/06/20020624-3.html.

_____. "President Bush Outlines Iraqi Threat," 7 October 2002. Available online at http://www.whitehouse.gov/news/releases/2002/10/20021007-8.html.

_____. "President Delivers State of the Union Address" 28 January 2003. Available online at http://www.whitehouse.gov/news/releases/2003/01/print/20030128-19.html.

_____. "President George W. Bush's Inaugural Address," 20 January 2001. Available online at http://www.whitehouse.gov/news/print/inaugural-address.html.

_____. "Presidential Address to the Nation," 7 October 2001. Available online at http://www.whitehouse.gov/news/releases/2001/10/20011007-8.html.

_____. "Presidential Debate at Wake Forest University," 11 October 2000. Available online at www.issues2000.org/Archive_2000.htm.

_____. "Remarks by the President on Cuba Policy Review," 20 May 2002. Available online at http://www.whitehouse.gov/news/releases/2002/05/20020520-1.html.

_____. "Remarks by the President on Global Development, Inter-American Bank," 14 March 2001. Available online at http://www.whitehouse.gov/newsreleases/2002/03/2002200314.7.html.

_____. "State of the Union Address," 28 January 2003. Available online at http://www.whitehouse.gov/news/releases/2002/01/20020129-11.html.

_____. "Statement on Defense at Campaign Rally in Kansas City" 22 February 2000. Available online at http://www.foreignpolicy.org/library.

"Bush Vows 'Sustained, Comprehensive and Relentless Operations.'" *International Herald Tribune*, 8 October 2003.

Buzan, Barry. "From International System to International Society: Structural Realism and Regime Theory Meet the English School." *International Organization* 47, no. 3 (1993): 327–53.

Byers, Michael. "International Law and the American National Interest." *Chicago Journal of International Law* 1, no. 2 (2000): 257–61.

Cahill, Lisa Sowle. "Toward a Christian Theory of Human Rights." *Journal of Religious Ethics* 9 (1980): 277–301.

Calciano, Elizabeth M. "United Nations Convention on the Rights of the Child: Will it Help Children in the United States?" *Hastings International and Comparative Law Review* 15, no. 3 (1992): 515–34.

Callahan, David. *Unwinnable Wars: American Power and Ethnic Conflict.* New York: Hill and Wang, 1997.

Cameron, Maxwell A., Robert J. Lawson, and Brian W. Tomlin, eds. *To Walk Without Fear: The Global Movement to Ban Landmines.* New York: Oxford University Press, 1999.

Campaign Development Group. *Navigating the Ad Hoc Committee: A "Rough" Guide to NGO Participation in the Development of a Treaty on the Rights of People with Disabilities.* Washington, D.C.: Landmines Survivor Network, 2002.

Campaign for Tobacco Free Kids. "Memo on Tobacco Trends in the Twenty-first Century: Domestic and Global Outlook." *U.S. Newswire*, 16 December 1999.

Campbell, David. *Writing Security: United States Foreign Policy and the Politics of Identity.* Minneapolis: University of Minnesota Press, 1998.

Campbell, Duncan. "Bush Nominees under Fire for Link with Contras." *Guardian*, 6 April 2001.

_____. "Nominee to UN Linked to Deaths." *Sydney Morning Herald*, 7 April 2001.

Carey, Henry F. "U.S. Domestic Politics and the Emerging Humanitarian Intervention Policy: Haiti, Bosnia, and Kosovo." *World Affairs* 164, no. 2 (2001): 72–82.

Carothers, Thomas. *Aiding Democracy Abroad: The Learning Curve.* Washington, D.C.: Carnegie Endowment for International Peace, 1999.

Carter, Jimmy. *Keeping Faith: Memoirs of a President.* New York: Ballantine Books, 1982.

Carter, Ralph G., ed. *Contemporary Cases in U.S. Foreign Policy: From Terrorism to Trade.* Washington, D.C.: Congressional Quarterly Press, 2000.

Carter, Ralph G. and Donald W. Jackson. "Funding the IMF: Congress vs. the White House." In *Contemporary Cases in U.S. Foreign Policy: From Terrorism to Trade,* edited by Ralph G. Carter. Washington, D.C.: Congressional Quarterly Press, 2000.

Center for Defense Information. "Non-Lethal Weapons: War without Death?" Washington, D.C.: Center for Defense Information, 1995.

Center for Strategic and International Studies. "American Military Culture in the Twenty-first Century." Washington, D.C.: CSIS International Security Program, 2000.

Center for Strategic Leadership. "Peacekeeping Institute." U.S. Army, March 23, 2001. Available online at http://carlisle-www.army.mil/asacsl/divisions/pki/pki.htm.

Chairman of the Joint Chiefs of Staff. "Joint Tactics, Techniques, and Procedures for Joint Special Operations, Task Force Operations. Joint Publication 3-05.1," VI-7, 19 December 2001. Available online at dtic/mil/doctrine/jel/new_pubs/jb3_05_1.pdf.

Charlton, J. I. *Nothing about Us without Us: Disability, Oppression and Empowerment.* Berkeley and Los Angeles: University of California Press, 1998.

Chayes, Abram and Antonia Handler Chayes. *The New Sovereignty.* Cambridge, Mass.: Harvard University Press, 1995.

Checkel, Jeffrey. "The Constructivist Turn in International Relations Theory." *World Politics* 50 (1998): 324–48.

Chen, Martha Alter. "Engendering World Conferences: The International Women's Movement and the UN." In *NGOs, the UN and Global Governance*, edited by Thomas G. Weiss and Leon Gordenker. Boulder, Colo.: Lynne Rienner, 1996.

Chomsky, Noam. *The New Military Humanism: Lessons from Kosovo.* Monroe, Me.: Common Courage Press, 1999.

Chopra, Jarat, ed. *The Politics of Peace-Maintenance.* Boulder, Colo.: Lynne Rienner, 1998.

Christopher, Warren. "Overview of 1995 Foreign Policy Agenda and the Clinton Administration's Proposed Budget." Statement before the Senate Foreign Relations Committee, Washington, D.C., U.S. Department of State Dispatch 6, no. 8 (1995): 111–17.

Clark, Wesley K. *Waging Modern War: Bosnia, Kosovo and the Future of Combat.* New York: Public Affairs, 2001.

Clarke, Jonathan. "The Conceptual Poverty of U.S. Foreign Policy." *Atlantic Monthly*, no. 272 (1993): 54–66.

Clinton, William J. "Statement by the President to the Nation." The White House, Office of the Press Secretary, 1999.

_____. "Statement by the President on Signing the International Religious Freedom Act of 1998." *Weekly Compilation of Presidential Documents* 34 (1998): 2149.

Coady, C. A. J. "The Ethics of Armed Intervention." *Peaceworks*, no. 45. Washington, D.C.: U.S. Institute of Peace, 2002.

Cody, Edward and Molly Moore. "First Strikes in Daylight: UN Agency Urges Caution after Deaths of 4 Civilians." *International Herald Tribune*, 10 October 2001.

Cohen, Cynthia Price. "Implementing the U.N. Convention on the Rights of the Child." *Whittier Law Review* 23, no. 1 (1999): 95–105.

_____. "Role of the United States in Drafting the Convention on the Rights of the Child: Creating a New World for Children." *Loyola Poverty Law Journal* 4 (1998): 9–46.

_____. "Role of Non-Governmental Organizations in the Drafting of the Convention on the Rights of the Child." *Human Rights Quarterly* 12 (1990): 137–47.

Cohen, Eliot. "Twilight of the Citizen Soldier." *Parameters* 31, no. 2 (2001): 23–28.

Cohen, Harlan Grant. "The American Challenge to International Law: A Tentative Framework for Debate," *Yale Journal of International Law* 28 (2003): 551–82.

Cohen, Jeff. *The Return of Otto Reich: Will Government Propagandist Join Bush Administration?* FAIR, 8 June 2001. Available online at http://www.fair.org/articles/otto-reich.html.

Cohen, Roberta. "Human Rights Decision-Making in the Executive Branch: Some Proposals for a Coordinated Strategy." In *Human Rights and American Foreign Policy*, edited by Donald P. Kommers and Gilburt D. Loescher. Notre Dame, Ind.: University of Notre Dame Press, 1979.

Cohn, Elizabeth. "U.S. Democratization Assistance." *Foreign Policy in Focus* 4, no. 20 (1999).

Cohn, Gary, and Ginger Thompson. "Unearthed: Fatal Secrets." *Baltimore Sun*, 11 June 1995.

Coker, Cristopher. *Waging War without Warriors?* Boulder, Colo.: Lynne Rienner, 2002.

Cole, Timothy M. "When Intentions Go Awry: The Bush Administration's Foreign Policy Rhetoric." *Political Communication* 13, no. 1 (1996): 93–113.

Coliver, Sandra. "Centuries-Old Law is Critical for Torture Survivors." *San Francisco Chronicle,* 11 June 2003.

_____. "The U.S. Can Still Play a Role in Bringing War Criminals to Justice." *Legal Times,* 13 May 2002.

Collie, Tim. "The Civilian-Military Divide: Poorer Classes Serve Their Country While America's Elite Have Other Dreams." *Toronto Star,* 27 November 2001.

Consigny, Scott. "Rhetoric and Its Situations." *Philosophy and Rhetoric,* no. 7 (1974): 175–86.

Cooper, Belinda and Isabel Traugolt. "Woman's Rights and Security in Central Asia." *World Policy Journal* 20, no. 11 (2003): 59–67.

Cooper, Scott A. "The Politics of Airstrikes." *Policy Review* no. 107 (2001): 55–66.

Council on Foreign Relations. *The RMA Debate.* Available online at http://www.comw.org/rma/.

Cox, Larry. "Reflections of Human Rights at Century's End." *Human Rights Dialogue* 2, no. 1 (2000): 5.

Cox, Matthew. "Keeping the Peace Is No Easy Task: U.S Soldiers Try to Gain Control in Kosovo." *Army Times,* 5 July 1999.

Cox, Michael, John Ickenberry, and Takashi Inoguchi. *American Democracy Promotion: Impulses, Strategies and Impacts.* New York: Oxford University Press, 2000.

Coy, Patrick. "Cooperative Accompaniment and Peace Brigades International in Sri Lanka." In *Transnational Social Movements and Global Politics,* edited by Jackie Smith, Charles Chatfield, and Ron Pagnucco. Syracuse, N.Y.: Syracuse University Press, 1997.

Crabb, Cecil V., Jr. and Pat M. Holt. *Invitation to Struggle: Congress, the President, and Foreign Policy.* Washington, D.C.: Congressional Quarterly Press, 1994.

Crawley, Vince. "What's Wrong with Keeping the Peace?" *Army Times,* 22 May 2000.

Crossette, Barbara. "Bush Finding It Rough Going on U.N. Human Rights Issues." *San Diego Union-Tribune,* 8 April 2001.

Cumings, Bruce. "The Wicked Witch of the West Is Dead. Long Live the Wicked Witch of the East." In *The End of the Cold War: Its Meaning and Implications,* edited by Michael Hogan. Cambridge: Cambridge University Press, 1992.

Daalder, Ivo H. and James M. Lindsay. "Bush Has an Obligation to Build an Afghan Peace." *International Herald Tribune,* 24–25 November 2001.

Daalder, Ivo H. and Michael E. O'Hanlon. *Winning Ugly: NATO's War to Save Kosovo.* Washington, D.C.: Brookings Institution, 2000.

Dao, James. "Army Orders Peacekeepers to Sessions on Rights." *New York Times,* 2 December 2000.

_____. "Solitaire: One Nation Plays the Great Game Alone." *New York Times,* 7 July 2002.

Dardagan, Hamit. *The Iraq Body Count Project* 2003. Available online at http://www.iraqbodycount.org.

Davis, Tami and Sean Lynn-Jones. "City Upon a Hill." *Foreign Policy,* no. 66 (1987): 20–38.

De Neufville, Judith. "Human Rights Reporting as a Policy Tool: An Examination of the State Department Country Reports." *Human Rights Quarterly* 8 (1986): 681–99.

De Soto, Alvaro, and Graciana del Castillo. "Obstacles to Peacebuilding." *Foreign Policy,* no. 94 (1994): 69–83.

De Young, Karen. "Bush Says U.S. Will Help Train Afghan Army, Police." *Washington Post,* 29 January 2002.

_____. "U.S. Strives to Shore up Coalition." *International Herald Tribune*, 11 November 2001.

De Young, Karen and Dana Milbank. "Military Flaws Informed by Polls; Carefully Chosen Words Prepare Americans for Potential Toll in Ground War." *Washington Post,* 19 October 2001.

Defense Link. "Summary: Report to Congress on U.S. Military Activists in Rwanda, 1994–August 1997." Available online at www.defenselink.mil/pubs/rwanda/summary.html.

Deibel, Terry L. "Bush's Foreign Policy: Mastery and Inaction." *Foreign Policy*, no. 84 (1991): 3–23.

Deiss, Joseph. "The Geneva Conventions Must Be Applied in Full." *International Herald Tribune*, 18 April 2002.

Dejevsky, Mary. "Assault on Serbs: Clinton Team Launches a TV Offensive; Persuades America." *Independent*, 29 March 1999.

Dellios, Hugh and E.A. Torriero. "Sorting Fact from Fiction in POW's Gripping Story." *Chicago Tribune*, 26 May 2003.

Del Olmo, Frank. "In War, Diversity Can Be a Lifesaver." *Los Angeles Times*, 11 May 2003.

Dembart, Lee. "For Afghans in Cuba, Untested Legal Limbo." *International Herald Tribune*, 25 January 2002.

Dembour, Marie-Benedicte. "Human Rights Talk and Anthropological Ambivalence: The Particular Contexts of Universal Claims." In *Inside and Outside the Law: Anthropological Studies of Authority and Ambiguity*, edited by Olivia Harris. New York: Routledge, 1996.

Demchak, Chris C. *Military Organizations, Complex Machines: Modernization in the U.S. Armed Services*. Ithaca, N.Y.: Cornell University, 1991.

Dennis, Michael J. "Newly Adopted Protocols to the Convention on the Rights of the Child." *American Journal of International Law* 94, no. 3 (2000): 789–99.

Deptula, David A. "Firing for Effects." *Air Force Magazine*, 84, no. 4 (2000): 46–53.

Diehl, Jackson. "Russia and Israel Want to Hijack the Anti-Terror Campaign." *International Herald Tribune*, 18 October 2001.

_____. "U.S. Again Supports Unsavory Dictators." *International Herald Tribune*, 20 March 2002.

Dietrich, John. "U.S. Human Rights Policy in the Post–Cold War Era." Paper presented at the Annual Convention of the International Studies Association, 28 February 2002.

Di Prizio, Robert C. *Armed Humanitarians*. Baltimore: Johns Hopkins University Press, 2002.

_____. "Post–Cold War Humanitarian Interventions: What Motivated the Bush and Clinton Administrations?" Paper presented at the International Studies Association Northeast Conference, Albany, N.Y., 9–11 November 2000.

Dobbs, Michael. "Back in Political Forefront: Iran-Contra Figure Plays Key Role on Mideast." *Washington Post*, 27 May 2001.

_____. "For Wolfowitz, a Vision May Be Realized; Deputy Defense Secretary's Views on Free Iraq Considered Radical in Ways Good and Bad." *Washington Post*, 7 April 2003.

Dobriansky, Paula. "Feeding Vulnerable Afghans Is a Major Part of the Strategy." *International Herald Tribune*, 17 October 2001.

Dobson, Alan. "The Dangers of U.S. Interventionism." *Review of International Studies* 28 (2002): 572–97.

Donagan, Alan. *The Theory of Morality*. Chicago: University of Chicago Press, 1977.

Donnelly, Jack, C. "Post-Cold War Reflections on the Study of International Human Rights." In *Ethics and International Affairs,* edited by J. Rosenthal. Washington, D.C.: Georgetown University Press, 1999.

———. *Universal Human Rights: In Theory and Practice.* 2nd ed. Ithaca, N.Y.: Cornell University Press, 2003.

———. *Universal International Human Rights: In Theory and Practice.* Boulder, Colo.: Westview Press, 1998.

Donini, Antonio. "The Bureaucracy and the Free Spirits: Stagnation and Innovation in the Relationship between the UN and NGOs." In *NGOs, the UN and Global Governance,* edited by Thomas G. Weiss and Leon Gordenker. Boulder, Colo.: Lynne Rienner, 1996.

———. "The Social Construction of International Human Rights." In *Human Rights in Global Politics,* edited by Tim Dunne and Nicholas J. Wheeler. New York: Cambridge University Press, 1999.

———. *Universal Human Rights in Theory and Practice.* Ithaca, N.Y.: Cornell University Press, 1989.

Dorsey, Ellen. "Human Rights and U.S. Foreign Policy: Who Controls the Agenda?" *Journal of Intergroup Relations* 22, no. 1 (1995): 3–17.

———. "U.S. Foreign Policy and the Human Rights Movement: New Strategies for a Global Era." In *The United States and Human Rights: Looking Inward and Outward,* edited by David P. Forsythe. Lincoln: University of Nebraska Press, 2000.

Drew, Elizabeth. "The Neocons in Power." *New York Review of Books* 50, no. 10 (2003): 20–22.

Dreyfuss, Richard. "Missing More Intelligence." *Nation* 27, no. 1 (2003): 4–5.

Drezner, Daniel W. "Ideas, Bureaucratic Politics, and the Crafting of Foreign Policy." *American Journal of Political Science* 44, no. 4 (2000): 743–49.

Drohan, Madeleine. "Abusive Multinationals Have a Pal in Washington." *Globe and Mail,* 19 May 2003.

Drysdale, John. "Foreign Military Intervention in Somalia: The Root Cause of the Shift from U.N. Peacekeeping to Peacemaking and It Consequences." In *Learning from Somalia: The Lessons of Armed Humanitarian Intervention,* edited by Walter Clarke and Jeffrey Herbst. Boulder, Colo.: Westview Press, 1997.

Duffield, Mark. *Global Governance and the New Wars.* New York: Zed, 2001.

Dumbrell, John. *American Foreign Policy: From Carter to Clinton.* London: Macmillan, 1997.

Dunlap, Charles J., Jr. "The Origins of the American Military Coup of 2012." *Parameters* 22, no. 4 (1993): 2–20.

Dunne, Timothy. *Inventing International Society: A History of the English School.* New York: St. Martin's Press, 1998.

Dunne, Timothy and Nicholas J. Wheeler, eds. *Human Rights in Global Politics.* New York: Cambridge University Press, 1999.

Edwards, Jim. "Government Sued over Post–September 11 Detentions." *Legal Intelligencer* 226, no. 79 (2002): 4.

Ellis, Anthony. "Utilitarianism and International Ethics." In *Traditions of International Ethics,* edited by Terry Nardin and David Mapel. New York: Cambridge University Press, 1992.

Elshtain, Jean Bethke. "The Dignity of the Human Person and the Idea of Human Rights" (book review). *Journal of Law and Religion* 14 (1999–2000): 53–57.

Enloe, Cynthia. *Maneuvers.* Berkeley and Los Angeles: University of California Press, 2000.

Erlanger, Steven. "Europeans Take Aim at U.S. on Detainees." *International Herald Tribune,* 24 January 2002.

———. "NATO Allies Relieved at Calm U.S. Response." *International Herald Tribune,* 29–30 September 2001.

Evans, Gareth. *Cooperating for Peace.* St. Leonards, Australia: Unwin and Hyman, 1993.

_____. "Preventing Deadly Conflict: The Role and Responsibility of Governments and NGOs." Lecture at the Centre for Study of Human Rights, London School of Economics, 2 February 2001.

Evans, Tony. *U.S. Hegemony and the Project of Universal Human Rights*. New York: St. Martin's Press, 1996.

Evered, Timothy C. "An International Criminal Court: Recent Proposals and American Concerns." *Pace International Law Review* 6 (1994): 121–57.

Eviatar, Daphne. "Profits and Gunpoint: Unocal's Pipeline in Burma Becomes a Test Case in Corporate Accountability." *Nation*, 30 June 2003, 16–22.

Fainaru, Steve. "U.S. Jail Is Harsh Place for Terror Detainees." *International Herald Tribune*, 18 April 2002.

_____. "U.S. Judge Rejects Closed Immigration Hearings." *International Herald Tribune*, 5 April 2002.

FAIR: Fairness and Accuracy in Reporting. "Ashcroft Quizzed about Southern Partisan Endorsement," 19 January 2001. Available online at http://www.fair.org/press_releases/ashcroft.html.

Falk, Richard. "Clinton Doctrine: The Free Marketeers." *Progressive* 58, no. 1 (1994): 18–20.

_____. "Cultural Foundations for the International Protection of Human Rights." In *Human Rights in Cross-Cultural Perspectives*, edited by Abdullahi Ahmed An'Na-im. Philadelphia: University of Pennsylvania Press, 1992.

_____. *Human Rights and State Sovereignty*. London: Holms and Meier, 1981.

_____. *Human Rights Horizons*. New York: Routledge, 2000.

_____. *On Human Governance: Toward a New Global Politics*. University Park: Pennsylvania State University Press, 1995.

Faludi, Susan. "An American Myth Rides into the Sunset." *New York Times*, 30 March 2003.

Farrell, Theo. "Culture and Military Power." *Review of International Studies* 24, no. 3 (1998): 404–16.

_____. *Democracy by Force: U.S. Military Intervention in the Post–Cold War World*. New York: Cambridge University Press, 2000.

Farrell, Theo and Terry Terriff, eds. *The Sources of Military Change: Culture, Politics and Technology*. Boulder, Colo.: Lynne Rienner, 2002.

Fautua, David T. "Transforming the Reserve Components." *Military Review* 80, no. 5 (2000), 57–67.

Feaver, Peter D. and Richard H. Kohn. *Project on the Gap between Military and Civilian Society: Digest of Findings and Studies*. Chapel Hill, N.C.: Triangle Institute of Security Studies, 1999.

_____, eds. *Soldiers and Civilians: The Civil-Military Gap and American National Security*. Cambridge, Mass.: MIT Press, 2001.

Federation of American Scientists. *U.S. International Security Assistance Education and Training*, 2001. Available online at http://www.fas.org/asmp/campaigns/training.html.

Ferguson, Neil. "Power." *Foreign Policy* no. 134 (January/February 2003): 18–24.

Field, Kim and John Nagl. "Combat Roles for Women: A Modest Proposal." *Parameters* 31, no. 2 (2001), 74–88.

Finn, Peter. "Milosevic Fades Away, but an Old Issue Looms: Ethnic Albanians Vex Yugoslavia and NATO." *International Herald Tribune*, 26 December 2000.

Finnemore, Martha. "Constructing Norms of Humanitarian Intervention." In *The Culture of National Security: Norms and Identity in World Politics*, edited by Peter J. Katzenstein. New York: Columbia University Press, 1996.

_____. "International Organizations as Teachers of Norms: The United Nations Education, Scientific, and Cultural Organization and Science Policy." *International Organization* 47 (1993): 565–97.

_____. *National Interests in International Society.* Ithaca, N.Y.: Cornell University Press, 1996.

Finnemore, Martha and Kathryn Sikkink. "International Norm Dynamics and Political Change." *International Organization* 52, no. 4 (1998): 887–917.

Fitchett, Joseph. "Food Aid across Northern Border Called Key to Afghan Crisis." *International Herald Tribune*, 26 October 2001.

_____. "Pentagon in a League of Its Own." *International Herald Tribune*, 4 February 2002.

_____. "U.S. Policy on Terrorism: Think Globally and Don't Interfere Locally." *International Herald Tribune*, 28 September 2001, 10.

Flood, Patrick. "Human Rights, UN Institutions and the United States." In *The United States and Human Rights: Looking Inward and Outward*, edited by David P. Forsythe, 367. Lincoln: University of Nebraska Press, 2000.

Fore, Matthew L. "And You Shall Weigh Your God: Assessing the Imperialistic Implications of the International Religious Freedom Act in Muslim Countries." *Duke Law Journal* 52, no. 2 (2002): 423–53.

Foreign Assistance Act. 94-329, 90 Statute 729 .

Foreign Policy Editors. "Clinton's Foreign Policy." *Foreign Policy*, no. 121 (2000): 18–29.

_____. "True Believer: Interview with Gareth Evans." *Foreign Policy*, no. 123 (2001): 26–41.

Forero, Juan. "Rights Groups Overseas Fight U.S. Concerns in U.S. Courts." *New York Times*, 26 June 2003.

Forsythe, David P. *Human Rights and Comparative Foreign Policy.* New York: United Nations University Press, 2000.

_____. "Human Rights and U.S. Foreign Policy: Two Levels, Two Worlds." *Political Studies* 43 (1995): 111–30.

_____. *Human Rights in International Relations.* New York: Cambridge University Press, 2000.

_____. "Human Rights in U.S. Foreign Policy: Retrospect and Prospect." *Political Science Quarterly* 105, no. 3 (1990): 435–54.

_____. "Human Rights Policy: Change and Continuity." In *U.S. Foreign Policy after the Cold War*, edited by Randall B. Ripley and James M. Lindsay. Pittsburgh: University of Pittsburgh Press, 1997.

Forsythe, David P. and Barbara Ann J. Rieffer. "US Foreign Policy and Enlarging the Democratic Community." *Human Rights Quarterly*, no. 22 (2000): 988–1010.

Foyle, Douglas C. "Public Opinion and Bosnia: Anticipating a Disaster." In *Contemporary Cases in U.S. Foreign Policy: From Terrorism to Trade*, edited by Ralph G. Carter,. Washington, D.C.: Congressional Quarterly Press, 2000.

Franke, Volker C. "Generation X and the Military: A Comparison of Attitudes and Values between West Point Cadets and College Students." *Journal of Political and Military Sociology* 29, no. 1 (2001): 92–119.

Friedman, Thomas L. "Democracy or Anti-Terrorism?" *International Herald Tribune*, 9 May 2002.

Fulbright, J. W. *The Arrogance of Power.* New York: Vintage, 1966.

Gabelnick, Tamar. "Turkey: Arms and Human Rights." *Foreign Policy in Focus* 4, no. 16 (1999).

Gaer, Felice D. "Reality Check: Human Rights NGOs Confront Governments at the UN." In *NGOs, the UN and Global Governance,* edited by Thomas G. Weiss and Leon Gordenker. Boulder, Colo.: Lynne Rienner, 1996.

Galtung, Johan. "Violence, Peace, and Peace Research." *Journal of Peace Research* 6, no. 3 (1969): 109–34.

Garamone, Jim. "Bush, Rumsfeld Announce Food Aid for Afghan Refugees." Washington, D.C.: American Forces Press Service, 2001.

Garcia, Victoria. "U.S. Military Aid for Allies in a War against Iraq." Washington, D.C.: Center for Defense Information, 2003.

Gellman, Barton. "CIA Seeks Rules from Top Leaders on Assassinations." *International Herald Tribune*, 29 October 2001.

Gerges, Fawaz A. "It's Time for Muslims Suspicious of America to Think It Over." *International Herald Tribune*, 9 October 2003.

Geyer, Georgie Anne. *When Force Fails: Flawed Intervention*. Special report of the Cantigny Conference Series. Chicago: McCormick Tribune Foundation, 2001.

Gilbert, Felix. *To the Farewell Address: Ideas of Early American Foreign Policy*. Princeton, N.J.: Princeton University Press, 1961.

Gingras, Jeffrey and Rudy Tomslav. "Morality and Modern Air War." *Joint Air Forces Quarterly* 25 (2000): 107–11.

Girion, Lisa. "1789 Law Acquires Human Rights Role." *Los Angeles Times*, June 16, 2003.

Glennon, Michael J. "The New Interventionism: The Search for a Just International Law." *Foreign Affairs* 78, no. 2 (1999): 2–7.

Gordon, Michael, and Bernard Trainor. *The Generals' War: The Inside Story of the Conflict in the Gulf*. Boston: Little, Brown, 1995.

Gordon, Michael R. "Aspin Overhauls Pentagon to Bolster Policy Role." *New York Times*, 28 January 1993.

——. "Mission to Haiti: Military Analysis Pentagon's Haiti Policy Focuses on Casualties." *New York Times*, 6 October 1994.

——. "Mission to Somalia: U.S. Is Sending Large Forces as Warning to Somali Clans." *New York Times*, 5 December 1992.

——. "Pentagon Limits on the Media Tighter Than in Earlier Wars." *International Herald Tribune*, 22 October 2001.

Goulding, Marrack. "The Evolution of UN Peacekeeping." *International Affairs* 69, no. 3 (1993): 451–64.

Graham, Bradley. "Joint Chiefs Doubted Air Strategy." *Washington Post*, 5 April 1999.

——. "Pentagon Shifts, Seeks Laser Weapons Curbs; U.S. Joins Move on Arms Designed to Blind." *Washington Post*, 20 September 1999, A3.

Gray-Briggs, Abigail and Michael MacIver. "Preparing the War Fighter for the Sojourn to Peacekeeping." *Airpower Journal* 13, no. 2 (1999): 15–26.

Green, M. Christian. "The 'Matrioshka' Strategy: U.S. Evasion of the Spirit of the International Covenant on Civil and Political Rights." *South African Journal of Human Rights* 10 (1994): 357–58.

Guay, Terrence. "Local Government and Global Politics: The Implications of Massachusetts' 'Burma Law.'" *Political Science Quarterly* 115, no. 3 (2000): 353–76.

Gunn, Jeremy T. "A Preliminary Response to Criticisms of the International Religious Freedom Act of 1998." *Brigham Young University Law Review* 2000, no. 3 (2000): 841–65.

Gutmann, Amy, ed. *Human Rights as Politics and Idolatry*. Princeton, N.J.: Princeton University Press, 2001.

Haass, Richard N. "The Squandered Presidency: Demanding More from the Commander-in-Chief." *Foreign Affairs* 79, no. 3 (2000): 136–40.

Hafen, Bruce C. and Jonathan O. Hafen, "Abandoning Children to their Autonomy: The United Nations Convention on the Rights of the Child." *Harvard International Law Journal* 37 (1996): 449.

Halberstam, David. *War in a Time of Peace.* New York: Scribner's, 2001.

Hallion, Richard P. *Precision Guided Munitions and the New Era of Warfare.* Australia: Air Power Studies Centre, 1995.

Halverson, Ronald and Paul Bliese. "Determinants of Soldier Support for Operation Uphold Democracy." *Armed Forces and Society* 23 (1996): 81–96.

Harrell, Margaret C. and Laura L. Miller. *New Opportunity for Military Women: Effects upon Readiness, Cohesion, and Morale.* Santa Monica: Rand Corporation, 1997.

Harris, John and Ruth Marcus. "U.S. Sends Military Police; Aristide Thanks Clinton, Carter; Scenes of Violence Prompt a Shift in Troop Policy." *Washington Post,* 22 September 1994.

Hart, D. G. "The Mid-life Crisis of American Evangelicalism: Identity Problems." *Christian Century* 109, no. 33 (1992): 1028–31.

Hartz, Louis. *The Liberal Tradition in America: An Interpretation of American Political Thought since the Revolution.* New York: Harcourt Brace Jovanovich, 1955.

Hass, Richard N. *Intervention: The Use of American Military Force in the Post–Cold War World.* Washington, D.C.: Carnegie Endowment for International Peace, 1994.

Hatch, Orrin G. "Religious Liberty at Home and Abroad: Reflections on Protecting this Fundamental Freedom." *Brigham Young University Law Review* 2001, no. 2 (2001): 413–28.

Healy, Gene. "Arrogance of Power Reborn: The Imperial Presidency and Foreign Policy in the Clinton Years." Cato Institute, Cato Policy Analysis no. 389, 13 December 2000. Available online at http://www.cato.org/pubs/pas/pa-389es.html.

Hendrickson, David C. "The Recovery of Internationalism." *Foreign Affairs* 73, no. 5 (1994): 26–43.

Henkin, Louis. "U.S. Ratification of Human Rights Conventions: The Ghost of Senator Bricker." *American Journal of International Law* 89 (1995): 341–52.

Herold, Marc W. *A Dossier on Civilian Victims of United States' Aerial Bombing of Afghanistan: A Comprehensive Accounting [Revised],* 2002. Available online at http://www.cursor.org/stories/civilian_deaths.htm.

Hicks, Neil. "The Bush Administration and Human Rights." *Foreign Policy in Focus, Global Affairs Commentary,* 2001. Available online at http://www.foreignpolicy-infocus.org/commentary/2001/0101humrights.html.

Hillen, John. "Must U.S. Military Culture Reform?" *Parameters* 29, no. 3 (1999): 9–23.

Hiltermann, Joost, and Vikram Parekh. "Beware of Unsavory Afghan Allies." *International Herald Tribune,* 10 October 2001.

Himmelfarb, Gertrude. "The Illusions of Cosmopolitanisms." In *For Love of Country: Debating the Limits of Patriotism,* edited by Martha C. Nussbaum. Boston: Beacon Press, 1996.

Hinds, Lynn Boyd and Theodore Wendt. *The Cold War as Rhetoric: The Beginnings, 1945–1950.* Westport, Conn.: Praeger, 1991.

Hoagland, Jim. "Day One of the Air Strikes Shows Force and Mercy." *International Herald Tribune,* 9 October 2001.

Hoffman, Mark. "Normative International Theory: Approaches and Issues." In *Contemporary International Relations: A Guide to Theory,* edited by Margot Light. New York: St. Martin's Press, 1994.

Hoffman, Stanley. *World Disorder: Troubled Peace in the Post–Cold War Era.* Lanham, Md.: Rowman and Littlefield, 1997.

Hoffmann, Stanley, ed. "Out of the Cold: Humanitarian Intervention in the 1990s." *Harvard International Review* 16, no. 1 (1993): 8–9.

Holbrooke, Richard. *To End a War.* New York: Random House, 1998.

Holsti, Kalevi J. *International Politics: A Framework for Analysis*. 7th ed. New York: Prentice-Hall, 1995.

Hook, Steven W. and John W. Spanier. *American Foreign Policy since World War II*. 16th ed. Washington, D.C.: Congressional Quarterly Press, 2003.

_____. *American Foreign Policy since World War II*. 15th ed. Washington, D.C.: Congressional Quarterly Press, 2000.

Hosmer, Stephen T. *The Conflict over Kosovo: Why Milosevic Decided to Settle When He Did* (MR-1351-AF prepared for the United States Air Force), Rand Corporation, 2001. Available online at www.rand.org/publications/MR/MR1351.

Hoversten, Paul and Judy Keen. "Troops Learn 'Specifics' on Intervention; Rules of Engagement Still a Case-by-Case Basis." *USA Today*, 23 September 1994.

Howard, Rhoda E. *Human Rights and the Search for Community*. Boulder, Colo.: Westview Press, 1995.

Howard, Rhoda and Jack Donnelly. "Human Dignity, Human Rights and Political Regimes." *American Political Science Review* 80 (1986): 801–17.

Huang, Margaret. "U.S. Human Rights Policy toward China." *Foreign Policy in Focus* 6, no. 8 (2001).

Hubert, Don. "Inferring Influence: Gauging the Impact of NGOs." In *Toward Understanding Global Governance: The International Law and International Relations Toolbox*, edited by Charlotte Ku and Thomas G. Weiss. ACUNS Reports and Papers no. 2. Providence, R.I.: ACUNS, 1998.

_____. *The Landmine Treaty: A Case Study in Humanitarian Advocacy*. Occasional Paper no. 42. Providence, R.I.: Watson Institute for International Studies, 2000.

Human Rights Watch. *Annual Report* 1994. Available online at http://www.hrw.org/reports/1994/WR94/Middle-06.htm.

——. "The Crisis in Kosovo: Civilian Deaths in the NATO Air War Campaign." New York: Human Rights Watch, 2000.

——. *Human Rights after September 11*, 2003 [cited 11 May 2003]. Available online at http://www.hrw.org/campaigns/september11/.

——. *Leave None to Tell the Story: Genocide in Rwanda*. Washington, D.C.: Human Rights Watch, 1999.

——. *Race and Incarceration in the United States*, Human Rights Watch, 2002. Available online at http://hrw.org/backgrounder/usa/race/.

——. "The Ties That Bind: Colombia and Military-Paramilitary Links." *Human Rights Watch* 12, no. 1 (2000).

——. "U.S. State Department Trafficking Report a "Mixed Bag." Press release, Washington, D.C., July 12, 2002. Available online at www.hrw.org/press/2001/07/traffick-0712.htm.

——. "U.S. State Department Trafficking Report Undercut by Lack of Analysis." Press release, Washington D.C., June 11, 2003. Available online at http://www.hrw.org/press/2003/06/trafficking report.htm.

Hunt, Swanee. "Gender and the American Experience." Address before the IPI World Congress. Available online at http://www.freemedia.at/Boston%20Congress%20Report/boston32.htm.

Hunter, Robert. "Think Tanks: Helping to Shape U.S. Foreign and Security Policy." *U.S. Foreign Policy Agenda* 5, no. 1 (2000): 33–36.

Hurrell, Andrew. "Power, Principles, and Prudence: Protecting Human Rights in a Deeply Divided World." In *Human Rights in Global Politics*, edited by Tim Dunne and Nicholas J. Wheeler. New York: Cambridge University Press, 1999.

Hutchinson, Earl Ofari. "Ashcroft Poses a Moral Threat to Civil Rights." *San Francisco Chronicle*, 28 December 2000.

Ignatieff, Michael. "The Attack on Human Rights." *Foreign Affairs* 80, no. 6 (2001): 102–16.

_____. "Human Rights as Politics." In *Human Rights as Politics and Idolatry*, edited by Amy Gutmann. Princeton, N.J.: Princeton University Press, 2001.

_____. "The Virtual Commander: How NATO Invented a New Kind of War." *New Yorker*, 2 August 1999.

_____. "Will the Quest for Security Kill the Human Rights Era?" *International Herald Tribune*, 6 February 2002.

International Human Rights Law Group. "IHRLG in the United States." Available online at http://www.hrlawgroup.org/country_programs/united_states/advocacy.asp.

Ivie, Robert. "Metaphor and the Rhetorical Invention of Cold War 'Idealists.'" *Communication Monographs*, no. 54 (1987): 165–82.

_____. "The Metaphor of Force in Prowar Discourse: The Case of 1812." *Quarterly Journal of Speech*, no. 68 (1982): 240–53.

Jablonsky, David. "A Tale of Two Doctrines." *Parameters* 31, no. 3 (2001): 43–62.

Jackson, Patrick Thaddeus and Ronald R. Krebs. "Twisting Tongues and Twisting Arms: The Power of Political Rhetoric." Paper presented at the Annual Meeting of the American Political Science Association, 28–31 August 2003.

Jane's Information Group. *'Non-Lethal' Weapons May Have Significant Impact on International Law,* 2000. Available online at http://www.janes.com/press/pc001214.shtml.

Jensen, Holger. "NATO at the Crossroads: U.S. Alliance Must Reconsider Their Roles at Critical Juncture in Post Cold War Era." *Denver Rocky Mountain News*, 15 December 1996.

Jentleson, Bruce W. *American Foreign Policy: The Dynamics of Choice in the Twenty-first Century.* New York: W. W. Norton, 2000.

Jepperson, Ronald L., Alexander Wendt, and Peter J. Katzenstein. "Norms, Identity and Culture in National Security." In *The Culture of National Security: Norms and Identity in World Politics*, edited by Peter J. Katzenstein. New York: Columbia University Press, 1996.

Jervis, Robert. *The Logic of Images in International Relations.* Princeton, N.J.: Princeton University Press, 1970.

Joint Non-Lethal Weapons Program. *Joint Non-Lethal Weapons Program History.* Available online at http://www.jnlwd.usmc.mil/Programs/History.htm.

Joint Warfighting Center. "Joint Task Force Commander's Handbook for Peace Operations." Fort Monroe, Va.: Joint Warfighting Center, 1995.

Kagan, Robert. "American Power: A Guide for the Perplexed." *Current*, no. 383 (1996): 12–21.

Kancis, Jyothi. "Trafficking in Women." *Foreign Policy in Focus* 3, no. 39 (1998).

Kaplan, Lawrence F. "Colin Powell's Out-of-Date Doctrine" *Pittsburgh Post-Gazette*, 7 January 2001.

Karsten, Peter. "The U.S. Citizen-Soldier's Past, Present, and Likely Future." *Parameters* 31, no. 2 (2001): 61–73.

Katzenstein, Peter J. "Introduction to Alternative Perspectives on National Security." In *The Culture of National Security: Norms and Identity in World Politics*, edited by Peter J. Katzenstein. New York: Columbia University Press, 1996.

Kaufman, Marc. "Negotiator in Global Tobacco Talks Quits, Official Said to Chafe at Softer U.S. Stands." *Washington Post*, 2 August 2001.

Kaufman, Marc and Peter Finn. "Aid Experts Skeptical on U.S. Food Airdrops." *International Herald Tribune*, 10 October 2001.

Kaye, David. "Are There Limits to Military Alliance? Presidential Power to Place Troops under Nonpresidential Command." *Transnational Law and Contemporary Problems* 5 (1995): 339–443.

Keck, Margaret E. and Katherine Sikkink. *Activists beyond Borders: Advocacy Networks in International Relations*. Ithaca, N.Y.: Cornell University Press, 1998.

Keith, Linda Camp and Steven C. Poe. "The United States, the IMF, and Human Rights: A Policy Relevant Approach." In *The United States and Human Rights: Looking Inward and Outward*, edited by David P. Forsythe. Lincoln: University of Nebraska Press, 1999.

Keller, Bill. "It Will Take a New Cold War to Defeat the Terrorists." *International Herald Tribune*, 13–14 October 2001.

Kelly, Claire R. "The Value Vacuum: Self-Enforcing Regimes and the Dilution of the Normative Feedback Loop." *Michigan Journal of International Law* 22 (2001): 673–731.

Kelly, Michael. "The Design Flaws in Clinton's Foreign Policy." *National Journal*, no. 23 (1998): 1160–61.

Kennedy, David. "The International Human Rights Movement: Part of the Problem?" *Harvard Human Rights Journal* 15 (2002): 101–25.

Kennedy, Kevin M. "The Relationship between the Military and Humanitarian Organizations in Operation Restore Hope." In *Learning from Somalia: The Lessons of Armed Humanitarian Intervention*, edited by Walter Clarke and Jeffrey Herbst. Boulder, Colo.: Westview Press, 1997.

Kenny, Karen. "When Needs Are Rights: An Overview of UN Efforts to Integrate Human Rights in Humanitarian Action." In *Occasional Paper #38*. Providence, R.I.: Thomas J. Watson Jr. Institute for International Studies, Brown University, 2000.

Keohane, Robert O. "International Institutions: Two Approaches." *International Studies Quarterly* 32 (1988): 379–82.

Kerr, Elizabeth. "Homosexuals in the U.S. Military: Open Integration and Combat Effectiveness." *International Security* 23, no. 2 (1999): 5–39.

Kilbourne, Susan. "Placing the Convention on the Rights of the Child in an American Context." *Human Rights* 26, no. 2 (1999): 27–31.

Kimmey, Mark L. "After the Deployment: The Impact on Peacekeeping and Readiness," *Army* (July 1999): 11.

Kirschten, Dick. "Pinched Pitchmen." *National Journal*, no. 14 (1995): 2529–31.

Kissinger, Henry. "Beyond Baghdad, after Regime Change." *New York Post*, 12 August 2002.

_____. *The White House Years*. Boston: Little Brown, 1979.

Klein, Naomi. "Bush to NGOs: Watch Your Mouths." *Globe and Mail*, 20 June 2003.

Klotz, Audie. *Norms in International Relations: The Struggle against Apartheid*. Ithaca, N.Y.: Cornell University Press, 1995.

_____. "Norms Reconstituting Interests: Global Racial Equality and U.S. Sanctions Against South Africa." *International Organization* 49 (1995): 451–78.

Knowlton, Brian. "Bush 'Very Pleased,' Though He Told Opposition Not to Enter Kabul." *International Herald Tribune*, 14 November 2001.

_____. "Rumsfeld Replies Firmly to Allies on Prisoners' Treatment." *International Herald Tribune*, 23 January 2002.

Kocs, Stephen A. "Explaining the Strategic Behavior of States: International Law as System Structure." *International Studies Quarterly* 38 (1994): 535–56.

Koh, Harold Hongju. "The 1998 Frankel Lecture: Bringing International Law Home." *Houston Law Review* 35 (1998): 623–35.

_____. "1999 Country Reports on Human Rights Practices." *Defense Institute of Security Assistance Management Journal* 22, no. 3 (2000).

_____. "Review Essay: Why Do Nations Obey International Law?" *Yale Law Journal* 106 (1997): 2599–665.

_____. "Transnational Legal Process." *Nebraska Law Review* 75 (1996): 181–202.

_____. "A United States Human Rights Policy for the 21st Century." *St. Louis University Law Journal* 46 (2002): 293–332.

Kohn, Rebecca Rios. "The Convention on the Rights of the Child: Progress and Challenges." *Georgetown Journal on Fighting Poverty* 5 (1998): 139–70.

Korey, William. *NGOs and the Universal Declaration of Human Rights.* New York: St. Martin's Press, 1998.

Kornbluh, Peter. "Bush's Contra Buddies." *Nation* 272, no. 18 (2001): 6.

Kornbluh, Peter and Malcolm Byrne, eds. *The Iran-Contra Scandal: The Declassified History (The National Security Archive Document).* New York: New Press, 1993.

Kosterlitz, Julie. "Occupational Hazards." *National Journal,* 22 March 2003.

Kourous, George and Tom Berry. "Protecting Human Rights." *Foreign Policy in Perspective* 1, no. 1 (1996).

Kozaryn, Linda D. *No Silver Bullet to Stop Serb Aggression.* American Forces Press Service, 1999. Available online at http://www.defenselink.mil/news/Mar1999/n03311999_9903311.html.

Kratochwil, Freidrich. *Rules, Norms, and Decisions: On the Conditions of Practical and Legal Reasoning in International Relations and International Affairs.* New York: Cambridge University Press, 1989.

Kratochwil, Freidrich and John Ruggie. "International Organization: A State of the Art or the State of the Art." *International Organization* 40, no. 4 (1986): 753–75.

Krauthammer, Charles. "The Unipolar Moment." *Foreign Affairs (America and the World 1990/91),* no. 70 (1991): 23–33.

Krisch, Nico. "Legality, Morality, and the Dilemma of Humanitarian Intervention after Kosovo." *European Journal of International Law* 13, no. 1 (2002).

Kull, Steven and I. M. Destler, *Misreading the Public The Myth of a New Isolationism.* Washington D.C.: Brookings Institution Press, 1999.

Kuperman, Alan J. *The Limits of Humanitarian Intervention: Genocide in Rwanda.* Washington, D.C.: Brookings Institution Press, 2001.

Lakoff, George and Mark Johnson. *Metaphors We Live By.* Chicago: University of Chicago Press, 1980.

Lambeth, Benjamin S. *NATO's War over Kosovo: A Strategic and Operational Assessment.* MR-1365-AF ed. Washington, D.C.: Rand Corporation, 2001.

Lapid, Yosef. "Culture's Ship: Returns and Departures in International Relations Theory," in *The Return of Culture in International Relations Theory,* edited by Yosef Lapid and Fredrich Kratochwil. Boulder, Colo.: Lynne Rienner, 1997.

Lawyers Committee for Human Rights. "Women Asylum Seekers in Jeopardy." Press release. New York: Lawyers Committee for Human Rights, 2003.

Lebovic, James H. and Deborah D. Avant. "U.S. Military Responses to Post–Cold War Missions." In *The Sources of Military Change: Culture, Politics and Technology,* edited by Theo Farrell and Terry Terriff. Boulder, Colo.: Lynne Rienner, 2002.

Leffler, Melvyn. *A Preponderance of Power: National Security, the Truman Administration, and the Cold War.* Stanford, Calif.: Stanford University Press, 1992.

Lego, Jeffrey W. "When Norms Matter? Revisiting the 'Failure' of Internationalism." *International Organization* 51 (1997): 31–63.

Leoran N. Rosen, Kathryn H. Knudson, and Peggy Fancher. "Cohesion and the Culture of Hypermasculinity in U.S. Army Units." *Armed Forces and Society* 29, no. 3 (2003): 325–51.

Lewis, Anthony. "Cooperation Instead of Unilateralism: Bush Changes His Spots." *International Herald Tribune,* 15 October 2001.

_____. "World without Power." *New York Times,* 25 July 1994.

Lewis, Neil A. "Aftereffects: Detainees: More Prisoners to Be Released from Guantanamo, Officials Say." *New York Times*, 6 May 2003.

——. "Bush Team Drafts Tribunal Rules." *International Herald Tribune*, 29–30 December 2001.

Lewis, Norman. "Human Rights, Law, and Democracy in an Unfree World." In *Human Rights Fifty Years On: A Reappraisal*, edited by Tony Evans. Manchester, England: Manchester University Press, 1998.

Liang-Fenton, Debra. "United States Human Rights Policy: A Twenty-Year Assessment." Washington, D.C.: United States Institute of Peace, 1999.

Lindqvist, Bengt. "Standard Rules in the Disability Field." In *Human Rights and Disabled Persons: Essays and Relevant Human Rights Instruments*, edited by Theresia Degener and Yolan Koster-Dreese. Dordrecht, the Netherlands: Martinus Nijhoff, 1995, 63–68.

Linklater, Andrew. "Citizenship and Sovereignty in the Post-Westphalian State." *European Journal of International Relations* 2, no. 1 (1996): 77–103.

Lippman, Thomas W. "Ambassador to the Darkest Areas of Human Conflict." *Washington Post*, 18 November 1997.

——. "Madame Secretary." *National Journal*, no. 3 (2000): 1736–43.

——. *Madeleine Albright and the New American Diplomacy*. Boulder, Colo.: Westview, 2000.

Liu, F. T. *United Nations Peacekeeping and the Non-Use of Force*. Occasional Paper Series. New York: International Peace Academy, 1992.

Livingston, Stephen. "The Politics of International Agenda-Setting: Reagan and North-South Relations." *International Studies Quarterly* 36 (1992): 313–30.

Lobe, Jim. "Rights—U.S.: Ashcroft Attempts to End Victims' Rights Law." *Inter Press Service*, 15 May 2003.

——. "Bringing the War Home: Right Wing Think Tank Turns Wrath on NGOs." *Foreign Policy in Focus* (June 13, 2003). Available online at http://www.foreignpolicy-infocus.org/commentary/2003/0306antingo.htm.

——. *Army Peacekeeping Institute Sent Packing*, 2002. Available online at http://www.tompaine.com/feature.cfm/ID/5799.

——. "The Return of Elliott Abrams." *TomPaine, CommonSense*, 11 December 2002. Available online at http://www.tompaine.com/feature2.cfm/ID/6895/view/print.

Lord, Janet E. "International Disability Rights: Challenging Traditional Theory in the Emergence of a New Transitional Advocacy Network." Paper presented at the Forty-Fourth Annual Convention of the International Studies Association, Portland, Oregon, 26 February–1 March 2003.

Lui, Andrew. "Do Human Rights Have a Future? A Study of Transformation in International Relations." Paper presented at the Forty-Fourth Annual Convention of the International Studies Association, Portland, Oregon, 26 February–1 March 2003.

Lumsdaine, David. *Moral Vision in International Politics*. Princeton, N.J.: Princeton University Press, 1993.

Lund, Michael S. "What Kind of Peace Is Being Built? Assessing Post-Conflict Peacebuilding, Charting Future Directions." Ottawa: International Development Research Centre, 2003.

Luttwak, Edward. "Where Are the Great Powers? At Home with the Kids." *Foreign Affairs*, no. 73 (1994): 23–28.

Lyons, Gene M. and Michael Mastanduno, eds. *Beyond Westphalia? State, Sovereignty and International Intervention*. Baltimore: Johns Hopkins University Press, 1995.

MacKenzie, Donald. *Inventing Accuracy: A Historical Sociology of Nuclear Missile Guidance*. Cambridge, Mass.: MIT Press, 1990.

Malcolm, David J. "Tobacco, Global Public Health, And Non-Governmental Organizations: An Eminent Pandemic Or Just Another Legal Product?" *Denver Journal of International Law and Policy* 28, no. 1 (1999): 1.

Malinowski, Tom. "Court-Martial Code Offers a Fair Way to Try Terrorist Suspects." *International Herald Tribune*, 29–30 December 2001.

Mandelbaum, Michael. "Foreign Policy as Social Work." *Political Science Quarterly* 74, no. 1 (1996): 16–32.

_____. "The Bush Foreign Policy." *Foreign Affairs* 70, no. 1 (1991): 5-22.

_____. "The Reluctance to Intervene." *Foreign Policy*, no. 95 (1994): 3–18.

Marine Corps Doctrine Division. *Joint Vision 2020*. Washington, D.C.: U.S. Government Printing Office, 2000.

Mariner, Captain Rosemary. "Public Attitudes towards the U.S. Military." Paper presented at The Women in International Security Conference, Chicago, 14–15 September 2000.

Maynard, Edwin S. "The Bureaucracy and Implementation of U.S. Human Rights Policy." *Human Rights Quarterly* 11 (1989): 175–248.

Maynes, Charles William. "A Workable Clinton Doctrine." *Foreign Policy*, no. 93 (1993): 3–20.

Mazarr, Michael J. "Clinton Foreign Policy, R.I.P." *Washington Quarterly* 21, no. 2 (1998): 11–14.

Maze, Rick. "Defense Officials: U.N. Peace Missions 'Useful' for Military." *Army Times*, 5 May 1997.

McAlister, Melanie. "Saving Private Lynch." *New York Times*, 6 April 2003.

McElroy, Robert. *Morality and American Foreign Policy: The Role of Ethics in International Affairs*. Princeton, N.J.: Princeton University Press, 1992.

McGee, Jim. "Ex-FBI Officials Criticize Ashcroft's Tactics as Counterproductive." *International Herald Tribune*, 29 November 2001.

McGinnis, John O. and Mark L. Movesian. "The World Trade Constitution." *Harvard International Law Journal* 114 (December 2000): 511–86.

Mead, Walter Russell. *Special Providence: American Foreign Policy and How It Changes the World*. New York: Routledge, 2002.

Mearsheimer, John. "Disorder Restored." In *Rethinking America's Security: Beyond Cold War to New World Order*, edited by Graham Allison and Gregory Treverton. New York: W.W. Norton, 1992.

Melvin, Edward C., R. Manning Ancell, and Jane Mahaffey. *Who Will Lead? Senior Leadership in the United States Army*. Westport, Conn.: Praeger, 1995.

Mendelbaum, Michael. "The Bush Foreign Policy." *Foreign Affairs* 70 no. 1 (1991): 5–22.

Meron, Theodor. "On a Hierarchy of International Human Rights." *American Journal of International Law* 80, no. 1 (1986): 1–23.

_____. "The Continuing Role of Custom in the Formation of International Humanitarian Law." *American Journal of International Law* 90 (1996): 238–43.

Mermin, Jonathan. "Television News and American Intervention in Somalia" *Political Science Quarterly* 112, no. 2 (1997): 385–403.

Merritt, Jeffrey D. "Unilateral Human Rights Intercession: American Practice under Nixon, Ford, and Carter." In *The Diplomacy of Human Rights*, edited by David D. Newsom. Lanham, Md.: University Press of America, 1986.

Mertus, Julie. *Kosovo: How Myths and Truths Started a War*. Berkeley and Los Angeles: University of California Press, 1999.

_____. "From Legal Transplants to Transformative Justice: Human Rights and the Promise of Transnational Civil Society." *American University International Law Review* 14, no. 5 (1999): 1335–77.

_____. "Human Rights and the Promise of Transnational Civil Society." In *The Future of International Human Rights*, edited by Burns H. Houston and Stephen P. Marks. Ardsley, N.Y.: Transnational, 1999.

_____. "The Liberal State and the National Soul: Rule of Law Projects in Societies in Transition." *Social and Legal Studies* 8, no. 1 (1999): 146–54.

Meyer, Edward C. and R. Manning Ancell with Jane Mahaffey. *Who Will Lead? Senior Leadership in the United States Army*. Westport, Conn.: Praeger, 1995.

Midgely, Mary. "Towards an Ethic of Global Responsibility." In *Human Rights and Global Politics*, edited by Timothy Dunne and Nicholas J. Wheeler. New York: Cambridge University Press, 1999.

Miller, Arthur. "Rhetorical Exigence." *Philosophy and Rhetoric*, no. 5 (1972): 111–18.

Miller, David. *On Nationality*. Oxford: Clarendon Press, 1995.

Miller, Eugene. "Metaphor and Political Knowledge." *American Political Science Review*, no. 73 (1979): 155–70.

Miller, John M. *Congress Bans Military Training for Human Rights Violators*. Press release, East Timor Action Network, 1998. Available online at http://www.etan.org/et/1998/september/sep22-30/29congre.htm.

Miller, Laura. "Do Soldiers Hate Peacekeeping? The Case of Preventive Diplomacy Operations in Macedonia." *Armed Forces and Society* 23 no. 3(1997): 415–49.

Miller, Laura and Charles Moskos. "Humanitarians or Warriors? Race, Gender, and Combat Status in Operation Restore Hope." *Armed Forces and Society* 21 (1995): 615–37.

Mills, Kurt. *Human Rights in the Emerging Global Order: A New Sovereignty?* New York: Palgrave, 1998.

Minear, Larry, Colin Scott, and Robert Weiss. *The News Media, Civil Wars and Humanitarian Action*. Boulder, Colo.: Lynne Rienner, 1997.

Mirsky, Jonathan. "Remind Beijing: Human Rights and Arms Control Do Matter." *International Herald Tribune*, 22 October 2001.

Moeller, Susan D. *Compassion Fatigue: How the Media Sell Disease, Famine, War and Death*. New York: Routledge, 1999.

Moravcik, Andrew. "The Origins of Human Rights Regimes: Democratic Delegation in Postwar Europe." *International Organization* 38 (2000): 217–52.

Morgan, Matthew J. "Army Officer Personnel Management and Trends in Warfighting." *Journal of Political and Military Sociology* 29, no. 1 (2001): 120–39.

_____. "Army Recruiting and the Civil-Military Gap." *Parameters* 31, no. 2 (2001), 101–17.

_____. "Melancholy Reunion: A Report from the Future on the Collapse of Civil-Military Relations in the United States." *Airpower Journal* 10, no. 4 (1996): 93–109.

Moskos, Charles C., Jr. "From Citizens' Army to Social Laboratory." *Wilson Quarterly* 17, no. 1 (1993): 83–94.

_____. *The American Enlisted Man*. New York: Russell Sage, 1970.

Mottern, Jacqueline A. "1995 Gender Integration of Basic Combat Training Study: Army Research Institute Study Report." Alexandria, VA: U.S. ARI, 1997.

Mufson, Steven. "American Foreign Policy Suddenly Shifts Course." *International Herald Tribune*, 28 September 2001.

_____. "U.S. to Alter Color of Air-Dropped Food Packs." *International Herald Tribune*, 3–4 November 2001.

Murphy, Sean D. "Contemporary Practice in the United States Relating to International Law." *American Journal of International Law* 93 no. 2 (1999): 470–501.

_____. *Humanitarian Intervention: The United Nations in an Evolving World Order*. Philadelphia: University of Pennsylvania Press, 1996.

Murray, Kevin. "Iraq: The Challenge of Humanitarian Response." *Foreign Policy in Focus: Global Affairs Commentary,* 2 June 2003. Available online at http://www.fpif.org/commentary/2003/0306humane.html.

Murray, Williamson. "Does Military Culture Matter?" *Orbis* 43, no. 3 (1999): 27–42.

Nanda, Ved P. "U.S. Forces in Panama: Defenders, Aggressors, or Human Rights Activists?: The Validity of United States Intervention in Panama under International Law." *American Journal of International Law* 84 (1990): 494–504.

Nardulli, Bruce R. *Disjointed War: Military Operations in Kosovo.* Publication MR-1406. Washington, D.C.: Rand Corporation, 2002.

Nash, William L. "The Laws of War: A Military View." *Ethics and International Affairs* 16, no. 1 (2002): 14–17.

National Council on Disability. *A Reference Tool: Understanding the Potential Content and Structure of an International Convention on the Human Rights of People with Disabilities,* July 2002. Available online at http://www.ncd.gov/newsroom/publications/understanding_7-30-02.html.

Natsios, Andrew S. *U.S. Foreign Policy and the Four Horsemen of the Apocalypse: Humanitarian Relief in Complex Emergencies.* Westport, Conn.: Praeger, 1997.

Nauck, Barbara J. "Implications of the United States Ratification of the United Nations Convention on the Rights of the Child: Civil Rights, the Constitution and the Family." *Cleveland State Law Review* 42 (1994): 675–702.

Nazarova, Inna. "Alienating "Human" from "Right": U.S. and U.K. Non-Compliance with Asylum Obligations under International Human Rights Law." *Fordham International Law Journal* 25, no. 5 (2002): 1335–1420.

Neack, Laura. *The New Foreign Policy: U.S. and Comparative Foreign Policy in the Twenty-first Century.* Lanham, Md.: Rowman and Littlefield, 2003.

Newsom, David D. "The Diplomacy of Human Rights: A Diplomat's View." In *The Diplomacy of Human Rights,* edited by David D. Newsom. Lanham, Md.: University Press of America, 1986.

Nino, Carlos Santiago. *The Ethics of Human Rights.* Oxford: Clarendon Press, 1991.

Noonan, Michael P. and John Hillen. *The Coming Transformation of the U.S. Military?* Foreign Policy Research Institute e-notes, 2002. Available online at www.fpif.org/ enotes/military.20020204.noonanhillen.comingtransformationsmilitary.html.

Noyes, Lt. Col. N. Winn. "Peacekeepers and Warfighters: Same Force, Different Mindset." Newport, R.I.: U.S. Naval War College, 1995.

O'Connell, Mary Ellen. *The Myth of Preemptive Self-Defense.* Washington D.C.: American Society of International Law Task Force on Terror, 2002.

O'Connor, Michael. "GI Disinterest is a Casualty in Bosnia." *New York Times,* 4 January 1998.

Office of the High Commissioner for Human Rights. *Fact Sheet No. 13, International Humanitarian Law and Human Rights.* Available online at http://193.194.138.190/html/menu6/2/fs13.htm.

O'Hanlon, Michael. *Saving Lives with Force: Military Criteria for Humanitarian Intervention.* Washington, D.C.: Brookings Institution Press, 1997.

Olson, Elizabeth. "UN Rights Panel to Hear Criticism of War on Terror." *International Herald Tribune,* 18 March 2002.

Omestad, Thomas. "Why Bush Lost." *American Foreign Policy,* no. 89 (1992): 70–81.

Onuf, Nicholas G. *World of Our Making: Rules and Rule in Social Theory and International Relations.* Columbia: University of South Carolina Press, 1989.

Paarekh, Bhikhu. "Non-Ethnocentric Universalism." In *Human Rights in Global Politics,* edited by Tim Dunne and Nicholas J. Wheeler. New York: Cambridge University Press, 1999.

Parks, W. Hays. "Teaching the Law of War." Department of the Army pamphlet 27-50-174. Washington, D.C.: U.S. Department of the Army, 1987.

Pastor, Robert. "George Bush and Latin America." In *Eagle in a New World: American Grand Strategy in the Post–Cold War Era*, edited by Kenneth A. Oye, Robert J. Lieber, and Donald Rothchild. New York: Harper Collins, 1992.

Paust, Jordan J. "Customary International Law: Its Nature, Sources and Status as Law of the United States," *Michigan Journal of International Law* 12 (1990): 59–91.

"Pentagon Speaks about Operation Restore Hope." Television interview. CNN, 1992.

Perlstein, Rick. "Goodbye to the Vietnam Syndrome." *New York Times*, 15 October 2002.

Perry, Michael. *The Idea of Human Rights*. New York: Oxford University Press, 1998.

_____. "What Is 'Morality' Anyway?" *Villanova Law Review* 45, no. 1 (2000): 69–105.

Pfaff, Tony. *Peacekeeping and the Just War Tradition*. Carlisle Barracks, Penn.: Strategic Studies Institute, U.S. Army War College, 2000.

Pfaff, William. "As Captor, U.S. Risks Dehumanizing Itself." *International Herald Tribune*, 31 January 2002.

_____. "In Its Quest for Supremacy, U.S. May Squander Partnerships." *International Herald Tribune*, 15–16 December 2001.

Phinney, David. "Less Than Deadly Force: New World of Military Conflict Calls for 'Non-Lethal' Weapons," 10 May 1999. Available online at http://www.abcnews.go.com/sections/us/DailyNews/weapon990510.html.

Picken, Margo. "Ethical Foreign Policies and Human Rights." In *Ethics and Foreign Policy*, edited by Karen E. Smith and Margot Light. New York: Cambridge University Press, 2001.

Pickering, Thomas R. "The Changing Dynamics of U.S. Foreign Policy-Making." *U.S. Foreign Policy Agenda* 5, no. 1 (2000): 5–8.

Pike, John. *What's New with Smart Weapons*. Federation of American Scientists, 4 March 2000. Available online at http://www.fas.org/man/dod-101/sys/smart/new.htm.

Pincus, Walter. "Silent Suspects: U.S. May Get Tough." *International Herald Tribune*, 22 October 2001.

Pine, Art. "On the Offensive; New Pentagon Boss Makes Big Changes." *Chicago Sun-Times*, 13 March 1994.

Pomper, Miles A. "The Religious Right's Foreign Policy Revival." *Congressional Quarterly Weekly*, 8 May 1998, 1209–10.

Powell, Catherine. "Dialogic Federalism: Constitutional Possibilities for Incorporation of Human Rights Law in the United States." *University of Pennsylvania Law Review* 150 (2001): 245–91.

Powell, Colin. "U.S. Forces: Challenges Ahead." *Foreign Affairs* 71, no. 5 (1992): 32–45.

Powell, Colin, with Joseph E. Persico. *My American Journey*. New York: Ballantine, 1996.

Power, Samantha. "Bystanders to Genocide." *Atlantic Monthly* 288, no. 2 (2001): 84–108.

Press, Eyal. "In Torture We Trust?" *Nation* 276, no. 12 (2003): 11–16.

Price, Richard. "Reversing the Gun Sights: Transnational Civil Society Targets Land Mines," *International Organization* 42, no. 3 (1998): 613–44.

Prins, Gwyn. *Understanding Unilateralism in American Foreign Relations*. London: Royal Institute of International Affairs, 2000.

Proctor, Dick. "*President Bush's Appointment of Elliot Abrams*," August 2001. Available online at http://www.dickproctor.ca/ndp.php/columns/21/.

Project on Peacekeeping and the United Nations. "African Crisis Response Initiative: A Peacekeeping Alliance in Africa." Washington, D.C.: Council for a Livable World Education Fund, 2001.

Reisman, Michael. "Preparing to Wage Peace: Toward the Creation of an International Peace-making Command and Staff College." *American Journal of International Law* 88 (1994): 76–79.

Reus-Smith, Christian. "The Constitutional Structure of International Society and the Nature of Fundamental Institutions." *International Organization* 51 (1997): 555–69.

Richardson, Michael. "Asian Regimes Appear to Use War on Terror to Stem Dissent." *International Herald Tribune*, 21 November 2001.

Richmond, Oliver P. *Maintaining Order, Making Peace*. New York: Palgrave, 2002.

Ricks, Thomas E. "The Great Society in Camouflage." *Atlantic Monthly* 278, no. 6 (1996): 24–29.

Risse, Thomas. "Let's Argue! Communicative Action and International Relations." *International Organization* 54 (2000): 1–39.

Risse, Thomas, Stephen C. Ropp, and Katherine Sikkink. *The Power of Human Rights: International Norms and Domestic Change*. New York: Cambridge University Press, 1999.

Risse, Thomas and Kathryn Sikkink. *The Power of Principles: The Socialization of Human Rights Norms in Domestic Practice*. New York: Cambridge University Press, 1999.

Robberson, Tod. "Aid Workers Say Food Drops Could Prove Deadly, Starving Afghans Could be Lured into Mine Fields, Officials Fear." *Dallas Morning News,* 12 October 2001.

Roberts, Adam. "Apply the Law of War in an Anti-Terror War, Too." *International Herald Tribune*, 4 October 2001.

_____. "Humanitarian Principles in International Politics in the 1990s." In *Reflections on Humanitarian Action: Principles, Ethics and Contradictions*, edited by Humanitarian Studies Unit. Sterling, Va.: Pluto Press, 2001.

Roberts, Brad. *U.S. Foreign Policy after the Cold War*. Cambridge, Mass.: MIT Press, 1992.

Robinson, Piers. "The News Media and Intervention: Critical Media Coverage, Political Uncertainty and Air Power Intervention during Humanitarian Crisis." Paper for the Annual Meeting of the Political Science Association–UK, 10–13 April 2000, London. Available online at http://www.psa.ac.uk/cps/2000/Robinson%20Piers.pdf.

Rohde, David and John F. Burns. "Afghan Alliance's Checkered Past Casts Doubt on How It Might Rule." *International Herald Tribune*, 8 October 2001.

Rorty, Richard. *Contingency, Irony and Solidarity*. New York: Cambridge University Press, 1989.

_____. "Human Rights, Rationality, and Sentimentality." In *On Human Rights: The Amnesty Lectures*, edited by Stephen Shute and Susan Hurley. New York: Basic, 1993.

Rosecrance, Richard. *America as an Ordinary Country: U.S. Foreign Policy and the Future*. Ithaca, N.Y.: Cornell University Press, 1976.

Rosemond, John. *A Family of Value*. Kansas City, Mo.: Andrews McMeel, 1995.

Rosen, Leoran N., Kathryn Knudson, and Peggy Fancher. "Cohesion and the Culture of Hypermasculinity in U.S. Army Units." *Armed Forces and Society* 29 no. 3 (2003): 325–51.

Rosen, Stephen Peter. *Winning the Next War: Innovation and the Modern Military*. Ithaca, N.Y.: Cornell University Press, 1991.

Rosenberg, Tina. "Conference Convocation, War Crimes Tribunals: The Record and the Prospects." *American University International Law Review* 13 (1998): 1406–8.

Rosenthal, Eric, Elizabeth Bauer, Mary F. Hayden, and Andrea Holley. "Implementing the Rights to Community Integration for Children with Disabilities in Russia: A Human Rights Framework for International Action." *Health and Human Rights* 4 no. 1 (1999): 83–113.

Ross, John G. "The Perils of Peacekeeping: Tallying the Costs in Blood, Coin, Prestige, and Readiness." *Armed Forces Journal International* 131 (1993): 13–17.

Rostrup, Morten. "'Humanitarian' and 'Military' Don't Go Together." *International Herald Tribune*, 18 October 2001.

Rota, Dane L. "Combat Decision Making in Operations Other Than War." *Military Review* 76, no. 2 (1996): 24–26.

Roth, Kenneth. "Sidelined on Human Rights." *Foreign Affairs* 77, no. 2 (1998): 2–6.

Roy, Oliver. "Europe Won't Be Fooled Again." *New York Times*, 15 October 2003.

Ruby, Jeffrey L. and Tomislav Z. Gingras. "Morality and Modern Air War." *Joint Forces Quarterly* 25 (2000): 107–11.

Ruggie, John G. *Constructing the World Polity: Essays on International Institutionalization.* London: Routledge, 1998.

Rumsfeld, Donald. "Interview with Secretary Rumsfeld," by Christane Amanpour, CNN, 18 March 2001. Available online at http://usinfo.state.gov/topical/pol/terror /01101908.htm.

———. "Secretary Rumsfeld Speaks on "Twenty-first Century Transformation' of U.S. Armed Forces (Transcript of Remarks and Question and Answer Period)." National Defense University, Fort McNair, 31 January 2002. Available online at http://www.defenselink.mil/speeches/2002/s20020131-secdef.htmlb.

Rutenberg, Jim. "Media Stoke Debate on Torture as U.S. Option." *International Herald Tribune*, 6 November 2001.

Safire, William. "Bush Brings Back Dark Ages of Military Justice." *Baltimore Sun*, 28 November 2001.

Salzberg, John P. "The Carter Administration and Human Rights." In *The Diplomacy of Human Rights*, edited by David D. Newsom. Lanham, Md.: University Press of America, 1986.

———. "A View from the Hill: U.S. Legislation and Human Rights." In *The Diplomacy of Human Rights*, edited by David D. Newsom. Lanham, Md.: University Press of America, 1986.

Sanger, David E. "Molding a Nation: Events Force Bush to Take Course He Has Derided." *International Herald Tribune*, 13–14 October 2002.

Sarkesian, Sam C. *Combat Effectiveness: Cohesion, Stress, and the Volunteer Military.* Beverly Hills: Sage, 1980.

———. "The Price Paid by the Military: Humanitarian Aid and United States Military Policy." *Orbis* 45, no. 4 (2001): 557–68.

———. "The U.S. Military Must Find Its Voice." *Orbis* 42, no. 3 (1998): 423–37.

Saur, Mark. "Today's Recruits Reflect Brighter, Leaner Military." *San Diego Union-Tribune*, 21 January 2002.

Scales, Robert H. "America's Army in Transition: Preparing for War in a Precision Age." Washington, D.C.: U.S. Army War College, 1999.

Schabas, William. "Spare the RUD or Spoil the Treaty." In *The United States and Human Rights: Looking Inward and Outward*, edited by David P. Forsythe. Lincoln: University of Nebraska Press, 2000.

Schaefer, Brett D. *Keep the Cap on U.S. Contributions to the U.N. Peacekeeping Budget.* Washington, D.C.: Heritage Foundation, 2001.

Scheffer, David J. *Seeking Accountability for War Crimes: Past, Present, and Future.* U.S. Department of State, 13 May 1998. Available online at http://www.state.gov/ www/policy_remarks/1998/980513_scheffer_war_crimes.html.

Schiffer, Adam, I'm Not *That* Liberal! Explaining Conservative Democratic Identification." *Political Behavior* 22, no. 4 (2000): 293–310

Schlesinger, Arthur, Jr. "Human Rights and the American Tradition." *Foreign Affairs*, 57, no. 3 (1978): 503–26.

Schlessinger, Stephen. "The End of Idealism: Foreign Policy in the Clinton Years." *World Policy Journal* 15, no. 4 (1998–99): 36–40.

Schmitt, Eric. "It Costs a Lot More to Kill Fewer People." *New York Times*, 2 May 1999.

Schmitt, Eric and James Dao. "Use of Pinpoint Air Power Comes of Age in New War." *New York Times*, 24 December 2001.

Schoultz, Lars. *Human Rights and United States Policy toward Latin America*. Princeton, N.J.: Princeton University Press, 1981.

Schrader, Esther. "Response to Terror; Pentagon Defends Strikes as Civilian Toll Rises." *Los Angeles Times*, 30 October 2001.

Schultz, George. *Triumph and Turmoil: My Years as Secretary of State*. New York: Scribner's, 1993.

Schultz, William F. *In Our Own Best Interest: How Defending Human Rights Benefits Us All*. Boston: Beacon Press, 2001.

Schwartz, Eric P. "Tools of Engagement: Saving Lives, Restoring Community, and the Challenge of Humanitarian Response in U.S. Foreign Policy." Washington, D.C.: United States Institute of Peace, 2002.

Sciolino, Elaine, and Alison Mitchell. "Clamor to Oust Saddam Grows." *International Herald Tribune*, 4 December 2001.

Scott, James M. *After the End: Making U.S. Foreign Policy in the Post–Cold War World*. Durham, N.C.: Duke University Press, 1998.

Second Presidential Debate, ABC News, 11 October 2000. Available online at http://www.foreignpolicy2000.org/library/.

Segal, David R. *Recruiting for Uncle Sam: Citizenship and Military Manpower*. Lawrence: University of Kansas, 1989.

Segal, David R., Brian J. Reed, and David E. Rohall. "Constabulary Attitudes of National Guard and Regular Soldiers in the U.S. Army." *Armed Forces and Society* 24 (1998): 535–48.

Sewell, John W. "Sign up to the Common Agenda." *International Herald Tribune*, 5 December 2001 .

Shanker, Thom. "Pentagon Hawk on Iraq Says Islam Isn't the Foe." *International Herald Tribune*, 6 May 2002.

Shattuck, John. "Religion, Rights, and Terrorism." *Harvard Human Rights Journal* 16 (2003): 183–88.

Shaw, Martin. "Global Society and Global Responsibility: The Theoretical, Historical and Political Limits of 'International Society.'" *Millennium: Journal of International Studies* 21, no. 3 (1992): 421–34.

Shue, Henry. *Basic Rights: Subsistence, Affluence, and U.S. Foreign Policy*. Princeton, N.J.: Princeton University Press, 1996.

Shull, Steven A. *A Kinder, Gentler Racism?* Armonk, N.Y.: M.E. Sharpe, 1993.

Sigal, Leon V. "The Last Cold War Election." *Foreign Affairs* 71, no. 5 (1992/1993): 1–15.

Sikkink, Kathryn. "The Power of Principled Ideas: Human Rights Policies in the United States and Western Europe." In *Ideas and Foreign Policy: Beliefs, Institutions, and Political Change*, edited by Judith Goldstein and Robert O. Keohane. Ithaca, N.Y.: Cornell University Press, 1993.

Simonovic, Ivan. "Relative Sovereignty of the Twenty-first Century." *Hastings International and Comparative Law Review* 25 (2002): 371–78.

Slaughter, Anne-Marie. "Good Reasons for Going around the U.N." *New York Times*, 18 March 2003.

Slevin, Peter. "Bush Sees Trade Change as Gift." *Washington Post,* 7 January 2002.

_____. "US Renounces Its Support." *Washington Post,* 7 May 2002.

Smith, Jean Edward. "Firefight at the Pentagon." *New York Times,* 6 April 2003.

Smith, Kevin Mark. "The United Nations Convention on the Rights of the Child: The Sacrifice of American Children on the Altar of Third-World Activism." *Washburn Law Journal* 38, no. 1 (1998): 111–49.

Smith, Michael Peter, and Luis Eduardo Guarnizo, eds. *Transnationalism from Below.* New Brunswick, N.J.: Transaction, 1998.

Smith, Thomas W. "The New Law of War: Legitimizing Hi-Tech and Infrastructural Violence." Paper presented at the International Studies Association Conference, Chicago, 20–24 February 2001.

Snider, Don M. "America's Postmodern Military." *World Policy Journal* 17, no. 1 (2000): 47–54.

Snyder, Jack. *Myths of Empire: Domestic Politics and International Ambitions.* Ithaca, N.Y.: Cornell University Press, 1991.

Solana, Javier. "International Court Signals a New Era." *International Herald Tribune,* 11 April 2002.

Sonnenfeldt, Helmut. "Foreign Policy for the Post–Cold War World." *Brookings Review* 10, no. 4 (1992): 33–35.

Sorenson, Theodore C. "America's First Post–Cold War President." *Foreign Affairs* 71 (1992): 40–44.

_____. Commencement address, American University, Washington, D.C. On file with author, 2003.

Spinelli, John J. "Peacetime Operations: Reducing Friction." In *QDR 2001: Strategy-Driven Choices for America's Security.* Washington, D.C.: National Defense University, 2001.

Spiro, Peter J. "New Global Communities: Nongovernmental Organizations in International Decision Making Institutions." *Washington Quarterly* 18 (1995): 45–56.

Stacy, Helen. "Relational Sovereignty." *Stanford Law Review* 55 (2003): 2029–56.

Steinberg, Donald. "The Role of Women in Peace Building and Reconstruction: More than Victims." Address before the Council on Foreign Relations, New York, 6 March 2003.

Steinfels, Peter. "Evangelicals Ask Government to Fight Persecution of Christians." *New York Times,* 23 January 1996.

Steinhardt, Ralph. "Fulfilling the Promise of Filartiga: Litigating Human Rights Claims Against the Estate of Ferdinand Marcos." *Yale Journal of International Law* 20 (1995): 65–106.

Steinmetz, Sara. *Democratic Transition and Human Rights.* Albany: State University of New York Press, 1994.

Stewart, David. "Ratification of the Convention on the Rights of the Child." *Georgetown Journal on Fighting Poverty* (1998): 173–76.

Stimson Center. "U.S. Funding for Peace Operations: A Look at the FY '03 Budget Request and Selected State Department Programs." Washington, D.C.: Stimson Center, 2002.

Stohl, Michael, David Carleton, and Steven E. Johnson. "Human Rights in U.S. Foreign Policy from Nixon to Carter." *Journal of Peace Research* 21 no. 3 (1984): 215–26.

Stork, Joe. "Human Rights and U.S. Policy." *Foreign Policy in Focus* 4, no. 8 (1999).

Stouffer, Samuel A. *The American Soldier.* Princeton, N.J.: Princeton University Press, 1949.

Strobel, Warren. *Late Breaking Foreign Policy.* Washington D.C.: United States Institute of Peace, 1997.

Suro, Robert. "Quick Strike Forces Urged for Military; Pentagon Study Gives Multiservice Units 30 Days to Control Outbreak of Trouble." *Washington Post,* 13 June 2001.

SustainAbility. "The 21st Century NGO: In the Market for Change." Washington, D.C., June 2003. Available online at http://www.sustainability.com/publications/latest/21C-ngo.asp.

Taft, Julia. "An Interview with Assistant Secretary of State Julia Taft." *U.S. Foreign Policy Agenda* 5, no. 1 (2000): 28–32.

Tamayo, Juan O. "Private Firms Take on U.S. Military Role in Drug War." *Miami Herald*, 22 May 2001.

Tapper, Jake. "The Last Place We Liberated." *Salon*, 10 April 2003. Available online at http://archive.salon.com/news/feature/2003/04/10/afghanistan/index_np.html.

Tarrow, Sidney. *Power in Movement: Social Movements and Contentious Politics.* Cambridge: Cambridge University Press, 1998.

Tasioulas, John. "In Defense of Relative Normativity: Communitarian Values and the Nicaragua Case." *Oxford Journal of Legal Studies* 16 (1996): 85–128.

Taylor, Allyn L. "An International Regulatory Strategy for Global Tobacco Control." *Yale Journal of International Law* 21 (1996): 257–301.

Taylor, Allyn L. and Ruth Roemer, "International Strategy for Tobacco Control." World Health Organization Doc. WHO/PSA/96.6 (1996). Available online at http://www5.who.int/tobacco/repository/stp41/Taylor.pdf.

Thakur, Ramesh. "Human Rights: Amnesty International and the United Nations." *Journal of Peace Research* 31, no. 2 (1994): 143–60.

Thomas, Daniel. *The Helsinki Effect.* Princeton, N.J.: Princeton University Press, 2001.

Thomas, Ward. *The Ethics of Destruction: Norms and Force in International Relations.* Ithaca, N.Y.: Cornell University Press, 2001.

Thompson, Kenneth. "Clinton's World: Remaking American Foreign Policy." *Political Science Quarterly* 115, no. 4 (2000).

Thompson, Mark. "Mission Underlines New Scope of U.S. Military after Cold War." *Houston Chronicle*, 5 December 1992.

Thomson, Janice A. "Norms in International Relations: A Conceptual Analysis." *International Journal of Group Tensions* 23 (1993): 67–84.

Tiefer, Charles. "Justing Sovereignty: Contemporary Congressional Executive Controversies over International Organization." *Texas International Law Journal* 35 (2000): 239–70.

Toffler, Alvin. *Power Shift.* New York: Bantam, 1950.

Turley, Jonathan. "Camps for Citizens: Ashcroft's Hellish Vision." *Los Angeles Times*, 14 August 2002.

United States Agency for International Development. *Foreign Aid in the National Interest: Freedom, Security, and Opportunity.* Washington, D.C.: U.S. Agency for International Development, 2002.

United States Army Judge Advocate General's School. *Operational Law Handbook.* Charlottesville, Va.: U.S. Judge Advocate General's School, 2000.

United States Army Special Forces Website, 2003. Available online at http://www.goarmy.com/sf/flindex.htm.

United States Congress. *Foreign Relations Authorization Act, Fiscal Year 1994 and 1995*, 103, House Record 2333.

————. House of Representatives. Armed Services Committee. *Fiscal Year 2000 National Defense Authorization Act—United States Policy in the Balkans: Hearings on Authorization and Oversight*, 106, 1999.

————. House of Representatives. *Omnibus Consolidated Appropriations Act, Fiscal Year 1997.* House Report 3610.

————. *Reservation I(1).* 140, Record 7634.

————. *Reservation I(1), Understanding III(2).* 138, Record 4783.

_____. *Reservation I(4)*. 138, Record 4783.

_____. *Restatement (Third) of the Foreign Relations Law of the United States.*

_____. *Understanding II(4)*. 136, Record 17,492.

United States Department of Defense. "Report to Congress: Kosovo/Operation Allied Force: After Action Report." Newport, R.I.: Naval War College, 2000.

United States Department of Justice, Office of the Inspector General. "The September 11 Detainees: A Review of the Treatment of Aliens Held on Immigration Charges in Connection with the Investigation of the September 11 Attacks." 2003.

United States Department of State, Bureau of Democracy, Human Rights, and Labor Affairs. "United States Policies in Support of Religious Freedom: Focus on Christians." 1997.

United States Department of State, Office of International Information Programs. "Summary of the African Crisis Response Initiative." 2001.

United States General Accounting Office. "Kosovo Air Operations: Need to Maintain Alliance Cohesion Resulted in Doctrinal Departure." Washington, D.C., 2001.

United States Institute of Peace. "Whither the Bulldozer? Nonviolent Revolution and the Transition to Democracy in Serbia." Special Report 6. August 2001.

United States Institute of Peace Working Group on International Humanitarian Law. *Law of War Training*, 24 May 2001.

United States Senate Committee on Armed Services. *Policy Concerning Homosexuality in the Armed Forces: 20 July 1993*. Washington, D.C.: U.S. Government Printing Office, 1995.

"U.S. Eager to Bolster Bioterrorism." *International Herald Tribune*, 2 November 2001.

Van der Vyver, Johan D. "American Exceptionalism: Human Rights, International Criminal Justice, and National Self-Righteousness." *Emory Law Journal* 50 (2001): 775–822.

Vickery, Scott A. "Strategic Coercion in the Kosovo Air Campaign." Washington, D.C.: Joint Military Intelligence College, 2000.

"Vienna Declaration and Programme for Action." Paper presented at the World Conference on Human Rights, Vienna, 14–25 June 1993.

Vincent, R. J. *Human Rights in International Relations*. New York: Cambridge University Press, 1986.

_____. "The Idea of Rights in International Ethics." In *Traditions of International Ethics*, edited by Terry Nardin and David R. Mapel. New York: Cambridge University Press, 1992.

Vogel, Steve. "Rwanda Mission's Timing Vague; U.S. Task Force in Uganda Delays First Kigali Deployment." *Washington Post*, 29 July 1994.

Vogelsang, Sandy. *American Dream, Global Nightmare: The Dilemma of U.S. Human Rights Policy*. New York: W. W. Norton, 1980.

Wagenseil, Steve. "Human Rights in U.S. Foreign Policy." *Journal of Intergroup Relations* 26, no. 3 (1999): 3–13.

Wapner, Paul. "The Democratic Accountability of Non-Governmental Organizations. Paradise Lost? NGOs and Global Accountability." *Chicago Journal of International Law* 3 (2002): 155–59.

_____. "Politics beyond the State: Environmental Activism and the World Civic Politics." *World Politics* 47 (1995): 311–40.

Warren, James. "Small Wars and Military Culture." *Society* 36, no. 6 (1999): 56–63.

Washington Post Editorial. "Detainees and Disclosure." *Washington Post*, 18 March 2002.

Wayne, Stephen J. "The Multiple Influences on U.S. Foreign Policy-Making." *U.S. Foreign Policy Agenda* 5, no. 1 (2000): 25–27.

Wedgewood, Ruth. "Testimony before the Subcommittee on the Constitution." Paper presented to the Senate Foreign Relations Committee, Washington, D.C., 17 April 2002.

Weidner, Glenn R. "Obligatory Training in International Humanitarian Law in the United States Army," 2001. Memorandum, on file with author.

Weil, Prosper. "Towards Relative Normativity in International Law." *American Journal of International Law* 77 (1983): 413–43.

Weisman, Steven R. "Pre-Emption: Idea with a Lineage Whose Time Has Come." *New York Times,* 23 March 2003.

Welch, David A. *Justice and the Genesis of War.* New York: Cambridge University Press, 1993.

_____. "Morality and the 'National Interest.'" In *Ethics in International Affairs,* edited by Andrew Held and Virginia Valls. Lanham, Md.: Rowman and Littlefield, 2000.

Weller, M., ed. *Iraq and Kuwait: The Hostilities and Their Aftermath.* Cambridge: Research Centre for International Law, University of Cambridge/Grotius Publications, 1993.

Wendt, Alexander. "Anarchy Is What States Make of It: The Social Construction of Power Politics." *International Organization* 46 (1992): 391–426.

_____. "Constructing International Politics." *International Security* 20 (1995): 77–78.

_____. *Social Theory of International Politics.* New York: Cambridge University Press, 1999.

Wendt, Alexander and Raymond Duvall. "Institutions and International Order." In *Global Changes and Theoretical Challenges: Approaches to World Politics for the 1990s,* edited by Ernst-Otto Czempiel and James. S. Rosenau. Toronto: Lexington, 1989.

Wheeler, Nicholas J. "Pluralist or Solidarist Conceptions of International Society: Bull and Vincent on Humanitarian Intervention." *Millennium: Journal of International Studies* 21, no. 3 (1992): 463–87.

_____. *Saving Strangers: Humanitarian Intervention in International Society.* New York: Oxford University Press, 2000.

_____. "The Legality of Allied Force." Paper presented at the Conference on the Future of Humanitarian Intervention, Durham, N.C., 19–20 April 2001.

Wheeler, Nicholas and Timothy Dunne. "Good International Citizenship: A Third Way for British Foreign Policy." *International Affairs* 74 (1988): 847–70.

Willetts, Peter. "Consultative Status for NGOs at the United Nations." In *The Conscience of the World: The Influence of Nongovernmental Organizations in the UN System,* edited by Peter Willetts. Washington, D.C.: Brookings Institution, 1996.

Wilson, Richard A. *Human Rights, Culture, and Context: Anthropological Perspectives.* London: Pluto Press, 1997.

Winfield, Nicole. "Report on Rights Hails Kosovo, Trial of Pinochet." *Salt Lake City Tribune,* 10 December 1999.

Witte, John, Jr. "A Dickensian Era of Religious Rights: An Update on Religious Human Rights in Global Perspective." *William and Mary Law Review* 42 (2001): 707–51.

Wood, David. "Cheney Jabs at Old Defense Plan; He Wrote Policy, Now He Scorns It." *Times Picayune,* 17 September 2000.

"The World in Their Hands." *Economist* 357, no. 8202 (2000): 59.

Wright, Jonathan. "Senate Panel Backs Negroponte for UN Post." *Reuters,* 14 September 2001.

"Wrong Man for the Job." *San Francisco Chronicle,* 23 April 2001.

Wuerffel, Kristin N. "Discrimination among Rights?: A Nation's Legislating a Hierarchy of Human Rights in the Context of International Human Rights Customary Law." *Valparaiso University Law Review* 33 (1998): 369.

Wurmser, David and Nancy Bearg Dyke. *The Professionalization of Peacekeeping: A Study Group Report.* Washington, D.C.: United States Institute of Peace, January 1994.

Zaid, Mayer. "Culture, Ideology and Strategic Framing." In *Comparative Perspectives on Social Movements: Political Opportunities, Mobilizing Structures, and Cultural Framings,* edited by Doug McAdam et al. London: Cambridge University Press, 1996.

Zimmerman, Tim and Linda Robinson. "The Art of the Deal: Forget Idealistic Foreign Policy. The Name of the Game is Trade." *U.S. News and World Report* 118, no. 6 (1995): 57.

Zisk, Kimberly Martin. *Engaging the Enemy: Organizational Theory and Soviet Military Innovation 1955–1991*. Princeton, N.J.: Princeton University Press, 1993.

Zunes, Stephen. "U.S. Arrogance on Display in UN Human Rights Commission Flap." *Foreign Policy in Focus*, 2001. Available online at http://www.foreignpolicy-infocus.org/commentary/0105unhr_body.html.

INDEX